THE
ALPINE JOURNAL
2001

1. Late afternoon view of the summit of Mount Aspiring reflected in a melt-water pool just below the Colin Todd Hut. (*John Slee-Smith*) (p37)

THE
ALPINE JOURNAL
2001

The Journal of the Alpine Club

A record of mountain adventure
and scientific observation

Edited by Ed Douglas

Assistant Editors:
José Luis Bermúdez and Geoffrey Templeman

Production Editor: Johanna Merz

Volume 106
No 350

Supported by the
MOUNT EVEREST FOUNDATION

Published jointly by
THE ALPINE CLUB & THE ERNEST PRESS

THE ALPINE JOURNAL 2001
Volume 106 No 350

Address all editorial communications to the Hon Editor :
Ed Douglas, 181 Abbeydale Road South, Sheffield S7 2QW
e-mail : ed_douglas@compuserve.com

Address all sales and distribution communications to:
Cordée, 3a De Montfort Street, Leicester, LE1 7HD

Back numbers:
Apply to the Alpine Club, 55 Charlotte Road, London, EC2A 3QF
or, for 1969 to date, apply to Cordée, as above.

First published in 2001 jointly by the Alpine Club and the Ernest Press
Typesetting by Johanna Merz
Illustration reproduction by Digital Imaging, Glasgow
Printed and bound in Great Britain by St Edmundsbury Press Ltd,
Bury St Edmunds, Suffolk

A CIP catalogue record for this book is
available from the British Library

ISBN 0 948153 66 0

Foreword

Many readers abroad will have read about the crisis in British agriculture prompted by the Foot and Mouth outbreak that began at the end of February. Great suffering has been endured by livestock farmers already reeling from the BSE crisis and a collapse in prices. Nor should the psychological pressure of watching herds of sheep or cattle – a lifetime's work for many – consumed on vast funeral pyres be underestimated. But there has been another story on the mountains and uplands of Britain this year which has largely been ignored.

While government ministers and the media have acknowledged the immense impact the crisis has had on tourism generally, few have reported thoroughly on how the thousands who earn their living from the hills have found their businesses undermined by the removal of access to the countryside. (It is important to remember that the scientific advice available to policy-makers was quite clear from the start of the crisis on how tiny the risk posed by walkers and climbers was.)

It may seem incredible, but the outdoor industry is now a significant business, comparable to agriculture. In upland areas, it far outstrips farming in terms of the turnover it generates and the jobs it secures. And yet the case for what is effectively our community was barely heard. We can only hope that in the enquiry which may have already taken place by the time you read this, the relevant agencies who speak for the outdoors will have had the opportunity to make our case clearly heard.

I think readers of the *Alpine Journal* a hundred years ago would be astonished by the size and scale mountaineering as a sport has now reached around the world. It is still obviously a minority interest, but mountains, apart from those with developed skiing industries, are traditionally poor places and have benefited greatly from mountaineering. One has only to think of Nepal, which suffered its own terrible tragedies this year with the murders of King Birendra and his family and the continuing Maoist insurgency, to find an example of how climbing and trekking can make a significant contribution.

This increasing influence enjoyed by mountain climbing is a double-edged sword. While it increases the sport's political influence, opening up new areas to explore, securing access for future generations and allowing local people a higher standard of living, it also increases the pressures on mountain environments. Businessmen without the depth of feeling for mountain landscapes that readers of the *Alpine Journal* share will continue to seek inappropriate development in mountain areas. But the activities of climbers themselves will increasingly come under the spotlight, as examples like the garbage on Everest are reported.

Most climbers, I hope, are sympathetic to the environment in which they pursue their sport. But there are plenty of environmentalists who look on the climbing community with some hostility and see us as a soft target that can be managed more easily than, for example, a multinational oil company or a government agency. This has already been the experience of climbers in Germany, where the Green Party has severely reduced access to German crags.

Part of the appeal of climbing is freedom from the complexity and pettiness of much of modern life. The thought of getting involved in planning controls and detailed environmental debate is too much for many of us. But next year the world will celebrate the International Year of the Mountains and in this edition of the Journal, climber and mountain environment campaigner Martin Price outlines some of the events and programs planned for 2002. Whether we like it or not, it is the work of people like Price which will shield us from the attention of bureaucrats and maintain the integrity of the wild landscapes we love so much.

Elsewhere in this year's Journal, the richness and diversity of that experience is shown to be in good health. Doug Scott reports on an aborted expedition in one of the toughest environments he has yet experienced – Arunachal Pradesh – and Tamotsu Nakamura reveals his latest explorations in the eastern Himalaya. Both men show that there are still areas of the world where talk of management plans and access legislation is a little premature.

There is plenty of excellent, adventurous climbing too, from young climbers like Ian Parnell and older hands like John Barry, still climbing extreme routes in his 50s. Past President George Band reports on his trek up the Rishi Gorge into the Nanda Devi Sanctuary, an environmental touchstone like almost no other. And Robert Roaf shares his memories of another age, when such issues were far in the future, climbing with Marco Pallis in Sikkim. I want to thank all this year's contributors for their time and effort and for making this year's Journal such an interesting collection.

Ed Douglas

Contents

ISSUES

HISTORY

Contributions from:
Kelly Cordes, Derek Fordham, Lindsay Griffin, Harish Kapadia, Paul Knott, Bill O'Connor, Simon Richardson, Javier Sanchez.

SKETCH MAPS AND DIAGRAMS

Illustrations

29. The unclimbed North Face of Xiashe (5833m), Shaluli Shan, photo graphed from the Zhopu Gompa. (*Tamotsu Nakamura*)
30. Mt Siguniang (6250m) in the Qiolangai was first climbed by a Japanese expedition in 1981 via the East Ridge, but the Japanese have also climbed the South Face, in 1992. To the north, Nakamura reports a number of granite towers up to 5500m. (*Tamotsu Nakamura*)
31. The highest peak in the Dangche Zhengla massif, photographed from the south-west. This peak is unclimbed. (*Tamotsu Nakamura*)
32. Lengo Gomba and rock peaks, Sichuan Province. The monastery was founded 600 years ago. (*Tamotsu Nakamura*)
33. Climbing Mount Korakas, Central Greece. (*J G R Harding*)
34. Skiing down Korakas. (*J G R Harding*)
35. The Cordillera de Santa Vera Cruz, Bolivia. The leftmost peak is Pico de la Fortuna (5493m), that second from right is Cerro Santa Vera Cruz, at 5560m the highest in the massif. (*Javier Sánchez*)
36. and 37. *Left and Above*
   The tin and card of Joseph Prem, left in 1939 on the summit of Cerro Santa Vera Cruz, and the archaeological remains – offerings from the Tiwanaku culture – discovered near the same place. (*Javier Sánchez*)
38. The SE Face of la Fortuna (5493m). The line of the first ascent, *Khespiqala*, goes up the middle of the snowy face at Difficile, 70°, reaching the ridge on the left just below the summit. (*Javier Sánchez*)

Appearing between pages 308 and 309
39. Ginette Lesley Harrison (1958-1999) (*South-west News Service*)

SOME NOTABLE FEMALE CLIMBERS FROM THE 20TH CENTURY:

40. to 45. *Clockwise from top left*: Alison Hargreaves on the S side of Everest in 1994; Catherine Destivelle in the Exit Cracks, North Face of the Eiger; Wanda Rutkiewicz, the first woman to climb K2, along with seven other 8000ers, before her death on Kangchenjunga in 1992; Jill Lawrence (*left*) the leading 1980s female rock climber, talking to the late Janet Adam Smith at the 1988 Festival of Mountaineering Literature at Bretton Hall; Chantal Mauduit who climbed six 8000ers before her death on Dhaulagiri in 1998; and Beatrice Tomasson, who kicked off the century with a futuristic guided ascent of the South Face of the Marmolada di Penia. The portrait is by the fashionable late 19th century artist John Singer Sargent. (*Sprayway; Destivelle collection; Rutkiewicz collection; Ed Douglas; Mauduit collection.*)
46. Nicholson, Cooke?, Roaf, Chapman, and Pallis, from the 1936 Zemu Valley expedition. (*R C Nicholson*)

Expeditions

MICK FOWLER

Mount Kennedy – North Buttress

Paul Ramsden was waving a book about with increasing excitement. 'You asked about Alaska, look at all these lines!'

I struggled to focus on the photographs. They all looked to be of disturbingly steep mountains. It had been a testing evening at the infamous Eastwood rocks; the slimy and depressingly undergraded gritstone cracks had spat me out with even greater ease than usual and I was nursing my flattened ego and bleeding hands. But it had to be said that these photographs were giving me quite an urge. Meanwhile, Paul was moving onto the finer detail.

'You'd love it. Only 24 hours from the UK to base camp, wonderful lines, nice and cold. Lots of snow. . .'

'And the downside?'

'Well the weather might not be too good. Geoff Hornby had 14 feet of snow in 23 days last year. But at least he got there. I've heard of some people who don't even get a good enough weather window to fly in.'

This suddenly wasn't sounding so good to a civil servant with limited holidays. We ordered more beer and the conversation moved onto the perennial problem of where our group should climb the following Wednesday evening.

But the photographs had unsettled me. I'd never even been to North America let alone climbed on the mountains of Yukon and Alaska. And to adopt the attitude that the weather might be bad so 'I'll never go' didn't really sit very comfortably with my underlying enthusiasm for climbing in new areas. There was no doubt about it, I would have to go for it and risk the weather. But who with and what exactly should we try and climb?

The first question was easily solved. Andy Cave had also not climbed in this part of the world before and was quick to show his whippet-like enthusiasm for anything that looked remotely inspirational. I hadn't been in the big mountains with Andy since Brendan Murphy's tragic death on Changabang three years previously. I enjoyed his company and looked forward to climbing with him again. Duncan Tunstall and Chris Pasteur, two old friends of mine, were keen to join us and so we were set as a team of four.

The second question was more problematical. We were starting from scratch and it seemed a bit of a tall order to expect others to simply send us lists of wonderful unclimbed objectives. A round of library searching led to a series of pleading e-mails to well-known North American activists. Andy and I considered the results together. People had been amazingly helpful.

'What about the North Face of Devil's Thumb? Randy's been there twice and the weather was terrible. A couple of Canadian kids sat in there last year for about two months and it never froze.'

That one didn't sound very hopeful. We moved on to the next.

'You could aim for a line on the East Face of Moose's Tooth and find it too dry – without ice. Some guys get lucky their first time out (in Alaska), others spend a lot of their time and money before tasting a morsel of success. How lucky do you feel?'

Andy and I contemplated these messages and the various photographs that we had managed to get hold of. One photograph in particular grabbed our attention; Bradford Washburn's of the north side of Mt Kennedy.

Kennedy stands in the St Elias range just on the Canadian side of the border. It was named after the American President John F Kennedy, assassinated in 1963, as a sign of respect and to mark the good relationship between Canada and the USA. When it was named, in January 1965, it was the highest unclimbed peak in North America. Senator Bobby Kennedy, JFK's younger brother, although not a mountaineer, promptly expressed an interest in climbing it. With assistance from the National Geographic Society an expedition was organised and in March 1965 Bobby Kennedy became the first non-mountaineer ever to make the first ascent of a major North American mountain. Amazing what can be arranged if you carry enough influence.

The Bobby Kennedy team had climbed from the south side but it was the tremendous 6000ft high north side which attracted our attention. The North Buttress had been climbed twice before, once in 1968 and again in 1977. Both ascents had used siege tactics and a couple of alpine-style attempts had been made. It was an obvious objective and the discovery that Andy Kirkpatrick at Outside in Hathersage had the same mountain in mind helped to focus our attention and prompt a decision. Mount Kennedy it would be.

In fact, though, it was the face to the right of the spur that was to become our prime objective. Sporting 3000ft of hard, mixed ground followed by 3000ft of easier terrain it looked to be a superb challenge, albeit possibly threatened by a menacing looking line of séracs. Four years previously two American superheroes, Jack Tackle and Jack Roberts, had spent nine days forcing a route to within 1500ft of the summit before bad weather stopped play. They had covered the difficult ground but the face itself was still unclimbed.

Yakutat (population 600) nestles on the South Alaska coastline and is apparently the smallest community in America to be served by a daily scheduled air service. The convenience is such that, within 24 hours of leaving Britain it is possible to be on the glacier beneath Mt Kennedy. From Yakutat it takes only 45 minutes or so but the terrain that we saw out of the window left us with no illusions about the remoteness of the area and the difficulty we would have walking out. There was no habitation or vegetation whatsoever in the valleys around Kennedy. Nothing but snow, ice and rock. The name Canadian Icefields Range was more descriptive than I imagined. For us there was no way out to Yakutat except by plane.

First impressions of Mt Kennedy were memorable. Andy was in full optimistic mood.

'Not as steep as I'd expected. Looks fine.'

Positive noises continued to emanate from the Cave body whilst I fought to overcome my feeling of nausea as Kurt put the aircraft into a tight circle for his final approach. Perhaps it was the angle of the plane, but the glimpses that I was getting from my side didn't sit comfortably with Andy's comments. It looked horrific. But my priority was to take some photographs and not be sick. I pointed the camera in vaguely the right direction and tried hard to ignore the sensation of being on a wild fairground ride.

The plane only took two passengers so it was an hour and a half later that Duncan and Chris joined us. By then my nausea had subsided and I felt well enough to join half-heartedly in the collective 'oohs!' and 'aahs!' and camera clicks. It did look very fine, but I couldn't help but notice the séracs overlooking the righthand side of the face. Perhaps I'm getting old. My wife tells me that I worry more than I used to. I'm sure that I wouldn't have focused on such things 20 years ago, but now I found the binoculars trained, not on the technical joys of the climbing, but on the steely blue ice walls forming the lower edge of the summit icefield. Interestingly, I noticed that Andy too seemed to be paying close attention to such things.

The lines on the face were not as obvious as we had expected. We spied possible connecting streaks of ice towards the right-hand side but they were definitely in the fall zone of the séracs. Perhaps it was the all-concealing smattering of snow, but it took us some time to work out the exact line taken by Jack Tackle and Jack Roberts.

Even peering through the binoculars, it was still impossible to decide whether or not it was ice or powder snow stuck to rock on their line. The line itself seemed to be just out of the fall line of the séracs, but a semi-permanent thundering cloud of spindrift brought it sharply home to us that it was the main, albeit shallow, funnel draining snowfall from the 3000ft upper face. We decided that we had enough excuses to adopt that wonderfully sensible middle-aged approach of sitting back, eating, drinking and observing.

Observing too much can be a bad idea. Inevitably we observed spindrift. Lots of it. Lying in nice warm sleeping bags on the glacier it was easy to talk ourselves out of anything too masochistic. With regular spindrift and temperatures in the shade plunging to –25°C or so, the chance of freezing solid on a hanging bivouac looked high. The tone of our conversations moved steadily away from Andy's initial optimism.

'Don't fancy getting flushed off by that lot.'

'Looks much safer on the North Buttress.'

'Brilliant line too. Gives me quite an urge.'

We did try skinning up the glacier to look at the face from different angles, but it didn't change anything. There was no doubt about it, we had subtly changed objectives. We would go for an alpine-style attempt of the North Buttress.

No sooner had the decision been made than the sun came out and having heard plenty of St Elias weather horror stories we felt obliged to stir ourselves into action.

The buttress did look an excellent climb. It was one of those lines that it's very difficult to say how hard it might be. From the glacier the first two-thirds looked Okay, but in the upper third mixed buttresses could be seen to block progress.

We had the first ascensionists' report which referred to A3 aid climbing and included a disturbing photo of someone aiding up a decidedly blank-looking wall. Clearly we would need to carry a fair amount of technical gear to stand a chance of coping with this.

With more or less 24-hour daylight and an obvious bivouac spot after 1000ft or so, an early morning start somehow didn't seem very necessary. Relishing the luxury of being able to leave our head torches behind, we relaxed over a leisurely breakfast of fried halibut and it wasn't until around midday that we felt obliged to haul our bursting stomachs towards the toe of the buttress.

One of the good things about steep lines is that fresh snow tends to slide off rather than accumulate. Even better, the polishing effect of frequent snow slides tends to create streaks of squeaky white ice – perfect for climbing on. Andy and I wavered up the lower slopes, picking out the 'squeaky' lines wherever possible. Much as the weather was perfect and the climbing easy it was unsettling to have heavy waves of spindrift engulfing us every now and then. We made quick progress trying not to think how the spindrift might look if it started to snow.

Gaining height brought home to us the scale and spectacular remoteness of the St Elias range. Below us the Kennedy glacier presented a flat white expanse, perhaps two miles wide, which wound its way majestically down to the Lowell Glacier, ultimately emptying into the Alsek River and the sea south of Yakutat Bay. There weren't exactly a lot of people around. In fact, no one. In a way, despite the ease of access (in good weather!), it seemed more remote than the Himalaya. Walking out with all our equipment was definitely not on. Even just carrying survival gear, it would be testing enough to get out to the Alaskan Highway. But as we had to get back to Yakutat, which is not connected to the main road network, that wasn't exactly much use. Walking to Yakutat from Kennedy would involve 70 miles or so of crevassed glacier, ice block ridden inlets and mosquito-ravaged bogs. There was no doubt about it – we were dependant on Kurt Gloyer, pilot extra-ordinaire, to pick us up. It was a strange and slightly uncomfortable feeling to be so dependant on someone else.

I suppose we should have been rushing, but good weather, scenic views and an idyllic safe bivouac site on a projecting crest prompted a relaxed approach and a short day.

Needless to say by mid-afternoon on day 2 we were experiencing 'full' Yukon conditions.

Although our chosen line primarily followed the crest it was quite a broad crest and we tended to veer backwards and forwards between subsidiary ribs. It was whilst making one of these rising traverses that the occasional gentle flurries of snow built up into something more substantial. With near on 5000ft of mountain above us, it was perhaps unsurprising that the intermittent clouds of spindrift soon developed into roaring snow slides. It was also disturbing to note that the slope was not of a good consistency for reliable ice screws and communication was near impossible. An uncomfortably dangerous situation was beginning to develop. Another short day was called for.

The rib on our right gave a ray of hope, but this Yukon snowfall was something else. Even the crests of the buttresses were mercilessly raked by the ongoing deluge of spindrift.

Andy appeared philosophical.

'Glad we're not on the face.'

I had to agree – although somehow my mumbled response didn't sound so calm.

'Perhaps head for that one ?' I pointed hesitantly through the mist at an indistinct rib adorned with a fragile cornice. It appeared to stand sufficiently proud of the slope to escape the worst of the spindrift waves. It took half an hour of wallowing against the flow before Andy was somewhere near it.

'Am I in the right place?'

This didn't sound good. Much cursing and excavating was followed by a welcome call for me to climb.

The sensation on reaching Andy's powdery perch was memorable. It felt like sitting on a small island in the middle of a raging river. All was safe for the moment but added interest was guaranteed if the spindrift rivers rose much more. We looked glumly at each other.

'Can't just stand here. Best get the tent up.'

In my previous experience even the softest and most fragile snow edges tend to have good ice somewhere deep down inside. This one, though, seemed to defy normal characteristics; it appeared to be simply powder snow resting on granulated snow. Reliable belays were distressingly non-existent.

'The ice screw I put in up there's not bad,' announced Andy, pointing at a screw 20 feet above and 10 feet to one side.

I silently imagined the two of us fighting claustrophobic fabric while ensconced in a tent penduluming off the crest and being battered by snow slides.

'Perhaps a couple more would be nice?'

And so with snow still falling (where does it all come from in Yukon?) the two of us squeezed into our little tent secured by a selection of ice screws well above us and way to one side. Within minutes the snow had completely blocked the entrance and we had merged into the profile of the crest.

We had a radio with us but this was not over-helpful as contact with the outside world was impossible. Also, after 24 hours there was little in the way of exciting news to report to the boys at base camp. Our exchanges were becoming a touch repetitive.

'Base camp here. What's it like up there? Over.'

'Snowing. How about down there? Over.'

'About a metre now. What are your plans? Over.'

'More reading. Over and out.'

I had chosen light-hearted reading. My children having developed into avid Harry Potter fans I relished the opportunity to catch up on some of Harry's latest adventures, my aim being to attain an even playing field on Hogwart's tittle-tattle. I lay engrossed, exploring the absorbing world of Harry and his friends and beginning to understand for the first time what inspires London commuters to the extent that some go as far as to blank out the cover to anonymise their trips into Harry's world. I felt no such need to disguise my apparently childish choice of reading and chuckled contentedly in a world away from spindrift-ridden mountain faces. Andy had chosen deep and meaningful reading to further his thesis on mining dialects. Somehow he seemed to find it difficult to concentrate, although perhaps this was more to do with his position in the tent than his choice of reading material.

We lay head to tail with Andy's head by the entrance. It must be said that the constant roar of spindrift avalanches was not the most relaxing of background noises – and the action was uncomfortably close to the Cave head. A particularly loud roar followed by a severe pummelling of the fabric at the mountain end was enough to make the Cave body look uncharacteristically uneasy.

'Not very pleasant, Michael.'

I mumbled agreement whilst trying to concentrate harder on Harry.

By the morning of day 3 the team was tiring somewhat of inactivity. Andy squeezed back inside, after one of the least comfortable craps imaginable, reporting an apparent easing of the flow. It didn't sound that way but any incentive to move was welcome.

'Tent excavation underway.'

The message sent on the morning radio call was loud and clear. Deep down inside though I didn't feel quite so positive. The tent had the appearance of having been sucked into the bowels of the mountain. In clearings in the cloud Duncan and Chris had failed to spot us through their binoculars, even though we were in direct line of sight from base camp. In terms of progress everything would hinge on how much snow was lying on the snow slopes we would have to cross.

The weather though was still not exactly at its best. Cloud hung thick and persistent above us and the air was still heavy with falling snow.

We waded off our protected little ridge crest and back into action. Invisible granite slabs grated unnervingly against crampon points but our guarded optimism proved correct in that the angle was such that most of the new snow had simply slipped off the face.

By late afternoon we were halfway up and, more importantly, the skies had cleared. A glorious panoramic view had opened up. Any doubts we had over the wisdom of continuing evaporated. Pinnacle Peak now soared spectacularly above an intervening ridge and we were looking obliquely downwards across the northwest face onto the huge Kennedy ice shelf slanting up towards Mount Alverstone.

Another fine snow crest, with big overhangs below, made for a spectacular bivouac. The atmosphere had totally changed. Smiles came readily; we were in with a chance. But the obvious crux of the line was still above us.

Aid climbing is definitely not my forte so we were working on the basis that we would be able to find interlinking ice streaks and avoid time-consuming aid pitches. (It's amazing how optimistic it is possible to be when viewing from a position of comfort.) Now we had our noses up against the problem that the lines we had spotted through binoculars from base camp were far from obvious. In fact we couldn't see them at all. We peered closely but unproductively at the old Bradford Washburn photograph that we had brought with us. Creases had appeared in all the wrong places and these made it almost impossible to pin-point our position.

'Perhaps we're just here. Or ought we to be over to the right a bit?'

Andy pointed at a vague couloir almost entirely obliterated by a crease. Our on-the-spot assessment didn't add much, although there was certainly a line of sorts up to our right and not very much in the way of other options.

Everything always seems to look so much more difficult from directly below. I could only hope that this generalisation applied to the feature that we were now looking at. The weather was worsening again. By the time we reached it, the steepening spindrift was pouring over an overhang 40 feet or so up, spraying out and catching us squarely in a fine mist of snow. At least it was intermittent – for the moment.

One of the good things about climbing with Andy is that he is a great all-rounder, equally at home on rock and ice. Regardless of the terrain he can be put in the lead whenever there is a hint of any kind of difficulty.

I recalled a rock-climbing evening at Stoney Middleton in the Peak District, when he had surged up an E5 in the rain, leaving me to attempt to second but end up dangling in front of a large appreciative audience. At least there was no audience here! And at least I climbed comfortable in the reassuring knowledge that I had a secret weapon to tackle any really nasty bits that we might come across.

Unfortunately, though, we were leading strictly alternate pitches and somehow the first pitch on this steeper ground was mine. Soon I was thrashing in an acute-angled, slanting groove. The spindrift had swept the loose snow away leaving squeaky white ice but it was right at the back and my sack kept forcing me out.

'Adrenaline flowing, Andrew,' I grunted energetically.

By dint of far more brute strength than skill, I scraped the sack up the groove and emerged on to a small ledge with a good belay and sat down to bring Andy up. I suppose I should have expected it to be a 'bad for the ego' experience but it would have been nice if he had looked just a little bit more stretched.

Impressively, voluminous flakes now fell quietly from a bleak grey sky. In tune with the weather the rock changed from golden granite to slate grey dolerite. At least, though, we knew that the dolerite only appeared on the top third of the route. And once through this section we knew there was only 1500ft or so of ice slopes to the summit. But it was somewhere here that Jack Tackle and Jack Roberts had turned back in 1996. They had completed the technically difficult climbing on the northwest face, veered left to the point where we now were and then ground to a halt in the face of bad weather. They must have been gutted not to stand on the summit after nine days of effort. It was a sobering thought for us to know that it took them two full days and 36 x 60m abseils to get back down. The summit and a possible walking descent on the far side looked increasingly appealing. But even the upwards path of the ever-versatile Mr Cave had ground to a halt. Bad news indeed.

A sudden clearing of the skies revealed the Cave body poised precariously.

'I'm in the wrong place. Should be over there.'

Now that I looked closely it did all look horribly insecure. Crampons scraping unnervingly, Andy started to curse, down climb and traverse whilst I soaked up the sun's rays. The sky was now completely clear and the views stunning. I sat back clicking away with the camera while Andy inched himself out to the base of the summit ice field.

Soon we had found a spot where we could pitch the tent. Admittedly, one third of the floor space hung off the ledge we hacked out and I lost the toss and got the outside position. But it seemed to matter little in the face of the sun streaming through the door and the possibility of the summit the next day. If you are tired enough sleep comes easily!

I would say that the morning dawned clear but of course the sun doesn't really set in this part of the world; best to say that, remarkably, clear weather continued as we emerged into the crystal clear and frigidly cold morning air. Rare conditions indeed. Soaking in the scenery, we alternately led up the summit ice slope, a narrow connecting crest and finally moved together up the easing angle to the summit snow cone. Amazingly this was our sixth day out from base camp.

It was a great feeling to stand there in perfect weather on the summit of Kennedy. A cloud layer covered the sea but summits in all directions stood proud. It was a sobering thought that there might not be anyone at all within 30 miles or so of us. For ease of access combined with remoteness and solitude it's difficult to beat this part of the world.

Andy was on the radio trying to radio Kurt in Yakutat. We had been assured that it would be possible to make radio contact from the summit. But if we couldn't, our only sensible option was to descend the way we had come up. I didn't fancy that very much.

'Hello. Hello, Kurt. We're on top… Can you pick us up from the lower Cathedral Glacier? 5pm tomorrow?'

'No problem. See you there.'

All confirmed then. The next evening we were back in Yakutat Jack's bar drinking to Geoff Hornby's 23 days' inactivity and 14 feet of snow the previous year. The experience had ended as abruptly as it had begun.

Odd place, Yukon. Go there with your weather fingers crossed.

ATHOL WHIMP

Jannu - North Face

*I sit astride a small snow ridge and dig my heels into the snow. It's 5pm and Andy
Lindblade and I are only about 100 metres from the summit of Jannu (7710m).
'Okay,' I shout into the wind and swirling snow as I pull the rope tight. Eventually
Andy arrives. 'Across this gully and up the side of that rock buttress,' I tell him.
Andy heads off, traversing the steep gully. I can hear a buzzing, a crackling noise
– like an electrical appliance about to short out. The noise intensifies, and I realise
that it is coming from me, from my helmet. Static electricity surrounds me and
shocks start to shoot through my body. I feel as though I'm about to explode.
'Andy,' I scream, pulling at the rope, 'come back, come back!' He understands
what is happening and hurries back to me. He can hear the buzzing noise and it
starts to affect him too. 'Quick, there's a small ice cave about ten metres down
there. Go!' I shout.*

In 1986 I read the *Wall of Shadows*, an account of the 1975 New Zealand
expedition that first attempted to climb the mountain from the north.
The climbers tackled the 'Wall of Shadows' – vast ice fields of the North
Face – but failed below the summit ridge when winter storms and a
dwindling team effort forced them from the mountain. The next season the
Japanese reached the summit after fixing thousands of metres of rope up
the Wall of Shadows and following the precarious East Ridge to the summit.

Andy and I are drawn to the massive, unclimbed headwall of the North
Face and decide to attempt the unclimbed North Face 'direct'. This direct
route would present us with a myriad of logistical and technical challenges
and push us to the limit. Without doubt it is one of the most difficult and
prized unclimbed routes of the Himalaya. From a base camp at 4500 metres
on a terrace above the Jannu Glacier, the route crosses the glacier and climbs
up steep cliffs to the névé at 5400 metres. This is where the route really
starts. A steep, icy couloir shoots 1500 metres diagonally up the face to a
hanging glacier that clings precariously to the mountain at 7000 metres.
There, in the thin air and freezing temperatures of a cold Himalayan north
face, sits the sheer headwall, 700 metres of compact, vertical and overhanging rock leading to the airy summit.

After eight days' walking we reach the site of our base camp, a beautiful,
grassy terrace about 100 metres above the Jannu Glacier. Behind our camp,
granite cliffs rise up a couple of hundred metres to vast scree slopes. Opposite
base camp, on the other side of the glacier, massive cliffs rise 1000 metres
up to the névé. An almost unbroken line of ice-cliffs tops the faces and
huge avalanches thunder down into the valley throughout the day and night,
the biggest ones sending a cloud of ice particles floating over our camp.

We spend the next three weeks establishing a route and packing the gear we will need for our climb up to the névé below the wall. We pick a line used by most expeditions who have attempted Jannu from the north, and first established by the 1975 New Zealand expedition. It takes a couloir from the glacier up to the cliffs and then a rising traverse across the cliffs to a broad snow slope, where, at around 5100 metres, we establish an intermediate camp. From Camp 1 we climb up the snow slope, a couple of small rock buttresses and finally to the edge of the névé at 5400 metres where we set up Camp 2. Relics from past expeditions indicate that this site has been well used.

This is a period of acclimatisation and for getting in tune with the mountain. We also get an understanding of the weather, which proves to be unsettled and unpredictable.

On 6 April my girl-friend Panagiota and Andy's sister Katherine and her friend Dougal leave base camp to return to Australia. It is very sad as they disappear from view down the valley and we feel very alone. Now it's just Andy and me and our two Nepali base camp staff. Without any distractions we are free to commit ourselves to the climb.

On the same day our friends leave, we take our last loads up to Camp 2 and prepare for the route. Over the next few days we fix a couple of hundred metres of rope over the bergschrund at the base of the wall and up the bottom of the couloir that soars 1500 metres to the headwall. We haul the portaledge and haul-bag with 14 days' supplies up to the top of the fixed rope. Hauling is extremely strenuous, harder than the climbing. Even with the haul-bag on a two-to-one pulley system we have to throw our body weight against the rope to get it moving.

The first spindrift avalanches begin just as we finish setting up the portaledge. At first, small avalanches slither past us, hissing down the couloir, but within minutes huge torrents of snow are thundering down, spilling over the tiny rock outcrop above us, crashing down on the ledge, pummelling us as we hang on the belay. We finally manage to get inside the ledge, crampons and all. There is snow everywhere, but at least we have some shelter. We lie there in the chaos, panting and swearing. A couple of times each minute the ledge gets battered and the roar from the continuous spindrift in the couloir – only a metre away – intensifies. Slowly we get ourselves organised. Working one at a time on the confined ledge, we remove our crampons, boots and wind suits and get into our sleeping-bags. Every time the ledge is hit, fine snow floats in through the vents, adding to the mess. We assemble the stove and soon get a brew going. Outside it's getting dark, but there isn't any let-up in the snowfall. It is beginning to look like more than just a typical afternoon storm.

Andy and I are at 6000 metres on one of the hardest unclimbed mountain faces in the world. Our tiny portaledge, just 1½ metres wide by two metres long, is hanging off three tied-off ice screws on the edge of a steep, icy couloir 1500 metres above base camp and 1700 metres below the summit.

It is now dark outside and around us the storm continues to build. Flashes of lightning momentarily illuminate the interior of the ledge. Snow covers everything. Thunder crashes around us, echoing off the huge walls of rock and ice, so loud and sudden that it makes us jump even though we're expecting it. Spindrift avalanches continue to pummel us, and the roar from the couloir continues. We are in the centre of a huge storm. We have to shout at each other to talk. All night the storm continues unabated. Dawn slowly arrives and still the storm continues. Snow has built up behind the ledge, constricting the tiny space even more, and tilting the floor. Much of our gear is filled with snow and our sleeping-bags are damp. We realise that we cannot stay where we are; we must shift the ledge or descend. I dress and climb out into the storm. Spindrift cascades down on me, draining the heat from my body. I try to clear the snow from behind the ledge but I can't make any progress against the spindrift. We decide to pack up as best we can and descend. We dismantle the portaledge, attach it and the haul bag to the anchor and abseil off. We try to keep to the edges of the couloir, but even so we are engulfed by spindrift on many occasions. By the time we reach the névé in the early evening, the storm has all but finished but spindrift continues to cascade off the vast rock and ice faces surrounding us. Bathed in the beautiful glow of twilight, we plough wearily through half a metre of new snow back to Camp 2.

The next day we descend to base camp for a well-earned rest and to restock the depleted reserves of our bodies. We wash clothes, listen to music and read. A yak herder visits us and a keen trader from the village of Ghunsa arrives to sells us a couple of bottles of beer and some potatoes.

A week later we are once again at Camp 2 and ready for another attempt. After a 3am start we cross the névé and jumar up the couloir to the top of the ropes we fixed during our descent from the storm. We climb up to the ledge and haul bag and manage to climb and haul another 100 metres by late afternoon. After our last experience we want a sheltered site for the ledge, and find a small rock buttress we hope will give us some protection from the spindrift. Anchors are hard to find and I have to climb up a further 20 metres and place a couple of pitons. We hang the ledge from the rope and just manage to get inside as a snow storm sends spindrift down the couloir. It stops snowing during the evening and when the spindrift ceases the mountain is eerily quiet. We sleep well but very early in the morning are woken by a thunderous crash of rockfall down the couloir. We go back to sleep and wake up just before dawn. We make a couple of hot drinks and eat some breakfast and prepare for the day's climbing. Andy dresses first and is just about to exit the ledge when we hear a sickening crash above us. Suddenly the ledge is smashed by a hail of rock and ice. Rocks tear through the fabric and we are surrounded by flying débris. We hunch against the wall as the ledge kicks and shakes. As suddenly as it started, it is over. Small trickles of snow float down on us. The fly is shredded and the ledge is full of rocks and ice. Miraculously we are unhurt. For the next hour

Andy digs the haul bag out of the spindrift and packs our gear while I try to repair the ledge. Slowly the gravity of the situation dawns on us. The ledge is beyond repair, and without the ledge we cannot continue. We discuss our options and both feel sick with disappointment as we realise that we must again descend. We look across to the Wall of Shadows and decide to make an alpine-style ascent of the route.

After another spell at base camp we are back at Camp 2 and ready to go. Two hours before dawn we quietly pack up camp, leave a note among our gear should we not return, and head across the névé for what we hope will be the last time. We are fit and acclimatised and make good time to the base of the wall. We jumar 200 metres of rope that was fixed the day before up the steep, mixed buttress at the base of the wall and emerge into sunlight at the start of the ice fields.

A thousand metres above us, seeming to hang out over our heads, massive, leaning séracs challenge our existence, daring us to cross the exposed ice-slopes ahead. For the past week we have been mentally conditioning ourselves for this 'Russian roulette'. For the next hour or so we are in the firing line. With the rope packed away we climb up and across the steep, polished ice-slopes, constantly casting nervous glances above us. There is nowhere to run, nowhere to hide.

Without incident we make it to the relative safety of the lower of two hanging glaciers that are the dominant features of the Wall of Shadows. We traverse underneath the hanging glacier and emerge into a broad, steep couloir that winds up the side. By midday the oven-like heat from the sun is starting to sap our strength. A few hours later we are near the top of the hanging glacier at 6400 metres. In the shelter of a small ice wall we chop a platform for our tiny tent. Just as we finish pitching it, an afternoon snow shower sends waves of spindrift hissing down the face.

In the morning we climb to the top of the hanging glacier and then up a steep ice rib for 100 metres. Above us the face steepens, broken by several rock bands. We get the rope out, wind in a couple of ice screws and start to climb, pitch by pitch. The hard ice and heavy packs make for strenuous climbing. The second jumars the rope and we make steady progress. We get stunning, close-up views of the stupendous headwall of the North Face – our original objective – and speculate on the line, and how we would have gone. The sheer enormity and complexity of the headwall almost leaves us speechless.

By mid-afternoon we have climbed seven hard, steep pitches and, with the build-up of cloud and signs of snow, we decide to traverse to the second hanging glacier and look for a tent-site. Even before I start the pitch it is snowing and torrents of spindrift are hurtling down the couloir we have to cross. I traverse steep, bulletproof ice into the couloir. It's strenuous climbing and I struggle to wind in an ice screw to protect me when I launch into the river of spindrift. I fight to maintain my footing, my crampons scratching at the ice under the torrent. Finally, exhausted, I reach the shelter of an open-ended crevasse and belay Andy across. Like me, he battles the spindrift and arrives frozen and exhausted. We have a great tent-site, a natural ice cave with a roof to keep out the snow.

The next day we climb only a couple of hundred metres, up to the bergschrund at the top of the second hanging glacier. Here, at around 7000 metres, we pitch the tent under the huge, overhanging, upper wall of the 'schrund. We spend the rest of the day eating, drinking and sleeping in the sun. It is a magnificent site; the face drops away dramatically and the headwall looks close enough to touch. The Himalaya stretch away to the horizon and to the north the mountains fade into the brown plains of the Tibetan Plateau. The sunset is phenomenal; the headwall turns red, and the sun slowly sinks among the monsoon clouds, silhouetting the giants of the Everest group.

It's 1.30am, very cold and very dark. We pack only a little food, the stove, the rope and a couple of pitons and ice screws. With our head torches on we climb out of the 'schrund and on to the sweeping ice fields that lead up to the East Ridge. There isn't any moonlight but we can vaguely make out the huge, striped rock buttress above us, which we have to climb round. Front-pointing up the ice we make good progress, concentrating on the circle of ice illuminated by our head torches. I pause for a rest and turn off my head torch. I look across at Andy as he climbs towards me, a small circle of light playing over the glistening ice. He stops next to me and turns off his torch. As our eyes become accustomed to the dark we try and make out the route above. The cold quickly invades our clothing and we continue upwards, carefully climbing a thin ice ribbon through a small, steep rock band. The buttress looms above us and we traverse underneath it and up towards the ridge.

Dawn comes slowly as we near the top of the ice fields. The sky brightens and light invades the valley below. Our situation is outrageous. Beneath our front-points the face falls away 3000 metres to the Jannu Glacier; the towering rock buttress to our right is striped with horizontal bands of black shale that are tinged red in the morning light. We continue upwards towards the ridge, heading for a weakness in the rock band that guards the ridge. On the way I collect a piton and karabiner from the edge of the buttress for a souvenir. Below the rock band we get out the rope. Andy belays me as I climb up the steep rock step and on to the ridge at about 7400 metres. I sit in the snow, dig my heels in and call for Andy to follow. Our view to the summit is blocked by a step in the ridge. We climb over a small 'schrund and up steep, soft snow to the top of the step.

The view along the ridge to the summit fills us with despair. The ridge is long and intricate. Huge cornices hang off the southern part and the northern side drops away steeply to the North Face. Several steep steps finally lead to the precarious summit. It is obvious that we can't make the summit and return to our camp in one day. We haven't got any bivvy gear with us but we do have the stove. We decide to climb on and bivvy on the descent.

Like two very old men bent over their walking-sticks, we hunch over our ice axes, breathing deeply. I turn to look at Andrew, a few metres away. His red suit stands out brightly against the white snow and the almost black sky. Our meandering tracks in the knee-deep snow, like those of a small beetle foraging for food, trace our route back along the ridge. Behind Andy the steep, fluted flanks of the east peak of Jannu glisten in the sun while further away the mighty South Face of the five-summited Kangchenjunga massif completely dominates the view.

I straighten up and focus my camera on Andrew, framing the shot to catch the wisps of high cloud that could warn of the approach of the hurricane-like winds that batter this part of the Himalaya. The shot captures the essence of why we are here; the physical struggle, the awesome beauty, and our detachment from civilisation. The deliberate, mechanical sound of the shutter causes Andy to look up. 'Awesome shot, Andy,' I say. Andy straightens up, I put my camera away and once again we turn to the task at hand, climbing the last several hundred metres to the summit of Jannu.

After our static-electricity scare, the sudden tranquillity of the ice cave to which we retreated is as shocking as the chaos outside. We get ourselves organised, hang the stove from an ice-screw and get a brew going. A freezing wind blasts up through a gaping crevasse in the floor of the cave and the cold is intense. We change our socks and make ourselves as comfortable as we can for the long night ahead. It is soon dark and for the next 12 hours we concentrate on keeping our feet alive. During the night the temperature plummets to −20°C. We put chemical toe warmers in our socks and massage our feet to keep the circulation going. The night passes painfully slowly but the task of avoiding frostbite keeps us occupied. At 6am we make another hot brew and leave the cave for the summit.

A rising traverse on the south side of the ridge leads me to the airy summit. I stand just below the top and dig my tools into the snow. Andy arrives and we stand together, looking out over the Himalaya, choked with emotion. We spend about half an hour on the summit before starting the long descent. We slowly climb back along the summit ridge, the sun and soft snow sapping what little energy we have left. Darkness catches us just after we abseil the rock band to the top of the ice fields. For the next four hours we carefully down-climb the steep ice-slopes to our tent in the 'schrund. We arrive at 10pm, exhausted and dehydrated. The next day we rest, sitting and dozing in the sun, and the following day we down-climb and abseil the face to the névé and Camp 2.

I linger on a grassy moraine ridge and cast a final glance up at the mountain; Andy and the porters have gone on ahead. I look up at the face and slowly shake my head as I recall our incredible journey. The hours of endless front-pointing up and down the vast ice fields, our dance along the precarious summit ridge, the freezing night in the ice cave. Powerful memories to last a lifetime. A gust of cold wind brings me back to the present. Cloud drifts over the East Ridge and slowly obscures all the

mountain except for the summit ice cap, which glistens in the sun. I turn
and scramble down the moraine ridge. Before me the valley opens up and
I feel the weight of the expedition finally lift from my shoulders.

*This article first appeared in the Australian Rock magazine, with thanks to Chris
Baxter.*

IAN PARNELL

Arwa Spire

(Plates 2–3)

A female friend of mine back home had suggested that male mountaineers always exaggerate their expedition writings, obsessed with tales of macho survival, with the inevitable conclusion '. . . and then we almost died.' Of course, I knew she was right, but nevertheless at that moment I couldn't help feeling like I was being buried alive. I knew, suspended in my portaledge 800 feet up an unclimbed peak in the Himalaya, that I was not in excessive mortal danger. My dreams, on the other hand, were crushed.

Kenton Cool, fellow corpse in this nylon coffin, and I had painted our desires across an enlarged copy of a photograph taken by Indian mountain explorer Harish Kapadia. A few years back, wandering off the beaten track in the Arwa area on the northern edge of the Gangotri in the Indian Garhwal, Kapadia stumbled on two beautiful slender spires. Dubbing them Arwa Tower and Spire, Kapadia tantalised the mountaineering community with his published photographs. Typically, Mick Fowler was quickest off the mark, leading a trip to the area in 1999. Mick, together with Steve Sustad, forced a fine first ascent of the Tower while the other expedition members, Crag Jones and Kenton Cool, made several attempts on the Spire, only to be thwarted by appalling snow conditions.

Kenton wasn't put off though and a year later, eager for a return match, he put together a motley crew for a serious attempt on the unclimbed Spire. The plan was for our team of six to operate as three independent pairs. Al 'the Vegan' Powell and the ever youthful Dave 'Dad' Wills were heading to the North Face, applying their lightweight alpine-style approach towards a vertical couloir line dubbed, only partly in jest, 'the hardest mixed line in the world'. Their attempt would be one of absolute commitment typical of many of the pair's previous forays into the big hills. The albino twins Pete 'Piggy' and Andy 'Agresso-man' Benson hoped to make a dash up the compelling NE Ridge of the Spire. Both strong skiers, they packed their planks and hinted at capping the planned first ascent with a rapid first ski descent.

Kenton 'KC' and I had spent our time back home scouring our photocopy, tracing and retracing a seemingly invisible line. Imaginary seams connecting blurs we hoped were corners and dust specks that might be flakes. We filled the gaps with our self-belief, eventually persuading ourselves we could manage the hardest most direct route on the mountain: the central pillar of the North Face. Kenton had the reality from his previous year's attempt to base his belief on and I had two successful expeditions already that year to inflate my ability.

Now, listening to the rhythm of the snow avalanching over our suspended cocoon, the joyful naïvety of those distant planning evenings are replaced by the brutal truth that we are about to 'fail'. Even crueller is the knowledge that the line will probably go.

Our taste of the technical delicacies yesterday included thin ice, tension moves, aiding on axes, top step teetering and crampon-scraping Scottish mixed. But we were only just beginning to nibble at the base of the real meat of the tower. Twelve days in and at least another nine to the summit. We just don't have the time – or do we? The spindrift spills in under the flysheet, drifting over my down bag. I pay it little heed – there's not much melting going on at –20°C. A decision has to be made. Continue to the last days of our trip and see if we can beat the race of time to the summit or retreat now and save ourselves for an attempt on the much easier but quicker left-hand couloir? To add impetus to our decision I've been unable to keep what little food I have eaten in for longer than a few minutes. With no warning my guts take their revenge at least four times a day.

Kenton laughs. It's usually him that is ill on these trips, but I worry what effect this inability to take on energy will have after another nine days up this tower. I tell myself that it's better to make decisions while you can rather than try to rationalise when the body and mind are truly breaking. The pain and struggle of the last two weeks to reach this point make the right decision a hard one to make. We had spent nine days just reaching the base of the tower. Nine days hauling 200lbs of gear through thigh-deep snow on a mere 40° slope or alternatively stumbling head-over-heels as our haulbags took us crashing amongst the moraine boulders. Often we would end up side by side on all fours, our lungs grabbing for the thin air, alternately cursing and laughing in despair at the stupidity of the challenge we'd set ourselves. But when we finally crawled over the col beneath the Arwa Tower the dream became true, the game worth the pain. Flanked by precipitous runnels of ice, rose a sheer slender spur, maybe 3000ft high, with only the merest ripple of features across its pure sweep of granite – the central pillar of the Arwa Spire.

But the decision is made; the dream is shattered. We're not talking; there's little for us to say. Heads bowed we stagger down the glacier, our backs to the wall. It was depressingly easy to descend in minutes the first pitches that had taken us days to climb and haul. My mind is blank, my soul empty as I wander in zigzags, the horizon blurred. As long as it's downhill away from these mountains I don't care. Slowly however my perceptions begin to clear. Whether it's the rhythm of our retreat march or the very emptiness of my heart at this moment, but I'm struck by the beauty of everything that surrounds me. The glacier is a bowl filled with light dancing amongst ice crystals in the air. It runs in rivulets of melt channels across the frozen ice

2. Arwa Spire (6193m), Garhwal. (*Al Powell*)

3. Kenton Cool in yellow and Al Powell in red during the second ascent of Arwa Spire, via the East Ridge. (*Ian Parnell*)

pooling at the base of giant-mushroomed erratic boulders perched atop plinths of ice up to 20 feet above us. As the melt increases we splash amongst jagged penitents, the glacier surface fractured into sharp waves frozen at their crest.

Each way I look another wonder reaches my eyes, lifting my spirits. I've stumbled into nature's secret gallery of treasures. Even the terminal hours of moraine display their own delights, an iron ore infusion scoring fire through rock banding gold, sienna and crimson, gilding the monotonous greys. I'm too tired to laugh, to dance, but I feel like a child discovering reflections in water for the first time. Each turn brings new discoveries. The river slowly becoming trapped by winter ice mirrors our own struggles with the race of time. Dreamy sculptures of ice fringe the shore. We crash through six-foot plates of sugar paper while delicate crystalline structures belie their fragile appearance and take our weight.

Head torches left amongst the equipment pile at the Spire's base, we press on into the night balancing the sound of rushing water to our left with the rough touch of granite boulders. Sometimes we misread our Braille and fall splashing to our knees but we can sense we are getting closer to camp. The giant silver disk of the Moon suddenly bursts through, bathing the valley in icy light. Something glints below and we can hear our friends once again. We've made it, we are back home.

Three days later we couldn't find any more excuses. The albino twins, Andy and Pete, had crashed into the dinner tent the previous night, big smiles cracking their sunburnt faces, victorious on the NE Ridge and so making the first ascent of the Spire. Excitedly, they retold tales of wild climbing and aiding to the summit in a snowstorm. The lift for the rest of us was palpable. Inspired by their efforts Kenton and I joined with Al and Dave who had also been forced to retreat from their route, the right-hand couloir of the North Face. We had retreated from low down on our line, but Dave and Al's attempt was even more heart-breaking. Climbing in the boldest of lightweight alpine styles, they forced difficult mixed climbing and tenuous thin ice three quarters of the way up the mountain before reaching an impasse at an impending shield of 120-degree overhanging rock. Hopes of good granite faded into a giant pale scar riddled with unclimbable rotten rock. Unable to find the merest hint of a ledge, the pair were forced to carve one-cheek scoops from the ice for a couple of precarious bivis. These cold, icy perches had taken their toll particularly with Dave who had contracted a nasty haemorrhoid, which was sympathetically christened 'Emma' by his team-mates.

So it was a rather impaired four that made the return trek to the base of the Spire. At least this time we were armed with a significantly better knowledge of the approach, managing in a long day the struggle with haul bags that had previously taken over a week. Any advantage we felt we had gained was being steadily eroded by the onset of winter. The snow fell heavily as we retraced our steps across the glacier and the temperatures had dropped even further. Our second-choice line of the left-hand couloir was becoming steadily more lethal, ready to spring on any unwary climbers wandering into its avalanche-laden trap. So our eyes turned to the ridge, squinting to catch signs of the Benson brothers' first ascent.

Awaking after a frigid, restless night, we moved slowly and clumsily, our clothes cracking in temperatures of −25°C. Another perfect clear alpine blue sky offered hope but 'Emma', Dave's unwelcome growth, had got even worse and he reluctantly had to abandon the climb. Sadly, we left Dave alone on the glacier and began to plough a furrow towards the ridge. Al, one of Britain's best fell-runners, took the helm, steering us through thigh-deep powder concealing gaping crevasses we could only sense. The first pitches of any big climb always seem the crux to me. Retreat is still possible and the rhythm of ascent has yet to be established. On the dark-shadowed ice up to the ridge, doubts surrounded me like clouds. My right foot had lost all feeling and I wasn't relishing the return to hard graft after our days of relaxation back in base camp. Al and Kenton seemed full of energy, surging up towards the sunlight breaking over the crest of the ridge. Their enthusiasm pulled me along and as the sun's rays hit my face I felt a release of pressure. Above us snaked the perfect alpine ridge: a sinuous knife-edge dotted with precipitous gendarmes. All our obsessions with the North Face and self-professed hardest routes in the Himalaya evaporated as the heat of the morning sun filled us with energy.

We decided to move together as a trio on one rope. Everything seemed to click and we were no longer hauling, wading or plodding but finally moving, really moving in the mountains. And fascinating movement it was: teetering on front-points above a 2000ft drop, swinging wildly round hanging arêtes, our mitts full of granite, axes biting pure ice or torqued in tiny cracks. I was beginning to remember what mountaineering should be all about. Our days spent struggling on the cold North Face had acclimatised us and, unleashed from the heavy tether of the haulbags, we made great progress along the ridge.

The highlight for me came at the penultimate pitch, perched 300ft above the untrodden southern Arwa Glacier. Here, in a heavy whiteout snowstorm, the Benson brothers were forced to aid a narrow crack as they raced the deteriorating conditions for the summit. As I was the supposed aid-climbing expert of our little team I assembled a mixture of slings into foot loops and set off, unsure of how hard it might be. At first, for speed, I free climbed the initial groove, tentatively reaching round for the aid crack. My fingers sank into a perfect jam and I leaned out to see a slice of pure Millstone Edge laid out before me. My lungs seemed to forget the altitude, higher than I'd ever been before, as jam followed jam. My plastic boots skittered across the hard granite but protection was perfect. In the snowstorm the brothers must have missed this classic HVS and opted for a thinner seam further right. Kenton and Al were soon whooping their way up this and a final crack towards the summit. The brothers had mentioned that the final summit block had proved interesting. A smooth crackless standing stone, perhaps 15-20ft high, protected Arwa's highest point. I tried every trick in the book but despite half an hour of effort we shared the same highpoint as the Bensons. Back in the Peak this last monolith would offer a fine E5 6b but at well over 6000m and in plastic boots we accepted our limitations and celebrated at its base.

We soaked up a cloudless view across the Gangotri, the Nanda Devi Sanctuary and a thousand unclimbed peaks towards a huge mountain that must have been Dhaulagiri hundreds of miles away on the horizon. I'd forgotten the pain and struggles of the previous days. The quest for difficulty had been replaced by a lesson in simplicity. Working together with friends I had learnt again the joy of the mountains.

Summary: A personal account of the first ascent of the Arwa Spire (6193m), Indian Garhwal. First ascent of the NE Ridge by Andy and Pete Benson, followed three days later by Kenton Cool, Ian Parnell and Al Powell. Dave Wills reached a 5900m high point with Al Powell on the unclimbed North Face.

ACKNOWLEDGEMENTS

The expedition would like to thank: Nick Estcourt Award, Mount Everest Foundation, BMC, MC of S and UK Sport for generous financial support and Rab, Terra Nova, Paramo, North Face and Urban Rock for equipment support.

JOHN BARRY

Big Walls in Kenya

(Plate 20)

Beware encounters of the casual, insouciant kind. They end in tears. I was on the way to the post office, a harmless pursuit, when the dream of the day was broken by the toot from a car horn, and there he was, the tooter: Pat Littlejohn. Beware, too, boyish grins and torrential enthusiasm, for he has all of both. And so the 'what-you-been-up-tos' and the 'got-anything-planneds' led seductively to the 'd'you fancys', which led in very quick turn to Kenya, the North Face of Poi and me bruised, bloodied and about beaten, closer to the sky than the earth and hanging clear of the rock we'd come to climb.

There's more to it than that, of course, but not much. Littlejohn had said that Steve Sustad and he were off to Kenya to this fabulous chunk of rock, two-and-a-half thousand feet high and only one route so far, to have a shot at a spectacular-looking line on the north side, coupla-weeks February, wannacome? The answer was yes. The answer's always yes. So that was the trip planned. Pat bought a placcie water-container and that was the admin. Steve found some tickets on the Internet which was the logistics. And I failed on the easiest route on the local climbing wall: trained.

Two days north of Nairobi is Poi: a great loaf of a rock baked in the north Kenyan desert, miles around and half-a-mile high. As our truck bounced by, an eye of faith could trace the line: the mother of all *arc-en-ciels* from base to about two thirds, then overhangs – or were they ledges? And was that eyebrow insubstantial scrub or sturdy trees? And what above? It was hard to get the scale; hard to know if that crack or chimney or this slab, or yonder offwidth was indeed crack or chimney or slab or offwidth. Or whether they were ten feet or hundreds (they were hundreds). Anyway, my eyes were faithless both and as Ozymandias commanded, I looked on his works and despaired.

'What-dya think Pat?'

'Ye-eh'!

That's what Pat always only thinks, and ever voiced in a great affirmative plosion of grinning enthusiasm. Diamond geezer, diamond climber. Just as well.

The nearest village, N'gurunit, a collection of mud and wattle huts with a smattering of more substantial dwellings, is set amid a wonderland of Yosemite-esque walls. The desert scrub is laced with ribbons of lush green foliage where fountful rivers run and limpid pools lie beneath plashy rocks. Camels graze in herds, antelopes run in pairs and lions roam alone – and all under an azure African sky: gorgeous. The local tribesfolk are Samburu, a people improbably tall, implausibly handsome, improperly decent and impossibly elegant: gorgeous. That's the blokes. The women were of such dead-drop pulchritudity that even the uxorious Littlejohn could scarce forbear to steal a look. Sustad stared like a bachelor – which he is. I merely recorded this – and leered.

We recruited a dozen of the men to help with our wherewithal to the bottom of the crag; the wherewithal was mostly water. What it wasn't, this being a Littlejohn trip, was bolts. He don't bolt. Our climb lay a couple of miles uphill from a dirty track, through excoriating scrub to a thick strip of primary forest that girdled the base of Poi. The walk was hot, no hotter – and the scrub mordant.

'In Kenya everything you touch either bites, pricks or eats you', I said, adding, tongue in cheek so to speak, 'or gives you a dose of all three.'

Steve's only concession to climate and flora was a sun hat on a thinning pate. Otherwise it was black Levis, black 'Iron Maiden' T-shirt and once-black Doc Martens. He looked, for all the world, as if he was on his way to a meeting of the Chapter; while Pat, a Lowe sponsoree, from tip (also thinning) via tail to toe, sported all manner of casually smart leisure wear. I, meanwhile, sweated, got pricked, bitten, eaten … and not quite all four.

A few hours later, where rock and forest met, the Samburu shed their loads and joshed and chewed on tubers, watching intently as we readied for the off. One of the older of them, whether to show the way or the where or the why I'm not sure, pencil slender, lissomed up the first fifty feet, cast half-interestedly about as if spoilt for choice, and descended with the languid grace of Nijinsky at a village bop. He smiled at us. Sympathy? Pity? Or we-were-here-first primordial ownership? It was impossible to know. But of one thing I was certain.

'Looks bloody desperate, Pat.'

'Ye-eh.'

'Look at those off-widths' (for they were they).

'Ye-eah. They're yours mate. Fat man's pitches.'

'What about that roof – that one half way up?'

'Ye-eah. Lovely off-width right through. You'll love that. Fat man's pitch.'

'Nice slab to start though.'

'Ye-eah. But that's an off-width all up the edge. Fat man's pitch.'

I was somewhere after despair when he volunteered, 'we'll swing leads, 1, 2, 3.' Relief. Great deal.

Steve was uncoiling ropes, lots of ropes, and racking gear, great janglings of it. This was business. More Friends than Tony Blair and not a bolt to be seen. Nor any unseen. The man don't bolt. Simple as that.

'What if, Pat?', I asked.

'Adventure, mate. There's always a way.'

'Always?'

'Ye-eah – so far anyway.'

Pat stepped from forest floor to rock, dusted hands and feet and was away in that calm, purposeful climbing gait of his. It's not so much that he makes hard look easy, it's that he makes desperate routine. But I'd climbed with him before and I wasn't fooled. After about 140ft of routine, mundane, pedestrian E3 5c he belayed and Steve and I followed in tandem. Next pitch is Steve's. He says, Pateyesque, that he's a mountain man, not much of a rock climber. And so insisting, dispensed another 140ft E3 5c+ in ten minutes and a couple of grunts. The plus? I added that later – just now in fact. Fat man got the last pitch of the afternoon – a rounded off-width (made to measure, Pat said) and lubricated with dust and guano. Guano. I didn't tell you about the vultures, great hungry-looking Griffins that circled all day overhead (and as we got higher, underhead) with the vested interest of an undertaker and a nice line in guano. E3 5c. Have a nice day.

I lay comfortable on the forest floor and wondered how much more unknown E3 5c I could handle – especially since our three pitches plainly comprised the easy bit and Pat, reasonably, was insisting on a metronomic swinging of leads. Looking up into the quick tropical twilight I could see, maybe 1000ft above, the *arc-en-ciel*, the impending, to use the word favoured by guidebooks, crack, overhanging in two planes (more if you want) and capped by a sleepless roof. The one through which ran (disastrously for me) an off-width. In *extremis*, I thought (and, boy, would I be in *extremis*) I could always resort to jumars – a pair of which Pat had allowed.

Next morning, after a cuppa and something, we jumared to the ledge of our high point and set out again. Pat first. Gibbon moves on a too-slender branch. Steve follows and gibbons heavily and the branch cracks. I'm too heavy a gibbon and it breaks. Nothing to gibbon on, so I gibber on – and up – just. E3 5c. Then two more pitches, E3 5c. Nothing if not consistent; cracks, off-widths, walls, overhangs; nothing if not varied.

By now, the third day, we had run out of ropes to fix, so we quit the ground that morning, with water in gallon containers, pullovers for the night and a bar of chocolate. Pat don't eat either. We muscled up the six pitches, on jumars, and I belayed Pat for the next lead. Steve, despite twice the load I'd carried, made light work of the jumaring, and whereas I'd emerged sweating and bloody knuckled, he arrived coolly unscathed, declaring himself now a big-wall man. I felt a very small-wall man.

Above, Littlejohn was making light too, and soon, too soon, came the cry 'safe.' I followed the steep corner at – no prizes – a routine E3 5c. However, and that's a great big overhanging, *arc-en-ciel* of an however, the routine was over. What lay ahead seemed to arch over, beyond a single craning of the neck towards Cairo, several thousand miles to the north and looked about as appealing. I averted my eyes when they came to the capping roof, 15 feet across, and cleaved by – you got it – an off-width.

According to Pat it was my pitch. According to me it was impossible.
'Whaddya reckon Pat?'
'Ye-eah. Looks tasty.'
'Tasty? We got to climb the bloody thing, not eat it.'
'Fancy it?'
'Ye-ah.'
Tasty! I had surrendered. Capitulated. Pleaded. Too tasty a pitch. Pat led. And how the boy led! Certainly, inexorably, upwards.

Nor grunt, nor groan, nor lurch, nor scrabble; only deliberate jams and deft, precise feet: nothing hurried, plenty gained. Resting place, he said, at 70ft and after that much more of the same. A scarcely perceptible falter, a barely breathed grunt, and he was there. E5 6a – every move a hand jam. You'd never have known it. Pat's ease, falter and grunt apart, gave it the lie, but I can read geometry and a crane-sore neck tells only true. It looked a horror. It was horror. I jammed for all I was worth – which isn't much. I shed energy, showered grunts. I bled while calories fled my arms so by 70ft I not so much needed a rest as a sabbatical. Rest? 'Where's the rest?'

Pat called instructions and I bridged as he said. Just. No, not just but whatever is less than that, one foot on rock that was distantly attached to Kenya and one on rock that came down from the sky, or cyberspace. Between my legs I could see Africa – all of it, and a long way below. Above more *arc-en-ciel* and that roof. I was unhappy.

My fighting weight – and, was I fighting! – is 12 stones. Pat now knows that too. But he knows no quarter and, at the belay, allowed me only a minute to blow before handing me the gear and nodding at the roof. I slid my head into the rack much like a condemned man into a noose, with hangman Pat in close attendance, morbidly solicitous, professionally cheerful. I think he was enjoying himself. As far as I was concerned, hanging or climbing, the results were likely to be similar and a hanging the more humane. As I started he handed me a Camalot the size of a small house, assuring me that it was the bollocks.

In truth the crack across the roof was a horizontal, chimney-like climbing along a narrow corridor, a thousand feet up, with no floor. No protection either, but not bad once you'd got your arse into gear – which is what chimneys are all about. The corridor led to the roof's edge and the open-ended chimney closed, above, to an off-width. Here the Camalot was the bollocks and I thrust it anyhow into the crack, glad to be relieved of its half-hundredweight. Above that I fancied I could see heaven; as close as I ever expected to be. Then with the courage that crawls in after departed despair, I launched – I think that's the verb – heavenwards. Well upwards anyway.

Now it is said that there's technique to off-widths, but I'm not so sure. To me it's a bar room brawl; fists, elbows, shoulders, head, knees, feet, arse and belly, especially belly. I brawled. I won.

Beyond lay a hand crack and vertical. Immediately below, like at the end of my legs, a flat, room-for-two-feet, hold, the flattest, prettiest thing I'd seen all day. It felt like Nebraska. But I was out of gear that fitted; and guts. Could I belay? Pat wanted to know. Not on a single Friend, I yelled. Could I lead on? No. Could I be lowered? Yes. I lowered off. Well not off exactly, but to somewhere and Pat took over while Steve waited patiently several hundred feet below, having jettisoned our fixed-line umbilical. From now on retreat would be tricky. Pat disappeared around the roof going steadily (as you'd expect) as far as Nebraska, above which he slowed, the rope now consumed in inches per move rather than furlongs. Then nothing for ages. After an hour or so I ventured a 'how's-it-going-mate?'. There was a delay. Then, 'Bloody grim.' Grim! Grim from the man, that pathological optimist Littlejohn, was bad news indeed.

At last, a long last, the rope went tight and a couple of tugs signalled my okay and I set out again on recently quit ground, which went more easily this time round. Something to do with a top-rope perhaps? Minutes later I was able to reach high and get a solid two-handed grip on Nebraska and make a joyous heave onto the best hold in three days of climbing. But Nebraska wasn't having it and came away in a state-sized chunk while I hung aboard. As we parted company ten feet later, it caught my instep and left me to hang in space while it crashed past a startled Steve to Earth.

Everything I looked at was red, blood red. Hands, feet, rope, rock, there was freely gushing blood for everywhere. I tried so hard not to panic that I panicked; wriggling into an upside-down position to try to stem the flow. An intricate retreat was sounded and we were out of Africa, though avowed to return to the same fray same time next year.

At the post mortem, Pat put the last pitch at E6 6a, not counting ten feet of vertical and ungradable guano which he'd surmounted by chipping holds with his nut-key. The pitch had ended in a vulture ledge, the climb in tears.

February 2000 saw us back – with a vengeance. The vengeance being hammocks, a few more Friends, an even bigger Camelot, this one the size of a multi-storey car park, and Jan, a fourth climber – or, more accurately, jumarer (sorry mate).

I'm not sure why we were surprised but all the 5cs were still 5c, the 6as, 6a. And I still wanted that + on the 5c+ – too nice a distinction for Pat whose register doesn't clock on until somewhere in the senior sixes in any case.

We did it too, though not without a rattling good scrap. It took two days of climbing to gain Pat's vulture ledge. This time I belayed at what was left of Nebraska and Pat led through to his guano. Still a triple-X-rated, adults only, horror.

Next day we quit the ground to jumar 9 pitches, about 1200ft to the vulture ledge. The last 300 were on an 8mm rope which stretched shoe-lace-thin when weighted, and shoelace-thinner and flat where it ran over edges. It was sobering. The hell, it was terrifying, but just when I had concluded that I was getting too old for it all, Steve, a veteran of many a wild Yosemite wall, said that was one of the worst jumars of his life, which, in a perverse sort of a way, cheered me. Above Vulture Ledge, Steve, the non-rock-climber, led another horror (E5 6a), though not before averring that it was an off-width and, therefore, properly mine. I countered that it was a finger-crack and, therefore, properly Pat's. In fact, it turned out to be a round-shouldered layback and Pat (natch) made the best fist of it, Steve and I sneaking on a point (or two) of aid.

Then life got serious. Littlejohn climbed twenty feet and drew a blank. Went left, drew another. Tried right, and another. No-one said anything about retreat. We all knew there was none. Having dropped the jumar ropes we had burnt our bridges, boats and any other combustible metaphor you care to think of. On the menu of possibilities, down was off, love. Up didn't look very appetising either. Littlejohn, diamond geezer, you gotta get up. He fixed a good nut and climbed 'til he fell, which put him in space and well out from the rock. This was when I realised he was cool-hand crazy.

Above him, maybe 30 feet, grew a tree. Not a sturdy English oak or anything of the kind, but a tree, a bush of a tree, of sorts. Moreover, this tree had multifarious branches and roots but spindly and brittle. And Littlejohn saw hope – salvation – where I saw only tree. Hanging there in vast airborne space, he took from his armoury a Friend, and untying from one of his two ropes, he fashioned a bolas. Then, leaning back to get an angle, he wound up the improvisation for a hurl and after a dozen revolutions, set it flying upward towards the tree. Near miss. Another go – nearer miss. On the fourth or fifth attempt Pancho's Friend fell between root and rock and, with a deft tweak or two, lodged. Elsewhere, on Pampas terra-firma only full-blooded gauchos can do that, and when they do they win prizes at rodeos. Our prize was the climb.

Littlejohn threaded a couple of prusiks to our lifeline and, ginger as you like, crept to the tree as far as the first branch and gibboned into it. It was breathtaking, thirty foot hanging free from a Friend fluke-jammed between nothing much and nothing at all. Jan, Steve and me, we jumared all three.

Next day, after a night in the tree, came the highlights. Pat took maybe ten falls trying for a breakthrough up a short wall to easier ground. We gave up. Ten falls from Littlejohn means try elsewhere. We went left first and then a long overhanging traverse back to the point above where Pat had tried so hard, 200ft of 6a climbing to win 20 vertical feet, and Steve the non-rock-climber pulling out a big lead where I had failed. At last, though, we sensed we were winning and after a further 150ft pitch, 5c and about two runners, we abseiled back to our tree-of-life for a second night.

Now we were desperately short of water. We had to get up the next day. Which day began with a free-hanging diagonal jumar, a sharpener of the senses in a warm, sudden tropical dawn. First one of my jumars slipped from the rope, leaving me hanging from a single device. I clipped a second point faster than anyone before or since. The vultures looked disappointed.

Then an intermediate anchor failed and I fell fifteen feet attached to the rope only by jumars. I clipped a third point faster than the previous faster. The vultures were mortified, my senses fully honed.

At last an easy pitch, E2 5b, led to what looked certain to be the last – and less than vertical at that, though not much less. I volunteered. As if to compensate for its lack of plumb, the pitch offered no holds, or runners either. But we were fired-up and had, just had, to get up. E3 6a, rotten gear and yards in between. E2 scrambling remained. We stood on top with giant thirsts and foolish grins.

As Pat put it, the outcome had remained in doubt to the last, 'proper adventure that.'

We called it, *Dark Safari*. Pat says it's E6 – and he's the man. I say it had 17 or 18 pitches, but I was past counting. And who cares?

RICHARD PASH

The Lemon Mountains of East Greenland

(Plates 4–9)

R emember the last really grim climb you did? The desperate struggle in
the whiteout when you asked yourself 'What am I doing here?' The
time you wished you had realised the route was out of condition before
you'd started climbing or the frustrating walk back to the car following a
failure. Sometimes sunny days and good conditions seem a bit elusive.

So if I told you that there are some mountains in the world with almost
perfect weather would you believe me? A place where most routes are only
60 minutes from camp, somewhere you can climb 1000m lines without
bivvy gear? How about somewhere with unclimbed routes on solid granitic
gneiss or on good ice in deep-cut couloirs? Such a place exists: the Lemon
Mountains in East Greenland.

I'm lucky enough to have spent the last two summers climbing in the
Lemons. After our first expedition in 1999 we were tempted back, so I put
together a note of what was good about the place to help attract new
members.

You can climb six days a week. Stable summer weather typically means
blue windless skies; in six weeks this summer we were tent-bound for only
six days. Climb fast and light: 24 hours' daylight means no bivvy gear on
long routes and the low altitude means no acclimatisation and no headaches.
And the choice is wonderful: climb rock in the midday sun in your T-shirt
or climb ice in the midnight sun in your duvet. There are no walk-ins
because there are no valleys, only glaciers, so an hour's skiing takes you to
the bottom of the climb. How simple; a climbing expedition on which you
spend most of your time climbing.

Our two expeditions were a loose group of friends of mixed experience
and all aged 20-27. Some were Greenland and Arctic 'veterans' back for
their sixth expedition, while others were good technical climbers but in
Greenland for the first time. As well as a mix of ability it was great to have
a mix of sexes there. This summer, with three women, there was a lot less
puerile humour than before! Everyone had something to learn and everyone
had something to bring to the group. Our rock 'pros' got valuable Alpine
experience, our Scottish winter experts taught the rest a thing or two about
ice and Greenland taught us all about how to behave in the wilderness.

The jagged peaks of the Lemons are made of good stuff – the rock there
is unusually hard for the Arctic – and it is this which gives the area its

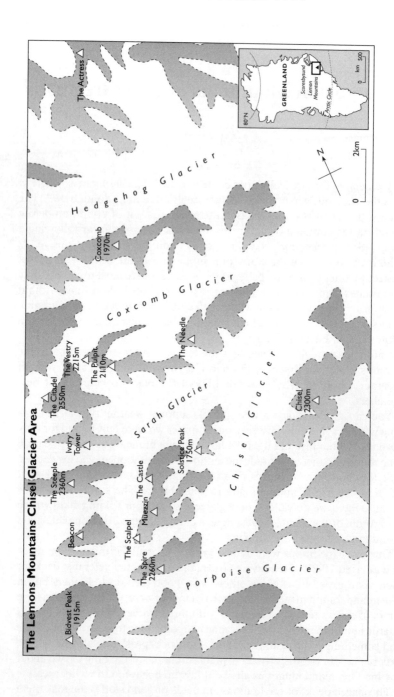

character. There are lovely Alpine peaks with fluted snow faces; giant teeth of mountains with impressive snow ridges; rock towers with faces cut by deep ice couloirs; and lots of fine rock spires. Because the rock stratum points up, everything points up: spires, towers, aiguilles, gendarmes.

The catch to the Lemons is that they are not easy to get to; they are in the middle of Greenland's desolate East Coast. Only 3500 people live on the whole of this coastline, which is half of the coastline of the second biggest island in the world. Our nearest town was in Iceland; the easiest way to the Lemon Mountains is to fly from there in a ski-equipped plane. As for our food and equipment, we dropped that from another plane in cardboard boxes, to save money. We had a few nervous moments opening the boxes to discover what had smashed, but apart from losing a third of our fuel everything else was remarkably unscathed. I say 'unscathed' because when you're hungry you don't mind a bit of jam on your fish. The fuel situation was worrying, given we had to melt all our water, but we solved that using blue plastic barrels in the sun. Once we settled in, the feeling of remoteness was fabulous. Standing on the summit of Solstice, our first peak, with thousands of mountains in every direction, it was spine-tingling knowing no one else there. How amazing for such a big view to be so silent.

The Citadel was one of the reasons we came back to the Lemons. It was just too far away from us in 1999, but from every peak we climbed we could see its striking rock profile towering above the other summits. This time we didn't hesitate: two days after making camp four tiny people skied up to its enormous South Face. Tackling several linked snowfields, we were aiming to hit the East Ridge as the sun swung round to warm the rock. This way we caught the snow at 'night' and then had 12 hours to get to the summit before the rock got too cold to climb. Excited to be on our first big mountain we raced up the snow and changed into our rock gear in a flash, leaving axes and plastic boots at the stance. The 6am sun was just starting to light the ridge so there was a bit of hand-shaking going on as we tried to keep warm. Soon though the orange rock was radiating with heat and what had looked like a desperate knife-edge from camp turned into eight pitches of Severe: the knife was 20 metres wide! As usual the scale of Greenland was bigger than anticipated. When we got to the summit ridge what had looked like small snow patches from camp was a two-metre snow crest. With no axes or plastics, the 45-60° snow and ice on the right looked a bit dubious. As for the left, an intermittent rock ledge over a 400m headwall didn't look too inviting either. We decided to head back, disconsolate to fail so close to the top. Rupert, however, wasn't having any of this, so as the rest of us stroked our beards and mumbled discouragingly, off he went. A fine lead with a lot of rope drag thrown in and suddenly a cheeky face appeared beneath the summit. Citadel was ours.

Percy Lemon first spotted the Lemons as he surveyed them with Gino Watkins in 1931 as part of the Trans-Arctic Air Route Expedition of 1930-33. Despite the interest of eight expeditions since then – most famously

Chris Bonington's visits in 1991 and 1993 – only 10 peaks had been climbed on the Hedgehog and Chisel glaciers when we first visited in 1999. Having seen stunning photos taken of the area, we aimed in our two expeditions to explore these glaciers much more thoroughly. Between the two trips we climbed 50 new routes, including 32 first ascents up to TD+.

I was pleased we didn't recce the Steeple properly. Aptly named by Chris Bonington in 1993, it looks impenetrable from all directions: a tower of rock with 60° sides. Its only flaw is a superb ice couloir that reaches from head to foot on its East Face. A magnet of a mountain, it was only unclimbed because of poor ice conditions on the crux in 1993. Deep ice couloirs are a feature of the Lemons, where eroded bands from a soft rock intrusion split the faces of a number of the mountains. On the Actress in 1999 we found several pitches of Scottish V ice: what was in store here? Climbing a nearby mountain to survey the route, we could see the whole line except a small part hidden by a buttress. It looked fine, in fact it looked no more than Scottish III or IV, even if it was 700m long. But what was behind that buttress? I was also concerned about the top of the peak: vertical rock from the couloir top to the summit. At the time I thought we had been quite thorough recce-ing the route, but as we skied to the foot of the climb my heart hit my mouth. The ice behind the buttress was vertical and the rock beneath the ice was also vertical, so falling off the ice could be iffy. To get there we came in from the side: delightful climbing on mixed III ice and rock up a meandering ramp. Round the corner and there it was, a large ice-filled slot, cut deep in the buttress. In I went, up 40 metres of 45-60° water ice, my axes biting into the plastic surface. Bridging out across the chimney I found plenty of pro and climbed with confidence towards a small boulder for a belay. I looked at the boulder, put a sling around it and gave it a tug. It promptly moved down, onto my shoulder. During the next few sweaty minutes I tried to push the rock back onto its ledge, but it felt like the whole mountain was trying to send me down the gully. Shouting to the others I told them to get out of the way while I guessed what would happen when the rock fell. Quite apart from bouncing off the chimney into them, it would almost certainly hit my rope and take me down too. There was nothing I could do; I gingerly took my weight off the rock and stepped aside, expecting the worst. Three crumbs of gravel held it in place. The world felt fluffy again. Looking across the chimney I saw the obvious belay with Bonington's sling. If I was a half-decent mountaineer I would have seen it ages ago. Time wasted, I brought Rupert up and he set off up the wall above. Unluckily for him things were not nearly as consolidated above as they were for me, a lattice of icicles covered snow that barely supported his weight. We could see why our predecessors were repelled in warmer conditions. Unluckily for me I was at the unprotected stance below, while Rupert – the ice destroyer – smashed his way upwards. Wham! Bam! Crunch! Everyone swore at Rupert while envying his excellent Scottish V lead.

Was that it? Above the falls things looked a lot simpler: a long broad gully stretched up as far as I could see. Off I went only to discover it was soft snow on ice; we moved together, but it was hard work and we weren't going as quickly as we hoped. As we sweated our way up, the snow thinned until we found ourselves again on beautiful hard grade III ice, pitches and pitches of the stuff. Lovely climbing but we'd now been going for 11 hours and my enthusiasm for kicking steps was starting to wane. I also had a horrible feeling that we wouldn't be able to get out of the couloir at the top. I wished I could stop worrying and enjoy what were superb conditions near the top of one of the finest unclimbed peaks in the area and one of the finest peaks I have ever climbed. Funny how it takes until you're sitting in the pub to realise that. At the top of the couloir we saw our way through. The rock was easy after all and we sped to the summit.

Good rock-climbing was something we had come to the Lemons for. There are no shortage of beautiful spires, towers and faces to climb. There are many, many unclimbed lines waiting for their first ascent. It seemed sacrilegious to me to go cragging when there were so many unclimbed summits, but some days there's nothing better than soaking up the sun on a 50-metre corner. Although scanning the route with binoculars, we were often way out on scale. That pile of rubble? Those are 60-metre slabs. What look like crack lines are arm jams, and off-widths turn into giant chimneys.

One of the peaks we 'worked' was the Castle, so called because of its four impressive looking turret-like buttresses. We camped right beneath it and scoured the rock for lines. Pippa and Tom were the first up on the SE Turret, climbing four fine pitches of 5c and 6a up a single spiralling crackline called *Never Mind the Crocodiles* (ED1). Four others attacked the twin summits of the castle from the west. Nic and I found a lovely four-pitch VS on the North Summit (*Cam-a-Little*, D) and watched Tom and Lucy on a very airy VS (*Cam-a-Lot*, D–) to the summit opposite. Our third pitch was a superb rising 4c hand crack right on the outside of the arête. I was almost laughing as I found move after move on beautiful rock, especially as it was really Nic's lead but she'd sent me up to remove a stuck friend and I kind of carried on. Watching Lucy and Tom on their 80° tower opposite, the feeling of the scale and space behind us was stupendous. Miles and miles of nothing between us and the Steeple in the distance.

Life on a four-mile wide glacier had a few surprises, like where to go to the loo when there are no convenient bushes, or where to put down your mug of tea. Living on an enormous block of ice means you can't drop your jumper on the floor, and sleeping on anything thinner than a Therm-a-rest can be rather chilly. We soon got more savvy: metal poles from our sledges doubled as clothes hangers, and stuffing shopping bags with bubblewrap from the airdrop made warm seats. We also had a superb mess tent which we dug two metres into the snow. It was just big enough for all eight of us to squeeze in, and was pretty cosy when the stoves were going. It was great to be able to eat together and chat about the routes of the day, or the state of Tom's dreadlocks.

Not all our climbing went to plan; we kept having problems with north-facing snow routes. The night temperatures weren't as cold as we would have liked which meant the north faces which get the weak midnight sun didn't consolidate properly. We were particularly disappointed to fail on the Scalpel, an evil blade of a mountain with a superb twisting ice gully running vertically up its north face. Only one pitch of rock is needed to access the gully, but we were deluged in water as we tried to climb it.

The Lemons are adjacent to one of the biggest fjords in Greenland, Kangerdlugssuaq, which is so large you can see it on every map of Greenland, two-thirds of the way from Ammassalik to Constable Pynt. There's something about the combination of mountains and fjords that's just magical; the starkness of the mountains combined with vivid colours of the coast and the contrast between mighty peaks and flat sea. With our explorers' hats on we went off to find the fjord, setting off from camp on ski with our bivvy gear to a remote peak at the foot of Sarah Glacier. Apart from the Scandinavians, I've never seen anyone Telemark ski with confidence, and our drunken path down the glacier was no exception; even gentle slopes look sinister in soft leather boots. Going uphill again we were back in control of our legs; we skied almost to the summit.

It was possibly the most chilled-out bivvy in the history of Greenland; we drank whisky and chatted in our sleeping bags while thousands of icebergs groaned in the fjord below our feet. A peachy glow from the low sun reflected off the Greenland Icecap to our right while we scanned the horizon of hundreds of unclimbed mountains waiting across the fjord. The scale of our vista was incomprehensible; the smallest of the glaciers across the fjord were several miles wide, the smallest mountains had 400m faces, and the tiniest icebergs were several storeys high. So how many thousand kilometres of icecap could we see? How many million tons of ice was floating in the fjord? It was one of those occasions when I felt I might have an impression of the real size of the Earth.

As the end of the expedition drew near, we were drained. Sore hands, aching legs and general lethargy set in. To begin with we kept going; saying that seeing as it was another nice day, we ought to make the most of it, then rest when the weather clagged in. Not that we wanted it to snow, but at least it would be a good excuse to stop. It was lovely lying around at camp, but somehow it felt wrong under a perfect sky. Then again, as I soaked up the Greenland sunshine, and took in the views, the weather would surely be good for another day – and those unclimbed peaks could wait. Next time you're fighting through in a blizzard, or reading the back of a Mars Bar wrapper in your tent, have a think about the Lemon Mountains. Maybe it's time you planned a trip there.

Reports from both 1999 and 2000 expeditions are at: www.wayupnorth.clara.co.uk

JOHN SLEE-SMITH

An Ascent of Mount Aspiring

(Frontispiece and Plate 10)

Towards the end of 1998 my wife and I went to New Zealand for a holiday. Even at the age of 65 I had not lost my love for high mountains and I was looking forward to the opportunity of climbing one of New Zealand's highest peaks, Mount Aspiring. An isolated mountain, 3027 metres high, Mount Aspiring is the most southerly of all the 3000-metre peaks in the Southern Alps. I had written to a New Zealand guide, Geoff Wayatt, who lived and worked in Wanaka, and we had provisionally put aside a week during the second half of November.

Mount Aspiring, known to the Maori people as *Tititea* or glistening peak, is situated about 35 miles from Wanaka and about 15 miles from the roadhead. If you are walking in, normally a two-day trek, there is a track to the French Ridge Hut and from there you would have a good glacial crossing to get you to Mount Aspiring. Spring in New Zealand can produce some fairly fickle weather and we wanted to make our attempt on this fairly remote peak in as stable weather conditions as possible. At ground level the weather was perfect – bright sunshine with a gentle breeze – but higher up, at 2000 metres, automatic weather station reports indicated winds reaching 60-70 mph. We decided to wait for a couple of days; the weather became more settled and we decided to go for it.

To replace the two-day walk-in, we hired a helicopter to take us and our gear to the Bevan Col just above the Bonar Glacier. From there we would have a fairly simple snow plod over the least crevassed area of the glacier to the Colin Todd Hut, perched on rocks at the foot of the northwest ridge of Mount Aspiring. The pilot, highly experienced in mountain navigation, brought us down amidst swirling cloud to a tiny, twelve-foot stony platform right on the col. He was naturally anxious to return to lower levels (small helicopters are notoriously bad at navigating in cloud) so we quickly heaved the sacks out of the rear compartment and, ducking low, bade farewell to our link with civilisation for the next four days.

The Colin Todd Hut was built of metal cladding, over a timber frame bolted and wired down to surrounding bedrock. Like many of the newer New Zealand alpine huts, the Colin Todd had been flown into position by helicopters in pre-fabricated units.

This was to be, probably, my only experience of climbing in the Southern Alps of New Zealand, and what an incredible area of natural wilderness it proved to be. Beautiful peaks, glistening out of surrounding glaciers and icefalls, rose above the clouds. Around the area of the hut I came across the *kea*, or mountain parrot – a bird that will eat anything, from the inner linings of boots, to gaiters or anoraks left out on the hut balcony to dry. Big notices were posted inside the hut: 'DO NOT FEED THE KEA – EITHER INTENTIONALLY OR UNINTENTIONALLY'. Most of the huts are equipped with two-way radio communication with a central base in Wanaka – a facility that has to be paid for! This is very useful for getting the latest weather information, avalanche warnings and other important data such as who will be attempting the peak in the following 24 hours. Every party has to register with the National Park authorities on the day they depart from Wanaka.

We were going to make our attempt on the northwest ridge the following day, so a fairly early start was called for. I had brought with me, from the UK, my own mountain equipment, such as snow boots, crampons, ice-axe and gaiters. I could have hired these, but borrowed gear is never quite so comfortable as one's own. Up at the reasonable hour of 4am, we were on the glacier just after 4.30. About three-quarters of an hour later we reached the foot of the ridge and put on crampons. Firm, good quality snow brought us to the lower rocks. Very loose rock reminded me of the Bernese Oberland peaks and needed careful handling to make rapid progress. As we were making excellent time, we could afford a breakfast stop before tackling the last third of the mountain.

We had been climbing, so far, through fairly heavy cloud, but from this point to the top we were bathed in beautiful sunshine and climbing on delightfully crisp *névé* with patches of water ice. The summit was a perfect cone of untrodden snow – another hidden joy! – while amazing views stretched for nearly 100 miles to the Fiordland peaks in the south-west and we also had a view of Mount Cook in the north. The guide was extremely pleased with our ascent, especially as I was his oldest client over a long career as a professional mountain guide. He added that, if I was typical of seasoned Alpine Club members, then he was impressed!

The snow on the glacier during the early afternoon was soft and heavy, making our return to the hut rather a tedious affair. On the descent route the bergschrund lay at an awkward angle of about 40 degrees. The guide told me that it was usual to jump it and turn at the same time, so that when you landed you were facing uphill. With slightly less flexibility than I used to have, my performance of this manœuvre must have been quite amusing to watch! The following morning we began a two-day walk-out to the roadhead where Geoff had arranged for a car to be waiting for us. To have managed this in a single day would have involved walking with a heavy pack for 12 hours or more and getting back to Wanaka after dark. From Bevan Col we descended a couple of thousand feet through soft snow at a convenient angle, abseiling down wet rock until we eventually reached the valley floor. We then had to ford five streams in spate and one glacial torrent up to our thighs, with a strong-flowing current.

As we approached the valley we saw thousands of Mount Cook lilies lining the hillsides and on the banks of the river and subsidiary streams. These magnificent multi-stemmed flowers with pale yellow centres are like very large buttercups; they appear in spring and can grow up to thirty inches from the gound. The majority of New Zealand alpine flowers, that appear just below the snowline, are white and are pollenated at night by moths. The wooded areas of the valley produced some of the most difficult terrain to walk through. There was no established track – just a hint, occasionally, that someone else had been that way. Tree roots, some as high as five feet, had to be negotiated, and what the locals called 'wash-outs', where winter avalanches had completely obliterated any evidence of a track.

Halfway down the valley, at a placed called Shovel Flat, the guide owned quite a comfortable hut, with a kitchen block and separate sleeping accommodation, surrounded by a balcony. He used this mainly for groups of young people whom he would take into the hills on training courses before venturing into the high mountains. We arrived there, with the hut to ourselves, at about 3pm, completely saturated. We had already decided to call it a day some miles back, but now, as soon as we had lit a fire in the wood stove, our decision was quickly confirmed. Instead of struggling back to Wanaka, wet and tired, we spent some pleasant hours talking over a long-delayed lunch.

There was a lot of bird life in the forest and those that we saw ranged from the 'rifleman', New Zealand's smallest bird at about 7 to 8cm, to the multi-coloured pidgeon, much the size of our own woodpidgeon or collared dove. We also saw relatives of the *kea* and a very attractive kingfisher. The following morning, in dry clothes, we reached the roadhead in beautiful sunshine, and returned to Wanaka in time for lunch with our wives. Although Geoff had made many ascents of Mount Aspiring, his wife Beryl had climbed the mountain for the first time only the previous year.

Those four days provided a vivid memory to bring back to England. So now it's back to Munro-bashing and an effort to complete them all by the time I reach 70.

Mountain Conservation

MARTIN PRICE

The Trails to 2002

The International Year of Mountains – and beyond

A re mountains important? The answer depends very much on who you are. For mountaineers, challenge and camaraderie are important values of mountains – though, in the Alpine Journal, the main emphasis is generally on the highest parts of the mountains, composed of rock, snow, and ice. We also value mountains as places to escape from the stresses of everyday life, and for their beauty. Yet to get to the high points, we usually pass through the inhabited parts of the mountains, and many of us are increasingly aware of how we can affect mountain environments, economies, and cultures. Mountaineering values are only one facet of why mountains are important, a global importance recognised by the UN General Assembly's declaration of the year 2002 as The International Year of Mountains.

Until relatively recently, most people – including international policy-makers – tended to regard mountains as eternal, remote, and unchangeable. Media coverage usually focused on dramatic mountaineering exploits, and human and 'natural' disasters. Yet, increasingly, a different view of mountains has begun to emerge – that they are fragile: endangered by pollution and climate change (especially the glaciers!), overuse by tourists, damage from ski area developers and 'development agencies' and, in many countries, population growth linked to deforestation and the erosion of soils. Linked to this view has been growing concern about the quality of life of mountain people, who are not insignificant by any measure. They comprise nearly one-tenth of the human population, including many of the last remnants of traditional cultures on Earth.

Today, mountains should no longer be regarded as distant places, of little importance except to those who live there and those who visit them. A glance through the adverts in any mountain magazine shows that tourism companies offer trips to almost every mountain range in the world. Mountains are second only to coasts and islands as tourist destinations, and 15-20% of the global tourist industry – $70-90 billion a year – is associated with mountain tourism. But tourism is only one aspect of the increasing integration of mountains into the global economic and political system – an integration that reflects their global importance. The reasons are clear. Mountain regions occupy almost a quarter of the Earth's land surface. They supply water, hydro-electric power, minerals, soil nutrients, timber and fuelwood, agricultural products, and places for tourism and recreation to more than half of the world's population. They are centres of biological diversity – housing not only wild species, but also the progenitors of many of the world's main food crops, a heritage of increasing importance as populations grow and the climate changes ever more rapidly. Many mountains are also borders and, as the inhabitants of Afghanistan, Kashmir, Kosovo, Kurdistan and many other mountain states and regions know to their cost, these regions are often militarised zones, where the well-being of mountain people plays second fiddle to political imperatives.

Although mountains supply many resources, as well as manpower, to neighbouring lowlands – and often more distant places – most have always been economically and politically marginal. There are exceptions, especially in the tropics where mountains usually have a more equable climate and a healthier environment than the lowlands. Few mountain countries are major players on the world stage, and mountain regions are usually far from capital cities – not just in terms of distance, but also in the minds of politicians. To start changing these perspectives, a small group of scientists and people from 'development agencies' formed the informal *Mountain Agenda* in 1990, with the aim of putting mountains on the agenda of the UN Conference on Environment and Development – The Earth Summit – due to take place in Rio de Janeiro in June 1992. With funding from the Swiss government, *Mountain Agenda* produced a draft chapter on sustainable development in mountain areas. In 1991 this was introduced into the preparatory meetings for Rio.

The Earth Summit was the largest-ever gathering of heads of state and government. One of their actions was to endorse 'Agenda 21', a plan for action into the 21st century. Chapter 13 of 'Agenda 21' – 'Managing Fragile Ecosystems: Sustainable Mountain Development' – was based on *Mountain Agenda*'s draft. Its inclusion in 'Agenda 21' effectively made mountain people and their environments a priority for global attention comparable to the depletion of tropical rainforests, desertification, ozone depletion, and climate change.

After the Earth Summit, the UN Food and Agriculture Organization (FAO) took responsibility for implementing Chapter 13. In 1994, FAO convened a task force of UN and other organisations that has met more or less annually; the World Mountaineering and Climbing Federation (UIAA) has participated since 1996. One of the task force's first recommendations was that inter-governmental consultations should take place in each region of the world, to encourage the exchange of experiences and increase aware-ness of common problems and possible solutions. From 1994 to 1996 such consultations took place on four continents, bringing together representatives from 62 countries and the European Union. The meetings all produced documents which provide overviews of issues of concern in the different countries, and final statements which identify areas for priority action. During the 1990s, a number of countries, including Bulgaria,

Macedonia, Romania, Slovenia, and Vietnam, established national-level institutions whose aims contribute to sustainable mountain development. Similar sub-national or local institutions have been created in other countries, such as Honduras, South Africa, and the United Kingdom (the Cairngorms Partnership). There are also a number of recent national laws (eg in Bulgaria, Italy, and Japan) and sub-national or local legal, land use, and planning instruments (eg in Austria, France, Germany, Greece, Ireland, Norway, Spain) which provide various means of support for mountain communities.

A second recommendation was that non-governmental organisations (NGOs) should be more closely involved in implementing Chapter 13. The principal outcome of this was the holding of non-governmental consultations both at global scales, and in Europe and the Indian Himalaya. The global meeting led to the establishment, in 1995, of the Mountain Forum, a global network for information exchange, mutual support, and advocacy for equitable and ecologically sustainable mountain development and conservation. It primarily functions through the use of the Internet, which is increasingly accessible in mountain areas all over the world; the Forum now links over 2000 members in over 100 countries. The European meeting was preceded by a questionnaire sent to over 5000 mountain NGOs across Europe, which achieved the very high response rate of 20% – reflecting not only the high level of concern among the respondents, but also the fact that the questionnaire was distributed in 16 languages; linguistic diversity is also characteristic of mountain areas. The meeting led to the European Mountain Forum, the European partner of the Mountain Forum, with nodes organised by NGOs in various parts of Europe.

All of these meetings and new structures and policies have led to a certain increase in public and political awareness of the importance of mountain areas. This is reflected to some extent in the greater attention given by some development aid agencies to mountain areas and in their recognition as a priority by the Global Environment Facility (GEF), a global financing mechanism operated by the World Bank and the UN Development and Environment Programmes, leading to major investments in mountain regions. Awareness has also been heightened by the many 'natural disasters' – often with at least partially human causes – that have struck mountain areas in recent years, particularly in Latin America and Africa, but also in Europe, where floods and storms have affected both large parts of mountain areas and those downstream. Yet, at the turn of the millennium, many of the challenges facing mountain people – such as limited access to resources, environmental deterioration, and economic and political marginality – still persist. This was the background to the movement, led by the government of Kyrgyzstan, to declare an International Year of Mountains (IYM): a movement eventually supported by 130 states in the UN General Assembly when it declared in November 1998 that 2002 would be the IYM.

The objectives of the IYM are to:

- ensure the present and future well-being of mountain communities by promoting conservation and sustainable development in mountain areas;
- increase awareness of, and knowledge of, mountain ecosystems, their dynamics and functioning, and their overriding importance in providing a number of strategic goods and services essential to the well-being of both rural and urban, highland and lowland people, particularly water supply and food security;
- promote and defend the cultural heritage of mountain communities and societies;
- pay attention to frequent conflicts in mountain areas and to promote peace-making in those regions.

What will be particularly critical is for the Year to be not just another series of events, but a further catalyst to actions which lead to concrete long-term improvements both for mountain people and in the environments on which they and a large proportion of the world's population depend.

In various countries around the world, national committees and other structures are being established to plan and implement activities during the IYM. At the time of writing (July 2001), such structures had been established in Australia, Austria, Bolivia, Bulgaria, Dominican Republic, Ecuador, France, Gabon, Germany, Italy, Kyrgyzstan, Madagascar, Mexico, Morocco, Nepal, Peru, Slovenia, Swaziland and Tunisia. While the UK government has indicated that it does not intend to establish such a structure, activities are developing in Scotland, where Scottish Natural Heritage, various NGOs, and the Cairngorms Partnership have provided the funds to support a project officer, Andrew Macpherson, who will work out of the Centre for Mountain Studies at Perth College, within the developing events, to involve both NGOs and the private and the public sector, throughout the year. These will aim to raise public awareness of the ecological and human importance and role of mountains; promote debate about their future and change towards more sustainable use; and encourage links between NGOs, government agencies and the private sector with an interest in mountains in order to facilitate more 'joined up thinking' and action in relation to sustainable mountain use and development.

These events should link closely to the two international meetings on mountain themes planned to take place in Scotland in 2002. The first of these will be the 3rd European Mountain Convention, to take place in Inverness in May; the second will be a conference on conservation and management in the mountains of northern Europe, in Pitlochry in November. At the global scale, the UIAA has established a working group for the IYM, and is planning a series of activities, including preparation of a charter, codes of conduct for expeditions or trekking groups, histories of mountaineering and ski alpinism, and various seminars.

The IYM represents a special opportunity for people who live in mountains and those who visit the mountains to give greater attention to their common interests and to work together to raise awareness of the manifold importance of mountains to a very large proportion of the world's population. 2002 comes just at the beginning of a century during which the importance of mountains as sources of water, energy, food, enjoyment, and challenge will increase for the inhabitants of an ever more urbanised and unpredictable world. Mountaineers often debate ethical issues, though the focus has generally been on how we should behave on rock, snow and ice. I hope that 2002 will provide an opportunity for all of us to give even greater consideration to the needs and efforts of mountain people who maintain the landscapes and cultures that are so important to us.

BIBLIOGRAPHY AND WEBSITES

Bruno Messerli and Jack D. Ives, editors, *Mountains of the World: A Global Priority*. Parthenon (Carnforth, 1997).
IYM website: http://www.mountains2002.org/
Mountain Forum website: http://www.mtnforum.org/

KATH PYKE

Giant Himalayan Woolly Flying Squirrels

(Plate 53)

Squirrels come in all shapes and sizes. There are the small fluffy ones that steal nuts from the bird-feeder in your garden. Then there are squirrels four feet long from snout to tip of tail that can fly from one side of a valley to the other. Am I serious? In August 2000, I was serious enough to join a Wildlife Conservation Society (WCS) project and galvanise a group of American climbers to travel to northern Pakistan in search of the animal. Declared extinct in 1924, the giant Himalayan woolly flying squirrel (*Eupetaurus cinereus*) created headline news with its rediscovery in 1996 by mammal researcher, Peter Zahler. He found that small populations existed in remote forested pockets at altitudes between 9,000ft and 13,000ft south of Gilgit district. It was our quest to see whether the animal existed in the Gulmit and Chalt valleys further north. Information we gathered would help in co-ordinating strategies and funding effort with mountain communities for protection of their forests and this unusual animal.

Unlike your common or garden squirrel, the giant Himalayan woolly flying squirrel is believed to live almost entirely on blue pine needles. It is nocturnal, lying up in deep crevices or caves in cliffs during the day. Its rediscovery and elevation to endangered status on international lists does not assure its continued existence. With growing populations in the valleys, its biggest threats are loss of forest from overgrazing by livestock and logging.

But in our four-week attempt to locate this animal we received a curious form of help. The animal's fate, and its best chance of survival, is inextricably linked to a crystalline urine-based product it produces called *salajeet*. This is widely used in Pakistan, partly as a prophylactic for aches and pains, but mostly as an aphrodisiac. Collected in lumps, it is refined to an oily dark liquid and sold in small vials. The prescribed use is three drops in a warm glass of milk before bed. Within this cultural tale lies a whole industry.

Arriving in Gilgit we were introduced to members of the exclusive workforce, the salajeet collectors – a thin wiry bunch who make a living by climbing cliff faces to collect the stuff. It didn't take long for our pasty, unacclimatised team to make an assessment on who would be the most useful in this venture. These boys are super-athletes; one wonders if Alex Lowe would have met his match. Born and bred in the mountains, you barely see them break into a sweat as they ascend several thousand high-altitude feet in less than an hour. Difficult to spot in the same earth-tone *shalwar kamiz* they would wear in their villages as crossing a glacier, they would scamper in plastic shoes across the worst type of loose, technical climbing that would reduce most Western climbers to a nervous wreck.

Salajeet collectors work in groups of three to five people. Their tools are simple. Occasionally they bring out the most frayed piece of rope to lower one of their team over a particularly steep section of cliff to check out a cave. They do this by tying the rope round their team member's waist and then lowering him hand over hand. Belays were simply not part of the equation, even if there was a tree or rock spike to hand. Within a few days of meeting it became very clear that our best role would be to hand over our ropes which I imagine will be used for a decade to come.

As a team of five US climbers and three salajeet collectors, we were wisely given different valleys to cover to accommodate our super-athlete friends. Daily surveys took us above glacier and moraine, sometimes to altitudes of 13,000ft. You might think these places were devoid of wildlife, but the alpine pastures were lush with herbs and we often found fresh tracks of ibex. As the designated climbing leader, I was always glad to see our team make it out in one piece; a careless step could be fatal with nothing to stop you rattling down a 1000-foot slope. At first we took a measure of climbing gear but as the project progressed, we imitated our salajeet friends and divested ourselves of almost everything, carrying just an 8.5mm coil.

Despite the salajeet team, our surveys yielded nothing more than aching muscles, a desiccated skeleton and some fecal pellets. Peter Zahler seemed satisfied enough since our research showed that the animals were not in this region. The salajeet collectors shifted their focus to collect the equally valuable deposits of the smaller and more common Kashmir squirrel that gave them a price per kilogram return in the markets that exceeded most salaried Pakistan schoolteachers. It's a fair-sized industry, and therein may lie the key. There are over 300 salajeet collectors in the Gorabad region returning income to their homes and villages. While sustainable forestry projects may not seem a priority to some, this is a demonstrable link that caring for these high elevation forests is key to sustaining their livelihood.

We never did get to see the squirrel. When you do this type of trip you have to accept this as a possible outcome. In the year 2000, there were over 120 US expeditions of varying technicality to the Karakoram. It seemed important that an animal as scarce as this, that lives in mountain areas so popular with trekkers and climbers, should be the focus of a conservation project. This field trip was a small venture by climbers to offer assistance and raise awareness about what makes these mountain communities and wildlife so special and deserving of protection efforts.

This project gratefully acknowledges receipt of the AAC Bedayn Fund research grant to support field survey work. Pakistan Field Project Assistant: Mayoor Khan. Salajeet collectors: Abdul Jabar, Mubeen Khan, Manawar Sheed. US climbers: Kestrel Hanson, Hiroki Ide, Paul Norburg, Kath Pyke, Amanda Tarr. Research leader: Peter Zahler WCS.

GEORGE BAND

Nanda Devi Reopened
A Short Walk in the Sanctuary

(Plate 13)

On 4 November 1999 I was sitting quietly in the departure lounge at Delhi Airport waiting for my flight to Srinagar, when an official handed me a note hastily scribbled by Ian McNaught-Davis who was on the other side of the security barrier. It read: 'George: Seven soldiers killed 6pm yesterday in Srinagar cantonment by militants. Conference to be rescheduled in Delhi. Mac.'

But I was committed, my baggage already loaded on the aircraft. I was eagerly looking forward to my first ever visit to Indian controlled Kashmir, the earthly paradise for so many tourists and climbers before partition in 1947. Mac and I, together with Steve Berry of Himalayan Kingdoms, had accepted invitations from the Indian Mountaineering Foundation (IMF) to a 'Millennium Meet' to be held in Gulmarg, Kashmir. As both Mac and I had been on separate treks in Nepal, we planned to arrive early and spend a few days trekking in Kashmir before the Conference. Mac had been warned just in time not to fly, but I was still expected and was warmly welcomed by Ashraf Khan, the Director General of Tourism for Kashmir. He put on a brave face to conceal his disappointment that, after all his organisation, I was the only Conference delegate to arrive instead of the hundred expected!

A week later we all reassembled in Delhi. Our presentations were well received and in the ensuing discussions we three made a plea for the reopening of the Nanda Devi Sanctuary which had been closed to foreigners since 1982. After all, the so-called Annapurna Sanctuary in Nepal was open to trekkers and it was quite within the remit of the Indian Government to open Nanda Devi for limited trekking and climbing and, if they wished, to charge a premium rate for doing so, as is the case for travel in Mustang and Bhutan.

Nanda Devi has a special attraction for the British, with our early history of attempts to penetrate the ring of peaks surrounding the Goddess, by the only obvious entry point through the precipitous gorge of the Rishiganga. Famous climbers like Graham, Longstaff, Mumm, General Bruce and Ruttledge, with their Alpine guides, had all tried in vain. The eventual success of Shipton and Tilman in 1934, and the brilliant ascent of the mountain itself at the first attempt by the Anglo-American party only two years later, are wonderfully told in Shipton's and Tilman's books. Bill Tilman and Noel Odell reached the summit and, in their excitement, 'so far forgot themselves as to shake hands.' Nanda Devi was the British Empire's highest peak, and at 25,645'/7816m was the highest climbed in the world until the French scaled Annapurna in 1950.

Why was the Sanctuary closed in 1982? We never received a clear answer from the authorities or our friends at the IMF. It was probably for a combination of reasons:

- Unacceptable rubbish left by uncaring trekkers and climbers in the 1970s.
- Overgrazing by sheep and goats on pastures in both the Outer and Inner Sanctuaries where the shepherds of Lata village considered they had hereditary rights.
- Excessive poaching of musk deer, blue sheep and snow leopard.
- The secret ill-fated attempt by American and Indian climbers in 1965 to place a nuclear-powered device near the summit to monitor Chinese missile tests. It was secured at 22,000'/6707m but in 1966 was found to have been swept away by avalanches and was never recovered. This extraordinary act has been suggested as the reason for closure, although it had happened 16 years previously.

Our petition to reopen the Sanctuary did not fall entirely on deaf ears. Colonel Narindar 'Bull' Kumar, who had led the first Indian expedition to climb high on Everest (1960), and to summit Nanda Devi (1964), and Kangchenjunga (1977) was long retired from the Indian Army, but kept his hand in by managing an adventure company, Mercury Himalayan Explorations, specialising in trekking and rafting. He made our petition a personal crusade. The newly elected President of the IMF, Mr N. N. Vohra, a former Defence Secretary and Home Secretary, was also sympathetic. Kumar advised Mac, as current President of the UIAA, the World Mountaineering and Climbing Federation, to write formally to the IMF to request permission for a trekking party to visit the Sanctuary. If granted, Mac undertook to write a report on our experiences for the IMF. The trek would be organised from the UK end by Himalayan Kingdoms and in India by Kumar's company. Steve happily persuaded John Shipton, Eric's son, to lead the trek and took the risk of advertising it in his brochure, subject to permit, and had little difficulty in raising a party. The trek was scheduled from 23 September to 18 October 2000, and I apologise if this personal account may not give due credit to all the members of a very congenial team.

Steve hoped that the permit would be granted by May, but it proved a real cliff-hanger. Kumar chased it round various government departments, even threatening to go to the Prime Minister's office. By August, he assured us that it was 90% certain, but it was not until we had actually been in Delhi for a day that Steve was able to hold the precious document. We were to be classed by the IMF as an expedition, rather than a trek. We required X-visas, and we had to pay an environmental fee and take a Liaison

Officer. Mac's wife, Loreto, used her charms to help persuade Surab Gandhi to join us at a few hour's notice, having only returned at 2am from being L.O. to an expedition in Spiti. He was a happy choice. One of the fittest in the party, the memory of his frequent and characteristic braying laugh still rings in my ears.

We left Delhi by bus at 3pm on 25 September and seven hours later stopped for the night in Rishikesh. Another full day on the bus took us to Joshimath. To ensure the success of our venture, we stopped for a dip in the Holy Ganges close to Mercury's permanent rafting camp and, at midday, reached Devprayag, the confluence of the Bhagrati and Alaknanda rivers before following the latter to Joshimath, perched on the steep hillside, some 1500ft above the river.

Above the town, much to our surprise, was a gondola lift, rising from 1905m to the ski resort of Auli at 3000m from which looking east we had our first stunning view of Nanda Devi. It was a chance to recover from the long road journey, stretch our legs and stroll up through the forest until we broke out onto open pasture. Had we continued a few more hours uphill we would have reached the Kuari Pass at 4268m which marks the cul-mination of the Shipton-Tilman trek, also called Curzon's Trail, starting from Gwaldam, which in the 1930s was the roadhead. Mac, Loreto and I had done the second half of this 10-day trek the previous year to pass the time before the IMF Conference. The Pass was famed as a viewpoint. Shipton wrote:

> ... we were privileged to see what must be one of the grandest mountain views in the world. As we raised our heads above the top of the pass a gigantic sweep of icy peaks confronted us, and it was difficult to refrain from gasping at the vastness of the scene. The serrated line of the Kedernath and Badrinath peaks, Kamet, Hathi Parbat, and the great cleft of the Dhauli Valley were easily recognised, but the glittering array of snowy peaks of all shapes and sizes which filled the gaps were easier to admire and wonder at than to identify. South of the Dhauli towered the graceful Dunagiri, but a sight of Nanda Devi, so soon to be our lodestone, was denied us.

We were there on an equally cold, clear morning, but I confess to a sense of anti-climax. To me, the view was fine, but hardly of a Himalayan dimension, and then I realised why. In the 1930s Nepal was still a closed country and Europeans were ignorant of its mountain wonderland. I had just come from a challenging and wondrously beautiful trek up the Buri Ghandaki, round north of Manaslu and the Annapurnas and down the Kali Ghandaki towards Dhaulagiri. I had skimmed the cream of Nepal and been thoroughly spoilt in comparison.

Our trek proper was to start from Lata up the Dhauli Valley where our bus deposited us the next afternoon. This was the last village, and counts

4. Chisel (*left and centre*) and Sheridan Peak (*right*) seen from the Chisel Glacier, Lemon Mountains, Greenland. (*Richard Pash*) (p31)

5. East Face of The Steeple. The line taken by Pash and partners follows the left-trending ramp just above the left snowfield, then into the obvious snow gully towards the summit. (*Richard Pash*) (p31)

6. Exploring crevasses on the Sarah Glacier. (*Richard Pash*) (p31)

7. Ski mountaineering in the Lindbergh Fjelde, north of the Lemon Mountains, with Jatteborg in the background. (*Richard Pash*) (p31)

8. This wide crevasse was crossed during a ski tour to the Lindbergh Fjelde.
   (*Richard Pash*) (p31)

9. Nic Faulks on the penultimate pitch of The Castle's South Summit, Lemon Mountains,
   Greenland (*Richard Pash*) (p31)

10. Mount Aspiring taken from a helicopter near the Bevan Col in early morning light. The NW Ridge seen over the Bonar Glacier is the prominent skyline ridge on the left. (*Geoff Wayatt*) (p37)

11a. Takpa Shiri (6885m), Arunachal Pradesh, in five minutes of clear weather. (*Greg Child*) (p59)

11b. One of the Apatani people. (*Greg Child*) (p59)

12a. An Apatani woman. The facial dis-
figurements and tattoos are designed
to prevent rival tribes stealing Apatani
women. (*Greg Child*) (p59)

12b. A Nishi porter, near the village of
Bakar, Arunachal Pradesh.
(*Greg Child*) (p59)

12c. Doug Scott crossing a river near Mille. (*Greg Child*) (p59)

13. A short walk in the Nanda Devi Sanctuary. George Band with the mountain in the background. Band reports that Indian expeditions have been active in the region during the 1990s. (*George Band collection*) (p50)

as being in the Outer Sanctuary, just above the Dhauli's confluence with the Rishi. Above it is the wooded Lata Peak from the summit of which Tilman had a magnificent view up the Rishi gorge – the key to the Sanctuary. Our first stage was to Lata Kharak, a grazing area above the tree line at 3700m, a good 1500m above the village and a strenuous first day. An acclimatisation rest day enabled us to stroll along the ridge towards Lata Peak until the view of the Rishi was revealed. We could see our next stage, crossing several rocky spurs to more grazing at Dharansi, where we were told there was insufficient water, so it was decided to do a double stage, continue over a saddle and down to a beautiful strip of pasture surrounded by a forest of tall pines called Dibrugeta. This was one of Shipton's favourite camp sites, but it was almost our undoing. We were not yet acclimatised and several were feeling poorly, so it was long after dark before we were all in camp, the porters lighting their way through the forest by flaming torches made from strips of resinous birch bark. A rest day gave the botanists, John and Howard, ample time to collect seeds and argue over the names of various plants. We were actually camped in a stand of wild angelica towering 6 - 9 feet around our tents – a far cry from the candied root in my mother's fruit cakes! The next day we entered the gorge of the Rishi and crossed the torrent to camp at Deodi in the forest on the opposite bank. We now began to feel we were really in the Sanctuary and could look back at a huge square-cut cliff resembling an outer curtain.

Here a little digression. Having understood that the Sanctuary was formally closed to all since 1982, we were very surprised when one of our party, Lena Dacunha, discovered through the Internet a book by the Indian Engineers describing their expedition to Nanda Devi in 1993. In their report they recommended that the Sanctuary should remain closed, but an expedition should be allowed every 5–10 years to report on the area's regeneration. Perhaps we were that expedition? But we were not alone. We were further surprised on arrival in Delhi to learn that a full-scale expedition by the Indo-Tibet Border Police was currently climbing Nanda Devi by the customary south ridge. They had built log bridges over the Rishi and Trisuli torrents and fixed ropes over the most exposed tricky sections of the entry to the Inner Sanctuary. We learnt that they had in fact summited on 30 September, eight eventually reaching the top, and were now on their way out. Kumar was able to agree with them that they would leave their bridges and ropes in place for us, provided we removed them on our way out, leaving the Sanctuary inviolate. This was a lucky break for us, removing the uncertainty of whether we would find the way in at all. However, the ITBP asked us to wait a further day at Deodi because the next camp site in the gorge at Ramani was constricted between a cliff and the river and there was not room for both groups. We could only agree.

Up to Ramani, although there had been no need for fixed ropes, the path along the side of the gorge was quite exposed in places. At one of these, a porter's load unbalanced, a small bag broke loose and tumbled out of sight.

As I rounded a spur, I could see people looking down, and at first thought someone had fallen headlong and probably been killed. It was with some relief to all but Loreto that it was only her Gucci bag containing her make-up, some jewellery and various accessories! Several porters risked their lives in descending to retrieve the scattered contents and she was not allowed to forget the incident.

We crossed the Rishi easily by the well constructed double-log bridge making use of a huge boulder jammed midstream., and we were humbled to think of Shipton, Tilman and their three porters, Angtharkay, Pasang, and Kusang just wading across the torrent. At Ramani, the impending wall of the gorge towered over us. It seemed incredible that there could be a viable path up, around and beyond the intervening spurs. We were a trekking party of varied abilities and this was the point at which each person had to decide whether to continue to the Inner Sanctuary. We agreed to split forces. Four 'clients' would return from here in leisurely stages together with Kumar. The rest of us including Kumar's son Akshay would continue. Steve had recommended we bring climbing harnesses so that we could clip on to the fixed ropes if necessary.

This was John Shipton's day, 6 October. It was his 50th birthday and he was leading us into the Inner Sanctuary, first penetrated by his father 66 years before. I had not known John before this trip, but he had much of his father's charisma and carefree nature. He was born in Kunming in 1950 during Eric's last Consular appointment, on returning from which he was invited to lead the 1951 Everest Reconnaissance. John had been something of a rolling stone, teaching English overseas, but now gathering moss as a 'bluebell farmer' in Carmarthenshire, with his partner Alison, growing native bulbs for wild-flower gardening. It seemed only in recent years that he had become interested in visiting the regions travelled by his father, and had led several treks for Himalayan Kingdoms. His considerable botanical knowledge added lustre to the party.

We started at 7.30am, nearly two hours before the sun reached us in the depth of the gorge. I cannot remember the intricacies of the route. We wound up, down and across several times, with fixed ropes here and there protecting moves that were never more than 'difficult' but were very exposed and intimidating with all too clear views of the river hundreds of feet below. A fortuitous natural ledge led us around the curtain of Pisgah, followed by an equally unexpected 50ft chimney giving us access to the slopes above. We had arrived at the overlapping slabs of Patalkhan, with water and convenient caves for the porters. Mac's cumulative altitude watch registered 985m for a height gain of only 650m. We now had a superb view of Nanda Devi and marvelled at the steepness of the prominent North Buttress route climbed by the Americans, Roskelley, States and Reichardt in 1976. At sunset all our cameras and telephoto lenses were trained on the summit. Hugh Thomson, one of the last to join the party, was the most meticulous photographer as, being both a BBC producer and a freelance writer, he had negotiated a contract for a well-illustrated book on the trek. We celebrated John's birthday and our entry to the Inner Sanctuary with the last of my Famous Grouse and a packet of tasty shredded *biltong*.

Next morning, we immediately had to cross some tricky slabs where a fixed rope was a welcome handrail. It was the point on the 1936 expedition where the heavily laden Sahibs in their clinker nailed boots had suffered some embarrassment. Tilman wrote:

> The Mana men waltzed across this with no more ado than crossing a road, ... and then they sat down on the far side to see how we, the eminent mountaineers, would fare. It was not a prepossessing place to look at and the first few tentative steps soon convinced us that this time appearances had not deceived us. The wretched loads were of course the trouble, for with those on one had not the confidence to stand up boldly and plank the feet down. Each man took the line that seemed good to him, but all got into difficulties, and then was seen the comic sight of seven Sahibs strung out over the slabs in varying attitudes, all betraying uneasiness, and quite unable to advance. The Mana men, having savoured the spectacle to the full and allowed time for the indignity of our situation to sink in, came laughing across the slabs to our aid and led us gently over by the hand like so many children.

Soon the path became broadly horizontal; the rocks and scree gave way to rolling downland. The view opened up and we could see up the valley to the north side of Nanda Devi, hemmed in by the chain of peaks from Mangraon to Saktam forming the east rim of the Sanctuary. Due north was Changabang but, from this southern viewpoint, totally unlike the much photographed granite fang of the north face familiar to top-flight British climbers. Indeed, there was considerable debate as to whether we were looking at Changabang or something else altogether. Sadly, we would not have time to explore the northern basin of the Sanctuary. Our aim was to camp on pasture at Sarsonpatal, 4100m, below the dark ramparts on the SW side of Nanda Devi and then continue to the site of the 1936 Base Camp in the cirque formed by the southern flanks of Nanda Devi and Nanda Devi East. In 1936, Tilman and Houston had forced a new route out of the Sanctuary by crossing Longstaff's Col, 5910m, to the east. It was tempting to think that we might do the same, but unrealistic in the time at our disposal. Indeed, the weather, which had so far been superb, began to show signs of breaking and we did not want to be caught on the trickier fixed-rope sections of the Rishi gorge in foul weather. So it was decided to spend just two nights at Sarsonpatal before returning, and on the intervening day walk either to the 1936 Base Camp and back, or on less energetic exploration.

In the event, only five of our party made it to the Base Camp, John Shipton, Jeff Ford, our sole American Gerry Becker, Surab and Deva. I started with that intention, getting as far as the Base Camp area of the tragic 1976 American expedition (in which Nanda Devi Unsoeld died), but seeing the seemingly endless hillocks of glacial moraine ahead, and rounding several spurs only to see more of the same, I gave up and compromised with the view of the upper half of the Longstaff Col. Others in the party walked up the hillside from our camp, gaining much the same view with less effort.

Our return journey was completed without incident, apart from one fixed-rope section where, becoming confused by too much advice, one of us let slip with both hands and feet and hung momentarily only from his harness. All the fixed ropes were retrieved and the log bridges over the Rishi and Trisuli rivers were demolished, leaving the Sanctuary inviolate. By doing a couple of double stages, we caught up with Kumar's party and avoided a serious change in the weather, although the now snow-covered slippery slopes above Lata Kharak required special care.

Travelling with Kumar's adventure company enabled us to spend two days unwinding, with a taste of white water kindly arranged by Akshay, at their very comfortable rafting camp on a sandy secluded forest-fringed shore of the Ganges just above Rishikesh. Mac and Loreto returned earlier to prepare for the annual Assembly of the UIAA, but on our trek back we had discussed what recommendations for opening up the Sanctuary Mac could reasonably propose in his report to the IMF. There seemed to us no reason for not allowing limited trekking and climbing, under careful supervision, for say 6 - 8 parties per year. To avoid congestion between groups entering and leaving the restricted camp sites in the narrow part of the gorge, it would be more satisfying if a circular route could be devised, entering by the gorge but departing by another route, possibly over a shoulder of the Devistan ridge between Sarsonpatal and the Trisuli nullah. Although I do not know whether any foreigners have crossed this way, there is said to be a route used by local shepherds and hunters over a reasonable pass. These local people could be contracted at the beginning of each season to build temporary log bridges over the Rishi and Trisuli torrents, as a welcome boost to their incomes.

We did not see a great deal of game. There were blue sheep here and there, and doubtless an unseen snow leopard or two preying upon them. There were certainly musk deer on Lata Peak. I kept a modest bird list and was pleased to see my first glistening blue grandala. Appendices on birds and plants may be included in the IMF report. We are very grateful to have been allowed – albeit briefly – into the Sanctuary. I was delighted while in Vermont the following month to stay and share reminiscences with Charlie Houston, co-leader of the 1936 Anglo-American team and still a sprightly 87-year-old. He was astounded to learn that we started our trek just by stepping off the bus at Lata. What a bunch of softies, he must have thought, but was far too polite to say so. 'Before we got to Lata,' he said, 'We had already walked for two weeks from Ranikhet!'

Exploration

Exploration

DOUG SCOTT

Arunachal Pradesh

(Plates 11a–12c)

The expedition left Delhi aboard the Rajdhani Express on 18 September 1999 for NE India, waved off by the President of the IMF, Dr Gill, who also happens to be the Chief Election Officer for India and therefore India's top civil servant. Thanks to him we had permission from all quarters – Ministry of Defence, local army and the Home Ministry – to make the first ever non-Indian visit to the mountains of central Arunachal Pradesh. Without his wholehearted support and connections, particularly with the Home Ministry, the expedition would not have been possible.

Although we foreigners were Greg Child from Australia and only myself from Britain, we were classed as a joint Indo-British team. The Indian members were Akhil Sarpu, into tea production, and my old friend Balwant Sandhu. It was Balwant who kept up the momentum for this expedition – a brave commitment I realised later. He had already, at my request, gone out to Arunachal on two reconnaissance sorties. In due course we were all to find that we had strayed into an environment where we did not belong, and suffered accordingly.

After passing the mangled and already rusting wreckage of a previous Rajdhani Express, near New Jalpaiguri, in which 600 people had died, we arrived at Guwahati in the wet lush green state of Assam. Akhill was there to meet us and accommodate the expedition in his company house. He was 32 years old and a big man at 15 stone, but fit from having lately played rugby for India.

We left for Itanagar, the capital of Arunachal Pradesh, on 21 September by a bus now full of final food purchases, all the equipment and our high-altitude Sherpas from Darjeeling: Pasang Futar Sherpa, Phurba Sherpa, Thukpa Tshering and Dorji Sherpa. En route Balwant cleared the first bureaucratic hurdle after consultations with the army HQ for NE India at Tezpur. Despite intense pre-expedition planning, Balwant forecast problems ahead. The army had mixed us up with a local military expedition to the eastern Arunachal mountains of Gorichen and had not fully briefed their local army commanders ahead. The most serious practical problem to confront us, apart from bureaucratic interest in our 'ground-breaking' visit, would be the shortage of porters due to the recent decision of the Indian government to call national elections. Electioneering was already taking place in some states, staggered throughout the nation. Unfortunately for us, elections would take place in Arunachal exactly when we planned to leave for the mountains. All available porters would be taken up with carrying election boxes and official baggage to remote villages.

We were, however, encouraged by the positive reaction to our plans of P M Nair, Chief Secretary of Arunachal Pradesh, and his Transport Secretary who both worked upon the idea of making a helicopter available to transport gear and maybe some of the team from the most important town in the region, Ziro, to the smaller administrative village of Sarli, thus saving two days on jeep track and two days walking. We continued our journey into forbidden Arunachal Pradesh.

Our excitement at climbing up onto the Apatani plateau – the heart of the region – was tempered on meeting, at Keming, the Commander of the 9th Assam Rifles, a paramilitary force attached to the Home Ministry. The scowling Colonel insisted that a detachment of soldiers, plus a radio operator and necessary porters, should accompany the Liaison Officer and ourselves to base camp. The Colonel was unable to answer the basic problem of how we were to obtain porters to accommodate this extra burden.

We continued up out of the mist onto the plateau and paddy fields bathed in moonlight and drove through Ziro and its surrounding villages to our lodgings at a government rest house where we retired under our mosquito nets at midnight. Early next morning we were collected by Sanjay Phukan of the Development Office and taken to see the DC Keshav Chandra, a young, intelligent bright-eyed young man of 28 who proved to be decisive and sympathetic to our plight. He agreed to the helicopter support and we worked out a schedule of portering to enable the porters to cast their vote – his main concern.

Greg and I were to spend four frustrating days on the Apatani Plateau. The Apatani people and the place were some compensation for being ordered off the helicopter after it had been loaded up, and a few minutes from take-off. The pilot had received a chitty – 'no foreigners allowed on the helicopter'. This had originated from the military.

Balwant had frequently telephoned the top brass at the Indian Army Eastern Command. As a retired colonel of the Parachute Regiment he had the extra army personnel reduced to just two radio operators. Now, mysteriously, others had pulled strings in the opposite direction.

Akhill and Balwant left with the equipment. Our Liaison Officer, Lt Raj Kumar Singh, who had turned up at Ziro two days ago, Greg and myself waved goodbye from the tarmac. Greg took this badly, declaring: 'I'm outta here.' I persuaded him otherwise, and the next day, with the help of the DC, we drove for two days in torrential rain with the radio operators in the official DC's jeep on very rough rain tracks and roads to the head town of Kloriang. At least we were at the start of the trek-in, despite one last effort by the Assam Rifles' Colonel to delay our departure by insisting we had two soldiers to protect the radio operators, when he knew our jeep was already over-full and no other was available. The DC had persuaded him to drop this requirement.

On 29 September we were given enough porters by the Subdivisional Officer, G L Roy, to manage our four light loads for the two-day walk to join up with Balwant and Akhil, now at Sarli. We walked up to the Administration Bungalow, with the Liaison Officer limping alongside having twisted his ankle. Mr Roy and the villagers we spoke to said we were the first foreigners ever to come here. Mr Roy gave us the cheery news that people were dying of cholera up the valley, and that a villager had been killed by a bite from a poisonous snake the previous night. His final advice was not to antagonise the jungle natives or they would cut us to pieces with their machetes, but then he mused we would probably not find any more porters so we could not proceed far anyway. I told him we could always wait for the election to finish. He said even if they were free to carry, the Indian Government provides so much subsidy to the villagers that they do not need extra money from carrying loads. This was eminently sensible but our prospects of even reaching base camp, two weeks away, now seemed remote.

The Jungle Journey

Every day saw torrential rain. On 29 September we left Kloriang, reaching Boweng in nine hours, lathered in perspiration, bitten by dim dim flies and leeches and cut from jungle thorns. Next day we trekked six hours to Sarli and met Balwant and Akhill who had been busy pushing gear up the valley with a small band of porters, working in relays. There we stayed for two days, as everyone was now preoccupied with the elections. The time was used trying to obtain more porters, organise the building of bamboo bridges and ladders up the jungle-clad Kurung river valley as well as touring around the fascinating Nishi homesteads. 4 October: Sarli – Palo (hamlet). Eight hours. 5 October: Palo – Mille (1550m). Four hours. This was the last permanent settlement. We stayed in a long house of bamboo set on stilts 10-15ft high where pigs and chickens scratched around for human waste dropped through the split cane floor. The men had up to four wives, each with her own fire place and collection of children screened off from each other.

On 7 October we trekked for nine hours from Mille to Wati (1890m). So far the path had never been anything like as good as those in Nepal. From now on, the path became indistinct. They do not move animals up the valley so the path is only trodden by the barefoot Nishi people treading nimbly and leaving hardly a trace. Rather than zigzag, they prefer to put up log ladders against steep rock steps, tied with bamboo strips, or to pull up creepers. The old ladders were fragile, jungle-rotted and frequently broken, especially when Akhill was on them.

8 October: Wati – Bibi (1830m). Eight hours. 9 October: Bibi – Watung. Eight hours. Because of the acute shortage of porters Balwant, the Liaison Officer and the two radio operators had to remain at Bibi until more porters came from down the valley. The going got more difficult. We rarely saw

the grey sky through the jungle green. There were huge drops to the Kurung river thundering down below. It was never possible to walk more than 15 paces without fear of tripping and slipping on the greasy boulders, mud and tangle of roots, ferns and creepers.

10 October: Watung – Semai: (2490m). Five hours. We recrossed the Kurung to camp under a rock overhang.

11 – 12 October: Semai. There were insufficient porters to move on, as some had disappeared and others had gone to relay gear left with Balwant.

13 October: Semai – Pi Chu –Bakar. Eight hours. It was another hard day of constant effort and concentration as though we were already on the climb. We recrossed the Kurung by a very rickety net of creepers and bamboo and began to meet rhododendrons and conifers.

14 October: Bakar – Kowachvi (3620m). Nine hours. Again we crossed back over the Kurung, at a gorge 150ft deep and so narrow it was possible to span it with 20ft logs. Greg now had blood poisoning from an infected cut in his leg. Pasang came down with malarial fever.

15 October: Kowachvi – Dolayang (3730m). Today we came out of the now alpine forest and into open pasture upon which the sun shone for the first time in days. We decided this would be base camp. Unfortunately, I had slipped off the trail earlier and torn a ligament in my knee. Thukpa Sherpa also now had high fever, probably malarial, like Pasang. They both retired early, as did Greg, whose fever was at its height. We retained three of the younger Nishi, who seemed children – probably between 13 and 18 years old. The others went down to bring up the rest of our group.

16 October: Dolayang (Base Camp) until 24 October. During this time we tried to recce the mountain above. Occasionally there were clear periods when we could see the snow-clad peaks of the Indo-Tibetan border. Takpa Shiri (6655m), directly above base camp, was the only named peak. Base Camp was on the bend of the Kurung where it swings west to its source. It was in that direction that the most attractive unnamed peaks were situated beyond the Mukhpa La, and between 6000m and 6800m all the way to Nyegy Kangtang (6983m) in the south-west.

During this period we heard that Balwant was suffering from typhoid at Semai; Akhill, whose wife was expecting their first child, had run out of time from his job; and I dislocated my big toe while hopping over a stream with my damaged knee. Greg decided to pull out with Akhill, and Pasang went down, completely debilitated from malaria and suffering from extreme high temperature. On 24 October the Liaison Officer arranged for a helicopter to take me out, and en route to collect Balwant, now totally emaciated from typhoid fever. We were flown to Din Jan Military Hospital in Assam, near Dibrugarh.

On 29 October we left by train and plane for Delhi. I arrived home on 8 November wondering if I should go back to Arunachal Pradesh.

We would not have made the eighteen-day journey through the jungle to the peaks on the Indo-Tibetan border without the help of the indigenous

Nishi tribesmen. We would not have managed a week on our own. As it was, we suffered typhoid, malaria, blood poisoning, torn tendons and festering sores from leeches and dim dim flies as well as a degree of despondency and helplessness not experienced on any other expedition.

Meanwhile, the Nishi, totally adapted to living on steep mountain sides covered in dense jungle washed by incessant rain, displayed all the attributes and energy of real mountaineers. They used, to ingenious effect, the jungle cane and creeper to bridge torrential side streams and the thunderous Kurung River. They were physically very strong, with exceptional balance, moving over the most precarious terrain with grace and an economy of effort that allowed them to cover in a day, barefoot and laden, what would take incomers four or five long exhausting days without a load.

One young man came up to base camp with a letter Balwant had written between bouts of fever, four days away down in the jungle. By the time I realised that the letter had been written that same morning and that I should really show more appreciation, the 'postman' had gone, melting back into the green. Not only were these people modest they were also honest. Not a single item of gear was missing despite it being scattered along 150 miles of jungle track awaiting relays of porters to move it up to base camp.

Each evening, usually after dark, we would reach camp wet and exhausted only to find that the natives, before attending to their own needs, had our fire going with ample dead wet wood drying on a rack alongside; they had filled our water butt with fresh spring water, made a frame for our tarpaulins and cut back vegetation to make a flat area for us to sleep on. And all this after carrying a heavy and sometimes awkward load through the tangle of root and mud, creeper and thorn bush, across innumerable side streams by slippery logs or slimy boulders.

Throughout this ordeal they remained stoically indifferent to the horrendous and often dangerous conditions of travel, where the slippery slope fell away towards monster cliffs above the Kurung River in full flood. Not only were the Nishi kind and generous in taking good care of totally inept strangers, they were also warm and spontaneous, producing laughter and amusement at every opportunity.

My lasting impression is of them as professional mountaineers. Small bands of hunters would suddenly materialise en route or in camp and vanish, before we could organise a photograph of them wearing thick homespun mosquito-proof jackets, carrying a lightly woven, snug-fitting bamboo rucksack and a woven bamboo sou'wester-shaped hat that overlapped a cape of animal fur. Across one shoulder hung their sword (*dao*) and on the other a bow and quiver full of arrows. Strong bare legs and feet bleeding from leech bites – and off they went with only rice and tobacco and wildlife they could shoot or trap on their journeys, sometimes lasting a month beyond their jungle village.

The Nishi seemed brilliant at living their entire lives on a 'slant,' as Verrier Elwin put it, summing them up thus:

A belief in the importance of truth, a hardness of moral and physical fibre, courage before impossible living conditions, the love of adventure and exploration, a fresh, candid simple attitude to life's problems are among the other qualities that the [Nishi] people have to give the world.

Time with the Nishi gives a snapshot of how, presumably, all our ancestors once were and for 120,000 years or so – a long time to have had the basic instinct of compassion for others.

TAMOTSU NAKAMURA

Untrodden Mountains of West Sichuan

(Plates 26–32)

'Today the map has no more secrets.' Idle minds repeat that parrot phrase. But who knows all Tibet, or its far-away frontier on western China? Even its own prayer-muttering tribes know only their own bleak, wind-swept valleys.'

National Geographic Magazine, February 1930

This is the opening paragraph of Joseph F Rock's account of his journey seeking the mysterious mountain, Amne Machen. The venture was carried out three-quarters of a century ago. However, the reader's attention is invited to the fact that, even today, Rock's words still apply widely to the Tibetan territories of southwest China. Once off the beaten track in the remote regions of southeast Tibet and West Sichuan, you will meet stunning untouched peaks and hidden valleys, with beautiful forests, pastures and, in some places, historic monasteries.

This article introduces the lesser-known mountains of West Sichuan (formerly Eastern Tibet), in two parts:

1 HENGDUAN MOUNTAINS EAST: UNCLIMBED PEAKS IN SICHUAN PROVINCE

Unlike southeast Tibet, where all the 6000m peaks remain untrodden, in Sichuan there are only a couple of unclimbed 6000m peaks. Nevertheless, countless alluring rock and snow peaks lower than 6000m are awaiting visits from climbers and trekkers. The first part of this article is an outline of the major mountain ranges/massifs in the eastern part of the Hengduan Mountains between Jingsha Jiang and Min Jiang of the Upper Yangtze River. These are described from west to east. It is noted that, unless otherwise specifically mentioned, all the peaks are unclimbed.

Chola Shan Range
Two 6000m peaks have already been climbed. Chola I (6186m) was first climbed by a joint Japanese-Chinese party in 1987 and Chola II (6119m) was ascended by an American solo climber in 1997. A UIAA team ascended some 5000m peaks in 1997. However, a 5816m peak at the northern end of the range is still unclimbed, and to the west there are some supposedly remarkable rock peaks surrounding an old monastery.

Shaluli Shan Range

This mountain range covers a vast area and there is no clear boundary between it and the other mountain ranges. Each massif is introduced in succession from north to south.

1   Gangga Massif

This massif stretches to the southeast from the end of Chola Shan, south of Yalong Jiang. The main peak, Gangga (5688m), and other 5000m peaks have small glaciers.

2   Jarjinjabo Massif

The highest peak is 5812m and the second highest is 5725m. The most impressive peak is a brilliant granite rock tower (5382m) soaring to the sky, like Fitzroy in Patagonia. These mountains are located along the northern rim of the wide Zhopu Pasture north of Xiashe (5833m) Massif. To the west there are several 5500m peaks and to the east the challenging fortress of Hati (5524m) rises proudly.

3   Xiashe Massif

Xiashe (5833m), the highest peak, has beautiful lakes on its southern side, while the north face seems to attract climbers. The massif also has 5500m-5600m peaks adjacent to the Sichuan-Tibet Highway.

4   Dangchezhengla Massif

This massif is situated 15-20km away from Batang to the east. There is short and easy access to base camp. Four principal peaks of 6060m, 6033m, 5833m and 5850m dominate, ranging from east to west. A Japanese party attempted the highest peak from the northern side in 1991, but they were unsuccessful owing to bad weather and avalanche danger. Since then no-one has attempted these mountains. On the southern side of the massif a heavenly lake called Yamochouken lies at the high altitude of 4800m.

5   Genyen Massif and neighbouring mountains to the north and northwest

To the south of the Sichuan-Tibet Highway, between Litang Plateau and Batang, lies a vast mountain area. The highest peak, Genyen (6204m), a divine mountain, was climbed by a Japanese party in 1988. However, more than ten peaks of rock and snow at over 5800m are awaiting climbers. In particular, a 5965m peak, towering like a sharp beak, looks magnificent, and the scenery surrounding the 600-year-old Rengo Monastery amid spiky rock pinacles is really enchanting.

6   Gongga Xueshan (Kongkaling) Massif

These mountains were known to F Kingdon Ward and Joseph Rock in the 1920s. There are three major peaks: Xianre Ri (6032m), Yangmaiyong (5958m) and Xaruo Doje (5958m). A Japanese party failed to climb Xianre Ri in 1989 and two Americans made a reconnaissance of Yangmaiyong in 1993. A perfect snow pyramid,Yangmaiyong, which Joseph Rock called 'Jambeyang', must be one of the most beautiful mountains in Sichuan.

Gongkala Shan Range

This is a small mountain range located 30km from Garze to the southeast. In 1998 a Japanese party made a reconnaissance from the south of the highest peak, Kawarani (5992m), and the second highest one, Peak 5928m. According to the topographical map of the Chinese Liberation Army (1:100,000), there seem to be well-developed glaciers on the northern side. No other record is available.

Daxue Shan Range

This range has the most famous mountains, including Minya Konka (Gonnga Shan, 7556m). The Tibet-Qinghai Plateau ends at Daxue Shan. The scope of the range is rather ambiguous. Each massif is described from north to south.

1   Haizi Shan - 'Ja-ra'

Tibetans called Haizi Shan (5820m) 'Ja-ra' to signify 'King of Mountains' and many explorers have noticed this outstanding peak. A good close-up view of the southwest side can be had from the Sichuan-Tibet Highway. The north face would provide a possible climbing route.

2   Mountains of Dadu River basin

Along the deep valley of Dadu He, one of the large tributaries of the Yangtze River, there exist many 5000m peaks both to the east and west. The highest is a 5712m peak on the left bank of the river. The eastern end shares a boundary with the Jiaojin Shan, a minor range, and the Qionglai Shan ranges.

3   Cheto Shan

This is a minor mountain with the highest peak, 4962m, located between Haizi Shan and Minya Konka.

4   Lotus Flower Mountains

Although no glaciers have developed, eminent rock peaks can be seen north of Kangding, the capital of the Garze Tibetan Autonomous Prefecture. A Japanese party climbed the highest peak, 5704m, in 1998.

5   Lamo-she Massif

This massif, east of Kangding, has been called the 'Mountains of Tachienlu'. In 1993 its highest peak, Lamo-she (Tianhaizi Shan, 6070m) was scaled by Americans and the fourth highest (Shehaizi Shan, 5878m) was climbed by an American-Canadian-NZ team. The other two peaks, 5924m (Baihaizi Shan) and 5880m, are guarded by rocks and hanging glaciers.

6   Minya Konka (Gonnga Shan, 7556m) and its Satellite Peaks

All the ascents of Minya Konka, from the first ascent by Americans in 1932 to the sixth ascent by Japanese in 1997, were made via the northwest ridge. In 1998, however, a Korean party made the 7th ascent, via the northeast ridge, an enterprise which had taken the lives of 12 Japanese climbers in three expeditions. Future problems are the difficult south ridge and southwest ridge.

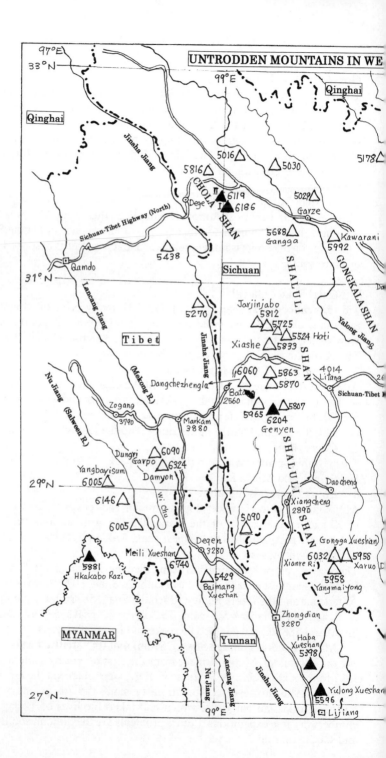

UNTRODDEN MOUNTAINS IN WE

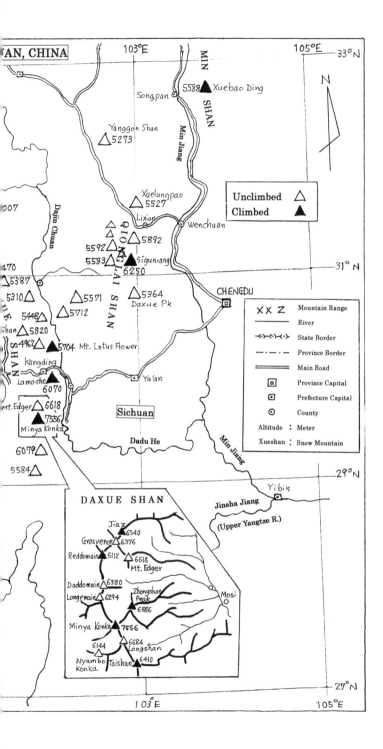

SICHUAN, CHINA

Unclimbed △
Climbed ▲

Mountain Range: X X Z
River
State Border
Province Border
Main Road
Province Capital
Prefecture Capital
County
Altitude : Meter
Xueshan : Snow Mountain

DAXUE SHAN

Min Jiang (Upper Yangtze R.)
Jinsha Jiang
Dadu He
Sichuan

Jiaz 6540
Grosvenor 6376
Reddomain 5112
6618 Mt. Edger
Daddomain 6380
Longemain 6294
Zhongshan Peak 6886
Minya Konka 7556
6144
6684 Longshan
Nyambo Konka Taishan 6410
Mosi

Xuebao Ding 5588
Songpan
Yanggon Shan 5273
Xuelungpao 5527
Lixian
Wenchuan
5892
5592
5533 Siguniang 6250
CHENGDU
5387
5310
5571 5364 Daxue Pk
5448 5712
5820
4962 5704 Mt. Lotus Flower
Kangding
Lamo-she 6070
Mt. Edger 6618
7556 Minya Konka
6079
5584
Yibin

007
470

There still remain unclimbed satellite peaks over 6000m. The following list shows the most important peaks still to be challenged:

Northern part	Grosvenor	6376m
	Mt. Edger	6618m (E-Gonnga)
Central part	Daddomain	6380m
	Longemain	6294m
Southern part	Longshan	6684m
	Nyambo Konka	6144m

7   6079m Massif
This is an independent massif with an unclimbed 6000m peak in the vicinity of Minya Konka to the south, though it is not on a large scale. No one has yet made a reconnaissance of the highest peak at 6079m. Further south, a 5584m mountain is shown on the Chinese map, but no specific information about it is available.

Qionglai Shan Range
This range forms the Min River–Dadu River divide and the highest peak is the famous Mt. Siguniang, 6250m, first climbed via its east ridge by the Japanese in 1981. Japanese mountaineers were also the first to climb the south face in 1992. The southern side of Mt. Siguniang is now a popular place for tourists, but to the north a splendid climbing field is expanding along beautiful valleys. Many granite rock spires of some 5500m soar, peak upon peak, and two major peaks of 5892m and 5712m with glaciers can be seen in the distance at the northern end.

Apart from Mt. Siguniang, Americans climbed the following peaks:

1983   Celestial Peak, 5413m (Tibetan name: 'Punyu'), a complete rock pyramid
1994   5484m and 5383m peaks
1996   a 5666m peak

Further north, there is an unknown massif of five 5000m peaks, of which the highest is 5527m.

Min Shan Range
The Min Shan range, at the eastern end of the Hengduan Mountains near Jiuzhaigou and Huanlong, is registered as a UNESCO World Heritage site. The highest peak, Xuebao Ding (5588m), was first climbed by Japanese in 1986. This area is now more suitable for tourists than for those seeking pioneer climbing.

2   JOURNEY TO UNKNOWN MOUNTAINS AND VALLEYS IN SOUTH KHAM

South Kham, which formerly belonged to Xikang Province, was incorporated into Sichuan Province in 1949 when Communist China imposed a new administration. Our trip during the first half of 2000 was focused on this unknown region. 'Seeking New Discoveries' was our primary aim, and consequently we planned the following objectives:

First round   Unclimbed 6000m peaks, Dangchezhengla Massif east of Batang
Second round   Jarjinjabo and Xiashe Massifs north of Litang Plateau

Dangchezhengla and Heaven Lake
Except for the satellite peaks of Minya Konka, only three mountain massifs in West Sichuan have unclimbed 6000m peaks. These are Xianre Ri (6032m) in the Gongga Xueshan massif, Peak 6079m south of Minya Konka, and Dangchezhengla.

Our party of two (total age 132 years) arrived at Chengdu via Shanghai on 26 May 2000. We were well received by the Zhang brothers of Sichuan Adventure Travel and by our guide, Lenny Cheung. The Zhang brothers have gained a reputation in the USA as the most experienced guides for rafting on both the Yangtze and Tsangpo rivers.

On 27 May we reached Kangding from Chengdu in eight hours in a Toyota Land-Cruiser via the newly opened Erlangshan Tunnel. On 28-29 May we proceeded westwards in the rain along the Sichuan-Tibet Highway to Batang (2560m). The road lies at an altitude of over 4000m for about 200km as it traverses the Litang Plateau. Lenny made the necessary arrangements for our party at Dongba village (2690m) near Batang.

On 31 May, after it had rained for several days, we heard that a cycle of favourable weather was moving in our direction. So we left Dongba and ascended a trail along a mountain ridge to the east. Our party consisted of two Japanese, a Chinese guide, three Tibetans (the local Communist Party Secretary and two muleteers), nine horses and one yak. We lost half a day waiting for the Secretary who had difficulty finding us. This was very frustrating. We stayed overnight at one of the Tibetan houses in Zhomba village at 3740m.

In the spring season it is not easy to employ local people as porters, or bearer animals such as horses, mules and yaks, because the villagers are busy gathering caterpillar fungus (a Chinese traditional medicine) from locations at over 4000m; at this time, animals are moved to high pastures for grazing. The fungus is a substantial source of income for local Tibetan people, one piece selling for a quarter dollar.

On 1 June the fine weather returned. Our caravan started with five horses and seven porters. The trail ascended along the left bank of the valley to the east through a primeval conifer forest. Rhododendrons were in full bloom. On the opposite side of the valley there was an isolated monastery. Before long the valley ended, blocked by an overwhelming 5148m rock peak beyond which must be heaven lake. We set up our base camp (BC) at 4450m by the main stream, near a temporary summer grazing hut.

On 2 June it was cloudy with some sunshine. Our path climbed up a steep zigzag slope and then followed a stream leading us to the right shoulder of the rock peak. This was likely to be the only outlet for heaven lake, Yamouchouken (4800m). The horses were gasping. Off the trail we could see many *Meconopsis integrifolias* with its yellow flowers, but *Meconopsis horidulas*, the so-called 'Blue Poppy' were not to be found anywhere. I described the scene in my diary:

> At last we reached the outlet at 10:30am from the western end of the lake. Total tranquillity rests over the entire area. No sounds of animals are heard, and the scenery before me is quite different from how I had imagined it. The sight is breathtaking. In spite of early summer, the lake is almost completely frozen and the surface glitters in silvery white. I was reminded of the salt lakes in the highlands of the Bolivian Andes and Ethiopia in East Africa. If you took one day's walk down to the Jinsha Jiang river basin from the lake, you would suddenly suffer from a dry and hot blast running up the valley. It is a wonder of nature, indeed, in South Kham.

We dismounted and continued our march further to the east, tracing a footpath along the north bank of the lake, until all the three peaks (at 6060m, 6033m and 5833m from east to west) of Dangchezhengla Massif came into view. We stopped trekking at 4900m. Peak 5833m had a large glacier. The southwest side of the highest peak appeared to be not too difficult to climb. In the late afternoon we returned to BC having accomplished a preliminary reconnaissance of the mountain massif.

On 3 June our caravan went down to Batang and spent one day there to prepare for the next round.

The heart of South Kham – Zhopu Pasture and Jarjinjabo Massif
One is apt to overlook something important if it lies near at hand: a hidden paradise exists not far north of the main Sichuan-Tibet Highway. The local chief of Dongba village gave us some information, summarised as follows:

1   Zhopu Pasture and its surrounding nature reserve is the most beautiful in Batang County. A wide grassy valley, rock and snow mountains, primeval forests, a blue lake and wild animals – all are in perfect harmony. It could be compared with Jiuzhaigou.

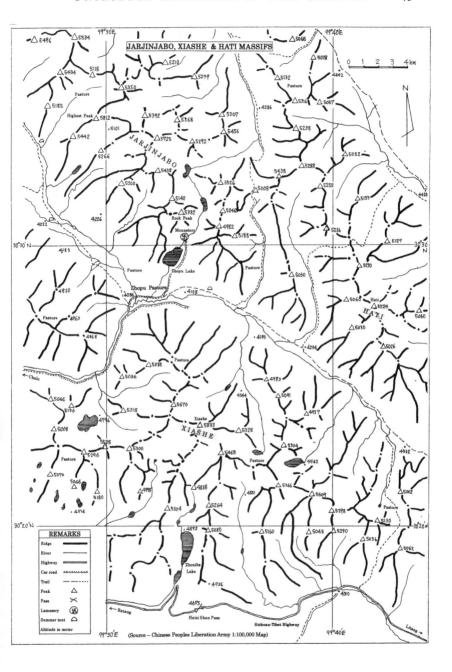

JARJINJABO, XIASHE & HATI MASSIFS

(Source – Chinese Peoples Liberation Army 1:100,000 Map)

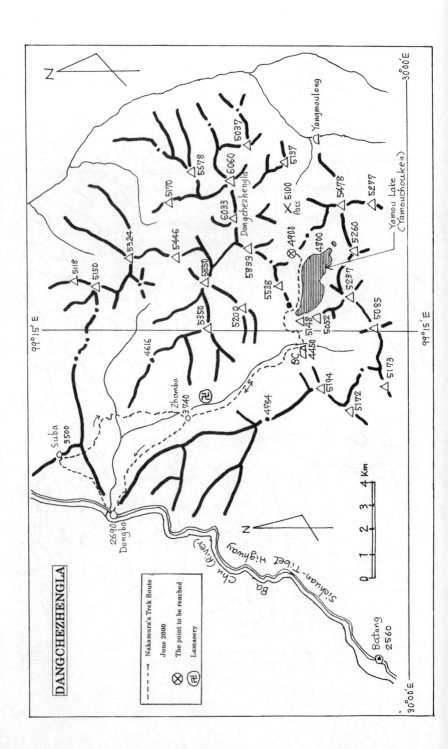

74

2   Zhopu Monastery, with its 700 years of history, is a holy place of the Red Hat sect. Vehicle access is now possible, since a road to carry mining products has been constructed from Chalu to a silver mine beyond Zhopu Pasture.

On 5 June we left Batang in the early morning for Zhopu Monastery with a great deal of expectation, as if we were entering into a secret and isolated world, like James Hilton's *Lost Horizon*. We turned north at the junction of the highway to Chalu and Zhopu. From Chalu a young local government officer accompanied us as a pilot. He had the task of watching the foreigners too. Our land-cruiser proceeded along the left bank of the valley to the northeast. We passed by a hot spring where old lamas were bathing. Conifers and oak trees grew freely on the mountain. The oak trees yield pine mushrooms that are exported to Japan. Soon an old monastery and then a ruined stone defence tower appeared. At about 4.00pm, we reached a point where the valley merged with a vast and flat pasture where hundreds of yaks and sheep were grazing.

Zhopu Pasture lies at an altitude of 4050m-4100m, spreading for about 20km from WNW to ESE and 2km-4km wide. Here the Khamba people live the life of nomads in black tents, looking after yaks, sheep and horses. Jarjinjabo mountain massif stretches in a panoramic view over the pasture. The grandeur of a 5382m granite rock peak, viewed head-on, is outstandingly impressive. But we were disappointed that there are no glaciers.

In the late afternoon we arrived at Zhopu Monastery (4120m), the neighbourhood of which supposedly has an atmosphere of 'Shangri-La'. Many lamas and students received us warmly but curiously, as we were the first foreigners to visit them.

On 6 June it was fine. After taking photographs of the challenging north face of Xiashe (5833m) in the early morning, we ascended a gully between granite rock walls just behind the monastery to the upper lakes for some hours. It was hard work and we could not help turning back halfway. At 3:00pm we had an interview with Living Buddha, who is the supreme lama in this monastery. He explained that the monastery had been opened in AD 1260 and now had 30 lamas and 300 students, of whom 100 were nuns. We came back to Zhopu Pasture and stayed at a villager's log house.

On the morning of 7 June the weather was settled. We spent one day exploring the two highest peaks, at 5812m and 5725m. Then, riding on horses, we moved calmly to the northwest. Fertile grasslands, yaks, sheep, black tents, Khamba girls and Tibetan dogs presented a typical picture of Eastern Tibet. We spent a couple of hours in a Tibetan black tent where only women and children were based, on their own, almost throughout the year. Tibetan women look after animals and children in the pasture, whilst males remain in their villages to take care of houses and barley fields.

The top of Peak 5725m is snow-covered and the southern side looks gentle. A profile of the highest peak, 5812m, looks very different. The broad southeast face is guarded by precipitous ridges and gullies, with hanging glaciers. But from a climbing point of view, it would not be very attractive. Further to the northwest are more ranges of 5500m peaks. In the evening it rained a little and we heard the rumbling of thunder, indicating that the weather was changing.

On 8 June it rained. We said 'Zaijian' ('See you again') to the warm-hearted Zhopu people. On 10 June we returned safely to Chengdu. We felt well satisfied with the outcome of our journey.

MAPS

1. Map of Mountain Ranges in China, 1:6,000,000 (Chinese version)
2. Map of Mountain Peaks on the Qinghai-Xizang Plateau, 1:2,500,000 (English)
3. Garze Tibetan Autonomous Prefecture, Sichuan, 1:500,000 (Chinese)
4. DMAAC (USA) – TPC Aeronautical Chart, 1:500,000 (English)
5. Chinese Peoples Liberation Army, Topographical map, 1:50,000 & 1:100,000 (Chinese)
6. Russian Topographical Map, 1:100,000, 1:200,000 & 1:500,000 (Russian)
7. Sketch maps of 'JARJINJABO, XIASHE & HATI MASSIFS' and 'DANGCHEZHENGLA' are included in this article.

SVERRE AARSETH

Three Solo Adventures in the Atacama

(Plates 18, 19)

This article is dedicated to the memory of Giancarlo Fiocco, who pioneered the route to Pissis from Chile and perished from exposure within sight of the Mina Marte.

Ojos del Salado (1991)

Immersed in a thermal pool in the middle of nowhere, I try to forget about my next move which is going to be a back-breaking experience. Instead I count my luck at having met Hugo in Santiago, who put me in touch with the only driver likely to take me to the base camp of Ojos del Salado, at 6883m the acclaimed second-highest peak in the Western Hemisphere. The day before, Giancarlo had driven me up from the oasis of Copiapo to the border police station at 4500m which would be a suitable staging-post after my previous acclimatisation in lovely San Pedro de Atacama, with visits to the geysers and ascent of the active volcano Lascar (5600m). To my surprise, I am supposed to have a permit but this obstacle is surmounted by my driver promising to get it from a friend in the local police on returning. His jeep could reach the first hut at 5200m but this would be too high so I put up my tent next to the burnt-out refugio. After next day's excursion to the azure-coloured Laguna Verde with its primitive spa facility, I spend one more day psyching myself up for the big carry. It was not exactly encouraging to have read of another party – in cars – who had taken several days finding the hut.

On the dreaded day I trace the tyre tracks along the bleak desert trail. The tent and ice axe are left behind but my extra load of six litres of water and one kilo of marzipan makes 20 minutes' carry an agony. When I finally reach an area at 5000m which corresponds to the description 'here we parked and walked up', the track becomes invisible but I spot an object with sharp edges and head up some hills. Having expended extra energy I realise it is not the hut, but the view now brings out faint markings. I descend a little and follow their direction. My spirits are revived when the road from the upper refugio can be seen and it is only a question of time before the Atacama refugio comes into view. Reaching it, my weary body collapses on a bed after 10 hours' hike. Following a restful Christmas Day, I do an easy carry to Tejos (5750m) and find a small source of water. On the way down my peace is disrupted by a truck; the passenger, whom I met at the roadhead, is hoping to get a summit picture of his sponsored mountain bike – named the 'Oxford' of all things, whereas I am a Cambridge man.

Two days later I join him in the comfortable hut after a brisk hike which beats the book entry of 90 minutes by two Brits. On summit day we leave together at six but an hour later my companion reaches his bike and falls behind. The first part is up rocks which makes for good progress but then comes the inevitable scree slope. The crater rim (6700m) is gained in 5½ hours but there is a sting in the tail. Hugo has warned me of the final summit towers – and advised against doing them alone – but their appearance still has a dramatic impact. After some rest, I follow a trail which skirts the snow-filled caldera and leads to the col, where as advertised there is a rope for assistance along the summit ridge. The last 25 metres is a walk and soon I stand on the summit 7½ hours after setting out. The wind is biting cold and my camera only manages an inferior picture of my sack by the cairn. Having ascended the official summit, I am tempted by the other one which rises from the col. The height is modest but the ground is unstable. Using the loose end of the rope, I lower myself over the col from where it is easier to gain access. Hugo, who has guided on Ojos before, was right: if you fall here, you fall a long way. But I scramble up without mishap and find a second summit book. The Thommen altimeter shows almost 6780m, whereas the reading was 6770 on the main summit – the deficiency of 110 metres is typical – but at least I have made sure.

Taking a rest halfway down the boulder field, I see Louis pushing his bike along the snow. He carries it up and desperately wants to make the summit. By now it is nearly 4pm and I insist it cannot be done; in any case there is no time. He accepts my spare bottle of water and agrees to delay his attempt. Next day still leaves me feeling weak but it is an easy stroll to the lower refugio where my driver is supposed to pick me up. With no vehicle appearing by 2pm, I decide to walk out and hope that one litre of water will be enough. The sack is light but the desert wind dries my mouth. Around 5.30pm I see a car standing in a flat spot. However, my spirits are dashed when I find it empty and see foot prints leading back. All the water is gone when I reach base at 7pm to find Giancarlo and two companions in my tent and one belonging to another expedition. The four-wheel drive had failed and the six kilometre walk required many rests for the Copiapo (altitude 300m) residents. I give them all my warm clothes and spend a sleepless night but at least the police radio has called for a rescue vehicle and nobody asks about the non-existent climbing permit. As it turns out, the Hertz car is unable to pull the stranded jeep out but we all squeeze in and head back to civilization. After experiencing the desert in slow motion, it is exhilarating to move along at speed and take in the vast and wonderful scenery which leaves an unforgettable imprint.

Pissis (1994)

Having spent the previous year, accompanied by my friend Edgar and with Giancarlo as driver, in an unsuccessful search for an approach to Pissis from Chile, I decide to try my luck again going alone. This time Giancarlo has done his research and together with a mining engineer found a more direct route on the return trip with a client. A rarely visited mountain, Pissis provides a unique opportunity for using my newly acquired 60th birthday present to make a GPS determination of its uncertain altitude. Unlike Ojos, there are no huts and its extreme isolation presents a daunting challenge for an unsupported visit. My preparation for the expedition consists of spending seven nights in the splendid Parinacota National Park, albeit with three nights at sea level before leaving for base camp. Again Giancarlo is at the wheel but he is retiring and handing over to Patricio and a friend who are coming along to learn the route.

Soon after passing Mina Marte (4000m) we leave the road and head for the Valle Ancho Pass (4500m) which also sports a border marker. Crossing illegally into the old adversary Argentina is especially exciting for the Chileans. There are no trails to be seen and the route-finding becomes tricky, with occasional backtracking. Soon Pissis shows itself; it is an impressive sight although partly engulfed in a snow storm. We are aiming for a well-defined spot at the bottom of a huge glacier which is reached after 7½ hours and 270km. At $400 per trip, it feels like the cheapest taxi ride in the world, considering the terrain which is littered with rocks. The three locals celebrate with a 12-year whisky on the snow before leaving me to my uncertain fate. The first task of erecting the tent proves tricky in the fresh breeze; losing the fly now would be a bad start. The platform is sloping slightly but arriving at 5400m from the lowlands is not conducive to great exertion and my stay will be short.

My first day should be restful but I wander up a possible route to the next camp and find a small snow field at 5700m. Ascending further, I reach the top of a ridge at 6000m which yields good views of five well separated peaks but it is impossible to pick out the highest. In any case, proceeding up the eastern side of the glacier appears the best bet since no obvious camp site – with level ground and snow – can be seen on the other side. The food sack is carried up to a safe place the following day and I return to endure hail and thunder which prevent cooking. Fortunately next morning is perfect and early dinner is prepared, although now the stove – my only one – is rather reluctant. I move camp and manage to level a platform before the afternoon hail sets in. Miraculously a small trickle of water appears when digging a hole at the edge of the snow field. Enduring some frightening thunder and lightning over several days, I am thankful for not having placed my tent on the exposed ridge above.

Two days later I brave the elements and return to the ridge for a final assessment. My initial plan still looks good and I decide to ascend the scree slopes and cross the glacier higher up where it seems to level out; then traverse to the most distant and probably the highest peak which is barely visible. Accordingly I place some markers along the route as guides for a possible late return or in bad visibility and get back in time to avoid a vicious snow shower. Christmas Day is my last chance to gain altitude before the final climb. I explore further to the east, reaching the end of a ridge at 6300m. A tempting summit is in full view across a small valley and I give myself three more hours to reach it. The hike is easy and I actually beat my estimate. This eastern outlier is at 6446m and does not show any evidence of previous visits. On returning I find the tent compressed by a strong gust of wind and the conditions do not favour any cooking, so there is not even a cup of tea for my Christmas dinner; however, the marzipan proves its worth. Next day I make sure of an early dinner. It is also my last chance to gain strength before gambling everything on the ultimate day. True to form, some late snow showers develop but the thunder seems more distant, which makes me hopeful that the gods will relent when I go for the top.

I get off to a good start and watch the sunrise shadows shortening in the desert below as the ridge is gained. The next stage turns out to be much longer than the two hours envisaged. There are a number of hidden depressions and I sit out a snow shower, the only one that day. The glacier crossing is reached at 1pm, some three hours later than estimated. The glacier appears safe at this point since the curved parts further down do not show any crevasses. I keep my crampons on to save time and proceed over gently sloping rough ground partly covered by snow. Once more it is a good deal further than first impressions indicated but my summit fever is too strong to permit me to turn back. Gaining a false summit, I notice that half a crampon is missing. Finally I reach the highest point shortly before 5pm and find a cylinder containing names but no official statement. Looking around, I see two other humps of similar height but there is no time to investigate so I hope the cylinder is placed correctly. Several measurements are made with the GPS which gives strong signals and small errors (50 metres either way). The best determination, of 6874m, is arrived at after deducting 20 metres due to the local deviation from the geoid, whereas the altimeter which was calibrated in camp shows an expected lower reading of 6710 m.

After a brief stay and some picture-taking I head for home. The altitude confuses my sense of direction since the summit area is featureless but a few foot prints point the way. It is cold and already my pace is slow due to lack of energy. The missing crampon is recovered but not reinstated. On crossing the glacier I gain some time by avoiding part of the scree slope and descend near the edge of the snow field, which has icy patches, hoping the faulty crampon will not let me down. It is my luck that the visibility holds up until sunset. Reascending the final ridge is painfully slow, with frequent rests, but there is no other way. I reach the tent around 9pm, with ten minutes to spare before it gets dark, but the location at the bottom of a snow field would have acted as a guide later. Going without dinner, I derive inspiration and satisfaction by admiring the incredibly sparkling sky.

My last day provides a complete contrast from ten days of solitude. The vehicle has been booked to arrive at 1pm, so I am in no hurry. Coming down the slopes, however, I see the jeep standing next to my red marker flag. The drivers were so excited that they left Copiapo long before dawn and got here hours ago. I open a small bottle of brandy to mark the happy event, trying not to think of the alternative scenario with them or me not making it. Immediately on leaving base, the car hits a big rock and gets stuck. This requires building a stone bridge which we can slide over, and amazingly there does not appear to be any damage. Later the engine begins to lose power for unknown reasons and is very hesitant uphill. Not surprisingly, it is more difficult to find the way without an obvious landmark but after several false trails we eventually reach town by 9pm, in time to celebrate our success.

Llullaillaco (1998)

After four years, the memories of hardship fade away and I find myself on the Atacama trail yet again. This time I am sharing transport and camp sites with Bob who has visited the desert many times. We are driven to 5000m on the remote Llullaillaco (6732 m) which ranks seventh in the Western World and is known for its ancient temple on the summit. (See *National Geographic*, November 1999, for description of treasures found at the summit.) With no prior acclimatisation, except for a night on the way at Aguas Calientes (3600m), it is necessary to take it easy at first. After three days of hanging around, I hike up to our next prospective camp and find a tiny snowfield next to the only flat area at around 5500m. Following a day's food carry, we move up in shirt-sleeve weather but four hours is long enough in my present condition. After a sleepless night we set off for the next stage with food sacks. The scree slopes are agonizing but I am not prepared for the shock announcement from Bob, who is trailing. He has had enough and is quitting. I reach the crater rim (6100m) in six hours and have a stunning view of the false summit some distance away. There is a big snow field close by and plenty of level ground.

After a well-deserved rest day I leave Bob behind but benefit from exchanging my temperamental stove which still fails to inspire confidence in spite of being checked out. This time it takes 7½ hours but there is still ample time for cooking. Two days later, after a night of −10°F outside, I make my first attempt without moving higher, which was suggested by Bob who has climbed the false summit. However, the route is problematic and I choose the eastern side, hoping to gain the long summit ridge. The early part is easy and only one snow field requires crampons, after which they are left behind to save weight. I gain the ridge and proceed upwards for a while before realising that the actual summit ridge is the next one over, separated by a valley which would take too much time. My eyes have been misled by foreshortening and now there is no choice but to carry on, hoping for the best. There are large blocks to negotiate and the wind becomes intensely cold. In addition, I have to contend with the most debilitating dry cough which has bothered me since day one. At 3pm I reach a point where the ridge abuts slightly before the col, although it should be possible to complete the climb with a scramble. The pointed summit looks tantalisingly close some 200 metres above. However, the weather conditions make such thoughts impossible and I have no choice but to retreat: it is the first time I have turned back on a solo climb.

On the way down I avoid the tricky ridge by ascending the adjacent snow field which starts at the col. However, care is needed to avoid falling into large holes near the rocks and my lack of crampons makes it hazardous to negotiate icy patches. I am greatly relieved when the ordeal is over. The rest is a stroll, but I am weak and need frequent stops before reaching the tent with two hours until sunset. With an extra day in hand, I do not have the energy for another attempt and must be content with carrying back images of magical Atacama.

Postscript
It appears that in the GPS altitude determination, the deviation from the geoid should not be subtracted when using the WGS 84 datum. In that case the measurement for Pissis should read 6894 metres, with an error of 50 metres.

EVELIO ECHEVARRÍA

The Cordillera Huarochirí, Peru

(Plates 14, 15)

It is commonly accepted that the Andes of Peru comprise 24 well-defined districts or *cordilleras*. Expeditionary activity has, on the whole, been quite well reported and recorded, but there is an exception. Orographic and expeditionary information about the Cordillera Huarochirí of central Peru has been confusingly reported and documented and there has been no attempt to correct this situation. Even the very name of the range may come as a surprise to many aficionados of the Andes; names previously known are all erroneous.

I have to start by saying outright that this Peruvian cordillera badly needs a few studious, dedicated souls who would take it under their wing and endeavour to solve the geographic and mountaineering problems that have hampered exploration. One was the problem of having an important mountain range without a definite name. Another was the problem of how to gain access to the higher peaks and valleys. So it is comforting to learn that these two problems have been almost completely solved by Peruvian climbers. But the third riddle, unfortunately a major one, has so far no solution in sight: existing maps differ widely as to the names and location of peaks, which, in turn, leaves us unable properly to survey the mountaineering history of the range.

First, a brief introduction. The Cordillera Huarochirí, also locally called Cordillera Pariacacca, is located south of the mining town of La Oroya (pop 41,000; 3700m). La Oroya is 187km east of Lima and sits astride the well-paved central highway running between Lima and Huancayo. The range, so far as peaks over 5000 metres are concerned, is estimated to be some 35km in length, north to south, and 18 to 20km in breadth. There are a few isolated massifs here and there. Streams that descend from the heights flow into the Canete river to the south, the Mantaro to the north and the Rimac to the northwest. Population in the higher valleys is extremely small. The village of Yuracmayo (population 400) exists only to provide the work force for a major dam. In the highlands one seldom finds hamlets of more than ten people. These highlanders, descendants of the Quichua race, are now wholly Hispanised. They tend their flocks of sheep and llamas and also do some fishing in the bigger lakes that dot the area. In their rather cold uplands there is very little natural life. Stunted bushes exist only near lakes and streams. The coarse *ichu* grass grows abundantly everywhere. Services in the district are scarce, owing to the reduced population.

The mountaineering season during the dry Peruvian winter is from May to October; halfway, by the end of June, the cold becomes intense and in some years, a persistent icy breeze roams the higher valleys. Good water can be found everywhere.

Names and access

In the last decade, several Lima mountaineers entering the district's valleys learned that the current, widely accepted local name for the range was Cordillera Huarochirí (Quichua: *huayra*, wind; *chiri*, cold). A second local name, Cordillera Pariacacca, was also discovered. Names used by mountaineers other than Huarochirí and Pariacacca are unknown to the local inhabitants and should therefore be discarded. 'Nevados de Cochas', after a local farm, was the name applied by some German surveyors. 'Cordillera Central' was the name consistently used by the 1967 Munich expedition, and this unfortunate denomination, actually belonging to another Peruvian range to the west of the Huarochirí, has been repeated everywhere. Still other names like 'Tunshu Group' and 'Tullujuto Group', after some major peaks, were applied to the entire range. They were equally inappropriate, since they referred to massifs known only to the inhabitants of a few valleys. And so on.

The best policy is to refer to this range with either of the names in use by the local population. Incidentally, Pariacacca, the second name found, is locally given both to the entire range and to the twin Tullujuto or Pariacacca Nevados (5700m and 5751m) located at the southern end of the range. Pariacacca was an Andean titan who, in a fierce struggle, defeated the perverse cannibal Huallallo and forced him to abandon the Inca lands.

The second confusing problem, finding ways of access to the peaks, was also solved by Lima climbers. Before the end of the last century, books and guidebooks suggested some less practical approaches. No wonder, since the authors of such books had never visited the range and one of them had never been in South America at all, let alone in the Andes! The San Mateo-Huayca valley, a long march over trails, and the long, devious Huarochirí town to Tanta route, in the south, were ways listed by such authors. Both, and indeed every other route, should be discarded in favour of any of the following, which have been opened and well-reconnoitreed by Peruvians:

1   Lima-Pachacayo – a station east of La Oroya. Taxis carry passengers to nearby Canchayllo, where vehicles can be hired for the run to the hamlet and dam of Huayllacancha (also called Jailacancha); the cost of a vehicle is about 80 soles ($1 = 5.20 soles). This route yields access to the south and east sides of the range, where the highest peaks are located (*see map*). The Pachacayo-Huayllacancha gravel road may have been the route used by the earliest mountaineers who visited the region, perhaps in the year 1927. It has been repeatedly used by Peruvians and by some foreign expeditions.

4. The Cordillera Huarochirí, Peru. Nevados Panchacoto (5450m) and Tranca (5250m) from the south. (*Evelio Echevarría*) (p83)

15. Cordillera Huarochirí, Peru. The Paca-Antachaire group seen from the west. (*Evelio Echevarría*) (p83)

16. The stunning prow of Nalumasortoq, Tasermiut Fjord, Greenland, first climbed via its great dihedral by an Italian and French team comprising Jerome Arpin, Mario Manica, Giancarlo Ruffi and Francesco Vaudo. The 850-metre line was graded ED/6c/A3 and called *Non c'è due senza t* ('If it happens twice, it will happen again'). The team placed one bolt. (*Mario Manica*) (*See* Area Notes: Greenland)

17. Climbing on Nalumasortoq's prow. (*Mario Manica*)
    (*See* Area Notes: Greenland)

18. Looking out of his tent at Camp 1 on Pissis towards the Ojos del Salado. (*Sverre Aarseth*) (p7

19. The desolate landscape of the summit region of Pissis. (*Sverre Aarseth*) (p77)

20. The North Face of Poi, Kenya, with the line of *Dark Safari* taking the big curving corner just left of centre. An American expedition also climbed a new line on Poi in early 2000, but chose to rappel the mountain first to bolt and clean their intended line. This irritated local activists. (*Pat Littlejohn*) (p24)

21. The North Face of Strandåtind, Arctic Norway. (*Anders Lundahl*) (p181)

22. Eva Selin overcoming the roof pitch on the first free ascent of *Lille Peder Edderkopp* (E5 6b), Strandåtind North Face, Arctic Norway. (*Anders Lundahl*) (p181)

23. The North Face of Strandåtind, Arctic Norway. (*Anders Lundahl*) (p181)

24. A lithograph by James D Forbes of the Strandåtind massif from his work of 1853, *Norway and its Glaciers.* (p181)

25. Believed by Anders Lundahl to be an unpublished photograph of Carl Wilhelm Rubenson (1885-1960) and William Cecil Slingsby (1849-1929) after their successful ascent of Strandåtind at Kjerringøy, in 1912. (*Unknown*) (p181)

2   Lima-San Mateo. From the latter large village, a van travels once a week through the Yuracmayo (or Rio Blanco) valley en route to Lake Paccha and the hamlet of Carhuasmayo. The cost is about 15 soles. This route leaves most western valleys open to visitors. It was discovered and used by the Peruvians Jose Pinzas and Alberto Murguia.

3   Lima-La Oroya-San Cristobal. At La Oroya, vans, locally called *combis*, can be taken to Yauli and the active San Cristobal mine. The cost is about 20 soles. This route offers access to the icy Chumpe group (5250m) that rises steeply above the mine, as well as to the northernmost peaks of the range. It was inaugurated in July 2000 by Alberto Murguia, accompanied by the writer.

Maps and peaks
Now for the main riddle. In 1969 the Deutscher Alpenverein, Munich section, published a map of the area known as 'Cordillera Central', scale 1:60,000, with names of peaks its expedition ascended and the subsequent routes. A few years later there appeared in Lima the Carta Nacional del Peru, scale 1:100,000, which, in comparison, showed a much larger number of peaks, with names, heights and location so vastly different to those of 1967 that it is not possible to reconcile one map with the other. Very few of the peaks ascended by the Germans, and indeed by all expeditions before 1967, can be located on this Peruvian map. And yet the latter, besides being the official national chart, is in my opinion far better. The Peruvian Alberto Murguia, at present the finest connoisseur of the range, and I, in our own forays into several valleys, were able to verify its accuracy in every respect. But how to reconcile names and, therefore, to rewrite the history of Huarochirí climbing according to the numerous new names found on the good Peruvian chart?
      It is certain that Nevado Shallanca (5400m), on the German map, is the same as Nevado Yantayo (5300m), on the Peruvian work. The Twins, or Zwillingen of the Munich group, seems to correspond to the Nevados Putca, of the Peruvians. The German Nevado Tembladero (5595m) could well be the Peruvian Nevado Ninaucro (5550m). But what about the rest? On their map the Munich climbers showed 35 named elevations. The three Peruvian sheets covering the Cordillera Huarochirí included some 40 named summits, plus some 50 other unnamed elevations over 5000m. In all, less than half of the 100 or so peaks that make up this district seem to have been ascended.
      With its proper name now established and its valleys of access well tested, there remains the unpleasant job of identifying, on the spot as well as from photographs, the peaks ascended before 1967 and reconciling their names, heights and locations with those that appeared on the Peruvian chart. There is much work ahead. The need is not for pure climbers but rather for dedicated souls endowed with characteristics that the pioneer alpinist

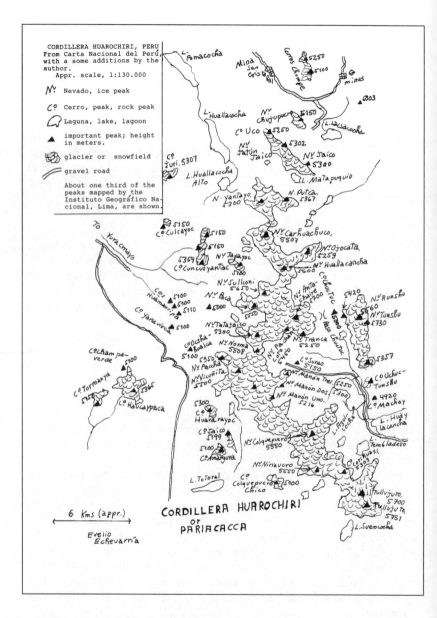

Douglas W. Freshfield once confessed to possess: 'I was a topographer; a geographer mixed with a mountaineer.'

It will be necessary to travel to the Huarochirí district with both German and Peruvian maps in hand; the only way to identify each mountain peak and thus to learn which peaks in the Range of the Cold Winds remain unclimbed.

History after 1967

In my surveys of Andean ascents, published in the *American Alpine Journal*, I covered all reported ascents that took place before the year 1970; and those ascended after that date were often noted in the same journal. Therefore, I am referring readers to the Bibliography and am listing below the little unrecorded activity that should be added.

• In 1979, a French-Peruvian group entered the range by the not-recommended route of the extreme south town of Huarochirí-Tanta and repeated ascents of the two Nevados Tullujuto and Pariacacca (5700m and 5751m, the latter is the highest in the range) and of Colquepucro.
• Before 1985, the Peruvian José Pinzas, perhaps alone, made the first ascent of Nevado Vicunita (5500m), located in the southwest part of the range. On this occasion, access by the Yuracmayo, the second option detailed above, was probably pioneered. It was repeated several times by Lima climber A. Murguia.
• My own experiences: in May 1999, alone, using the Pachacayo route (see above), I made the first ascent of Cerros Surao (5150m) and Uchuctunshu (5050m). A week later, June 1999, Alberto Murguia and I made the first ascent of Cerro Chuctuc (5000m), and an attempt on Cerro Entabladas (5100m) whose smooth, steep rock wall easily repulsed us. A year later, in July 2000, Murguia and I inaugurated the hitherto untried north access via the San Cristobal mine, the third route outlined above. Without proper acclimatisation, I was dragged by my enthusiastic companion to the top of Nevado Jatun Jaico (5302m). Murguia then had to return to Lima and after three days marooned in my tent by snowstorms, I climbed Chujupucro (5150m), and Pt 5200, which I christened Yurachucllu (Quichua: 'White Cricket'). All three were first ascents of very attractive ice peaks. Finally, a week later, still in cold July, alone, I entered via the San Mateo-Yuracmayo route and made the first ascent of rocky Cerro Riguis (5000m), and climbed two other 5100-metre rock peaks, crowned by cairns, probably erected by highlanders.
• In July 2000, Murguia and Guillermo Portocarrero climbed Nevado Paccha (5350m). Two weeks later, Murguia returned alone and made another first ascent, that of the ice peak located between Paccha and Vicunita (c5300m).
• several purely rock peaks, not above 5100m, may also have been ascended by local highlanders, who erected on their summits cairns or piles of stones. These ascents have gone unrecorded.

Some advice to future visitors to this range could be drawn from the experience accumulated by my Peruvian comrades as well as by myself. This is a range that offers mountain climbing only. There are no attractions for tourists, trekkers, hunters or archaeologists. The small amount of available fishing should be left to the highlanders, since it is a part of their sustenance. Small groups are recommended, owing to the lack of steady transportation and the scarcity of services and supplies in the high valleys. Very light equipment should be taken, since everything will have to be carried on one's back. There are no porters. As for horses, to my knowledge, only in the hamlet of Huayllacancha could a few be found, the owner being the capable *arriero* Moises Morales, whom I warmly recommend. Finally, in Lima, members of the Club de Montaneros Americo Tordoya could be contacted: the current president, Gonzalo Menacho; Guillermo Portocarrero, an active member of the American Alpine Club; and my good friend Alberto Murguia, will all give advice, as well as good companionship.

Further information

Club de Montaneros Americo Tordoya, at Avenida Tarapaca 184,
    Barrio Magdalena, Lima.
Instituto Geografico Nacional, at Avenida Aramburu 1190,
    Barrio Surquillo, Lima.

Books

Deutscher Alpenverein, *Munchner Anden Kundfahrt 1967*. Munich, 1969,
    with map 1:60,000,
Heim, Arnold, *Wunderland Peru*. Bern, Huberverlag, 1951,
Schmid, Karl, *Eisgipfel unter Troppensonne*. Bern, Aareverlag, 1950.

Articles

Echevarría, Evelio, 'A survey of Andean Ascents.' *American Alpine Journal*
    36, pp. 155-192, 1962 and 47, pp339-402, 1973. Most ascents that took
    place after 1970 were noted in later issues of the same journal.
Emslie, Myrtle, 'Conquering Peru's virgin peaks.' *The Scotsman*, 4 and 5
    November, 1958.
Jenks, William F., 'Climbing in the high Andes of Peru.' *American Alpine
    Journal* 4, pp157-176, 1940-42.
Kinzl, Hans, 'Die Anden-Kundfahrt des Deutschen Alpenvereins nach Peru
    in Jahre 1939.' Deutscher Alpenverein, *Zeitschrift* 72, pp1-24, 1941.

Current maps

Deutscher Alpenverein, Cordillera Central. 1:60,000, Munich, 1969
Instituto Geografico Nacional del Peru, Carta Nacional del Peru, *hojas* or
    sheets 24-K, 25-K and 24-L, 1:100,000, Lima, 1971.

J G R HARDING

In Praise of Greek Mountains

(*Plates 33, 34*)

No country has captured the romantic imagination more completely than Greece yet few are subject to greater misconceptions. In this birthplace of Jason, Odysseus, Niarchos and Onassis, the sea is omnipresent, with no part of the mainland more than fifty miles away from it. To those who know only its beaches, its coast and islands, Greece personifies the quintessential Mediterranean paradise – the gift of sun and sea. Yet in reality, four-fifths of mainland Greece is mountain and the stark limestone ranges that stretch out into the Aegean, like the fingers of a skeletal hand, mirror the harsher face of a country whose hard-edged character is personified in the life of its mountain peoples.

This paradox is reflected in commonplace British perceptions of Greece. Although, year in and out, Greece and its islands are amongst the most popular British summer holiday venues, it also vies with Switzerland as the most mountainous country in Europe. Furthermore, unlike Switzerland, it still retains those raw, rough edges much cherished by mountain travellers. For all this, the mountains of Greece remain a blank on the map for most British climbers. In British mountaineering compendia, such as Wilfrid Noyce's magisterial *World Atlas of Mountaineering*,[1] the mountains of Greece get no mention, while Edward Pyatt's *Guinness Book of Mountains*[2] confines its comments to classical mountain mythology and the monastic sanctuaries of Meteora and Athos.

Why should this be and was it always thus? To Western Europe, Greece became something of a land apart after the fall of Rome and the rise of Greek Byzantium. Sultan Mehmed's capture of Constantinople in 1453 may have brought down the final curtain on the Holy Roman Empire, but it was the earlier, Venetian-backed Fourth Crusade's sack of Constantinople in 1204 which dismembered the Byzantine Empire, accelerated the expansion of the Turkish Ottoman Empire into the Balkans and exacerbated a schism between the Roman and Orthodox Churches which has lasted to this day. During four hundred years of Ottoman rule, mainland Greece and Ionia became fragmented and disengaged from mainstream Western Europe. Although the recollection of classical Greek art, literature and philosophy remained a cultural inspiration, by the early 19th century general British interest was minimal in what was perceived to be an impoverished land populated by illiterate peasants and ferocious bandits.

Alexander Pope's 18th century translations of Homer's *Illiad* and *Odyssey* might have anticipated what became the vogue of Romantic Hellenism, but it took the Greek War of Independence (1821-1832) to switch the European spotlight onto Byron's 'Land of Lost Gods'. This revolutionary struggle, seen as a modern crusade to liberate Christian Greece from the Islamic yoke, was crystallised by Byron's death at Missolonghi in 1824. In the aftermath of independence, Greece suddenly became a magnet for the more intrepid traveller, topographer, antiquary, botanist, archæologist and, most particularly, the artists and writers who vied in their portrayals of Hellas's departed classical glories.

To the ancients, the magic of the hills was not interpreted by references to mountain scenery but rather, by association, to the spirits of nature. Yet to the artists of the Romantic Movement mountain scenery, previously regarded with aversion and distaste, became an object of inspiration. This change of attitude foreshadowed alpinism's Golden Age when British mountaineers made the Alps their stamping ground and much of the world their bailiwick. It is therefore curious that so little interest should have been shown by the Victorian climbing fraternity in the very mountains – Olympus, Parnassus, Taygetus, Ossa and Pelion – which had long been part of poetry's lexicography and whose myths were familiar to every educated Englishman. Patently, size, scale and challenge had much to do with it. Although the Greek mountainscape is steep, harsh and unyielding, it boasts no Matterhorns or ice-clad giants. And so it was, as it had been in the Alps and Pyrenees, that artists and writers pioneered the routes into the mountains of Hellas, with none more prominent than Edward Lear.

Lear made the first of his many visits to Greece in 1848. Although an epileptic and forever dogged by ill health, he was a resolute and compulsive traveller whose topographical landscape painting was to take him into many mountain regions besides Greece, including the Abruzzi, Albania, the Alps, Corsica and the Himalaya. From Darjeeling he sketched '*the very godlike and mysterious Kinchinjunga*' and back in England painted three oils of the great mountain including one for Lord Aberdare, father of General Charles Bruce, leader of the 1922 Everest Expedition and Alpine Club President from 1923 to 1925. This 'supreme example of the sublime' now hangs in the stairwell of the Aberdare Library as Lord Aberdare's bequest, yet for Lear, there were no mountains more beautiful than those of Greece whose 'divinest beauty' enchanted him from the start. Another of Lear's sublime paintings, *Parnassus* (1862), may have inspired a handful of Victorian mountaineers as it later inspired me to attempt its traverse on ski.

Notwithstanding the popularity and publicity of the Greek Revolution and the outpourings of poets and painters, the physical difficulties and dangers of mountain travel through Greece's inaccessible and often bandit-ridden country proved a deterrent to any but the most intrepid travellers. One such was that energetic clergyman the Rev H F Tozer, the outstanding classical geographer of his day, who travelled widely through the Sultan's domain – Greece, Asia Minor and Armenia – and gained election to the Alpine Club on the strength of mountain exploration. Although the British diplomat, D Urquhart, may possibly have climbed Skolio (2,911m), a prominent subsidiary peak of Mt Olympus and only six metres lower, Tozer was the first to make a serious, though unsuccessful, bid to reach the mountain's aiguille-like apex, Mytikas 'The Needle' (2,917m). This was in 1865 – the same year in which Whymper climbed the Matterhorn.

Twelve years later, in 1877, F F Tuckett, the man credited with popularising both the rucksack and the sleeping bag, launched an 'attack' on the Peleponesian Taygetus (2,407m). Tuckett, a distinguished Alpine Club pioneer who had climbed in the Alps, Pyrenees, Corsica, Spain, Norway and beyond, wrote lyrically, with a plethora of Greek and Latin tags, about

... this memory haunted peak whose name has been a household word from childhood ... bold in outline, vast in extent, and rich beyond description in all the unequalled glory that the colouring and sunshine and brilliant atmosphere of Greece can produce.[3]

To conclude his Greek campaign and inspired perhaps by Lear, Tuckett went on the climb the 2,458m Parnassus.

Seventeen years on, in 1894, Douglas Freshfield, almost unrivalled as a mountain traveller and pontificator, visited Greece. He recorded his impressions in 'Classical Climbs', following Tuckett up Taygetus, but was pipped up Parnassus by another distinguished AC member C E Matthews. Freshfield praised Greece's natural scenery, though he considered that it failed in its 'attempt at the sublime', and opined that 'a man of many mountains may sometimes smile at the adjectives lavished by the scholar on the cliffs of Parnassus.'[4]

Although neither Taygetus nor Parnassus can be classified as anything but strenuous walks in summer, Freshfield's conclusion that Greek mountains would be 'unpalatable food for the robust appetites of Alpine Clubmen' was based on a somewhat superficial acquaintance. In the course of his visit, he had sighted from afar the less digestible Mt Olympus but decided that this was not a morsel to whet his appetite. Years later, Colonel Strutt, as editor of the *Alpine Journal* and author of Freshfield's panegyric obituary in 1934, described Freshfield's 1904 Olympus venture (it was actually in 1894) as an 'attempt, defeated by brigands'.[5] Certainly, Greek brigands were a hazard at the time but whether the outcome of Freshfield's imaginary tryst with Olympus would have been different had he been accompanied by his devoted guide François Dévouassoud, we shall never know.

Another Alpine Clubman, Captain Monck Mason, who skirted Mt Olympus in 1918, assured readers that the summit 'can almost be reached by mules' and apologised for not reaching the top himself on account of the snow'.[6] Did he know that the summit peak, Mytikas, had been climbed five years earlier, on 2 August 1913, by the Swiss climbers Baud-Bovey and Boissonnas with their Greek guide Kakalos? It was another eight years before Marcel Kurz, pioneer of the High Level Ski Route, climbed its adjacent summit the 'Throne of the Gods', again with Kakalos. Only in 1926 did a British party led by W T Emslie climb Mytikas. Sadly, his photographs do little justice to the mountain.[7] Modern mountaineering came to Greece in 1934 with Comici's routes on the great walls of Olympus's Megala Kazania, yet the mountain was still virtually unknown when John Hunt was organising his mountain warfare training on its slopes at the close of the Second World War.

When I made a solo visit to Mt Olympus in November 1961, I knew little of its topography. Lured by its mythological associations, I only discovered something of its true nature from photographs in a book bought in Athens. When I saw for myself the Megala Kazania's awesome amphitheatre of 500m limestone cliffs encased in snow and ice from the discreet distance of Skolio's summit, I reached different conclusions to those of Douglas Freshfield as to this mountain's palatability.

After the war, John Hunt remained a champion and devotee of Greek mountains and in 1963, ten years after Everest, he made the first south to north traverse of the Pindos. Running for 160 miles NNW from the Gulf of Patrai to the Albanian frontier, this complex of ranges forms the backbone of mainland Greece and is unmatched for average height, continuity and impenetrability. Hunt's international party of mixed age and ability (which occasionally went up to 54 and included Tony Streather, George Lowe and John Disley) wrote a new chapter in trekking history but was more concerned with youth training and geographical science than with exploratory mountaineering. Yet it was this remarkable journey, undertaken in April often through heavy snow and rain, which heightened interest in Greek mountains for those with a bent for the unusual.[8]

One such connoisseur of the unfamiliar was the fastidious Robin Fedden. In 1972 his party visited Epirus and the Pindos. They put up a new route on the NW face of Astraka in the Tymphi massif and followed this up with a north to south foot traverse of the range from Konitza to Karpenisi on a line somewhat to the west of Hunt's. Fedden's verdict was that 'for all its wild scenery and impressive gorges, the Pindos range ... offers little serious climbing. The exception is the Tymphi massif [whose] climbs on the great north faces are comparable to classic Dolomite routes, with walls of up to 800m'. Lindsay Griffin's more recent climbs in the Tymphi excepted, this might have been the last word an Alpine Clubman would utter on the mountains of Greece.[9]

The Greek mountain scene was much changed when I revisited Mt Olympus in June 1985, 24 years after my first visit.[10] By now, skiing on snow had become almost as popular as skiing on water and new resorts were sprouting countrywide. John Hunt and Edward Peck had done some tentative Greek ski-touring in 1945 but, by the early 1980s, reports of serious ski-mountaineering ventures were percolating through. In 1981 the redoubtable French duo of Berruex and Parmentier made a circuit of the Ghiona and Vardousian massifs in Sterea,[11] and in 1984 an RAF team spent three days in the Tymphi before launching out on an ambitious north to south traverse of the South Pindos Ridge. Starting from Antochori they hit bad weather on the main ridge and had to abandon their bold attempt at Matsouki. When we found ourselves sharing the old Agapitos hut on Olympus with Ronald and Tilleke Naar I was intrigued by their excursions on short skis, for it was beginning to dawn on me that the most interesting way of getting to know these Greek mountains might well be on ski.

However, owing to other commitments it was another ten years before this came to pass. And so it was that on 4 March 1995 a predominantly AC party – David Williams, Rodney Franklin, Derek Fordham, Richard Cowper and I – slipped the Athens-Thessaloniki Express at Kato Titherea for a late afternoon start up the inhospitable Velitsa Gorge for what was intended as a tented three-day ski traverse of Parnassus. The story of that venture has been told elsewhere[12] but, as we discovered, the sparse flesh of these boney mountains is not easily digestible. Owing to the exaggerated freeze-thaw effect that often afflicts Mediterranean mountains, Parnassus was encased in ice. On the second day Derek Fordham suffered a bad fall and injured himself. On the morning of the third day we were still 250m below the 2,457m summit, pinned down by a blizzard; so we decided to stay put and dig in. Throughout that night we kept digging, fearful that the continuous build-up of snow would collapse our tents. Next day, with avalanches threatening, we gave Parnassus away to Apollo, Dionysius and any other interested muses and retreated down the same Velitsa Gorge up which we had so laboriously slogged four days before.

Derek had to retire home hurt but the rest of us had better luck in Sterea doing a pioneer circuit traverse of the Vardousian massif – an area some-times described as Greece's 'Little Switzerland', minus any recognisable Swiss facilities. The return leg to our Stavros Col camp gave an epic day with the last 1½ hours skied in total darkness. Next day we climbed the group's highest peak, Korakas (2,437m), and completed the programme with a traverse across the Ghiona massif taking in the shapely Pyramida, at 2,510m the highest peak in Central Greece. Exit involved a third and final bone-jarring walk-out down the spectacular Rekka Ravine to Viriani.

This bruising experience confirmed that, while there is enough steep rock in Sterea to keep climbers busy for years, few are likely to follow our ski mountaineering itinerary. These steep and stoney limestone peaks, inter-spersed with disconcertingly deep gorges, involve big ascents to and long descents from the snowline, with little continuously skiable terrain. Add to this the barest smattering of invariably locked huts, incomprehensible maps and you get the general picture. Yet for all this, the novelty, uncertainty and powerful personality of the country had caught my imagination and I had already determined to trek through the Tymphi massif the following year to recce a future winter visit on ski.

The Tymphi massif is the culmination and glory of the Greek mountain-scape. Set deep in Epirus Province, the homeland of Alexander the Great's mother Olympias and King Pyrrhus whose armies marched to within 24 miles of Rome, this is Greece's most scenic and atypical province. Byron's *Childe Harold's Pilgrimage* was largely based on his visit to the court of the legendary Ali Pasha at Ionanina and it was from the Epirot landscape that Edward Lear drew particular inspiration. Its wild peaks, dizzying gorges and fierce mountaineers set it apart from the rest of the country and although it took no part in the Greek War of Independence (Arta was only freed from Ottoman rule in 1881 and Ionanina still retains a distinctive Turkish flavour), its mountain redoubts were always a refuge for the outlawed, oppressed and dispossessed. Here the brave, brutal and anarchistic brigand/patriots known as Klephts followed no man's writ and here Mussolini's Italian expeditionary forces were routed in 1940/41. But here too, the darkest side of Greece was revealed in the terrible excesses of the Greek Civil War that are so harrowingly recounted in Nicholas Gage's *Eleni*.

Lonely Planet's *Trekking in Greece* offers some perceptive seasonal advice about trekking in Epirus. Don't do it during the last week in September when the autumn rains arrive with unswerving regularity. John Blacker, Peter Lowes, David Seddon and I paid the price for disregarding this unexceptionable advice. In consequence, our walks through the magnificent Vikos and Aoos gorges, and our strolls up two easy Tymphi peaks including Gamila II and the traverse of the Tymphi massif from Megalo Papingo to Tsepolovo, were all undertaken in an almost unremitting downpour. Although this trek finally did for my dicky hip, I resolved that one day I would come back, with my skis, to this dramatic part of Greece.

Three years on, in March 1999, Derek Fordham, Roger Childs, John Ducker and I picked up our hired Nissan 'Serena' van at Thessaloniki airport, drove northeast to Thrace and from the pretty village of Volokas skied to the topmost point (2,232m) of the Falakro massif. These giddy limestone walls are probably unknown to British climbers but this attractive mountain was useful to us as a warm-up for the more serious business of Smolikas (2,637m), Greece's second summit. To get there we had to drive across the breadth of northern Greece, unaware that we had already enjoyed our last fine day for a week.

Consultation with the oracle at wintry Dodona did nothing to improve the weather forecast but after various other diversions we eventually reached the unfussy Naneh hut, two hours or three above the Alpine village of Paleoselli. After two abortive attempts to find a skiable route up Smolikas, we were forced to retire. But disappointment was tempered by an undeserved hero's welcome and wild boar lunch back at Paleoselli. Fearing that we had perished on a mountain not previously attempted on ski, the local rescue party of two lads plus motor scooter had come up the mountain to find us, having already alerted the police helicopter at Konitza of our likely fate.

Much the same party, strengthened by David Seddon, was back again in Greece in March 2000 for another round with Smolikas. For this trip, I had also revived an earlier project of attempting a tented south-to-north traverse along the main Pindos Ridge from Vougareli to Metsovo – reversing, in effect, the 1984 RAF party's intended line. Running some 55km from Tzourmerka (2,393m) to Peresteri (2,295m), this, the longest continuous stretch of high mountains in Greece, maintains the 2,000m contour for most of its length; it has few break points and traverses country as wild, steep and dramatic as anything in southern Europe.

In the event, battle with the ridge was never joined. From Vougareli, the menacing, ice-encrusted cliffs of Tzoumerka looked impregnable, so we settled for a training climb up a virginal ski peak, Astri (1,853m), on the fringes of the Agrapha in surroundings reminiscent of the Spanish Pyrenees. Next day, really dirty weather made the prospect of two pensioners humping tents and impedimenta up and along an unforgiving crest of snow-encrusted limestone preposterous. We swiftly reappraised objectives and headed north in our hired van. The day-long drive from Vougareli to Ioannina through mist, cloud and rain on unsealed mountain roads overlooking dizzying gorges, riding switch-back ridges and slithering up and down double hairpin bends in search of deserted villages perched on mountain tops was more nerve-wrecking than anything we were later to attempt. It also convinced me that we might have taken weeks to have done this same stretch on ski.

From the comforting base of the Galaxy Hotel in the ancient Vlach capital and now popular ski resort of Metsovo, we made one cautious incursion onto the Mavravouni Ridge in the teeth of a paralysingly cold northeast wind. Following this up with a tentative recce of Peresteri (2,295m), it became obvious that this fine triangular peak was going to be a tough mouthful. Although we never properly deciphered Mr Sfikas's *The Mountains of Greece* sketch map,[13] we disentangled a segment of the mountain's complex topography second time round and reached its 2,100m North Col. But without a rope – no further. In recompense, the descent down Peristeri's Vallée Blanche, in a setting which almost rivalled its Mont Blanc counterpart, must be one of the finest ski runs in Greece.

And now for Smolikas. Its noble dome, dominating the northeast skyline, and framed by converging pine-covered ridges, had become a tantalisingly familiar sight from the spectacular mountain road that links Konitza to Paleoselli. After a night in the now familiar Naneh hut, we made our bid on a cold but brilliantly fine day. I now knew well the likely route to the crest of the long, rolling ridge that leads to Smolikas's summit pyramid.

Swopping crampons for skis for the steep top section, our first pair made the summit at 11.35 hours. A vast array of snow-capped ranges stretched away northwards into Albania and the Balkans, while to the south, the ten-kilometre-long, dark shadowed north wall of the Tymphi, presented us with Greece's grandest mountain tableau.

Certainly the mountains of Hellas will always gladden the hearts of painters and poets, yet their limestone faces will also test most rock-climbers and, during the harsh Greek winter, their wild peaks and ridges offer challenge enough to ski mountaineers. To my knowledge the complete Pindos ski traverse remains an unplucked plum.

SKI- MOUNTAINEERING SUMMARY

1995

4-7 March	Parnassus	Attempt by Velitsa Ravine
10-11 March	Vardousian massif	Ski traverse from Stavros col to Artotina. Return via West Soufles & Meteritza cols.
12 March	Korakas (2,437m)	
13-15 March	Ghiona massif	Traverse from Sekea to Viriani with ascent of Pyramida (2,510m) and descent by Rekka Ravine.

1999

3 March	Falakro (2,232m)	
8-9 March	Smolikas	Two aborted attempts.

2000

4 March	Astri (1,853m)	
6 March	Mavravouni Ridge	to Point 1,900m.
8 March	Peresteri Col (2,100m)	
11 March	Smolikas (2,637m)	

REFERENCES

1   Wilfrid Noyce, *World Atlas of Mountaineering*. Nelson, 1969.
2   Edward Pyatt, *Guinness Book of Mountains*. Guinness, 1980.
3   F F Tuckett, *'An Ascent of Taygetus' in AJ8, 316, 1877.*
4   Douglas Freshfield, 'Classical Climbs' in *AJ 22, 413, 1905.*
5   Col E L Strutt, obituary of Douglas Freshfield in *AJ 46*, 166, 1934.

6   Captain Monck Mason, 'From Spercheios to Acheloos' in *AJ 32*, 315, 1919.

7   W T Emslie, 'Mount Olympus' and photographs of Mytikas in *AJ 39*, 86, 1927.

8   John Hunt, 'A Journey through the Pindos Mountains in 1963' in *Geographical Journal 130*, Part 3, September 1964 and *Life is Meeting*, Hodder & Stoughton, 1978.

9   Robin Fedden, 'Pindos Range: Tymphi Massif' in *AJ 78,* 25, 1973.

10   J G R Harding, 'Olympian Triad' in *AJ 92*, 136, 1987.

11   Berruex and Parmentier, *Les Grands Raids a Ski*, AGLA Paris, 152, 1981.

12   J G R Harding, 'Hellenic Ski Tour' in *Eagle Ski Club Yearbook*, 7, 1995. and 'Grecian 2000' in *Eagle Ski Club Yearbook*, 54, 2000.

13   George Sfikas, *The Mountains of Greece*. Athens, 1982.

See also:
Angus Davidson, *Edward Lear*. John Murray, 1938.
Peter Levi, *Edward Lear*. Macmillan, 1995.

Women and the Mountains

SUE BLACK

Ginette Lesley Harrison

(Plate 39)

There can be few reading this who are unaware of Ginette's death in an avalanche on Dhaulagiri in Nepal on the 24th October 2000. It is really only since her death that much has been written about her achievements and character but it is no surprise to those who knew her personally not only that there is recognition now, but also that the memory of her is as clear and strong as when she was alive. She was a remarkable woman but one of her most endearing traits -- her genuine and unassuming modesty – meant that she made light of her achievements and, before one success could be registered properly, whether another peak conquered or another medical exam passed, she was away and on to the next.

She continues to make her mark through the Ginette Harrison Memorial Fund. This was set up by her friends to help children in Nepal in her memory. Through the Shiva charity, based in Bristol, the Fund is supporting a school in a valley near Kathmandu which has been renamed the Ginette Harrison school. Children at this school can be sponsored in her name: see website details at the end of the article.

I first met Ginette in 1986 at Ham Green Hospital near Bristol. I had returned to medicine in my 40s and she was my immediate 'senior'. I was very lucky to work with her as she was calm, unflappable and had a facility for solving problems using a combination of natural intelligence and downright common sense. Above all, she was compassionate and shared others' problems, whether patients or colleagues.

To start with, I was unaware of her climbing achievements; she spoke occasionally about her climbing and expeditions, always in passing, and would sometimes disappear for several weeks at a time. She lived very simply, had no car and thought nothing of cycling back and forth between her digs and the hospital, a distance of ten miles.

Ginette's interest in climbing started while she was at school at Katherine Lady Berkeley School in Wotton-under-Edge, Gloucestershire, where she started climbing with the Ranger Guides. At medical school in Bristol, she followed her developing passion by climbing in the Avon Gorge and elsewhere, with the University's climbing club.

Ginette kept in touch after we finished working together and soon I found myself agreeing to become a medical officer on the 1989 Everest Marathon, as she had been asked to organise the 10-strong medical team. (Says I: 'I'm 45, unfit and heights make me dizzy.' Says Ginette: 'You can do it.' – and I did!)

By this time, 1989, Ginette, at 31, had done two years of research in high-altitude physiology at the Cardiovascular Pulmonary Research Laboratory at Denver, Colorado, and been awarded her MD; was nearing the end of her general practice training posts, gruelling junior jobs with tough on-call rotas; had worked for four months at the Himalayan Rescue Association medical post at Manang in Nepal; and had been medical officer on the 1986 British Bhutan expedition and the 1989 British Masherbrum expedition, which she also led. She had published six scientific papers and eight abstracts and presented four papers at conferences in the UK and North America. She had been on five research expeditions, to Mount Kenya, Mount McKinley, Nepal, Karakoram and Peru, all but Mount McKinley with the Birmingham Medical Research Expeditionary Society. She had summited Mount Kenya (normal route) 1982, Mount McKinley (West Buttress) 1983, Island Peak 1984, Ghondo Khoro, Gundang, Pisang, Thorong, Chulu East 1987, Huascaran (Peru) 1988 and reached 22,500ft on Masherbrum.

Very few, let alone all, of these achievements were known to her friends, as she rarely spoke of them unless it was to relate in passing a funny story or an exciting episode. However, it was obvious to her friends that she wasted not a single minute of any day. I can't remember ever seeing Ginette sitting watching television. She would write letters in the most unlikely places, any time, anywhere. She would cook for her friends at a moment's notice, large delicious meals usually in a borrowed kitchen. She liked nothing better than a beer and chat down the pub or a wild stomp if there was music.

She was a good organiser. On the Everest Marathon expedition we lacked for nothing medically. The whole expedition went very smoothly and competently, Ginette even on several occasions treating the yaks for infected saddle sores. They lined up outside the medical tent along with their owners. At one point, worried about the condition of someone who had been left behind by a day's march, she ran back the way we had come, checked her patient and then ran back again in the dark to join us before we'd gone to sleep in our tents. We were exhausted, she wasn't, despite having done the day's route three times.

Ginette's stamina was always remarkable. Many of her friends will doubtless have postcards and letters saying things like 'kayaked ten miles to the island by moonlight for a lobster BBQ, went for another 21 miles paddle the next day before paddling back – it was brilliant.' A postcard from her honeymoon commented that she'd scratched her ring 'after climbing a desperate crack climb'. She was physically small but her stamina and determination were prodigious, which was probably the secret to her success at extreme high-altitude climbing.

After the 1989 Everest Marathon, Ginette came back and forth to the UK, always 'touching base' with us and meeting up for meals or walks. We spent hilarious hours in an informal revision group before taking the

MRCGP, the final exam for general practice. She left to work at medical jobs all over Australia in the early 1990s, and in between jobs she climbed Aconcagua in 1990, Kosciosko, Mera Peak in Nepal, and Kang Yatse in Ladakh in 1991. In Australia, with her usual enthusiasm and sporting ability, she also pursued a whole range of lower altitude sports including canoeing and scuba diving. But she was drawn back to the mountains. In 1993 she got the opportunity to climb Mount Everest with a Himalayan Kingdoms expedition. She met and fell in love with Gary, an American also on the expedition and they summited hand in hand. They married in 1997. Together they went on to complete the ascent of the highest peak in each of the seven continents – once again, as with Everest, she became the second British woman to achieve this, following Rebecca Stephens. By 1998, she had a further batch of summits: 1994 was Carstenz Pyramid (Irian Jaya), Ngga Pulu (Irian Jaya), Mount Kenya by the Diamond Couloir, Kilimanjaro and Elbrus. In 1995 it was Ojos de Salado in Chile, Mount Vinson in Antarctica and Mount Logan.

Mount Logan was an epic. She and Gary were helicoptered in and dropped on a glacier ready for a traverse; climbing the East Ridge and descending the Trench. The going was more difficult than expected and, owing to bad weather after they'd summited, they arrived at the other end after four weeks instead of the planned three weeks. An extreme test of a relationship.

In 1997, she and Gary summited Ama Dablam and Cho Oyu and then spent a month in New Zealand doing the Grand Traverse of Mount Cook, Mount Aspiring, the Silberhorn/Tasman/Syme ridge and Mount Dixon. A postcard from Ginette in New Zealand says: 'climbed initially on Mount Aspiring – a 17-hour climb with descent to a snowhole in a white out. This was a mere warm up to the next climb on Mount Cook which took 32 hours!– we got a bit lost. Got a little faster from then on and climbed Mount Tasman, Mount Dixon and did a traverse of Mount Cook.'

Ginette and Gary started to lead climbing expeditions to the Himalayan peaks over 8000 metres, and in 1998 she became the first woman to reach the summit of Kangchenjunga, the fifth she had climbed of the fourteen 8000-metre peaks. She went on to reach the summit by herself after meeting two fellow climbers just below the summit on their way down, as Gary had turned back. She felt she still had enough strength and pushed on without oxygen despite passing the body of a recently dead climber from a Japanese expedition.

By this time Ginette was living in Massachusetts with Gary, and had thrown herself into the American Family Medicine training programme (as general practice is known in the States). As ever, she was determined to finance her expeditions through her medical work and was undeterred by the rigours of undergoing more medical exams and hospital training in the American system. When she was killed on Dhaulagiri, she was hoping to settle down to a part-time job in family medicine near her home in Monson, Massachusetts, and the rest of the time to continue her aim of conquering the 14 highest peaks.

It was not to be. An avalanche swept her and a fellow climber, a Sherpa, to their deaths on 24 October 1999. We were all stunned. Ginette had seemed quietly invincible. But she died in the only way she would have wanted, striving to achieve her next summit in her beloved mountains and in the company of the man she loved. She was 41 years old.

Ginette Harrison Memorial Fund: http://www.shivacharity.org
or e-mail bobuppington@hotmail.com

HERMANN REISACH

Beatrice Tomasson and the South Face of the Marmolada

(Plates 42, 58)

Beatrice Tomasson (1859-1947)

Some ten years ago I climbed with friends up the South Face of the Marmolada. The climbing was very difficult and the commitment demanding. Who had put up this route? It turned out to be an Englishwoman, Beatrice Tomasson, who had done the first ascent almost 100 years before with two of the best mountaineering guides in the Dolomites. This much I could read in every Dolomite guidebook but could find nothing more about her, either in Alpine literature or a women's bibliography. It was a long trail from the Marmolada to archives in England, to her husband's nieces in London and, finally, to a very complex set of relatives, the descendants of her father's brother in Paris. All other branches of the Tomasson family had died out.

Beatrice Sybil Tomasson was born on 25 April 1859 as the second child of William and Sarah Anne Tomasson (née Hopkinson, b.1835) on the estate of Barnby Moor in the parish of Blyth, in Nottinghamshire. According to the census of 1861 there were over 30 people employed on the 711-acre farm. Beatrice's father (b.1832) was the son of a textile industrialist from Thurlstone, Yorkshire; her mother a farmer's daughter born at the village of Oxton, Nottinghamshire. In 1868, when Beatrice was just ten years old, the family moved from Barnby Moor to Ireland, to settle at a country house named Gortnamona near Tullamore in King's County.

There is nothing to be found about the course of her formal education in the family chronicle. It was usual in the English landed gentry at this time for tutors to be hired for the education of the children. Certainly the linguistic training by a tutor was not sufficient for her later occupation as a private tutor in the houses of Prussian Generals. It is known that she studied German and was fluent in Italian and French. Although it was unthinkable for a German woman in this period to study, there were already women in England at the universities. By the late 1870s women were studying at many universities apart from Oxford and Cambridge and were even beginning to get degrees. A pioneer in this respect was University College London, which began awarding degrees to women in 1878. The educational system was developed in the reign of Queen Victoria, and so was sport for women. I assume Beatrice was educated for several years at such an institution.

Family portrait
Beatrice's upbringing was not typical of Victorian society. She spent her childhood at Barnby Moor and her teens on a farm in Ireland. Her father had emigrated from Nottinghamshire for economic reasons and was a tenant on cheap land there. The children of the Tomasson family, the two girls as well, grew up with horses and shotguns, more the wild west than a typical bourgeois family. William, Beatrice's older brother, took part in the Zulu Wars in 1879 during which the Empire overwhelmed the army of Cetewayo. William wrote a book about this 'exciting campaign': *With the Irregulars in Transvaal and Zululand* (Remington & Co, 1881). At the age of 30, he started his career as the Chief Constable of Nottinghamshire and he was given a peerage in 1906. Thomas, the younger brother, emigrated to America. The last known photo, dated 1895, before the start of the Spanish-American war, shows him in uniform on horseback.

The 22-year-old Beatrice went to Prussia as a private tutor to one of the noblest households, the house of General Bülow in Potsdam and to manors in Silesia. Her sister Nelly went to Russia as a governess; soon after her departure came news of her drowning while swimming. These events from her family history and youth certainly formed Beatrice's character, especially her determination to cope, her toughness and her tenacity.

Literary and intellectual works
In 1883, at the age of 23, Beatrice lived in Potsdam, Prussia. She worked for the Prussian General von Knobloch as a companion. In that year she began her translation into English of the four-volume work *A Fight for Rome* by Felix Dahn, then a bestseller. The negotiations with the publishers, Bentley & Sons, are kept in the manuscript department of the British Library. Beatrice could not afford to undertake a complete translation at her own expense and suggested Bentley agree to accept half the profits. The contract was never signed.

She was successful with her next project. Together with Cäcilie Wüstenburg she wrote and translated *The Chimes of Erfurt, a Tale*. This book was published in 1885 in London by the Literary Society. These literary works occupied Beatrice for at least a few years. Apparently after that she had no further literary ambitions and according to my present knowledge did not publish her mountain adventures. There are no diaries in the family archives. When I carefully read the documents, a handful of letters and references for her mountain guides, written in German, Italian and English, a precise phraseology and a clear capacity for judgement become apparent. It is this capacity and not any evidence of a formal education which causes me, without hesitation, to describe Beatrice as an intellectual.

Mountaineer
The portrayal of Beatrice as 'an intrepid mountaineering woman', is found repeatedly in Alpine literature. Apparently she had concluded her literary

activities in about 1885 and transferred her ambitions to climbing. A photo of her in alpinist's clothes, with ice-axe and crampons, was taken at the Innsbruck photo studio *Senorer*, dated 1883. Beatrice lived in Innsbruck for a few years where she became a member of the Austrian Alpine Club in 1893, together with about a dozen other women; for example, Marie Geisberger, the owner of the hotel Zur Stadt München. Here Beatrice was employed as a governess to Edward Lisle Strutt (1874-1948), nephew of Lord Belper, the textile magnate. She was 15 years his senior. He had been a student in Innsbruck since 1892 and went into the diplomatic service after his studies and later became President of the Alpine Club, as well as a distinguished Editor of the *Alpine Journal*. Strutt wrote that Beatrice had accompanied him from 1892 on many expeditions in the Tyrol, the Ötztaler, Stubai and the Karwendel ranges. They climbed together for two seasons and family lore reveals that 'the student eloped with his governess'. From 1896 Beatrice enjoyed mountain ventures in the Dolomites where she stayed at Cortina and returned for several seasons.

With the mountain guide Michele Bettega, she made several first ascents in the Pala group and went on adventurous climbs with the guide Arcangelo Siorpaes in the area around Cortina. I think she was a proficient mountaineer herself after a decade of climbing with Strutt and the Dolomite guides. Strutt wrote in his mountaineering memoirs in 1942: 'In later years she achieved for the first time the two best snow and rock expeditions in the Tyrol: the East Face of Monte Zebru and the South Face of Marmolada'.

First ascents with the best mountain guides
Beatrice took trips to a variety of mountain ranges, always with the best guides of the time, predominantly in the Dolomites:

1897 With mountain guide Michele Bettega in the Pala range. First ascents of: Cima d'Alberghetto, Torre del Giubileo, Campanile della Regina Vittoria, Monte Lastei d'Agner, Sasso delle Capre.

1898 With guides Hans Sepp Pinggera and Friedrich Reinstadler, the NE Face of Monte Zebru in the Ortler range, rock III, 55° ice, a first ascent and at this time the most difficult ice wall in the Tyrol; with Hans Sepp Pinggera, the SW Face of Ortles, rock III, 50° ice, another first ascent; with Luigi Rizzi from Canazei, the second ascent of the Laurinswand West Face, up until then the most difficult rock wall in the Dolomites.

1900 With Luigi Rizzi on the Dent di Mesdi South Face in Sella range, a first ascent at grade IV in July.

1901 Her greatest adventure was the widely desired South Face of the Marmolada di Penia, with the guides Michele Bettega and Bartolo Zagonel.

1911 In the last year of her Alpine career she made the first traverse of Campanile Basso with guide Angelo Dibona, the most successful rock climber at this time; they were accompanied by her esteemed Michele Bettega.

Beatrice's most important undertaking was the first ascent of the Marmolada South Face with the guides Bartolo Zagonel and Michele Bettega from Primero at the foot of the Pala range. Zagonel and Bettega began the age of the professional mountain guide in the Eastern Alps. It signalled the end of the romantic and naïve age of Alpine mountaineering. With the start of the First World War – the guides were in the war – Beatrice's mountaineering exploits ended.

Marmolada expedition

The best climbers of the time had already repeatedly tried the face. Most notable was Luigi Rizzi's attempt in the autumn of 1900 when he found a route up to the first terrace, the most difficult part of the wall; he sooed up and down it without rope or pitons. Rizzi had been engaged by Tomasson to reconnoitre a route up the face; but in spite of this achievement I don't know why she didn't employ him as guide on the 1901 expedition. Beatrice made reconnaissances and several attempts; the last survey was with Michele Bettega. The entry in Bettega's Führerbuch reads: 'June 20th 1901 Passo Ombretta to see the South Wall of the Marmolada".

The Marmolada South Face is, in my view, the most prominent in the Dolomites. The ascent took twelve hours of climbing. Equipment consisted of ropes, pitons and specialist climbing shoes. They bivouacked at the foot of the wall to ensure an early start, there being then no huts on this side of the mountain except for the shepherd's hut on the Malga Ombretta. Two porters carried the nailed boots as well as warm clothing and champagne over the Fedaja glacier to the summit. There were, of course, critics and sceptics in the Alpine journals and several people voiced their doubts over this first ascent, like Edward Broome who wrote in the *Alpine Journal* of 1907: 'Details have never transpired, nor is it even known if and how the summit was gained, and,' he continued, 'from time to time we saw small pitons which were of course useless for ascending, so could only be supposed to have been fixed by a former party with a view to possible descent.'

The guides Zagonel and Bettega were generously rewarded. They received a whole year's salary for their Marmolada success. The reward of 400 Kronen would have the value of some £50 at the time. On their way up the South Face they had left several pegs in the rock as unmistakable signs, as well as newspaper wrappers, addressed to Miss Tomasson, Cortina. A description of the first ascensionists' route was never published, a shortcoming for which Beatrice was blamed. The guides also never forwarded information, even when asked. Successors were supposed to have a tough time of it.

Evidence of the first ascent

The Italian captiano of the Marmolada Front, Arturo Andreoletti, had investigated and collected all available information about the climb of the Marmolada South Face in researching his area of command. He was with the first Italian party to climb the wall in August 1908 with his friend Carlo Prochownick and guide Serafino Parissenti. To do his job thoroughly, Andreoletti climbed the route three times before the Great War. He had also interviewed Beatrice and reported on it.

The most valuable documents which have been handed down to us are the entries from Zagonel's and Bettega's Führerbücher. For sceptics there is Bettega's letter to Andreoletti. Bettega wrote on 4 July 1908: 'We climbed from Caprile to the Malga Ombretta and bivouacked on the Ombretta pass. The wall and the chimneys are the most difficult that I have ever done. It was on 1st July 1901.' He remarked that some colleagues had failed in spite of various attempts. In other words, Bettega was proudly reporting this first ascent.

There is also the detailed report of the whole expedition by Nina Callegari, the proprietor of the Hotel Belvedere at Caprile, to the secretary of the Italian Alpine Club, a paper unearthed recently by Bepi Pellegrinon, the eminent author of Marmolada books.

Early accounts

Within the next ten years, half a dozen essays appeared in the European Alpine magazines by subsequent ascensionists:

• Georg Leuchs – second ascent – made a 12-page report in the *Deutsche Alpen Zeitung* (Munich, 1903). Leuchs had written to Zagonel but had not received any route description from him. The Leuchs brothers' team had great problems with route-finding and finally on the top third of the wall lost trace of the first ascentionists' route and struggled to get to the top via a new exit. After a reconnaissance of three days, a rest day and two days of climbing with a bivouac, their expedition took a week in total. Incidentally the Leuchs brothers were acclaimed as among the greatest heroes of their day.

• Ferdinand Langsteiner in the *Österreichische Alpenzeitung* (Vienna 1905)

• Edward Broome in the *Alpine Journal* (London 1907). The party considered the expedition to be the finest in the Dolomites. Broome was one of the most remarkable climbers of his day. He concentrated on the most difficult expeditions of the time, particularly at Zermatt, Chamonix and in the Dolomites. He repeated the Marmolada climb three times within the next five years.

- Etienne Renaud wrote in *La Montagne* (Paris 1908), after the eighth ascent of the wall, that the Marmolada wall was twice as long and as strenuous as the Grépon East Face in the Mont Blanc Massif. The ascent of the Grépon East Face was then considered one of the most famous climbs in the Alps.

- Arturo Andreoletti in *Revista del Club Alpino Italiano* (Turin 1910)

- The first topo appeared in 1905 in the *Österreichische Alpenzeitung* by the artist and climber, Gustav Jahn.

- The *Alpine Journal* published the first detailed route description in 1907 by Edward Broome.

The ascent of the Marmolada South Face was regarded then, and for more than a decade, as the longest and the most difficult climb in the Alps.

Assessment from today's perspective

The summit of the Marmolada di Penia is only one of several on the three kilometre wide and 500 to 800-metre high South Face of the Marmolada which is, in my opinion, the most prominent climbing wall in the Dolomites, and the most inviting. Today there are almost 100 different routes up this face. I have climbed seven of them, which I consider to be among my best memories.

Ken Wilson describes this route in Bâton Wicks' new topo guide *Classic Dolomite Climbs* as follows : 'A 650m route of sustained grade 4 with some 5–, on a major and quite serious unclimbed face, completed in a day – a major landmark in both Alpine and women's climbing. Also of note is Rizzi's initial solo climb and descent.'

Women's climbing in Cortina

Cortina d'Ampezzo, in the central Dolomites, was at the turn of the century the meeting-place and the playground for a handful of ambitious women climbers. From a present day tourist's perspective it was described as the 'salon of the Alps'.

A month after the first ascent of the Marmolada South Face, the Hungarian Baronesses Ilona and Rolanda Eötvös climbed the South Face of Tofana, a similar undertaking, with the renowned Dolomite guides Angelo Dibona, Giovanni Siorpaes and Agostino Verzi. Other women belonging to this scene in Cortina were Maud Wundt, the wife of General Theodor von Wundt, the Dutch Jeanne Immink, and the Berlin pianist Käte Bröske with an early ascent of the Marmolada South Face in 1906. The subject of women's climbing, at the turn of the century is an absolutely untilled field in the history of Alpine climbing. From 1918 on, male heroes and their myths dominated the scene; for example, Sepp Innerkofler and his death on the Paternkofel.

Governess by profession

Until the beginning of the War Beatrice worked as a governess, mostly abroad. As we know from family history, 'she lived at an awful lot of places'. This nomadic life made reaserching her biography a detective story; the sketch of her by John Singer Sargent, for example, was provided by a relative living in Paris.

During the years of her mountaineering career she lived and worked as governess at Innsbruck, London, Copenhagen, Graz, Cortina, Nottingham, and Brierley, to name just a few of the places. She must have learned to be at home with a wide range of social types, not only the English gentry but Prussian generals, the Austrian bourgeoisie, and Italian aristocracy.

How could she have afforded these costly mountaineering holidays with guides? We know Beatrice worked as governess for wealthy families. In 1901, the year her Uncle Dymond died, she worked for her Aunt Anne at Burntwood Hall, Brierley, Yorkshire. As I learned from her publishing venture, Beatrice knew all about contracts. At Burntwood Hall she was employed as private secretary with an income of about £150 a year, compared to the £450 her brother earned as Chief Constable of Nottinghamshire. In this way she could pay her guides very generously for the Marmolada venture.

Horse riding

According to Strutt, Beatrice was 'an accomplished horsewoman'. When she was in Prussia, she was known as a daring horserider. Family legend has it that she broke in horses that even the Prussian officers could not tame. There's supposed to be a photo of her 'capturing a horse by a forward dive'. General Bülow presented her with a horse which she took back to England. A stable stands today next to the house in Little Benhams where, until the age of 80, Beatrice kept two riding horses. Every year she went on hunting and riding trips to Ireland. In one interview she was described by a friend, still living today, as 'a terrific horsewoman'.

Mrs Mackenzie

Beatrice Tomasson was aged 42 when she climbed the Marmolada South Face. She remained a spinster until the age of 61. In spring of 1921 Beatrice married Patrick Chalmers Mackenzie, of Scottish gentry, in London. They moved to Mackenzie's estate, Little Benhams near Rusper, Sussex, where they spent the rest of their lives. Beatrice wrote in her last Will: 'the many happy years of our life together will ever be for me a treasured memory'. Although she employed staff and a gardener in her household and on her small farm, she chopped her own firewood at the great age of 80. Her husband died on 9th March 1944. Beatrice died on 13th February, 1947, at the age of 87. Her obituary recounts her activities in the parish and various local women's clubs, and describes her physical and intellectual vitality right up to her death.

Independence and pride

Beatrice was financially as well as intellectually totally independent. I think the completely different periods of her life prove this. It was perhaps her independence that led to the misogynistic assessment of her Marmolada achievement in Alpine literature. A photo in an Alpine history book from Cortina shows Beatrice in a fashionable outfit. She is proudly wearing a hat of peacock feathers. Her confident manner and her appearance are probably a reason why Beatrice fell into disfavour with Alpine historians. When Beatrice celebrated her 50th birthday she had her portrait painted in Florence by the famous portrait artist John Singer Sargent. It was eight years since her first ascent of the Marmolada South Face, 'the finest hours of my life'. The Viennese, Hubert Peterka, characterised Beatrice in the *Österreichische Alpenzeitung* in 1974 as 'a young English woman who was infected with pride and ambition' [*'einem englischen Fräulein, das hochgradig von Stolz und Ehrgeiz befallen war'*].

As another example of misogyny, it has to be noted that although Beatrice went on several trips with Strutt, neither the Alpine Club nor its archive acknowledge her. When I asked the club several years ago the answer was simply 'we had no female members then'.* It would be interesting to browse through Colonel Strutt's diaries of his time at Innsbruck.

Determination and happiness

After the Marmolada climb, Beatrice wrote in Zagonel's Führerbuch: 'Zagonel showed splendid qualities, climbed magnificently & faced the intense cold and every difficulty with a pluck worthy of the best traditions of an Alpine guide.'

I think this description of Zagonel is also a fundamental part of her own personality, characterised by courage and determination. This is one side of her character. The other side reads: 'the many happy years of our life together will ever be for me a treasured memory', which sounds more like a 'Beatles' song than a passage from her Will. This is, in her own words, a concise view of the last 25 years of her resolute and fortunate life.

Character

Beatrice was an 'extraordinary character, very determined', according to a statement by her relative Paul Démogé of Paris. Her determination was in those days a completely unfeminine attribute. Her niece Mrs Philomena Baynes (b.1928) from her husband's side of the family described her simply as 'masculine' and 'wiry'. 'Wiry' is an appropriate description of her character. No curls, hair combed straight back into a bun, and no smile on her face, a completely unEnglish aunt in her wonderful country house down

---

* *Editor's note*: The Ladies' Alpine Club was founded in 1907. It would be interesting to hear from any former members who can offer an insight.

in Sussex, was her niece's memory of Beatrice. 'We cousins in London had a nickname for our aunt: "the old hairpin".'

Further reading:
Bepi Pellegrinon & Hermann Reisach: *Salve ... Regina! La Marmolada dei Pioneri*. Nuovi Sentieri Editore, Belluno, 2001. ISBN 88-85510-14-0 (trilingual).

This is an updated version of an article that was first published in High *magazine, No 203. For information I wish to thank first of all Paul Démogé, Philip E. Jones, Robin Chalmers, Mrs Philomena Baynes, Mrs June Rickett, Mrs Margaret Ecclestone, Claudio Ambrosi, Carlo Gandini, Bepi Pellegrinon and Klaus Nuber.*

ED DOUGLAS

Some Advice on Marriage

This is an edited version of a lecture given for the Banff Mountain Book Festival Tour on the sometimes lonely path taken by some of mountaineering's pre-eminent women.

I want to give you some advice on marriage:

> The right girl will come along sooner or later – if you have kept your head. You will find a girl whose character you admire and respect, whose tastes are like your own and whose comradeship you long for. It will not be merely her person that attracts you, but her personality. You will find a new, calmer and deeper form of love that links and binds you to her – one which, if you are wise, will never grow less.
>
> ... There may be times of trouble, little difficulties in the home which you don't foresee at first. Before you married you only did things for yourself; now that you are married you've got to chuck your self and do things for your wife – and later on for your children.
>
> 'Grousing won't mend matters; instead, give and take and SMILE all the time, but most especially at that time when most women get a little off their usual line, just before the first baby arrives. You've got to show your manliness and chivalry as her comforter and protector then.
>
> If she is a little fractious it is through her love for you that she is so. To such attention she will respond. Women are not only more grateful than men, but their character shapes itself according as it is led by their man.

Of course, it's easy to mock the moral attitudes of a man, in this case Lord Baden-Powell, writing in the 1920s for another generation. Although I should point out that my copy of Baden-Powell's manual for a happy life, *Rovering to Success*, is from the twenty-sixth impression of the second edition, published in 1963, the year that Philip Larkin said that sexual intercourse began in his poem *Annus Mirabilis*, between the Chatterley ban and the Beatles' first LP.

Baden-Powell's book had by this point sold over 200,000 copies. When he wrote it, the British Empire was intact, Everest was unclimbed and mountaineering was an activity practised, in Britain at least, by a handful of privileged men and a tiny number of equally privileged women like Lissie Le Blond and Lady Evelyn McDonnel.

In *Rovering to Success*, Baden-Powell writes: 'Under the head of a true sport, and one which is open to all alike without much expense, is mountaineering.' This wasn't true, remotely, in 1922 but Baden-Powell offers his own speculation on the reasons for this. 'The only wonder,' he writes, 'is that climbing is not better known as a sport. This is largely because fellows don't realise that they can carry it out in almost every part of Great Britain.' This would change during Baden-Powell's lifetime; that the wild tracts of British uplands offered freedom and learning, was well understood by the walking clubs in northern cities before the Second World War and by climbing clubs soon after it.

Baden-Powell, an icon of the imperialist age, the hero of Mafeking, the founder of the scouting and girl guide movements, has been so dismantled by the liberal establishment that it seems unfair to wheel him out again. In 1922 many young men would have thrilled to the word 'Mafeking', the thought of adventure in faraway lands a worthy prospect. Now the average teenager hasn't the faintest idea of where or what Mafeking was. There are fast-food joints in Kathmandu and traffic jams in Bangkok while many young men spend their lives playing computer games. I'll not dwell on Baden-Powell's shortcomings when our own age is awash with them.

All that I will add, is that the section on 'Women' follows those on 'Horses' and 'Wine', and includes the following scenario:

> I was in a 'Rovers' Den' when congratulations were being showered on one member on his engagement to be married.
> 'Who is the girl?'
> 'Oh, she's a Girl Guide.'
> 'Splendid! What a good idea! You couldn't do better.'
> But immediately two other men chipped in for part of the congratulations, saying that they also were engaged similarly to Girl Guides.
> I see promise in this.
>
> You get wives in this way who can be better pals because they have got the same keenness on camping and the out of doors with all the necessary handiness and resourcefulness, health and good temper that comes of such life. I feel certain that if I came to visit you in your home later on, when thus mated, I should find not only a happy home but a clean one; for the premises of campers, who were accustomed to leave their camp grounds as neat as they found them.

There's an innocence about this which is rather attractive, although I can't imagine what Lord B-P would have made of Snell's Field or Camp IV in the Yosemite Valley. Anyway, I am more interested in his automatic assumption that women in the outdoors are camp followers, that their independence out of doors ends on the day they marry and that any personal ambition or satisfaction will naturally be subsumed by the demands of family life. In *Rovering to Success*, Baden-Powell quotes General Bruce, leader of the first full expedition to Everest, on the appeal of climbing the world's highest mountain. Of course, for the General, the appeal was only to men.

A woman would apply to climb Everest for the 1924 expedition, Anne Bernard, about whom I know absolutely nothing. The Everest Committee, whose members I sometimes confuse with the Monty Python team, told her that it was impossible for them to 'contemplate the application of a lady of whatever nationality,' – I assumed she was French or possibly Belgian from this – because 'the difficulties would be too great.'

And yet it was around this time that the Pinnacle Club was founded, to generate the kinds of numbers that would get women's climbing taken seriously. 'Even then,' wrote Eleanor Winthrop Young, 'after all the madness and death, climbing was regarded as a strange activity. One had really done something drastic by becoming a climber. ... In those days, even up in the Lakes, a girl couldn't walk about a village in climbing clothes without hard stares from the women and sniggers from the youths.'

There were stranger things you could be, at least in public; a lesbian, for example. Freda du Faur, the Australian woman who in 1910 made the first ascent of Mount Cook in the Southern Alps, had a highly developed political sense and when she moved to London just before the Great War, she joined the Union for Women's Suffrage under Millicent Fawcett. Her later life was darkened by the loss of her lover and mental illness, culminating in her suicide in 1935. In some ways, her life echoes that of Menlove Edwards, also highly intelligent, also gay and also thwarted in unequal measures by his own inner demons, his obstinacy, and the rigidity of social attitudes. Du Faur could be obstinate too, turning her back on the Ladies' Alpine Club because she saw it as a compromise too far, despite the support it might have offered her. In a world as small as that of climbing, the political gains made by women in the early 20th century would take decades to filter through.

Of course, women's role, or lack of it, in mountaineering was, and is, so thoroughly influenced by social attitudes that it is hardly surprising they were largely absent from the scene for so long. Even when they arrived on the highest peaks of all, the stereotypical thinking endured. Walt Unsworth's exemplary history of Everest refers to Junko Tabei as the 'Japanese housewife' and later a 'bespectacled ex-schoolteacher from Tokyo'. Replace the word 'Tokyo' with the word 'Nottingham' and you have a fairly accurate description of Doug Scott.

Women nurture, they are coy, they are nest-builders. Men are the risk-takers, they are the ones who are out to impress with manly deeds like soloing gritstone slabs and hunting wildebeest. When women venture into the mountains, it is an eccentricity, their courage is remarked upon, as though it were the unlikeliest thing for a woman to show physical courage, and there is the constant subtext that any achievement is considered marvellous only insofar as it was done by a woman. 'If a bloke had done it,' men tell themselves, 'nobody would have been interested.' I want to give you an example of this, from the very start of women's mountaineering, the first female ascent of Mont Blanc.

There are myriad sources in English detailing the first ascent of Mont

Blanc in 1786, despite – or perhaps because of – the suppression of Michel-Gabriel Paccard's personal account and the heavyweight propaganda job done on Jacques Balmat by the jealous precentor, Marc-Théodore Bourrit and later on by Alexandre Dumas who interviewed Balmat in 1832 and whose fictitious, self-glorifying account could not be contradicted by Paccard, who had died several years earlier.

There are a number of books on this great achievement and the subsequent controversy, and Walt Unsworth gives it great attention in his history of Mont Blanc, *Savage Snows*. But to the first ascent by a woman, he gives only a few paragraphs. Nor is any other historian more generous, and there are all kinds of inconsistencies between their accounts. There is even disagreement on the date. Unsworth says 1808, others say 1809, some call her Marie Paradis, others Maria Paradis. Some say she was a serving girl, others that she ran a refreshment stall, or a café at her home in Les Pèlerins. I have read that she was even displayed at circuses as some kind of freakish exhibit. Her age is given variously as 18, 22 or 23 at the time of the ascent.

But one thing that all the accounts have in common is a dismissive tone about her climb, a description of how Paradis was dragged up the final slopes by her male guides, that she was in a semi-comatose state on the summit. It is also agreed that Maria – or Marie – chose not to describe her ascent beyond the briefest details on her return to Chamonix, inviting women of the village to go and do it themselves if they were that interested. And who took her on the ascent? Jacques Balmat, who had lied so aggressively about his role in the first ascent of the mountain a quarter of a century earlier. Among the accounts I've read in English of Maria's achievement, I prefer that by Charles Edward Mathews, alpinist, Brummie, friend of Joe Chamberlain and the first President of the Climbers' Club. It has the ring of truth and more detail than the dismissive accounts that have followed.

In 1809 a group of guides, led by Balmat, decide to make another ascent of Mont Blanc and as they are on the point of departure, two women, Euphrosine Ducroz and Maria Paradis, approach them and ask to go with them to the summit. Mathews says:

> The guides would have nothing to say to Madame Ducroz, but Maria was unmarried and Jacques Balmat, taking her by both hands, asked her if she had really made up her mind. She said yes. "Well," he replied, "I am an old wolf of the mountains, and even I will not promise to succeed. All I ask of you is to be courageous." Maria clapped her hands with joy, and they all started together.

The climb goes well, but Maria, Mathews tells us, is exhausted. 'Go more slowly, Jacques, my heart fails me – go as if you were tired yourself.' Then two guides take her by the arms, and partly by pushing her, and partly by carrying her, they arrive at the Rochers Rouges. Here Maria begs to be left behind, even thrown into a crevasse, but the guides continue to propel her upwards and so they continued to the summit. Mathews continues:

> The following day on reaching Chamonix, all the women in the village came out to welcome the young adventuress, and to ask for details of the journey; but she replied she had seen so many things that it would take too long to recount them, and such of them as were very curious upon the subject could make the journey for themselves.

She did open up later, according to Mathews, telling Captain Markham Sherwill, who made an early British ascent, about her climb, and also entertaining Henriette d'Angeville 30 years later after she made the second ascent by a woman.

I say Mathews has the *ring* of truth, because he quotes his main source as being Alexandre Dumas' account of the conversation he had in 1832 with Jacques Balmat. Dumas got Balmat drunk, so much of this version could very well be the self-aggrandising fantasy of a man so mistrusted that rumours he was murdered have a credibility even before you hear the facts. 'An old wolf of the mountains' is how he describes himself to Maria, at least in his own account, a predator taking the young, innocent girl into danger. It's like Little Red Riding Hood set at altitude.

Maria was also ill-served by Henriette d'Angeville, who discounted the first female ascent of Mont Blanc to promote her own: 'When I went up Mont Blanc,' she wrote afterwards, 'it had not been ascended by any woman capable of remembering her impressions.' As an antidote to such an unsisterly assessment, I think of Claire Evans' withering description of d'Angeville as 'a spinster who loved Mont Blanc because she had nothing else to love' who suffered from a 'morbid passion for self-advertisement'.

Whatever the truth of Maria Paradis' climb, the context is clear. She only succeeded because there were men close at hand to help and the climb didn't count anyway because it was simply not tolerable that a serving girl with no real ambition or position in society should have the honour. But I want to suggest to you that despite her own admission, assuming that even this is true, that she had to be half-carried to the summit, Paradis' achievement is astonishing. *

This was quite possibly the first significant ascent by a woman anywhere, even before mountaineering as a sport had gathered momentum. There were no ropes, no specialist clothing of any description, no ice axes, just unwieldy alpenstocks, and little understanding of altitude sickness. Less than a quarter of a century before it had been widely believed that anyone

---

* Someone who has taken Maria Paradis seriously is the poet and novelist Alison Fell whose poem *Marie Paradis, maidservant* shows more imagination of her than the dismissive histories. 'On the summit her anger arches / like an arrow, sickening and falling // Let them spread their own napkins / on the folds of the snow ... '

who spent a night on a glacier would die. And she was a *woman*, perceived by men as inherently inferior. I think Maria Paradis deserves rather more attention than she's got up to now.

Of course, that was all a long time ago. It's a different world now. Although I remember a couple of years ago helping my two young children out of the car outside my flat in London in the middle of the afternoon during working hours and being approached by an Italian man in his early 50s, who smiled at me sadly and said: 'You know this is for women to do. Women look after children. Men work. It's the way.' So maybe things haven't changed that much. Junko Tabei is still described even now as the 'Japanese housewife', as though being a housewife was an easy day for a lady.

More than a year after the publication of *Regions of the Heart*, the biography of Alison Hargreaves that I co-authored with David Rose, I am still discovering responses to her death which make me think afresh about the fundamental instincts that underpin our society. I recently met Peach Weathers, wife of Beck Weathers, the man who rose from the dead on the South Col of Everest during that infamous spring season on Everest in 1996 so memorably described in Jon Krakauer's *Into Thin Air*. In the account of his survival, entitled *Left For Dead*, Peach writes:

> While Beck was away, I watched a Channel 13 program about this Scotswoman who had died climbing in the mountains. Her husband later took their two children back to the Himalayas so they could see where their mother had died. I remember thinking at the time, Fat lot of good that's going to do them, telling a four-year-old and a two-year-old, "Mommy's up there in the clouds". I thought, That'll sure make them feel better. "Mommy was such a brave person." That's not going to help them when they fall down and skin their knees.

It seems a harsh assessment made worse by Peach Weathers not even bothering to find out the Scotswoman's name. But it is a judgement I have heard made more often than any other, and usually by women who instinctively avoid risk, who do not understand it, or even their own relationship to it. Because women do take risks, most unconsciously, some deliberately. Perhaps they do it less on the swell of testosterone that drives young men into dangerous situations, and with less bravado, but there is a commonality of motivation that overcomes the perceived differences in what is expected of us as men or women.

Alison did a number of remarkable things as a climber, making the first unsupported ascent of Everest without bottled oxygen being perhaps the most extraordinary. But there were other astonishing achievements, like her solo of the Croz Spur in winter conditions late in 1993 after her summer of soloing six north faces throughout the Alps. If you've ever done a north face like the Croz, even with a partner, then you will know viscerally that hollow, choked feeling you get as you cross the bergschrund, the mountaineer's regular Rubicon, and set off into the night. That fear takes a lot of self-control to overcome.

I think the idea of a woman, especially a mother, taking risks invites the kind of stunted judgements that coloured male ideas about women not just in Lord Baden-Powell's day but in the 1970s when Alison started climbing. Wanda Rutkiewicz, in my opinion the best female high-altitude mountaineer in the sport's history, suffered in a similar way and, again like Alison, the true story of her life was more inspiring and more courageous than she was sometimes allowed after her death. When Wanda was a little girl, during the Easter holidays in 1948, she was playing with her brother and his friends in bombed-out ruins of an apartment block in her home town of Wroclaw. They found an unexploded landmine buried in the rubble and decided to set fire to it. And Wanda's brother also decided that his little sister, then only five years old, shouldn't be allowed to join in with the boys, so she ran home to tell her mother how she had been cruelly excluded from this new, exciting game. The mine exploded as Wanda's terrified mother sprinted towards the ruin. All the boys were killed.

Wanda's share of personal tragedy didn't end with her brother. Her father was brutally murdered in 1972 by his own tenants, in his own home. He had offered lodging to a couple and then come home to find them robbing him. They assaulted him with knives and an axe. Wanda had to identify the body. She would say afterwards that people frightened her. 'I'm forever scared that something terrible might happen to me,' she once said. In the same way that Alison would find release from her unhappy marriage in the mountains, Wanda found freedom there from the ghosts that haunted her.

Alison didn't know Wanda, although she knew her reputation. She did, however, know Catherine Freer. They met at an international women's meet and hit it off. Catherine inspired Alison, showed her a glimpse of an altogether different world. They stayed in touch and Alison found her presence in the world encouraging. When Catherine died on Mount Logan's Hummingbird Ridge in 1986, Alison was stricken with grief, in a way she couldn't have predicted. Freer was an exceptional woman and an inspiration to the small group of Canadian women following in her footsteps.

One of her friends told me recently: 'Catherine was a powerful presence in our community. For younger women like me she was a goddess. Beautiful and climbing totally hard. I wanted to be just like her. I was awestruck by her, she didn't seem wimpy in the way I saw myself. Her eyes burned with this Maurice Richard intensity. I think she turned grown men to jello.'

Catherine was a psychologist and worked for a while in a home for abused wives. One evening, a husband who'd found out where his wife was hiding called round with a handgun and loosed off a shot at Catherine. It could have killed her. But if she had died that night, no obituarist would have dared suggest that she had died doing something useless, that she died pursuing her own selfish ends. And yet, climbing gave her a dimension she lacked before, or at least, helped her realise herself as an individual.

You could argue that she was a better psychologist, that she might have been a better mother, had she lived to bear children, because of that.

'You don't appreciate the full flavour of life until you risk losing it,' Wanda Rutkiewicz said once, and the obvious answer to that is that most of us know just how risky life is without leaving the ground, thank you very much. There is nothing heroic or glorious about dying in a mountaineering accident. But had Alison, like Cathy Freer, been killed anywhere but a mountain, then that side of her life would have been celebrated. There would have been no avalanche of criticism and moral judgements.

Of course, Alison had marital difficulties of her own although almost no one who heard of her death in August 1995 had any idea quite how much she had suffered. She had started climbing in a very male, very competitive English climbing scene where the last thing you did was reveal yourself or your emotions. But at the same time she felt unequal to the image she presented to the world. She often over-compensated for her lack of confidence, appearing brittle or ungenerous to her competitors. Plenty of people thought her selfish and self-obsessed. Cathy Freer, by contrast, was living her ambition and her fears out in the open; I think Alison envied that and while Cathy was around, she had a role model.

As she got older, and her climbing successes diluted her need to prove something to the world, then a different Alison began emerging. For much of her relationship with Jim Ballard, she had tried to conform to some kind of Baden-Powell notion of a good wife. (She was certainly organised enough when camping.) But there were times when she felt reduced, even crushed, and this led to disillusionment and bitterness. And she was alone with that, through fear mostly, much of it fear of failure, of admitting that she had been wrong about her marriage and the direction her life was taking.

Women like Alison Hargreaves and the others who dominated women's mountaineering in the 1980s and 1990s don't deserve that dismissive sneering challenge that what they did wasn't cutting-edge or innovative. Because, as Maria Paradis, cheated by history, might tell you, it was. 'Women are not only more grateful than men, but their character shapes itself according as it is led by their man,' Baden-Powell told his young readers. We laugh, we dismiss it, but the attitude was real, and I suspect still is for some men. Freda Du Faur, Alison Hargreaves, Wanda Rutkiewicz, Catherine Freer and others were the women who broke through these barriers. They were innovators for a future generation not by finding new routes in the mountains, but by finding new routes for themselves, by shaping their own characters. Most women don't climb mountains, most don't even understand climbing's appeal, but I think, in that regard at least, most women would sympathise with women mountaineers.

Further reading: *Wanda Rutkiewicz - A Caravan of Dreams* by Gertrude Reinisch (Carreg, 2000). *Between Heaven and Earth. The Life of A Mountaineer, Freda Du Faur* by Sally Irwin (White Crane Press, 2000).

The Diaries of Hester Norris

Edited and introduced by

DAVE ROBERTS

Hester Norris was born near Preston in 1910, one of two children of a clergyman; her brother also became a member of the clergy. She spent a large part of her working life as Secretary to the Headmaster of Rydal School in Colwyn Bay. She visited the Alps regularly from the early 1930s until the mid 1950s and was a member of the Midland Association of Mountaineers (MAM) for some time in the 1940s and 1950s.

After her death her climbing diaries passed to a friend, Tony Hughes of Windermere. He offered them for safe-keeping to the MAM, into whose care they came in 1995. Each diary is an account of one Alpine season from 1934 to 1956, written in a neat clear hand sometimes covering over 200 pages of hard-backed exercise books in great detail; the accounts of some of the best days are over 30 pages long. Her technique at first was to write it all out in the evenings and on rest days, copying it into the book once home. Later she took to making notes, often while on a climb, using these to jog her memory while writing up the diary later. There are many photographs and postcards, sometimes with the route taken on a mountain carefully marked in. She missed some seasons including, of course, the years of the second world war

The diaries are written in a fairly personal style; in places she almost talks to herself, and is quite prepared to share her feelings of joy on a successful climb and of frustration and despair if the weather caused an ascent to be called off. However, it is clear from a number of remarks that she intended them to be read and it becomes obvious that they were circulated among her friends, who she refers to as 'my regular readers'.

These were her Alpine diaries and they contain little other than passing remarks about climbing activities in Britain. Some exceptions to this will be mentioned, but it is probably because she makes no bones about her view that climbing is all about the Alps; Britain is fine for keeping fit and good enough fun, but the hills are too small and rock climbing is no good end in itself. We learn a lot about Hester's character and attitudes, but little about her life away from the Alps other than from passing remarks which sometimes intrigue rather than inform; no doubt her intended readers already knew all they needed to know about her.

As the diaries cover the 23 years from 1934 to 1956 they inevitably tell us a great deal about climbing in the Alps then: guides, equipment, transport, hotels, food, huts, all these and other topics are discussed extensively, and all are very different from the modern era. There is as much social comment about the Alpine scene as about the climbs themselves. Hester felt that she lived a busy, useful life, though far and away her happiest days were in the Alps, and she felt deeply sad when the time came to go home. We all feel this at times but I suspect that to her it was sometimes an almost intolerable wrench and on a number of occasions she discusses how the Alpine life is the only thing that truly matters. In her 1954 diary she speculates on the nature of happiness and asks if the readers can remember the happiest day of each year in their past. She can and lists them. The list starts with her first Alpine season and the happiest day in each year is a day of her Alpine trip. The only exception is for 1945, VE day, though there are gaps in the war years. This list will be referred to later as 'The 1954 List'. She worried about money, saving hard for her holidays, generally travelling third class on French railways and always watching the pennies, though one drain on her cash must have been the fact that she always climbed with a guide.

She first climbed in the Alps in 1934, when she was 24. For two years prior to that she had had skiing and skating holidays at Lenk in the Upper Simmental in the Bernese Oberland, staying in the Sternen Hotel, run by the Zahlen family with whom she became good friends. It is not clear how these holidays started though she obviously had contacts in Montreux. Being on her own was probably a bit unconventional for that period and she seems to have had a highly independent outlook with forthright views. Skiing was a minority sport then and instruction tended to be on a one to one basis. Her instructors were Victor Biner and Hans Griessen who were both mountain guides in the summer, Victor based in Zermatt and Hans in Lenk. Her first two climbing seasons were as a paying client of Victor. Thereafter she nearly always employed a guide as that was the established way of doing things; though a member of the Swiss Ladies Alpine Club she had no other climbing contacts for the Alps and she was not far removed in time from the era when alpinism amounted to a personal calling that only touched a few. There were no magazines, it was difficult to find anyone with useful knowledge of the Alps and the only guidebook she had was Ball's *Alpine Guide*, 1907 edition. Indeed, she only ever climbed with guides until 1949; she always held to the view that to climb guided was the ideal way. There was a greater chance of success on unknown ground, and the leader was always to be trusted in judgement as well as in technical competence. For Hester, climbing was all about successfully getting up mountains and big ones at that, Switzerland being her ideal. 'My beloved Switzerland' she called it, and she entertained ideas of one day living there. Easy snow plods were not of much interest, being dismissed as 'cow routes'.

Her relationships with her guides are interesting, though it was probably much the same as it was for most competent guided amateurs then. She only employed a few guides altogether, as she would engage one for the whole fortnight of the holiday and tended to return to the same ones. Thus they became good friends, but it was always a formal employer/employee relationship; Marcel Bozon of Chamonix with whom she climbed for three seasons and during some trying times always addressed her as 'Mademoiselle'. While Hester seems to have spent hours poring over her maps and climbing books, it was very much the choice and decision of the guide as to what they did on a given day; on a few occasions they left a hut in the dark with Hester not knowing where they were going. Her wish list of peaks for a holiday was her own affair and while she made it known what her hopes were she had little part in the actual decision-making. The security of the rope was very important, the more so as she never claimed to be expert, particularly acknowledging her shortcomings on snow and ice and in route-finding. Words of praise from her guide always made her very proud.

The diaries offer a worthwhile insight into the period in which Hester was climbing, although in these pages it is only possible to give the briefest details of her climbs, and almost nothing of the great range of content and comment in the complete version.

1934

This diary sets the pattern for most of the later ones. There is a sketch map of the area, an extract from *On High Hills* by Geoffrey Winthrop Young – she quotes Young quite a bit – and an index of contents which comprises List of Illustrations, Summary, Foreword and the location within the diary of the three best days. It is worth quoting a few phrases from the Foreword as they illustrate perfectly Hester's view of climbing in the Alps: 'September 6th was the best day of my life'; 'a wonderful, thrilling pastime'; 'the benefits and joys derived from [the holiday] are everlasting'.

She travelled to Newhaven on Archiebald, her motorbike, and by train to Zermatt. She met Victor, bought some boots, did some training on the Gorner Glacier and on the Riffelhorn; ' ... my first rock climbing of any sort ... I liked it'; and on the Furggengrat: 'I had no idea what a 'ridge' meant'; and then progressed to somewhat bigger things with a traverse of the Untergabelhorn and a night in the Schönbühl Hut, her first, followed by an ascent of the Pointe de Zinal. Times of leaving the hut, lengths of stops etc are carefully noted, something she continued to do throughout her climbing career.

Victor must have been satisfied with Hester's competence as he went up to the Hörnli Hut the same evening that they arrived back in Zermatt to guide two English clients up the Matterhorn, suggesting to Hester that she should bring some food up to the hut next day so that they could climb it the following day. At the hut 'I was excited, alarmed and amazed ... at the most wonderful mountain in the world.' They set off at 5am, overtook a few parties, rested for half an hour at the Solvay Hut and got to the top at 9 am. 'Surely this was, and always will be, the happiest day of my life.' It took them two hours and forty minutes, plus an hour sitting in the sun at the Solvay Hut, to get down. She almost envied the slow parties as they were still up there.

Two days later they traversed the Rimpfischhorn. Descent was made to Täsch; the start of the route down has a steep step ' ... the most ghastly place I have ever seen'. Hester slid down this on a very tight rope, while Victor abseiled, the first time she had ever seen this done. It had been a grand day and harder on the whole than the Matterhorn. They did the Riffelhorn again with Hester leading and Victor playing the part of an incompetent tourist, and then the Mettelhorn and the Plattenhörner and the Trifthorn by the Triftgrat, somewhat harder technically than the routes done so far. From the top there was a good view of the Zinal Rothorn; Victor said that on her next visit she should climb it: 'I'm sure I shall too, it looks <u>magnificent</u>'.

That was the end of the holiday, but the diary goes on to summarise her winter sports holidays in Lenk from 1932 to 1935, the first of these being in charge of a party of schoolgirls. In the Foreword she reveals that from 1933 she had longed to climb and Victor had told her that after a few days training with him, she could climb the Matterhorn. After all, he had already done it 52 times and by 1934 she had done it. The diary also describes a ski ascent of the Wildhorn with Hans Griessen in January 1935.

Her first rock-climbing holiday in England was at Wasdale Head over Easter 1935, one of her companions being Harry Lucas, of whom more later. This is just a short summary, but there is a long account of an ascent of North Climb on Pillar; quite an epic in terrible conditions, with hail and thunder. 'We were absolutely soaked to the skin and so we waded through the streams as it was pointless using the bridges. A <u>perfect end</u> to a <u>perfect day</u> and <u>I mean that.</u>'

1936

The only Alpine visit of 1935 was the winter sports trip to Lenk mentioned above; the 1954 List gives the ski ascent of the Wildhorn as the best day of the year.

The diary for 1936 starts with an enigma. The trip was marred by bad weather and in the foreword Hester bemoans the fact that they were unable to do the two biggest routes that she had set her heart on, the more so as: 'While enjoying this holiday so much there was just one thought which overshadowed everything at times – it was probably the last Alpine mountaineering holiday I should get for many years, as I had decided to save my money for a different kind of adventure. ... However the adventure failed and 1937 found me back in the Alps again ... seeking the one and only real adventure ... the mountains and all they stand for will never be put in the background again by me.' What adventure was this?

With Victor, she warmed up on the Riffelhorn and then went up to the Théodule Hut andthe Breithorn. She acknowledged the usefulness of this as altitude training and also the fine views, but 'it is nothing but a long weary trudge ... I came to <u>climb</u>, not to walk!' They added the Klein Matterhorn on the way down. Then they climbed the Dufourspitze of Monte Rosa from the Bétemps Hut, taking five hours and twenty minutes for the ascent of over 6000 feet. Hester found most of it to be a monotonous snow plod, but was quite worried by the final narrow ridge. Next they traversed the Obergabelhorn, up by the 'Old Route' via the Gabelhorn Glacier and down by the Arbengrat, on which Hester revelled in the exposure 'grand, thrilling and sensational!' A photo taken from the Obergabelhorn is captioned '<u>The Rothorn Ridge of the Zinal Rothorn.</u> Oh how I have set my heart on climbing this ridge. I wonder <u>when</u> I shall do it, if ever; <u>but I must!'</u>

Then the weather broke. They were turned back from an attempt on the Zinal Rothorn by wind and verglas and did not even leave the Hörnli Hut for a traverse of the Matterhorn as it was snowing heavily. All that remained were some of the harder routes on the Riffelhorn and some abseiling practice. Victor wanted her to stay on for the Matterhorn, but the weather looked poor and she had overspent. She makes the point that Victor is a great pal and a good guide but that he charges top prices '... just as well to know this beforehand which is more than I did'.

There is a supplement covering some other mountain activities in 1936. This comprises a short summary of a winter sports holiday at Lenk, Easter at Wasdale – another minor epic on North Climb on Pillar – and ten days with a novice in the Lakes in the spring, walking over most of the tops in the central area and some easy climbing. There is a clue here to the origin of Hester's concerns about not visiting the Alps again. The novice is identified as 'Lewis' and some photographs suggest a relationship rather more than just walking companions, the more so as at the end of the diary there are some similar shots which are among the very few indeed in the whole series of diaries taken away from mountains; one dates from 1933. There is also some other evidence to suggest that Hester was contemplating marriage at this time. We do not know what happened, but did she find herself having to make a decision between mountains and marriage? In the event she never married. She also visited Scotland and climbed the Buachaille Etive Mor and Ben Nevis via the Carn Mor Dearg arête; and with no explanation at all, there are a few photos taken in Newfoundland in November 1936. Perhaps this is something to do with Lewis.

1937

This time the Bernese Oberland with Hans Griessen: '... a genuine companion and friend ... a good all-round mountaineer and <u>not</u> one of the moneygrubbers!' They started with a training day on the Spielgarten – Hester's first serious abseil – and then a tour over country already known from skiing days; Wildhorn Hut, Wildhorn, Wildstrubel Hut, Wildstrubel by the North-west Ridge – 'Hans: "Today we go over everything and round nothing". I replied eagerly "That suits me fine" and pulled up my socks.' – and down to Kandersteg, a long way.

Then came another long trip, the route being the Blümlisalp Hut, Blümlisalphorn, Mutthorn Hut, Breithorn and on to Lauterbrunnen. Hans said that he never expected to cover so much ground in six days. 'No wonder we were divinely happy and walked on air without a care in the world.' From there they went by Kleine Scheidegg to Grindelwald, Hans spurred on at the thought of his girl friend, Gretel, who lived there, and who he married soon after. Grindelwald was buzzing with talk of an attempt on the as yet unclimbed North Face of the Eiger. (It was Vörg and Rebitsch, who retreated safely from the Death Bivouac.)

Hans had suggested the Mittellegi Ridge of the Eiger, but the weather was poor so they decided on the Andersongrat of the Schreckhorn together with a guide friend of Hans and his client. At the Strahlegg Hut the weather was still bad, though on the first day there they did the Strahlegghörner after a late start. The next day was a washout. Hester was not at all happy: ' ... the events of the past year [had] seemed long since forgotten. But this day of enforced inaction seemed to bring all those things right back in my mind ... so far as I know, this has been the only day of my life when I had nothing to occupy myself with, and I did not enjoy it.' Next morning there was new snow everywhere, so they retreated via Grindelwald to Boltigen where they spent a day on the crags used by the locals, the Jüngferli. Hester enjoyed this very much; the photos make it look quite interesting. There was just time for the Weisstadhorn, the only hill at Lenk which Hester had not been up by foot or ski, with the promise of the Mittellegi and the Andersongrat for the next year.

There is a supplement to this diary which is an account of Easter 1937 at Wasdale, mainly photos, the only lines of text being a lesson learned: ' ... don't go on trying to lead a pitch when you feel you can't or have lost confidence in yourself. It was only the enormous amount of new snow in Central Gully that prevented my fall, which involved my partner too, from being a serious one.' Tucked in the back of the book are a few photos taken on Tryfan of members of the family of Professor G I Finch, later to be President of the Alpine Club, and of Clare and Berridge Mallory, daughters of G L Mallory, and also of G W Young with the Finches at Pen y Pass.

1938

With Hans in the Oberland again. They traversed the Kingspitz from the Engelhorn Hut going up by the SW Ridge – 'what a fine ridge' – but easier than Pillar North Climb or Gashed Crag. Over lunch on the top, Hester marvelled at being there less than 48 hours after being on the Channel and how the views and atmosphere made what had been a difficult year at home now so easy to forget. Next day they traversed the Klein and Gross Simelistock; 'highly enjoyable', and on the top of the Klein Simelistock she wrote in her notebook: 'Hans said that we'd only just begun our climb and we've come up miles of glorious ridge. What wonderful mountains.' The descent was by abseiling down the McDonald Chimney in increasing mist.

Two days of unsettled weather saw them move to the Dossen Hut and up the Dossenhorn. This was a Sunday, and Hester allowed herself what is just about the only expression of religious faith to be found in these diaries; despite her family background she seems never to have had much interest in religious matters. 'I love being on an Alpine peak on Sunday mornings ... because I always think of the hundreds of people in church, and how <u>much</u> nearer the Almighty I feel on an Alpine summit than I ever do in church.' Next day, in better weather, they made a long trek to the Wettersattel and climbed the Wetterhorn, Hester telling herself sternly that her confidence on glaciers and on steep snow must improve. A long, rough descent in mist again led to the Gleckstein Hut, from where they teamed up with another guide, Christian Inabit, and his client and traversed the Klein Schreckhorn to the Strahlegg Hut.

After a day of rain they descended to Grindelwald for supplies before returning to the Strahlegg and a quick trip up the Strahlegghorn to spy out the route on the Gross Schreckhorn. The account for the day finishes: 'I summed up my feelings in my notebook thus: "Will it go? <u>Please, yes.</u>"'

Next day the weather was doubtful, and Hans led off without committing himself to the South Ridge, which was their ideal option, rather than the ordinary route. Hester willed him to plump for the harder route, as ordinary routes tend to be somewhat uninteresting. 'This is particularly so of the Matterhorn and until I have climbed it by the Zmutt and Italian ridges, I shall not feel I have justified my climbing career.' The weather looked doubtful; Hans looked at the ordinary route and said: 'That way means <u>nothing</u> to me except to come down by: I would so much rather climb the Sudgrat.' After some debate, Hester said, 'Let's risk it and we will climb together as much as possible.' So they did; the weather broke and the descent became a battle with mist, a fierce wind and driving hail and snow. At one point they took a wrong turn onto dangerous ground, eventually regaining the hut after 14 hours.

The weather stayed bad so they retreated to Grindelwald, teaming up with local guide, Fritz Kaufman-Almer and his two clients, to snatch the Eiger by the West Flank (not the Mittellegi, alas), in deep snow, getting back to the Eigergletscher station with half an hour to spare before the time of the last train Hester could catch to make her connections on the way home.

The supplement contains a two-page summary of her 1938 winter holiday in Lenk and a similar summary, but with many photos, of two weeks in Snowdonia in April 1938 with the Finches, meeting some members of the Climbers' Club and being taken up *Terrace Wall* by the well known climber Brenda Ritchie.

1939

In the previous diary Hester had mused on doing something different this year after having had four seasons in Switzerland, and it was *very* different.

For the first time she had a companion, Harry Lucas, from the Wasdale days; they were unable to engage a guide before setting out and 24 August 1939 was hardly an auspicious time to be heading for Chamonix. While they were there France ground to a halt; hotels closed down, guides were mobilised into the armed forces and some huts were taken over by mountain troops. But the food and drink were always a consolation and Hester loved the mountains of the area.

They hired a guide, Armand Couttet, and went up to Montenvers. On arrival there Armand was summoned by phone to report for military service at once, but Armand found a replacement by the name of Marcel Bozon who turned out to be ideal. The three of them did the Petits Charmoz (Harry's first Alpine climb) and the Pélerins and next went up to the Requin Hut. There is a splendid photo of a smiling Marcel, cigarette in hand, and Hester positively beaming, on the col between the Grands and Petits Charmoz, the caption reading: 'Here I am just itching to be off again for some more: <u>happiness personified!</u>' The Requin Hut was occupied by the military, but they were mainly guides in civilian life and friends of Marcel's so there were no problems.

From the Midi they had a long, hot descent in exasperatingly soft snow in which both Hester and Harry had some difficulty in keeping their feet. Hester records that Marcel, who was unfailingly patient at all times and somewhat laconic, remarked to her at one point: 'You know it is better to glissade on your feet for you have no nails in your behind!' An old Chamonix guide's joke, no doubt. Next day it was the Requin. Dorothy Pilley, who they had met at Montenvers, had worried Hester by taking her aside and saying, 'I wonder if your man is able to lead it properly?' Rather proudly, Hester records that Marcel climbed it with perfect ease, chain-smoking or whistling little tunes to himself all the while. And it was a splendid climb, just taxing enough.

Back in Chamonix things were falling apart; they had difficulty in finding somewhere to change money and Harry decided to make for home while the trains were still running rather than risk losing his job. Hester's secret wish was to do the Grépon; she did not dare to suggest such a relatively difficult climb to Marcel, so when asked what she would like to do merely said 'something fairly difficult'. She was overjoyed when Marcel promptly suggested the Grépon from the Plan de l'Aiguille. She left her luggage at Marcel's chalet at Les Pélerins and they took the téléphérique up to the Plan.

Next day was: 'A red letter day in my mountaineering career'. Marcel paced up and down looking at the doubtful weather, then suddenly sat down, ate his breakfast, packed and set off, only telling Hester that they really were going up the Grépon when she asked where they were going. Her account of the climb covers many pages, but it is enough to say all went well on a splendid climb. On the summit Hester allowed her mind to dwell on the thoughts that the mountains would always be there and that she would visit them every year that circumstances permitted, even when she could only do the easy ones and gaze at the big ones ' ... which have afforded me so many hours of unrivalled joy'.

The descent passed off without incident. Back at the hut someone had brought up a newspaper: *'Les Allemands attaquent La Pologne sans pitié.'* What should they do? In the event they did the Peigne and decided on the traverse of the Ciseaux and the Fou for the following day. That evening, though, an old man came up to drive down some sheep with the message: *'L'Angleterre a declaré la guerre aujourd'hui à 11 heures, et la France aussi ce soir à cinq heures!'* Next day the mountains were shrouded in mist anyway, so they descended to Marcel's chalet where she spent some time with his family, deeply worried about what would become of them. Eventually the time came to go; Hester and Marcel made the final mutual wish of 'À L'ANNÉE PROCHAINE!' Hester wanted to do Mont Blanc by the Brenva Route but, of course, next year in the Alps was not to be. The lights were going out all over Europe. Hester had become very fond of Marcel: ' ... he cycled away. I watched him disappear in the torrential rain and wondered unhappily if he will be spared from the firing line of this hateful war.'

The journey home took three and a half days of uncertainty, catching what sounds like one of the last ferries to leave Dieppe. ' ... it remains to be seen when the world will be able to resume its normal activities once more ... In the meantime I must be content with the glorious memories contained in my five Alpine diaries.'

The diary contains also a list of all the mountains she had climbed in order of merit – Matterhorn first, Grépon second – and Harry Lucas added a short summary of his recollections of the trip.

During the war the school moved to Loton Park in Shropshire. Visits to the hills were almost impossible; the only entries for this period in the 1954 list are for 1942 when she climbed Snowdon from Loton Park, travelling by motor bike, and for 1943 when she again climbed Snowdon, this time by push bike, sleeping out on Grib Goch. There exists a letter to Hester from T Graham Brown of Brenva fame, dated 7/12/44. This is presumably in reply to one she had written to him, recalling that they had met in the Strahlegg Hut in 1937 and asking for advice on the Brenva Face routes. Hester had commented favourably on his book *Brenva* – this letter was tucked inside her copy of the book – and he responded by looking forward to seeing her photos and her book, when she got round to writing it.

1946 (1)
Sunshine and snow

From this point onward Hester gave her diaries titles; there are two for 1946, both relatively slim. This first was written about a ski-touring and ski-mountaineering holiday in Lenk. Hester started with an extract from *Finale* by G W Young:

'I have not lost the magic of long days;
I live them, dream them still ... '
She also noted that the ban on private travel to Switzerland was lifted on
1 April; on 6 April she was on her way! The rail journey across France was
tedious but the welcome in Lenk, where not much had changed, made up
for it. They wasted no time, and set off for the Wildhorn Hut where Hester
spent a couple of days relearning all she had forgotten about skiing,
culminating in an ascent of the Wildhorn. They crossed the Rawyl Pass to
the Wildstrubel Hut from where they climbed the Rohrbachstein, the
Weisshorn and the Wildstrubel before descending to Kandersteg. One day
in the valley was enough, 'but as I only have money for the simplest of
souvenirs ... it is almost too much.' One consolation of a day in the valley
was a brief respite from having been badly sunburned: 'It was exceedingly
painful to smile.' Another consolation was the quantity and quality of the
food.

They took the train to the Jungfraujoch and then skied to the Concordia
Hut, touring around the Finsteraarhorn Hut and the Hollandia Hut. An
attempt on the Ebnefluh was called off in the face of mist and spindrift and
then it was time to go home. They made their way out to Goppenstein by
way of Fafleralp and thence back to Lenk. 'I thought for a moment of my
last departure at Chamonix in 1939 and how I had watched Marcel cycle
away through torrents of rain and how numb and dejected I had felt. Now
at least I was happy in the knowledge that I was not leaving the Alps
indefinitely and that it would only be a matter of months before I would be
among them again, if not among the Swiss Alps.'

1946 (2)
Making the Best of a Bad Deal
It was indeed only a matter of months, made possible by careful saving,
and to Chamonix and the guiding services of Marcel Bozon. Not only had
Marcel survived the war, he had been exempt from active service as the
father of seven children and as a guide he had spent the time training
mountain troops. France was difficult; Hester was held up on the way by a
sudden train strike at Dijon, everything seemed pretty chaotic, most things
were very expensive and food severely rationed, though at a price they ate
well enough from the black market. Stuck into one page are some French
food coupons: cheese, coffee, meat, vegetables, even wine. Perhaps these
memorabilia are now collector's items.

The main reason that this diary is short is that the weather was terrible
and there was little climbing to record. From the Couvercle Hut they climbed
the Moine before the weather broke, and then went down to Chamonix.
With no sign of improvement they wandered through the Aiguilles Rouges,
crossing into Switzerland before returning. They started with an ascent of
L'Index, 'the self-satisfaction that I was still able to climb,' stayed at the

Lac Blanc Hut, traversed the Aiguille de Belvedere in wintry conditions, descended to the Pierre À Bérard Hut, where Hester relates how she got stuck in the hole in the loo, then over the Buet and into Switzerland by the Col des Vieux and down to the Chalets of Barberine. The weather deteriorated as they climbed La Tour Salières. The photos they took of each other are captioned: 'An old man and an old woman, who looks at her last gasp!' After that they took the easy way back by Vallorcine and by bus over the Col des Montets and that was the end of the holiday.

On the last page of text Hester wrote: 'This concludes yet another of my Alpine Diaries, my seventh, and the least interesting of them all.' But there was always 'l'année prochaine'; and Hester was hoping to visit the Dauphiné. The diary ends with photos. Hester had become interested in photography and was doing a lot of her own developing and printing, often with the help of Mr Ross, father of one of the pupils at Rydal.

1947
Dauphiné; High Life in L'Oisans

Even before the holiday, Hester wrote that 1947 had been one of the most enjoyable years of her life. This trip with Marcel must have added to that enjoyment. They started by traversing from the Col de Lautaret to La Bérarde by the Tour Carrée and the Pic Nord des Cavales. Then, from the Promontoire Hut, they did the famous traverse of the Meije and carried on to La Grave in a 16-hour day. This had been one of Hester's great ambitions: 'I shall cherish my memories of the Meije among the very best of my mountain memoirs.'

Next, from the Evariste Chancel Hut, they traversed the Pic de la Grave and Les Têtes du Replat back to La Bérarde. A noisy night in the Temple-Ecrins Hut followed and then it was the South Face of the Ecrins. Marcel had not done it before: 'The ordinary way does not interest me ... because you love the mountains so much I like to take you up them by the best way.' Conditions were not good, windy and cold with verglas and Hester found it hard, though: 'It had been a dangerous, more than a difficult, day in my opinion but it was good to feel that we had accomplished my second ambition of the holiday ... '

They descended to the Ernest Caron Hut and did the Roche Paillon in poor weather before returning to La Bérarde, whence they went their separate ways. It had been 'one of the best of my Alpine Holidays'.

1948
Castles in the Air

Hester felt very positive about this year. 'I decided to "bag" as many Oberland giants with Hans Griessen as weather and funds would permit.' But the weather was very poor and these plans became so many 'Castles in the Air.' Hans was very pessimistic; many peaks had had no ascents yet that season and a leading Grindelwald guide, who had recently done the North Face of the Eiger, had just been killed in an avalanche. (Hans Schlunegger, who made the third ascent with his brother Karl and Gottfried Jerman in 1947.) Also, 'I felt that Hans had lost a great deal of his former pluck and determination.' Hans was 48 years old at this time; no excuse but perhaps he did not feel the need to try as hard.

However, in poor weather they pottered about on the lesser peaks near Lenk, climbing the Morgenhorn on a better day: 'Gosh! how <u>wonderful</u> everything was.' And then the Gspaltenhorn as the weather deteriorated, making a long trek out to the Fafleralp. From there they traversed the Mittaghorn ('Another peak for when I am sixty!') to Concordia and on to the Finsteraarhorn Hut. At least from there they managed the Finsteraarhorn, the highest point in the Oberland.

Back at Concordia it snowed. Hester admitted that she sulked and refused to talk to anyone until Hans persuaded her to come down for a meal. Later she berated herself; 'my mood that morning was despicable – utterly selfish, self-centred and inexcusable.' For once she met a large British party also marooned in the hut on an Alpine Club organised training trip; from them she learned to play liar dice, admitting that they cheered her up no end. They went out to Kleine Scheidegg, where she had a bust-up with the railway staff: 'The Kl. Scheidegg station officials must have a very low I.Q.' She was then offered a six-month job in the office of the Kleine Scheidegg Hotel for the next year; it was tempting, but her loyalty to Rydal would not allow it, though it made her wonder about such a possibility for the future.

She had been in correspondence with Arnold Lunn whom she had never met and had tea with him in Grindelwald, an appointment which she just managed to squeeze in before starting the journey home. He spent the time explaining copyright and she offered to help with typing manuscripts. This all seems a bit obscure, but near the end of the diary Hester wrote: 'When it comes to writing my book, however, this holiday will occupy no more than a paragraph.' So the book she had mentioned to Graham Brown was still in her mind. The journey home was enlivened by chance meetings with some of the crowd from the Concordia Hut.

The diary ends with a short essay on her improving skills as a photographer, and besides the Alpine photos there is a portfolio taken in the UK to demonstrate 'The Changing Seasons', not all of which are in the hills and many of which are missing. Some were taken in Snowdonia with the Rydal Hillwalkers, a group of pupils from the school. Some shots were taken on the Carneddau; one of the Hillwalkers remembers these being taken on a holiday granted to mark the birth of Prince Charles, while another relates the tale of being on the Glyders in thick mist, needing to return to Ogwen. Hester produced map and compass, emphasised how important it was to be able to navigate and then led them off confidently; straight down to the Llanberis Pass!

1949

Norsk Enterprise

In 1948, Hester had wondered about a trip to Norway. Two of the party she had met in the Concordia Hut had proposed her for membership of the MAM and she was delighted to find that the summer meet for 1949 was to be to the Sunnmøre area of Norway, led by Showell Styles and Cyril Machin. The diary is dedicated to the two of them, each adding a short contribution at the end; she climbed with Cyril and Olwen James. Cyril had the reputation of being a bit headstrong in the hills; he certainly gave Hester a few scares, being just about as different from an Alpine guide as it was possible to be, but: 'Such success as Olwen and I achieved was entirely due to his brilliant leadership.'

The first 50 pages are about the members, the journey out and her impressions of Norway. After training days on Slogen and Setertind the three of them did the SW Face of Smørskredtind, starting from the Patchell bothy. Hester honestly admitted that she was scared stiff; it was steep, mossy, difficult, lacking in belays, no obvious route and Cyril just forged on into the unknown without listening to her pleas to be allowed to traverse off onto one of the bounding ridges. At one point Cyril made a solo traverse to their descent ridge to leave boots and ice axes, returning to lead on but not allowing them to go to the ridge with him! After a desperate pitch off-route, where Cyril used a peg, they reached the top. The descent ridge was a long succession of towers; they got back to the Patchell at about 10.30pm. They found out later that they had made the first British and the first female ascents of the route.

At one point she had said to Olwen: '<u>I am never going to climb with Cyril again.</u>' She did, only a few days later. After a day's walking they climbed Brekketind, a good all-round mountaineering day, some more walks and then Råna. 'I had no qualms about what lay ahead ... Oh-ho, Hester, how are the mighty fallen and the dreams of the carefree perished.' It was a long approach, the climbing up an excellent ridge then taking four and a half hours. The descent was long and complex, followed by a struggle in the dark through scrub along the fjord side, eventually gaining access to the hotel through a toilet window. 'The time was 2.15 am. What <u>would</u> Hans, or Marcel, or Victor have said?'

Another walking day and then it was time to sail home. 'I had a wonderful holiday to relate and indeed I sincerely hope that next year I shall set off with the MAM to some new centre.' Talk of the Dolomites was in the air.

1950

Madness of the Heart

Hester's family could understand her wish to visit the Dolomites but not her wish to climb them. 'Madness of the Heart' they called it. This was quite a different MAM party from Norway, though Cyril Machin was there. The party had two guides, Johann and Toni Demetz. From the Sella Pass they did various routes on the First and Second Sella Towers and then the Gross and Klein Fermeda Towers from the Fermeda Hut. Hester felt that she was climbing quite well in an environment that was new to her, and was pleased to be included in a party which did the Kienekamin on the Funffingerspitze, along with Toni, Cyril, and two other MAM members. It went very well: 'Life was too good to be true … such confidence as I have never known before.' She did have considerable difficulty on a pitch now graded IV+.

The next day some of them trekked to Mount Boé by a primitive via ferrata, getting back in the dark, followed by a 13-hour day on the Langkofel. Then came the Adangkamin – some good photos – and a return to the Sella Towers, on harder routes this time.

Hester's private ambition for the trip was the South Face of the Marmolada, it being the biggest thing around. They never got to it, though Hester showed some signs of annoyance when a member of the party did it by slipping away and hiring another guide. They moved on to the Vajolet Hut to do the Winkler Turm on which she required a pull up on the rope on the notorious Winkler Crack, another IV+ pitch: 'Pull, pull!' I gasped … I crossed over to Priestley (Phillips) and Cyril to thank them, nay congratulate them, on their superhuman strength.' The Stabler Turm was much easier.

That was the end of the meet, but Hester and two others went on to the Ortler. Terrible weather prevented them from trying the Cevedale, though they did struggle up the lesser Punta Madreccino and Cima Pozzo. The photos which go with this diary show steady improvement over earlier years and Hester clearly looked on photography as a hobby in itself; indeed she records that she had two photos accepted for Blackwells Alpine Calendar, and years later some of her photographs were used in some of Showell Styles' books.

In the last section of the diary, 'Armchair reflections', Hester concluded that she was unlikely to go on the MAM meet in 1951, not because she failed to enjoy the meets, but because it was scheduled for Austria and she fancied something bigger. She admitted that a smaller party would be more to her liking and while she was aware that other MAM members were doing harder things in the Alps she did not know any of them. She also wondered if she should save her money for a winter holiday instead. In domestic climbing she was staying in Glan Dena, the MAM's hut at Ogwen, at times, often climbing the standard classics with the likes of Cyril and Showell 'Pip' Styles. Pip remembers her as a pleasant companion and as a competent climber, but with little desire to lead, preferring to be a good second, which is probably just what she would have said about herself. Jack Grant, who was on the Dolomites Meet, also remembers her as a competent climber and good company.

There are no diaries for 1951 or 1952. The 1954 list gives the a traverse of Cir Mhor as the best day of 1951, during a holiday in Arran reached on the pillion of a motorbike with her good friend Tony Hughes, at that time also a member of the MAM, and a ski traverse of the Mulkerblatt in January as the best day of 1952. By now she had another drain on her purse; Archiebald the motorbike was long gone and now there was Belinda the motorcar.

1953
Belinda's Great Adventure

Belinda was a small, red, pre-war MG convertible, registration number CTC 684, part of the Preston Mobile Police Force until 1945. Hester bought the car in 1949, her first, and imbued Belinda with a life and character of its own, talking as though the car was a member of the party rather than just a means of transport. Belinda appears to have brought out a new and not inconsiderable talent in Hester, as the diary is full of skilful pen and crayon sketches, virtually all featuring Belinda in a variety of situations. A large part of the plan was to have a driving holiday with a non-climbing friend, Sally Jones, and most of the diary concerns what turned out to be quite an adventure on the roads. Among other things they broke both a spring and a half shaft!

They drove out through Belgium, down the Rhine and into Switzerland. Plan 'A' then involved a short stay in Zermatt, hoping to afford a guide for at least one major route; plan 'B' involved a visit to Lenk with the hope of some lesser climbs with Hans, all of it depending on the weather. Hester was a little worried about both of these as she had sprained an ankle badly shortly before setting out. In the event the weather was terrible; they visited Lenk but climbed nothing.

They went home by a circuitous route; in the village of Aigle above the Rhône Valley Hester gave a glimpse of a former activity of which there is no more information at all: ' ... more memories of Mlle Bard's choral auditions came to my mind, for we had sung in the village church here in my "conservatoire days".' They reached home via the Italian Lakes, Genoa, Monte Carlo and Lyon.

1954
Part 1: Belinda Goes Abroad Again!
Part 2: Putting the Clock Back Twenty Years

This diary is divided into two distinct halves, the first concerning the drive out to Zermatt and home again and the second, the climbing. This time the driving was less eventful but Hester had doubts whether Belinda, now 17 years old, would be good for future Continental trips. Interesting though this part is, it is not relevant to cover it further.

Hester's companion was Marjorie Garner of the MAM, a walker rather than a climber. The idea was that Hester would do some walks with or without Marjorie to get really fit and then engage a guide to do what was still number one on her list since her failure on it in 1936: the Rothorn by the Rothorngrat. The training went well; Plattenhörner, Hotäligratt, etc.

In Zermatt she had met Victor Biner again but he was booked up and so he introduced Hester to Walter Biner (no relation). They went up to the Rothorn Hut but in the morning the weather was doubtful and soon it was sleeting. They descended to Zermatt in heavy rain. 'I was thoroughly despondent. ... I was dreadfully disappointed in a way I seldom feel in England and it just can't be thrown off lightly.'

After a few days to allow some of the new snow to melt they stayed in the Schönbiel Hut '. . . and I must give Walter full marks for being the only guide I've known who does not snore!!'. They left the hut at 3am and had a splendid climb in cold, windy conditions getting to the top of the Dent Blanche in six and a half hours. 'I felt exquisitely happy.' The wind increased and they had quite a rough descent, but without mishap. The only minor difference of opinion occurred as Hester found she needed to eat little and often but was a slow eater, whereas Walter never seemed to eat at all. Then it was time to go home: 'Yes, it was a wonderful climax to a most enjoyable holiday. Thank you, Walter Biner, for making it such a wonderful day ... the happiest day for years and years.'

1955 - 1966
Part 1: Belinda's Last Trip Abroad
Part 2: From Sea Level to 14,219ft

As before, the account of the 1955 Alps trip to join the MAM meet in Saas Fee is in two parts. Hester travelled out with Isabel Boag; again an eventful trip with a broken spring and a cracked chassis on the way out, repaired in Laon. At this early point in the story there is a short break in the narrative and a note dated 1978 inserted. In this, Hester tells how, at that point in writing up the diary after the holiday, the urge to write died and that most of this diary was written up 23 years later from notes made at the time and kept, with the result that the rest of it is in note form rather than the usual extended narrative. Strange for such a dedicated diarist, but she explains that in 1955 she took up the violin, spent much time practising each day, soon becoming good enough to play in an orchestra and organise musical soirées in the school. However, in view of some remarks in her notes for the rest of the holiday there may have been more subtle influences on her feelings and motivations which became alarmingly obvious in 1956, more of which shortly.

While at Saas, in various MAM groupings she climbed the Mittaghorn, Portjengrat, Weissmies and much the best of all, the Nadelhorn. '. . . felt quite depressed by my poor performance. I can recall feeling uneasy. . . I wonder now if this was the first flicker of warning.' However she must have felt better later as they did the traverse of the Fluchthorn and the Strahlhorn to finish a trip marred yet again by the weather.

In September 1955, with her brother John, she drove to Aviemore, left Belinda in the Rothiemurchus Forest, went by train to Blair Atholl and then traversed Glen Tilt and the Lairig Ghru back to the car, overnighting in Inverey. This was written up in 1978, of course, and she adds: 'I am so thankful that I made the most of those days when my energy never seemed to flag ... I accumulated a store of the happiest memories that life can offer.'

The 1956 notes in this diary are subtitled 'Nature's Decision'. She had been spending more time at the violin and less in the hills and had been helping her family move from one vicarage to another so that when she joined a small group of MAM members in Chamonix, travelling out by train, she was unfit and felt tired, hoping the Alpine air would buck her up. However, it soon became apparent that something was going badly wrong; even walking up to Montenvers was difficult.

First they did the Aiguille de l'M: ' ... ghastly gully which nearly finished me.' Then up to the Requin Hut where she met Marcel Bozon. She had mixed feelings; she longed to climb with him again but was depressed that he would be disappointed at her poor performance. They traversed to Courmayeur via the Torino Hut and back again. Hester had considerable breathing problems and feared that she had tuberculosis: 'I wanted to curl up and just be left in the snow.'

They decided to move on to the Alpes Maritimes. In Grenoble disaster struck; she suffered a minor stroke which affected her speech and her right hand. She was taken to a doctor who told her that her heart was 'fini' and that she must never do anything in any way physical again. ' ... whenever I thought about what he'd said about my future my mind seemed to cloud over and go blank ... my mountaineering days would come to an abrupt end with more than half my dreams unrealised.' She records that she was set against her companions sending for her brother, but common sense prevailed, as a member of the party recalls that in the event John came out and escorted her home by train.

She seems to have made a full recovery from the stroke. Investigation showed that she had a damaged heart valve, the legacy of rheumatic fever as a child. With characteristic optimism and single-mindedness she threw herself into her music, but ' ... my love for the mountains is always there,' so in 1958 she visited Skye in Belinda's replacement, an MG TF rather over-romantically christened Candlelight. She walked up into Coire Lagan and then went up Sgurr na Banachdich ' ... the pinnacled Cuillin ridge which I bitterly regret never having climbed'.

In 1959 it was Lenk again. Hans Griessen was in a sanatorium with TB; he recovered but died later from leukaemia. With the guide Arnold Ludi she did her last Alpine peaks, a two-day traverse of the old favourites, the Wildhorn and the Wildstrubel. She saw Hans in the sanatorium; ' ... sad about Hans, who will always be my most cherished mountain companion'.

It was 'My Last Ambition: Zermatt Once Again' in 1960. She went on a number of walks, including to the Hörnli Hut: ' ... there I was in a trance gazing up at the source of the happiest day of my life, 6 Sept 1934.' But sadly ' ... an alien feeling that I didn't belong to this mountain world any more ... I was a stranger up there in this climbers' world ... I felt shy of so much as peeping inside the hut.' She also reached the Bétemps Hut, which meant crossing the Gorner Glacier solo: ' ... revelled in the feeling of crossing a real glacier again.'

Further trips followed, the Shetlands with ascents of Ben Loyal and Ben Klibreck on the way home, a tour of Ireland by car and pony trekking in Scotland but in 1965 the big event of the year was surgery on her damaged heart valve. In spring 1966 she paid her last visit to Lenk, 'my second home,' staying with Gretel Griessen and doing some walking and skiing with Arnold Ludi; later in the year she went pony trekking in Norway. It was now 10 years since the Grenoble setback; as she was within four years of retiring she moved out of her rooms at Rydal and bought a small stone house overlooking the Conwy Valley and with views of the Carneddau. 'A new challenge confronted me, and at last the wanderlust has died.' And there her diaries finish.

A small outhouse was converted into a music room with the walls covered with her photographs. She retired in 1970, gave up the violin and, unable to walk the Welsh hills as she wished, drove around the lanes in her MG, occasionally visiting her old friends at Rydal. In 1978 she was in hospital again with further stroke symptoms and while these seem not to have been too bad it is tempting to wonder if it was this which prompted her to get out the final diary, at that time barely started, and to finish off the tale of her exploits. The 1978 note has the feeling of a summing up and signing off. It finishes: 'My house and garden are a delight and I have settled down to a solitary but happy existence looking after them. I am reluctant to admit the onset of old age but something has to suffer and since I lost my original music friends I decided to let Rydal have my instruments now rather than posthumously – mountains and music are still my greatest source of pleasure – my only regret being the physical limitation which prevents my undertaking long hill walks in fine weather which I had envisaged myself enjoying for many more years to come.

August 1978
The worst summer weather I've ever known
The comment about the weather was probably added later as it is in different ink; she would never miss the chance of commenting on something or anything! The very last entry, written after she had finished all the updating, is characteristically headed: 'Concluding clap-trap'. It reads: 'So ends my mountain saga, brought abruptly to its end by that childhood illness which I've outlined on pages 60-61. I enjoyed more than one more trip abroad since 1956 but now at 68+, my health is governed by pills and my home and garden are my chief source of happiness and I must be grateful that I remained active until the 45th year of my life.'

She seems to have accepted her later years in a philosophical if rather solitary style with her house and garden, music, large collection of mountaineering books and photographs and of course, her memories; but the surest reminders of the days when she took part in what was in her own view that most wonderful of all activities must have been these diaries which she must have read often. If only she had been able to climb the Zinal Rothorn! She continued to buy mountaineering books until late in her life and never lost interest in current climbing issues.

The diaries are fascinating to read and, by their candour, a wonderful and valuable record of the climbing life and times of a rather remarkable person. She left an impact on many who knew her by her sheer energy and enthusiasm. Rydal maintains a small exhibition in her memory; her ice axe and rope, some of her books and a few excellent enlargements of her alpine photos. In the Rydal library are two more volumes of diaries; these are the diaries of the Rydal Hillwalkers which existed from 1947 to 1951. They certainly covered northern Snowdonia thoroughly, with some very long walks, often in winter conditions. There is a further volume entitled 'Index of Mountains'. This is a gazetteer of all the world's mountains in alphabetical order, country by country, with first ascent information, short essays on the climbing history of a few main peaks and occasional potted biographies of the main protagonists. The historical information suggests it was compiled in the late 1940s, obviously a labour of love and perhaps the first real attempt ever to assemble this information.

Hester died at home at the age of 81, on 29 July 1991. Her ashes were later scattered on a mountainside above the Conwy Valley. In one of the 1946 diaries she quoted G W Young's poem *Exile*. In her later years she may have dwelt upon one of the verses of this poem, which also forms a fitting epitaph:

> What if I live no more those kingly days?
> Their night sleeps with me still.
> I dream my feet upon the starry ways;
> My heart rests in the hill.
> I may not grudge the little left undone;
> I hold the heights, I keep the dreams I won.

ACKNOWLEDGEMENTS

Thanks are due to the following: Sheila and Tony Hughes of Windermere for their courtesy, for their recollections, for the original gift of the diaries and the separate gift of the final diary; Mr J N Barry, Bursar of Rydal Penrhos, for information and for allowing access to the memorial to Hester Norris and the diaries in the library; Jim Milledge and Tony Young, once of the Rydal Hillwalkers, for recollections; Barbara McLauchlan, Jack Grant and Pip Styles of the MAM for their recollections, Pip Styles also for the gift of the 1949 diary.

Issues

PETER GILLMAN

The Yeti Footprints

(Plate 52)

Peter Steele gave me a hard time in his biography of Eric Shipton, published in 1998. Nine years before, I had written an article which doubted the authenticity of the celebrated yeti footprint photographed by Shipton during the Everest reconnaissance trip of 1951. In short, I suggested that Shipton had carried out a hoax by fabricating the footprint. Steele dismissed my article, which appeared in the *Sunday Times Magazine*, as 'difficult to take seriously, being so full of scurrilous invective'. And he was particularly aggrieved by my 'churlish appraisal' of Shipton's character.

How neat, I thought. Rubbish your opponent in ad hominem terms and save yourself the trouble of scrutinising arguments set out in an extensively researched article of almost 4000 words. I supposed that in the literary world these things were likely to happen, a prediction fulfilled when an anonymous reviewer in the *Economist* damned *The Wildest Dream*, the biography of George Mallory which I wrote with my wife Leni, as 'adding little' to an understanding of Mallory. I was astonished that someone could be so glibly dismissive of the product of years of work, particularly when I learned the reviewer's identity and remembered that he had told me how much he enjoyed the book when we had supper after an Alpine Club meeting a month or so before.

As for Steele, we met and shook hands at the Banff Mountain Festival last November, where Leni and I were giving a presentation on *The Wildest Dream* which by then had won the Boardman Tasker prize. We agreed to a concordat whereby we could continue the debate over the Yeti footprint in a more restrained and academic manner but since I have never replied to Steele's accusations, I would still like to have my say. I would also like to respond to Michael Ward's article 'The Yeti Footprints: Myth and Reality' in the 1999 AJ, in which I am once again taken to task. I have to say that reading their arguments has only strengthened my belief that the crucial footprint was a hoax, particularly in view of the way both treat a vital item of fresh evidence.

First, let us look at Shipton's primary account of what he found. Shipton, it should be recalled, had led the Everest reconnaissance expedition to the top of the Khumbu Icefall, where the route into the Western Cwm was barred by a monstrous crevasse. Instead of heading directly home, Shipton diverted the expedition into exploring the Menlung region 30 miles west of Everest. It was an enterprise entirely in keeping with the man, a romantic and adventurous diversion that satisfied his love for lightweight ventures into the wild places of the planet. It could have caused a major international incident, for at one point Shipton led the party into Chinese-occupied Tibet, and had to bribe their way to freedom when they were detained by Tibetan guards.

It was on the afternoon of 9th November that Shipton came upon the footprints that were to cause such excitement and controversy. He, Mike Ward and Sen Tenzing had crossed the Menlung La at 19,960 feet and headed south-west down the Menlung Glacier. Half an hour later, they came upon some tracks in the snow. This is Shipton's account for *The Times*, published on 6th December:

> The tracks were mostly distorted by melting into oval impressions, slightly longer and a good deal broader than those made by our mountain boots. But here and there, where the snow covering the ice was thin, we came upon a well preserved impression of the creature's foot. It showed three 'toes' and a broad 'thumb' to the side. What was particularly interesting was that where the tracks crossed a crevasse one could see quite clearly where the creature had jumped and used its toes to secure purchase on the snow on the other side. We followed the tracks for more than a mile down the glacier before we got on to moraine-covered ice.

Shipton took four photographs. Two showed a line of tracks stretching across the snow, one with Ward standing beside them. Two were close-up shots of a single footprint, which had a prominent big toe and impressions of perhaps four neighbouring toes. To indicate the size of the footprints, estimated at around 12" by 6", Shipton included an ice axe in one of the photographs and Ward's boot in the other. On 7th December *The Times* published three of the photographs – two long-shots and one close-up – together with the dramatic headline: FOOTPRINTS OF THE "ABOMINABLE SNOWMAN".

The footprint attracted immediate attention. Until then, the existence of the yeti had been almost solely a matter of Himalaya folklore, embedded in the legends of the mountain kingdoms and supported only by second- or third-hand travellers' tales. Among zoologists and anthropologists there was an air of excitement, since the footprint displayed a range of novel characteristics.

From the impress it had left, the ball of the creature's foot appeared to be concave, whereas on any known creature of similar size, including primates and humans, the ball is convex. There was an enormous difference in size between the 'thumb' and the other 'toes', and a marked gap between the thumb and toes – features also hitherto unknown. And there were sharp indentations apparently left by the outer part of the heel and the inner part of the sole, leaving it hard to conceive what kind of creature could have left these marks simultaneously.

When the scientific world tried to suggest what kind of creature could have left the footprint, it came up with some imaginative proposals. The Belgian zoologist, Professor Bernard Heuvelmans, concluded that it had to be a cross between an ape and a bear. It followed that the footprint had been made by a creature with unique morphological features that had developed in isolation in the equivalent of a Galapagos Islands style enclave deep within the Himalaya. It also had characteristics shared with other creatures of controversy such as the Loch Ness Monster, never leaving any other signs of its existence, such as dung or carcasses; and allowing only occasional imperfect glimpses of itself, instead – as in the case of the Loch Ness Monster – of surfacing in all its glory in full public view.

An early sceptic was Ed Hillary, one of the two New Zealanders who took part in the 1951 reconnaissance. Hillary noticed that there were striking differences between the nature of the tracks in the two sets of photographs. The single footprint is clearly new and fresh, whereas those in the line of tracks are blurred and indistinct, almost certainly the result of thawing and refreezing over a period of several days. Hillary questioned Shipton on the issue several times but always found him evasive. 'Eric,' Hillary told me, 'tended to rather dodge giving too much of a reply.'

A second sceptic was the anthropologist John Napier, a professor of primate biology at London University, who went on to write *Bigfoot*, an enquiry into the existence of a range of creatures of dubious provenance, published in 1972. As well as being baffled by the unique characteristics of the single footprint, he too noticed marked differences between the two sets of prints. The footprint in the close-up shot is almost rectangular, with the addition of the toes. The footprints in the long-shot are oval and there are no signs of toes.

During his research, Napier was so puzzled that he questioned first Ward and then Shipton about the discrepancies. It was Ward who proposed a novel explanation: there had in fact been two entirely different sets of tracks. Shipton supported Ward's account, agreeing with Napier that those in the long-shot were probably made by a goat; it was only those in the close-up which emanated from the unknown creature, yeti or otherwise. Shipton blamed the original confusion on a sub-editor at *The Times*; Ward suggested that the negatives had been mixed up in the archives of the Mount Everest Foundation.

What was particularly striking about this explanation was that it contradicted all previous accounts. Shipton, in *The Times*, had described seeing just one set of tracks, and repeated this in his book *The Mount Everest Reconnaissance Expedition* (1952) and his autobiography, *Upon That Mountain* (1956). Ward too had related the one-track version in his own autobiography *In This Short Span*, published shortly before Napier's *Bigfoot*. Further confirmation of the one-track account is to be found in the diary of Bill Murray. On November 11, two days after the sighting by Shipton and Ward, Murray and Tom Bourdillon came upon the footprints, which Murray described as 'a long line of spoor along the line of Eric and Michael's track'. I discussed the whole episode with Murray, who died in 1996, and he was certain that there was just one set of tracks.

I wrote my article for the *Sunday Times* in collaboration with Audrey Salkeld, who had previously voiced her doubts about the footprint in *Mountain* magazine. We obtained the full version of the 'ice-axe' photograph – the version that is usually published has been cropped – and found that it contained the top half of a second footprint. Unlike the full footprint above it, it had only vague impressions of the smaller toes; and where you would expect a big toe to match the one in the main footprint, there was nothing at all. It was after pondering all the evasions and inconsistencies that we concluded that the most obvious explanation for the unique and anomalous single footprint was that it had been fabricated by Shipton. It would have been the work of moments to enhance one of the oval footprints by adding the 'toe-prints' by hand, particularly a hand wearing a woollen glove. The crisp indentations delineating the inner side of the print could have been made by Shipton's ice axe. Hillary agreed with us, saying that he could quite imagine Shipton 'tidying up' the footprint in such a way.

It was for my temerity in arguing that Shipton could have been mischievous enough to perpetrate such a hoax that Steele attacked me so vigorously. After our rapprochement at Banff, he recommended that I read the diary of Tom Bourdillon, which I had not seen when I wrote my article in 1989. Steele told me that Bourdillon too had seen the crucial tracks and assured me that his diary entry supported the case for their authenticity.

At the time of the Everest reconnaissance, Bourdillon, a government physicist, was 27. Two years later, he and Charles Evans had the first shot at the summit of Everest, and could well have succeeded had Evans' oxygen equipment not proved faulty. They reached the South Summit where, before turning back, Bourdillon took one of mountaineering's most poignant and iconic photographs, with Evans in the foreground looking up at the tantalising final unclimbed stretch of the summit ridge. Three years later, Bourdillon died in a fall in the Bernese Oberland.

Jennifer Bourdillon – Tom's widow – kindly showed me the original manuscript of the diary he had kept in 1951. The key passage, in which he describes coming upon the footprints on 11 November, reads as follows:

> Most interesting thing of the day was about a mile of tracks of Abominable Snowman. This is not a myth. The tracks were about 18" apart, and staggered, and the pads 10" x 8", probably walking on two legs. Eric and Michael has [*sic*] seen and photoed them some days before when they were fresh, & saw the detail and claws of the pads – further, impressions of front pads where the beast had jumped a crevasse and scrabbled on landing. Sen Tensing had been familiar with the tracks and said 'big hairy man'. He distinguished between two sorts, one yak eating – this was – but this could have been on grounds of size and age only . . .

Peter Steele, of course, had argued that Bourdillon's account supported his cause. I believe that it does nothing of the kind. Bourdillon and Murray clearly did see the main line of tracks. But in the sentence beginning 'Eric and Michael ... ', the syntax of Bourdillon's description makes it equally clear that he did not see the close-up prints, and was instead reporting the description given by Shipton and Ward.

When I looked again at how Steele had rendered this crucial text in his biography of Eric Shipton, I had a further surprise. This is Steele's version, which should be compared with the verbatim extract above:

> The Abominable Snowman is not a myth. There were about a mile of tracks set 18" apart and staggered. The pads were 8" x 10" and he probably walked on two legs. There were impressions of the front pads where the beast had jumped a crevasse and staggered on landing.

I was astonished by Steele's selective editing of this crucial passage, as it removed the phrasing which makes clear that Bourdillon was reporting the description given by Shipton and Ward, rather than having seen the key footprint for himself. Since Steele accused me of being 'scurrilous', I felt like applying the same adjective to him. Steele has since told me, however, that he felt 'very contrite' for having 'condensed' Bourdillon's account in such a way. He explained that he had been pressed for time when Jennifer Bourdillon showed him the diary but now agreed that he should have recorded the passage word for word.

In his *Alpine Journal* article, Michael Ward also invokes Bourdillon to support his case. Before considering how he does so, it is worth examining in detail how Ward's own accounts have varied over the years.

This is what Ward wrote on page 83 of *In This Short Span* (1972):

> We descended a glacier and in the late afternoon found some large footprints which Sen Tensing declared without hesitation belonged to the yeti. We could see these tracks continuing down the glacier for a long way and in certain places, where crevasses had been crossed, obvious claw marks showed where the animal had taken purchase on landing. A number of very clear prints were photographed, with my feet or ice-axe alongside for comparison. We followed the tracks for a short distance and then made our way off the glacier which we did not wish to follow.

There is one obvious inconsistency with Shipton's account. Ward refers to 'claw marks' left by the creature as it jumped across glaciers, whereas Shipton had described the creature as 'using its toes'. But otherwise, in describing just one set of tracks, Ward's account is in keeping with the published reports by Shipton and the diary entries made by Murray and Bourdillon, amplified to me by Jennifer Bourdillon earlier this year. Tom, she said, had always spoken of just one set of footprints: 'I'm sure Tom thought it was one creature which had left the footprints. Nothing else had crossed his mind.'

It was under questioning by John Napier that Ward first changed his story and adopted the two-track account. He stuck to that version when I interviewed him for my article for the *Sunday Times* in 1989, and he again elaborated the two-track account. When I asked him why he hadn't described seeing two tracks in *In This Short Span*, he said he thought he had. He then added an intriguing variant. When I asked him why Murray and Bourdillon described seeing only one set of tracks in their diaries, he speculated that the other track must have melted. This explanation certainly did not accord with the weather at the time, Murray especially remembering the 'intense cold' at night. Nor is it easy to see why one set of tracks should disappear entirely while the other remained almost intact.

In his *Alpine Journal* article, Ward at first persists with the two-track account, although with caveats, such as the use of the word 'seem'. He relates how, at 15-16,000ft (Murray said the height was 18,000ft) they 'came across a whole series of footprints in the snow. These seemed to be of two varieties, one rather indistinct leading to the surrounding snowfields, while the other had in places a markedly individual imprint etched in the two to four-inch snow covering on the top of hard nevé.'

Shipton, Ward relates, took two photographs of the 'indistinct' prints – those in the long-shots – and two of the 'most distinct and detailed prints' – the close-ups. Ward added that he and Shipton followed the tracks down the glacier and noted that where the creature had crossed a narrow crevasse it appeared to have left claw marks in the snow.

Like Steele, Ward invoked Bourdillon to support his case, saying that Bourdillon 'comments on the tracks which, by the time he saw them, had become deformed by sun and wind'. He and Murray 'followed them for some way down the Menlung Glacier'.

Bourdillon did not in fact say that the tracks had become deformed by the sun and wind. More important than this minor distortion, however, Ward has subtly changed his ground, forgetting his previous distinction between the two sets of tracks, which now appear to be one and the same. He thus leaves the impression that Bourdillon saw exactly what he and Shipton had seen, including the footprint with the toes in the close-up shot. Later in his article, Ward asserts, without qualification, that Bourdillon had 'confirmed their existence' – when Bourdillon, as we have seen from his diary, had done nothing of the kind.

Ward goes on to dismiss my argument that the footprints had been 'a hoax' and to insist that events had been exactly as he and Shipton had described – although without specifying which of the various descriptions this applies to. At the same time Ward abandons the explanation that the footprints were evidence of the yeti or some other hitherto unknown creature, and goes on to consider just how they could have been produced.

Ward's latest proposal is that the footprints were made by 'a local Tibetan with abnormally-shaped feet'. Ward cites various precedents from medical literature and his own experience as a doctor. These include feet whose toes have fused together; feet with deformed big toes at right-angles to the rest of the foot; 'club' or 'lobster' feet which have just two toes; or even feet exhibiting the well-known surgical condition *onycho griffosis* ('ram's horn nail'), where the nail of the big toe becomes deformed and curves under the toe.

By now, however, we are back to the two-track explanation once more, for Ward reasserts the distinction between the 'indistinct' tracks leading off the snowfield, and those with the 'markedly individual imprints'. But we are also in the realm of the utterly fanciful. Leaving aside for a moment whether there are one or two sets of tracks, consider what ensues from Ward's theories, namely that a bare-foot Tibetan with a rare deformity has randomly wandered to a height of at least 17,000 feet on the Menlung Glacier.

None of the deformities Ward proposes in fact accounts for the most striking curiosities about the footprint, such as the enormous difference in size between the big toe and the lesser toes; or the concave ball of the foot. In passing, it is worth noting that we have now parted company with the claw-marks which Ward had previously described. And we face yet another problem, which Ward ignores. Ward says that the wandering Tibetan suffered from deformed *feet*, an explanation that is presumably required since he has not suggested that the feet were not uniform. It appears therefore that the Tibetan's two feet were deformed in precisely the same way – for which the chances must be small.

Perhaps aware of this difficulty, Ward proposes yet another alternative scenario: that 'one footprint was superimposed upon another'. This might account for the single footprint in Shipton's photograph; but it will hardly explain any sequence of footprints, for which so many other explanations have been advanced – from the claw marks left where the creature landed in the snow, to the Tibetan with two identical deformed feet or excessively long toe-nails.

Ward nonetheless concludes that these explanations 'are as plausible as any that have been put forward so far'. Well, hardly. I have already advanced one simple explanation which accounts for every anomaly which Ward wrestles with – and which Steele deals with by ignoring them entirely.

Which brings us back to the question of Shipton's character. Was he capable of playing a practical joke in this way? Unthinkable, says Steele, and utterly out of character. But in the *Sunday Times* article, Audrey Salkeld and I cited several instances showing that Shipton did indeed like to indulge in jokes of exactly this kind.

In 1938, soon after he had returned from Everest, Shipton gave a lecture on the effects of altitude on the brain. He described an incident that supposedly occurred high on the North Face of Everest in 1924, when Noel Odell attempted to eat some rock samples he had taken out of his pocket in the mistaken belief that they were sandwiches. Odell supposed that his sandwiches must have become frozen and threw them away. Odell told Audrey that the story was 'complete nonsense' and that he had in fact presented the samples in question to the Natural History Museum. Shipton told a similarly fanciful story about finding women's clothing and a 'sex diary' when he and Charles Warren located the body of the doomed aviator Maurice Wilson in 1935. Shipton related how he and Warren had tactfully buried the clothing and diary to avoid embarrassing Wilson. But Warren told Audrey that all of this was utterly untrue.

A further motivation could lie in Shipton's edgy relationship with the idiosyncratic Bill Tilman, his former partner on Everest and another who delighted in spinning travellers' tales. In 1949 Tilman claimed that while climbing at around 18,000 feet near Kangchenjunga before the war, he had come upon a line of footprints 'which could not be explained away'. He speculated that they had been made by 'a new erect being', perhaps wearing 'a primitive form of snow shoe', and went on to argue that if fingerprints could hang a man, 'footprints may be allowed to establish the existence of [the yeti]'.

Perhaps this implicit challenge gave a further spur to Shipton's imagination. However, while all these stories reveal elements of mischief-making on Shipton's part, I concede that it is a more serious step to mislead your expedition colleagues in this way. Jennifer Bourdillon, taking her husband's part, found the suggestion troubling: 'It would have been so alien from anything Tom himself would have done that it would have disturbed him profoundly,' she told me. Bill Murray told me that although Shipton had 'a peculiar sense of humour', and might even have played an initial joke on his colleagues, it was inconceivable that he would 'carry it on like that'.

Ed Hillary, however, believed that Shipton was capable of doing precisely that. 'He definitely liked to take the mickey out of people,' Hillary told me. 'He might have tidied it [the footprint] up, made it look fresh and new and photographed it.' As for Shipton letting the story run, Hillary said: 'He would think that was quite a good joke.'

The debate thus comes down to the issue of Shipton's character, and whether he could have done such a thing. Since Hillary for one believes that is possible, I am proposing a scenario which fits Hillary's reading and acts as an alternative to Mike Ward's deformed Tibetan.

Under my scenario, this is what could have happened. When Shipton and Ward came upon the line of prints, Shipton – unknown to Ward – added the crucial embellishments to the single footprint. He called Ward's attention to it, and joined in speculation that they had found evidence of the yeti. When they met up with their colleagues, it was in fact Ward who talked most volubly about finding the footprint, with occasional backing from Shipton. Shipton duly embellished the story in his account for *The*

Times, which appeared the day after his return from Kathmandu. He was taken aback to discover the furore it had caused, and perhaps relieved when the Natural History Museum, which staged an exhibition based on the photographs, concluded that the tracks could have been made by a langur monkey. Even so, he was irrevocably stuck with his account, for any recantation would expose his earlier deceit.

And Ward? It should be recalled that in 1951 Shipton was the most revered figure of active British mountaineers, who had been on all four British Everest expeditions of the 1930s. Jennifer Bourdillon recalls that Tom 'thought very highly' of Shipton and was reluctant to hear a word against him. He was also fiercely loyal to Shipton, resigning from the 1953 expedition when Shipton was replaced as leader by Hunt, until Hunt persuaded him to change his mind as he was needed to oversee the oxygen equipment. As a young man – 25 in 1951 – Ward was another fervent admirer of Shipton, although he later viewed him in a more realistic light. Even so, by my scenario, if Ward ever succumbed to doubts about the footprint he suppressed them, weighing in instead with new explanations and justifications when he was required to substantiate Shipton's original account. He too passed the point of no return, unable or unwilling to recast the episode in a way which might prove damaging to Shipton's reputation, and committed to endorsing it whenever the question was raised.

As an investigative journalist, I have learned one lesson which may be relevant. No matter how implausible a set of alternative theories may appear, there has to be one which is true. The best rule of thumb is to select the explanation which is both the simplest and least implausible – which in this case brings us back to the hoax.

Ward insists there was no hoax, and he's sticking to his story. It's a good story too, and one which has given us all great fun. There is a clue that Shipton would have enjoyed the fun too, since he remarked in one of his accounts for *The Times* that the footprints 'seem to have aroused a certain amount of public excitement'.

A 1935 Yeti on the Rongbuk?

(Plate 51)

A local friend, Patsy Craven, was reading a review by Stephen Venables in the *Sunday Telegraph* of 6 August 2000 on Reinhold Messner's recent book *My Quest for the Yeti*, when she remembered that she had a postcard-size photograph of yeti footprints which on the reverse was pencilled 'Photo taken by Eric Shipton about 1935'. It had come from her stepfather Michael Roberts, who had married her mother in 1975, but died in 1977 in his 80s. He had commanded the 10th Gurkhas, retiring as a Brigadier. He had travelled widely in Nepal getting to know Eric Shipton quite well. He had been gassed in World War I, but attributed his recovery to breathing the high altitude Tibetan air. As he had a son also called Michael, currently in his 70s, living in Oxford, I wondered whether he was related to another Michael Roberts, the late Janet Adam Smith's first husband, but apparently not.

I tried to trace some reference to the footprints, but no book was ever written on the 1935 Everest Expedition led by Eric. Another friend Tony Astill is collecting material to remedy this deficiency. He tells me that no personal diary by Eric of the 1935 expedition has been recovered or is known to exist by the Royal Geographical Society, or by Peter Steele, his biographer, or by his son John. So we do not know precisely when or where Eric took this photograph (*Plate 51*) which shows a couple of rounded footprints together with the imprint of a booted foot and part of the shaft of an ice-axe stuck in the snow, for comparison. However, Tony reminded me of an incident in James Ramsay Ullman's biography of Tenzing recorded on page 93. When Tenzing was on his first Everest Expedition in 1935, his father, who was then living in Thame in Nepal, decided to cross the Nangpa La to visit his son in Rongbuk. Tenzing is describing various encounters with yetis and reports his father's story:

> One night he stayed alone at Camp One, on the glacier, while the rest of us were either at the base camp below or at the other camps higher up, and in the morning, when it was just starting to be light, he heard a whistling sound outside the tent. He raised the flap and looked out, and there was a creature a little way off, coming down the glacier from south to north. Again, of course, my father was frightened. He did not want to look at the yeti, but also he did not want just to hide in

the tent, for fear it would then come closer, or even enter. So he stayed where he was until it had gone on down the glacier and was out of sight, and then he came as fast as he could up to Camp Two, where I was at the time. When he arrived he embraced me and said, "I come all this way to see my son. And instead what I see is a yeti."

One may conjecture that Tenzing's father relayed his frightening experience to Eric Shipton, who then went out in search of the tracks and took this photograph.

However, when Michael Ward was with Shipton in the Menlung basin in 1951 and they came across the 'yeti' footprints which have since been well publicised in the book of the 1951 Everest Reconnaissance Expedition and elsewhere, one might have thought that Shipton would have mentioned this 1935 incident. However, Michael tells me that he made no special mention of it other than to say, 'I have in the past found many sets of these curious footprints and have tried to follow them, but have always lost them on the moraine or rocks at one side of the glacier.' Nor do Warren or Kempson mention the incident in their 1935 diaries.

RAYMOND B. HUEY

The Economics of Adventure

On the high cost of Himalayan climbing permits

In this range [the Himalayas] are found the highest mountains in the world . . . we can count by the hundred summits of more than 6,000 metres; peaks less than 7,000 metres high are generally marked scornfully on the English maps by mere numbers: and it seems as if mountains do not deserve to have a name unless they reach a height of 8000 metres.

Paul Bert, 1878
Barometric Pressure: Researches in Experimental Physiology

Himalayan climbing has always been expensive. In 1953, Charlie Houston, Bob Bates and six other Yanks travelled to Pakistan and attempted K2. They spent $30,958 on equipment, travel and porters, or $3,869 per climber. That may seem cheap; but when inflated to year 2000 dollars, the cost amounts to roughly $24,200 per climber. Many contemporary Himalayan expeditions, especially guided ones, are still expensive. Some mountaineers shell out $65,000 to join guided Everest expeditions. Faced with such high costs, mountaineers may sometimes conclude that bankrolling a Himalayan expedition may be as challenging as the climbing itself. But one climber's obstacle is another's inspiration: Bill Tilman and Reinhold Messner both advocated climbing in small teams in part to beat the high cost of large-scale expeditions. In fact, Messner estimated that a four-person expedition to an 8000-metre peak in Pakistan in 1983 would cost only $6,800 per person in year 2000 dollars – vastly cheaper than large-scale expeditions. Whether climbing in a large or small team, prospective Himalayan mountaineers must budget for a climbing permit or 'royalty' from the host country. Such royalties didn't exist when the Houston-Bates expedition went to Pakistan in 1953. They certainly do now; in fact, the royalty payable to the Nepalese for attempting Everest via the South Col is a stratospheric $70,000 for a team of up to seven climbers! Added to that are additional fees for satellite phones, walkie-talkies, cine-films, environmental deposits and so forth. (See Box at end of article.) And, of course, basic expedition expenses must still be met.

It isn't surprising that the royalty for Everest is expensive in this era of the fourteen 8000-metre peaks and the Seven Summits. After all, Everest is Numero Uno, the ultimate mountaineering goal, and so will always be in high demand. But how expensive are royalties for 'lesser' Himalayan peaks? They should cost less than Everest, but how much less? How does the amount of the royalty 'scale' relative to mountain height? Does any peak that is lower than Everest carry a proportionally lower royalty? Or do climbers pay a premium for access to the 8000m peaks, which they prize so highly? This would be apparent if, for example, the royalty were $500 for a 6000m peak, doubled to $1000 for a 7000m peak, but then quadrupled to $4000 for an 8000m peak. Finally, do mountaineers pay a special premium for access to virgin peaks or virgin routes?

Someone pondering these issues is likely to conjure up memories of a class in introductory economics. The unifying tenet of such courses is that the 'Law of Supply and Demand' governs the cost of all goods. Are Himalayan royalties subject to this law? Let's briefly review basic economic concepts of the marketplace. The Law of Supply and Demand holds that the price of a commodity, be it an apple or a piton, charged by producers will be adjusted higher or lower depending on the relationship between the supply of that commodity relative to the demand by consumers wishing to buy it. If a given commodity is rare but in high demand, the producer will naturally start to charge more and will get away with this because consumers will have to compete for that commodity. The resultant higher prices raise producer profits, encouraging producers to make more of the commodity; but this increase in supply then leads to a lowering in prices.

Thus commodity prices evolve toward an equilibrium. Such price stability is inevitably transient: producers can change the supply, new competitors might offer cheaper substitutes, or consumer preferences might change – witness the demise of the hob-nailed boot. Further, if prices are raised too much relative to demand, consumers might even choose not to buy at all. The price of oil is a familiar example. A few years before this article was written, there was a glut of oil on the world market and oil was cheap relative to historical levels. This was great for consumers, but bad for producers and also for stockholders of oil companies. In response, OPEC cut production; and the cost of oil inevitably increased.

Mountains aren't barrels of oil, so does The Law apply to Himalayan royalties? Well, the basic players seem roughly comparable: host countries – Nepal, China, Pakistan, India – are equivalent to producers, mountains are the supply , and climbers provide the demand. Even so, mountaineering and traditional 'markets' do differ in important ways. For instance, the number of mountains of different heights is fixed geologically; so the only ways in which 'producing' countries can adjust the supply is by opening or closing access to specific peaks, or by controlling the number of expeditions. Furthermore, climbers unwilling to pay the royalty fees for an 8000m peak cannot opt for a substitute peak elsewhere, since 8000m peaks occur only in the Himalaya. Even so, we can still think of mountains and mountaineers from a crude supply and demand perspective.

Supply

To predict how costs of royalties should change with mountain height, we must first determine how the supply or availability of peaks changes with altitude. Everyone knows, of course, that small peaks are common, that big peaks are rare, and that there can be only one tallest peak in the world. But at the risk of quantifying the obvious, let's look at the actual numbers for supply versus height.

Figure 1

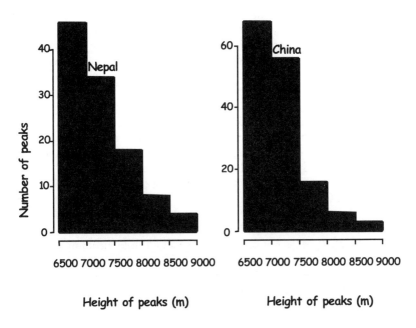

Figure 1 plots the number of peaks of different altitudes for Nepal and China. The Nepalese data are based on the number of peaks actually open to climbers as of spring 1999, whereas for China, the data are based on peaks above 6000 metres. (Information compiled by Jill Neate, in *Zhou Zheng* and Liu Zhenaki, in *Mountaineering in China*. Many of these peaks are not currently open.) As expected, the supply of peaks is inversely related to altitude – 6000m peaks are numerous, 7000m peaks are much less so, and 8000m peaks are decidedly rare.

Demand

Next, consider climber demand for specific peaks. The intrinsic value a climber places on a given mountain is highly subjective and necessarily somewhat idiosyncratic. Even so, climbers often place high value on peaks that are stunningly beautiful like Nanda Devi and Ama Dablam, or on those with a special history such as Nanga Parbat, K2 and Everest. Ease of access also increases demand. However, the most important determinant of value in the Himalaya seems to be altitude: bigger is better. Moreover, those few peaks that rise above 8000 metres – the 'eight-thousanders' – have epic value. Everest, of course, has the highest value of all. This special regard for 8000-metre peaks is hardly a late 20th century phenomenon, as Paul Bert's quote above attests. In any case, all else being equal, the bigger the peak, the bigger the demand.

However, two factors tend to decrease demand on the highest peaks, or on particular routes on the highest peaks, namely, the potential pool of mountaineers physically and technically capable of climbing them; demand should drop with an increase in altitude or in technical difficulty, although climber access to supplementary oxygen counteracts those trends. Assessment of demand can be made more objective by analysing the actual number of applications for permits to climb peaks of various altitudes. If climbers were to ignore height in selecting peaks to climb, then the number of permit applications per peak would be independent of the altitude of the peak. If, instead, climbers preferred big peaks, then the number of applications per peak should increase with peak size. Data for expedition permits granted by the Nepalese Government are available for 1994 and support expectations. Low-altitude peaks, between 6000 and 7999 metres, averaged far fewer than one permit per peak. The 8000-metre peaks averaged 3.7 permits, with Everest receiving eight permits, the maximum permitted in 1994. Interestingly, Ama Dablam (6812m) had the most permits with 17, undoubtedly reflecting its beauty, accessibility and the number of fixed ropes on its easiest route. For the spring 2000 season, the 8000-metre peaks in Nepal hosted more than 30 expeditions, of which more than half were for Everest, whereas all lower peaks (6500-7999m) had only 19 expeditions, with nine of these going to Ama Dablam.

Cost of Royalties

Given that big peaks are relatively rare (supply is low and fixed) but relatively prized by climbers (demand is high), The Law predicts that host countries will have adjusted fees so that the royalty increases with the altitude of peaks. In other words, bigger should be costlier. Moreover, the biggest and most highly prized peaks of all – the 8000-metre peaks – should be disproportionately costly.

That's the theory. What's the reality? I've compiled the costs of royalties for Pakistan (2001), China (1999), India (2001), and Nepal (2001). Comparing costs for different countries is complicated because the royalties are charged per expedition and host countries differ in the maximum number of climbers allowed per expedition. For example, royalties in China are currently based on expeditions with a maximum of 11 climbers, whereas the number is 12 in India, and seven in Nepal and Pakistan. So I've standardised royalties for each country to a cost per climber, assuming that an expedition has a full complement of climbers. For example, the royalty from Pakistan for K2 2001 is $12,000 per expedition, or $1714 per climber if the expedition has the full complement of seven climbers (but obviously more per climber if the expedition has fewer than seven climbers).

The range of royalties on a per-climber basis (from the cheapest to the most expensive) is 286 fold! At one extreme, the royalty for a Chinese peak smaller than 6000 metres is a bargain-basement rate of only $30 per climber. At the other extreme, the royalty for Everest via the South Col is a breath-taking $10,000 per climber. Let's examine each country separately to see whether and how royalties scale with the height of peaks.

Pakistan

Our expectation that bigger mountains are more expensive is clearly supported in Pakistan (Figure 2). For example, a royalty costs only $214 for peaks between 6000 and 7000 metres and $571 for peaks between 7501 and 8000 metres, but jumps to $1714 for K2. But are 8000m peaks disproportionately expensive, as would be predicted by The Law, because of their special value to mountaineers? This prediction can be checked by indirectly analysing cost data from the lower peaks and extrapolating to predict the royalty for the 8,000-metre peaks. If the actual 8000-metre royalty is higher than the predicted one, the expectation is supported.

Figure 2

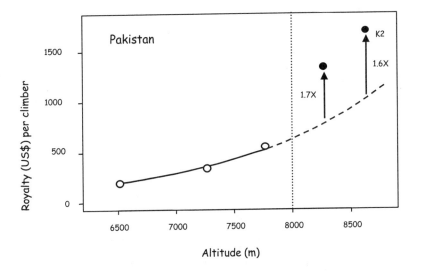

The approach involves first selecting only the peaks below 8000 metres (open circles), and then using a statistical procedure ('exponential regression', which assumes that the royalty increases in proportion to altitude) to quantify how the royalty changes with mountain height. The solid curve in Figure 2 shows that calculated regression for the lesser peaks. The dashed curve shows the predicted royalties for the 8000m peaks. The actual royalties for K2 and that for the other 8000m peaks (averaged) are shown as black dots.

The prediction holds. The actual royalty for K2 is about 1.6 times more expensive than predicted, and the royalty for other 8000m peaks is about 1.7 times more expensive than predicted. The Ministry of Tourism in Pakistan is seemingly well aware of the special attraction of 8000-metre peaks and charges accordingly! In Pakistan, bigger is more expensive, and the 8000-metre peaks are especially so.

Nepal

Royalty data for Nepal in 2001 are shown in Figure 3, and they also support the expectation that bigger is costlier. The royalty is only $214 per climber for a peak below 6501 metres, $571 for a peak between 7501 and 8000 metres, and a whopping $10,000 for Everest via the South Col.

Are the 8000-metre peaks disproportionately expensive in Nepal, as in Pakistan? Yes. Nepalese 8000m peaks (other than Everest) are 1.7 times more expensive than predicted. Everest via the South Col is 8-fold more expensive than expected!

Figure 3

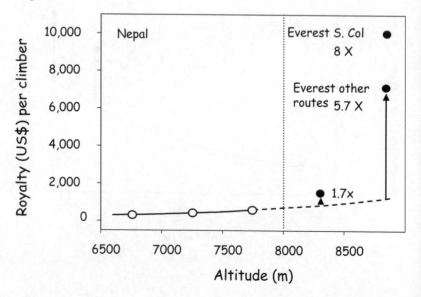

The Law even applies to different routes on Everest. The South Col route is of course in highest demand on Everest: other routes are either substantially more difficult and or more dangerous, and far less in demand. Not surprisingly, the royalty for the South Col route is 1.4 times more costly than that for an alternative route.

China

China has a complicated fee structure. A basic royalty in 1999 varied from only $30 per climber for peaks below 6000 metres to $455 per climber for Everest. However, the Chinese Tibetan Mountaineering Association has laid down special package costs for the three popular peaks: specifically, the cost per climber is $4300 for Everest, $3800 for Cho Oyu, and $3600 for Shisha Pangma (assuming 11 climbers per expedition). This CTMA fee covers not only the royalty, but numerous other fees as well, for example yak fees, transportation and liaison officer.

Figure 4

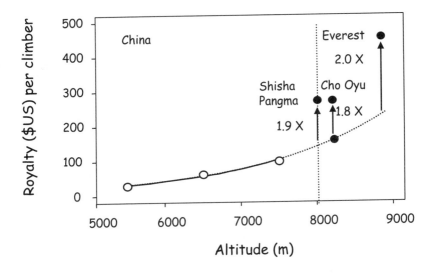

For present purposes I have analysed only the basic royalty, which increases with altitude of the peak (Figure 4). The popular peaks (Everest, Cho Oyu, Shisha Pangma) are 1.8 to 2.0 times more expensive than predicted. Curiously, royalties for the remaining 8,000 metres peaks of China (K2, Lhotse, Makalu, Gasherbrum I and II, Broad Peak) fall right on the predicted value and are thus not elevated. Thus China is exceptional in having elevated royalties only for certain 8000-metre peaks, but not for all. Why this is the case is not clear. The relatively low fee might be an incentive to attract climbers to China (see below), or perhaps it reflects the remoteness of access or route.

Sikkim

Indian Mountaineering Royalties are complex (www.indmount.com) and have changed recently. A base fee applies nationwide, but a supplemental fee is added in Sikkim. Also, special rates apply to peaks in the eastern Karakoram. Analyses here are on the cost to climb in Sikkim (IMF plus the Sikkim fee) and assume a full complement of 12 climbers per expedition.

Royalties in Sikkim – unlike those for other areas – increase only modestly with peak height, from $750 per climber for peaks below 6500m to $1000 for peaks above 8000m. However, Kangchenjunga (8586m) and its subsidiary summits are the only 8000-metre peaks in Sikkim, and Kangchenjunga is currently closed to climbing (Col. Ravinder Nath, personal communication). So it is unclear why Sikkim even lists a peak fee for peaks that can't be climbed. Prior to the ban on climbing on Kangchenjunga, Sikkim charged a special fee of $1667 for that peak, with the result that fees were elevated for the 8000m peaks, as in other areas.

Figure 5

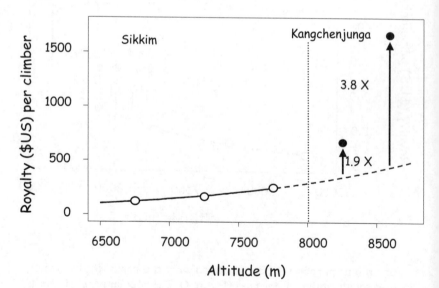

Competition between Countries

Comparing the above figures, one can easily see that cost of royalties differs rather strikingly between countries, even for the same peak. The royalty to climb Everest via Nepal costs $10,000 per climber, but only $454 via China (recall, however, that the CTMA imposes additional fees $4300 per climber). Similarly, climbing K2 via Pakistan costs $1714 per climber, but only $160 via China. Given such disparities, one might expect that climbers would flock to China, abandoning the traditional routes via Nepal and Pakistan. (Recall, of course, that the royalty is only a proportion of the total cost of an expedition, and extra fees and travel expenses might equalise total costs.)

To some extent this appears to be happening. Jon Krakauer (*Into Thin Air*) describes an incident involving the impact of changing Nepalese permit fees and regulations on Everest. In the autumn of 1993, the Ministry of Tourism in Nepal raised the permit fee to $50,000 for an expedition with five climbers, restricted the team size to a maximum of 12, and – perhaps most importantly – limited the number of expeditions to only four per season. At this time, China was charging only $15,000 per expedition and placed no restrictions either on the size or number of expeditions. As Krakauer notes: 'The flood of Everesters therefore shifted from Nepal to Tibet, leaving hundreds of Sherpas out of work. The ensuing hue and cry abruptly persuaded Nepal, in the spring of 1995, to cancel the four-expedition limit.'

Data on climbers who reached the summit of Everest via Nepal support Krakauer's conclusions. For the period 1988 to 1993, just before the restrictions were instituted, most summiters (84%) climbed via Nepal (averaging about 56 per year) rather than from Tibet (only about 11 per year). During the first year of the restrictions, the pattern remained similar: 45 summiters climbed via Nepal, and 6 climbed via Tibet. But after a lag of one year, patterns changed drastically: only 10 summiters climbed via Nepal, whereas 73 climbed via Tibet. Nepal was out; Tibet was in. When the Nepalese authorities removed restrictions on the number of expeditions, climber patterns rebounded back towards the norm: between 1996 and 1998 an average of 52 summiters per year climbed via Nepal, and 47 via Tibet. Note that the percentage of summiters who recently climbed from Nepal (53% for 1996-8) is still much lower than prior to 1994 (84%).* Whether this is due to the continuing disparity of permit fees, or simply an attempt by climbers to avoid crowds on the South Col route, or both, isn't clear. Although host countries adjust permit policies in an effort to compete for climbers, they are now beginning to co-operate in terms of permit fees and policies. In December 1998, delegates from mountaineering federations of the four Himalayan countries met to discuss common issues; and booking fees charged by all countries were circulated. From the summary of the discussions reported on the web (www.indmount.com/HIMCOM.html), the host countries were clearly in favour of exchanging information and ideas. Whether they form a high-altitude cartel remains to be seen.

* *Editor's note*: With the figures for 1999 and 2000 now available, the differential has widened. In 1999, 58% of 121 ascents were made from Nepal, while in 2000, 62% of 145 ascents were from Nepal.

The Costs of Climbing Virgin Peaks and Routes

We can extend our economic analyses by looking at another aspect of royalties. First ascents are highly prized in mountaineering, constituting a high demand. Host countries seem to appreciate this preference and charge extra for attempts on virgin peaks or even on virgin routes. In China, the cost of attempting a new route on a previously climbed peak is double that of attempting an existing route. Moreover, China adds a special fee for a virgin or newly opened peak: $1000 to $5000 per expedition for peaks between 6000 and 7000 metres; $1500 to $10,000 for peaks between 7000 and 8000 metres; and $27,000 to $41,000 for peaks greater than 8000 metres. (Given that all of main 8000m summits have long been climbed, the Chinese here are presumably referring to 'subsidiary' summits that top 8000m.) Until recently, the royalty for a virgin peak in Sikkim was double that of a climbed peak of the same height. However, this policy has apparently been discontinued (Col. Ravinder Nath, personal communication).

Historical Changes in Royalty Fees

Into Thin Air drew attention to the recent increases in royalties. In 1978, for example, the royalty for the South Col route on Everest was only about $1500 (around $4100 in year-2000 dollars) for an unlimited number of climbers, but is now $70,000 for a maximum of seven climbers. By any standards, and especially by those of climbers, this 17-fold increase above inflation in just over two decades is disconcerting. But is this dramatic increase for Everest typical of other peaks? How fast have royalties been increasing for the smaller peaks? Are they also increasing faster than inflation? Are fees for the biggest peaks increasing disproportionately fast, given the special attraction of the 8000m peaks?

For Nepal I've been able to obtain data from spring 1976 to the present. For Mount Everest on a per-climber basis (assuming seven climbers per expedition), the cost per climber has changed over that period from about $214 to $10,000 – nearly a 47-fold increase! This seems steep; however, the increase is really 'only' 15-fold, when the 1976 royalty is adjusted for inflation to year-2000 dollars ($681). Royalties for lesser peaks have also increased, but far less dramatically than for Everest. For non-Everest peaks above 8000m, the Nepalese royalty changed from about $200 per climber ($618 in current dollars) to $1428, a 2.3-fold increase when adjusted for inflation. For peaks between 7501 and 8000 metres, the royalty has changed from $171 per climber ($528 in current dollars) to $571, or only a 1.1-fold increase – thus barely changed at all.

In Nepal, therefore, the primary increase in royalties since 1976 has been on the 8000m peaks, especially Everest. For example, the royalty for an 8000m peak was only 1.2-fold higher than of a peak between 7501 and 8000 metres in 1976, but is currently 2.5-fold higher. The royalty for the South Col route on Everest was only 1.1-fold higher than that for other 8000m peaks in 1976, but is currently seven-fold higher. In other words, the relative royalty for 8000m peaks, especially that of Everest, have gone up far more than have the costs of lesser peaks. Demand comes at a cost.

My information from other countries is rather spotty. Reinhold Messner (*The Challenge*, 1977) reported that the royalty for his climb of Hidden Peak in Pakistan with Peter Habeler in 1975 was approximately $1000, or $500 per climber (about $1700 in current dollars). In 1983, he noted (*Mountain* 92:44-45) that the cost of a permit for a four-person expedition to an 8000-metre peak in Pakistan was £1000 (about $1620), or roughly $406 per climber ($790 in current dollars). In 2000, the rate per climber for a four-person expedition is $2375. For Pakistan, then, the increase per climber (1983 to 2000) is three-fold, after adjusting for inflation. For India between 1985 (cf *Mountain* 103:13) and 1999, permit costs have increased about 1.3 to 1.6-fold adjusted for inflation, depending on the height of the mountain. These crude analyses show that most royalties are increasing faster than inflation, but not hugely so. The real-dollar increase (excluding that for Everest, of course) over the past half century is roughly two to three-fold. What's driving this increase is, of course, the huge increase in climber-imposed demand (Figure 6).

For example, the number of climbers reaching the summit of Everest in 2000 was more than five times greater than in 1978, and in fact the number of summits in 2000 was greater than the total number of summits achieved for the years 1953 to 1981!

Figure 6

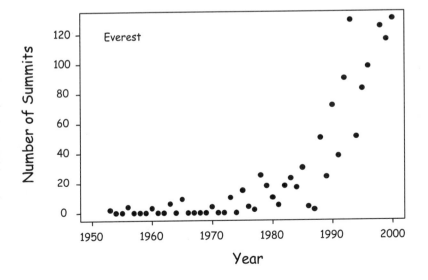

Subtle Impacts of Royalties

Royalties have an obvious impact on a climber's bank balance. But royalties may also influence climbers in more subtle ways. For example, because the royalty increases steeply with the size of the peak, budget-restricted climbers might choose to seek adventure on the many peaks smaller than 8,000 metres. The royalties of such peaks are less than the cost of a round-trip airfare from Europe or North America to Asia.

Royalties undoubtedly influence the size of expeditions. Recall that royalties are typically charged per expedition, not per climber. Thus, an alpine-style expedition to China with three climbers must pay the same basic royalty as an expedition of 11. Moreover, the CTMA special fee for Everest is $8,300 per climber for an expedition of one to three climbers, but only $3,300 per climber for expeditions of 28 to 30 climbers. Thus, a 'pay-by-the-expedition' policy in effect favors expeditions with a full complement of climbers and thus effectively discriminates against smaller ones (see also, L Griffin, High, June 1999, p. 3; and a private report by J McGuinness, http://www.project-himalaya.com/tourism-report/index.html).The motivation for a pay-by-the-expedition policy is probably economic as it directly increases revenues. Indeed, such policies may reflect intentional discrimination against small expeditions because they contribute relatively little to local economies. Galen Rowell (*In the Throne Room of the Gods*, p130, 1977) reports that Reinhold Messner, when applying for a permit to make an alpine-style attempt on Hidden Peak, was told by Pakistani officials that ". . . they would rather 'sell' the mountain to a large expedition that would employ more porters and bring more money into the country." Of course, climbers sometimes circumvent financial biases against small teams – two or more small teams can join forces to obtain a permit (and hence split the royalty and related fees), but then climb separately once on the mountain.

Royalty policies can also influence which peaks climbers attempt and when they attempt them. To achieve these ends, the Ministry of Tourism in Nepal has adopted rebates as incentives. For example, in an effort to increase economic growth in western Nepal, the Ministry can choose to give rebates to climbers attempting seldom-climbed peaks in this area. Similarly, rebates can be given to teams climbing outside the two traditional seasons (B. Shrestha, personal communication), presumably stabilizing the temporal input of foreign currency and jobs, and potentially reducing the seasonal impact on the mountains and peoples of Nepal.

Discounts can be available when expeditions include nationals from the home country, thereby encouraging local participation. In Pakistan, for instance, expeditions receive a 50% discount if half of the team is Pakistani. (In special cases the Tourism Division grants that discount if at least 1/3 the team is Pakistani.) Similarly, certain Nepalese peaks are completely closed to foreigners unless Nepalese climbers are included on the team.

Royalties could potentially be used to reduce crowding on popular routes. If, for example, the royalty is set relatively high for the standard route on a peak, climbers might be encouraged to try alternative routes, thereby allowing more expeditions on a given peak. To my knowledge, however, only Nepal has established route-specific royalties, and only on Everest.

Concluding Remarks

This article has outlined the economics of permits for the great Himalayan peaks. The basic patterns are clear: 1) pound for pound, bigger peaks (and especially the legendary 8,000-metre peaks) cost more, and 2) virgin peaks and virgin routes often cost more. These patterns are consistent with expectations based on economic fundamentals, namely, The Law of Supply and Demand. Big – or virgin – peaks cost more because they are rare, yet in high demand.

Although the economics of royalties seem understandable, the observation that royalties for the 8,000-metre peaks have been increasing much faster than inflation must be worrisome to mountaineers contemplating climbs in future years. Even so, mountaineers themselves are of course partially responsible for driving up royalties, simply because the increased number of mountaineers going to the Himalayan peaks (Figure 5) necessarily constitutes an increase in demand. One can't escape basic economics, even in thin air. The bottom line is that royalties are likely to continue to exist; and they will likely increase over the years. We can only hope that when mountaineers pay royalties to the governments of the Himalayan countries, they are thereby giving something back to the people who so graciously allow us to visit these special mountains that are their homes and sanctuaries. Ultimately, royalties constitute a reasonable mechanism to enable Himalayan host countries not merely to gain foreign currency, but also to control the impact that foreign climbers inevitably and increasingly place on a priceless environment and on unique cultures.

ACKNOWLEDGEMENTS

I thank C Bonington, G Brown, L Griffin, C Houston, J Karpoff, D Mazur, R Messner, Col Ravinder Nath, B Shrestha, and X Zheng for assistance or discussion and the J S Guggenheim Foundation for support.

What else is involved in obtaining permission to climb a Himalayan Peak?

The royalty is only one issue that climbers must deal with in obtaining permission to climb a Himalayan peak. Expeditions must of course apply for permission, pay various fees, as well as abide by mountaineering regulations and other laws and customs of the host country. Nepal is used here as an example. Complete details of regulations and procedures are given in a booklet *Some Provisions Relating to Mountain Tourism in Nepal*, obtainable from the Ministry of Tourism & Civil Aviation, Kathmandu. Note that different regulations can apply to so-called trekking peaks.

Application Procedures

An expedition must first submit an application requesting permission to climb a particular mountain and a particular route. A completed application includes miscellaneous details about the team (short biographical information and photographs of each member) plus descriptions of routes of access and of ascent, numbers of Nepalese workers who will be employed, etc. Each team must also submit an endorsement from their national mountaineering association. Applications should be submitted well in advance of a planned expedition, but no accompanying fee is required. A team must select a government-recognised trekking agency in Nepal to serve as a local liaison. Arrangements can be made after climbing permission is granted.

Assuming that the Ministry grants permission to an expedition, the leader is then required to pay the full royalty to the Ministry (in convertible foreign currency) within two months. Otherwise, permission is revoked.

Importation of Equipment

To obtain clearance to import food and equipment into Nepal, each expedition must submit a bill of lading or related documents to the Ministry. In addition, permission must be obtained to import communication equipment such as walkie-talkies, satellite links, as these are considered controlled articles. A new fee of US$5,000 is required for use of a satellite telephone. Special permission is required for filming (see below).

Miscellaneous Provisions

Each team will include one or more Liaison Officers, and will provide suitable provisions (equipment, clothing, food, medicine) for that Officer as well as for the Sirdar, guides, workers, etc. The team must also check the health not only of team members, but also of any workers (Liaison Officer, porters). Further, personal accident insurance must be provided for all Nepalese participants; and the expedition is responsible for compensation for death or injury of uninsured workers. All workers must have wills.

Expeditions are charged with not polluting the environment. Rules govern whether particular types of garbage should be incinerated, buried, recycled, or exported. A (refundable) environmental deposit is required, and ranges from $2000 for peaks below 8000 metres to $4000 for Mount Everest. Penalties for violating Nepalese regulations are severe. For example, anyone attempting to scale a peak without permission can be banned from entering Nepal for up to ten years. Moreover, the government can impose a fine equal to twice the royalty.

The expedition must file weekly status reports to the Ministry. At the end of the expedition, team members must contact the Ministry. Moreover, the team leader must submit reports (with photographs) of the expedition details (number of members, maximum altitude reached, accidents, and expenditures). Teams will also be interviewed by Miss Elizabeth Hawley. These reports and interviews serve as a valuable source of information not only for the Nepalese government, but also for mountaineering historians and ultimately future mountaineers.

Special Provisions for Filming
Expeditions making feature films are charged between $1000 and $1500, or between $100 and $500 for other types of film. A film may not be distributed until approved by a Nepalese embassy, and a free copy of the film must be sent to the Ministry of Communication. These figures should not be confused with traditional 'supply curves' in economics, which plot the quantity of a good that would be supplied at various prices. Consider a country that charges $1000 for an expedition of up to 10 climbers, or thus $100 per climber. If the country instead charges $100 on a per-climber basis, it would receive only $900 for a nine-climber expedition. So the host country either breaks even or does better with a per-expedition system (G. Brown, personal communication), unless many small-scale expeditions choose to climb elsewhere (see a private report by J. McGuinness, http://www.project-himalaya.com/tourism-report/summary-mountain-tourism.html).

Correspondence

Members are welcome to write to the Honorary Editor if they wish to comment on issues or omissions from the previous edition.

From Geoff Cohen

Being in exile in the US I only received my AJ 2000 today. As usual it's a wonderful read and I congratulate you on searching out good authors and some very moving photographs. It's because of that I found quite unaccountable the decision to include a single-photo advertisement opposite page 117. It jars completely with the preceding photos, and with the whole tone of the journal. I can't believe the fee from a single advert makes a significant difference to the journal's budget, so I'm at a loss to know why it was included.

Let the colour supplements intersperse pictures of disaster with adverts for ephemeral luxuries. I trust the AJ isn't going down this road. The British climbing magazines aren't as stuffed with adverts as the American ones but still provide a totally different reading experience to the AJ.

Editor's Note: Geoff Cohen is not the only member to complain about the reintroduction of advertisements. When the decision was taken to allow a very limited number of adverts, with a definite limit of two per issue, in a book of some 380 pages, only four companies with a longstanding and very real interest in mountaineering were approached. First Ascent, who import things that are actually useful, have generously supported the Journal since then. However, I share Geoff Cohen's dislike of commercial influences on climbing, and can assure readers that advertising will remain very limited, even though the income has offset rises in the Journal's overheads.

History

ROBERT ROAF

Sikkim, 1936

Climbing with Marco Pallis, Freddy Spencer Chapman and
others, in the Zemu Valley

(*Plates 46–50*)

By modern standards, our expedition in 1936 must appear to have been
a very amateur affair. Transport, clothing, equipment and local
conditions have all changed in the intervening years but it might interest
today's highly proficient climbers to read what it was like almost seventy
years ago. Marco Pallis was the leader and main organiser, obtaining the
necessary permits. He had extensive experience of guideless climbing in
the Alps; in 1933 he had led an expedition to the Himalaya during which
he had acquired an interest in Tibet and Buddhism and had since studied
both the language and the religion. He was a gifted musician and composer,
and a fine linguist.

Richard Nicholson was also a musician, an outstanding player of the
harpsichord. He had long been a climbing companion of Marco and was
equally experienced. Jake Cook was an experienced and skilled rock climber,
and had also climbed in the Alps; he was a very good companion, a reliable
photographer and an ornithologist. Freddy Chapman was extremely strong
and had immense powers of endurance. He had run up and down all the
major peaks in the Lake District within 24 hours and had been with an
expedition to Greenland. His experience on snow and ice was relatively
slight and he was in some ways a divided character. Although he could be
very charming and sociable, at heart he was solitary. He loved to pit his
strength against the challenge of physical forces. His fascinating book, *The
Jungle is Neutral*, illustrates this side of him.

I was the last member of the team, and relatively inexperienced as a
mountaineer. In addition to acting as a medical officer, I had learned Tibetan
from Marco. In those days, there were few medical facilities outside the
cities, but whenever we camped a mass of patients would come for
treatment. In 1933 Marco had been the interpreter, but he found that with
all his other responsibilities it was too much, so he wanted someone who
could deal with the patients without him. I was also responsible for medical
supplies and equipment.

We embarked at Liverpool on 22 February on the *SS Recorder*, a cargo
vessel with half a dozen cabins for passengers. The fare to Calcutta was
£14. Travel by cargo boat has many advantages and can be delightful. The
disadvantages were that they were slow and unpredictable, the food was

poor, only desalinated water was available and clothes and self had to be washed in salt water. In addition, there was the constant noise of the crew hammering away at the hull to knock off the rust. In spite of this, we enjoyed the trip. Our first stop was Port Said at the entrance to the Suez Canal. There I saw something which I found inexpressibly comic. A large P&O liner arrived full of 'mandarins' in dinner jackets with their wives in long evening gowns. They trooped into the Simon Artz emporium where they tried on a variety of pith helmets which gave them a bird-like appearance and reminded me of a play which I had just seen; it debunked their arrogance in a very humorous way.

We stopped again at Vizagapatan. Here we were told the ship would be delayed before continuing up the Hoogli, so Marco decided that he and I should go ahead to Calcutta by train. The train rattled through fertile agricultural land and I found this aspect of Indian life fascinating. In Calcutta we stayed a night at the Great Eastern Hotel where outside every room a servant sat cross-legged, presumably to protect his sahib or respond if anything was required. We took the night train to Siliguri, where the mountain railway to Darjeeling terminates. We took a taxi to Kalimpong and the ride through the lush vegetation was an eye-opener, not to mention the awe-inspiring hairpin bends with nothing to stop you if you left the road. Kalimpong was the main terminus for caravans of mules carrying wool from Tibet. It was also the site of the famous Dr Graham's homes for destitute boys. We stayed at the Himalayan Hotel which had originally been the family home of David Macdonald, who spoke Tibetan fluently and had previously been the Trade Agent at Gyantse.

The Himalayan Hotel was, and still is, an attractive two-storey building in the Tibetan style. Many well-known mountaineers had stayed there. David Macdonald was then an old man and the hotel was run very efficiently by his two daughters. (It is now managed by his grandson and his charming wife.) Everything was very pleasant except that then there was no plumbing. As was customary in India outside the cities, each bedroom had a small annexe containing a commode. This room had an outside door and twice a day a sweeper entered to empty it. Usually this worked well but, like many Europeans on a first visit to India, both Jake and I had enteritis and the system didn't cope too well with the extra load.

In Kalimpong there were many ethnic groups: Indian, Chinese, Tibetan, Nepali, Bhutanese and Sikkimese. It was known as the spy centre of Asia. Marco took the opportunity to master the local Tibetan dialect. He and I were invited by the Political Officer in Gangtok to visit him at the Residency. For a time, all went well. He showed us films of his sons playing football at Winchester where both he and I had once been scholars. Then he and Marco had a private talk and some time later Marco came out obviously very distressed. According to his account, he had been told that his request to enter Tibet could not be forwarded and that the Maharajah would not allow us to try either Simvu or Siniolchu. It looked as if our journey and preparations had been wasted. Later on we learned that the real reason behind these refusals was that the Officer was hoping to lead a high-level delegation to Lhasa later in the summer, and understandably did not want any other request to stand in the way of his own plans. At that time the project was still secret and could not be discussed with Marco. We returned to Kalimpong in low spirits, made worse by the fact that Marco had developed a severe upper respiratory infection. It was several weeks before he was fully fit.

In 1936 the previous Political Officer with whom Marco had corresponded, had recently died, and his replacement, Basil Gould, had been the agent at Gyantse. Marco was mistaken in thinking he had permission both to climb in Sikkim and to visit Tibet, because of Gould's plans to visit Lhasa and his reluctance to approve of anything that might undermine those plans. Theoretically, permission rested with the Maharajah, but occasionally the Political Officer needed to exercise his power to refuse permission on the Maharajah's behalf. He had a difficult balancing act which outsiders might not fully understand. It was a considerable relief when later on he changed his mind.

Marco had re-engaged from previous expeditions two porters from the once delightful village of Puh in Garhwal. Ishwar Singh was to act as Sirdar and his nephew Jun Singh as cook. We would need about twenty more porters. Richard and Freddy went to Darjeeling to choose them; they were helped by the secretary of the Himalayan Club who had the details of each man on a card: name, family, previous experience and thumb-print. The rate of pay was one rupee a day, roughly one shilling and sixpence. Three were easily chosen as having been on Everest; for the rest, hopefuls were told to run up a nearby hill and back, and the first 17 were selected.

The equipment they had to carry included the Grenfell cloth windproof jackets that each of us wore, thick and thin underwear and shirts, long grey flannel trousers and similar short trousers, a variety of thick and thin socks, light boots for trekking and heavier, better-insulated boots for climbing, gloves and mitts, two sleeping bags, crampons, an ice axe and skis. These were shorter than the usual alpine ones and there were detachable skins. For the porters who were going climbing there were windproof suits, boots and special short, wide skis with skins attached. For some inexplicable reason these were so constructed that the hairs pointed both fore and aft, so that the porters were denied the pleasure of gliding.

Apart from ropes, we did not have any special equipment such as pitons or ladders. Our food was mainly porridge, rice, dahl and chapatis. We had brought from England biscuits, tinned butter and tinned olives. While climbing, we lived almost entirely on pemmican. I had been responsible for medical supplies which were entirely in powder form in small tins with removable lids. Looking back, I think that I made a lot of poor choices and could have dispensed with many of them, but could have had more quinine tablets. I also had some dental forceps which were useful on occasion.

Although the bullock carts with the heavy luggage had not yet reached Gangtok, the mules which would carry the luggage as far as Lachen were there already, so we decided to go there too. Most of us stayed at the rest house but the Political Officer asked Richard and Freddy to stay at the Residence. Looking back, the reason was obvious. The Political Officer wanted a temporary personal assistant for his projected visit to Lhasa. From Freddy's curriculum Gould guessed that he might be suitable and wanted to assess him. Very soon, he decided to ask him if he was interested in going to Lhasa but emphasised that it was a very provisional offer and must not be mentioned. Naturally, Freddy agreed. I don't think that he realised that this might have disastrous consequences for Jake who would be left stranded without a climbing partner. In the end providence intervened and all was well.

The mules were not a good economic proposition. Our loads weighed 50lbs, a mule carries 150lbs but as the loads have to be equal on each side, each mule only carried two loads, or 100lbs. The load of 50lbs for each porter was also less than usual. We had the now familiar problem of porters being paid per day and their consequent reluctance to do proper stages. Marco was skilled in dealing with their tactics and often succeeded in making them laugh and carry on.

The first night we camped near Podang monastery. Sikkim is an exceptionally beautiful country. In a couple of days one can go from tropical to Arctic scenery and vegetation, and at frequent intervals there are spectacular views. From the balcony of the bungalow at Mangan, one could see the Teesta river at 2000ft and look, simultaneously, at the summit of Kangchenjunga at over 28,000ft. Other spectacular views were the receding and increasingly high forest-covered mountains, tier upon tier, with the green changing to blue and purple as the distance increased, and above and beyond one saw the snow-covered outline of the giants. It reminded me of Moses looking at the promised land and certainly conveyed a spiritual message.

The main problem was leeches, the voracious blood-suckers dropping onto our heads from trees, or getting inside our boots. The first we knew of them would be our heads dripping with blood or our boots filled with it.

After a few days we reached Lachen at 10,000ft. It was a charming little village, situated on a gentle slope. In order to get there we had to cross the Teesta by a swaying rope-bridge. No problem for the porters, but disconcerting for us. There was a small monastery whose head was a saintly *tulku* who had previously spent several years in solitary prayer. Marco had several sessions with him. The *tulku* conducted, at our request, a blessing ceremony for us and the porters, during which we were each given a pill of unknown content.

The mules had to return to Gangtok, so we needed to recruit about thirty local porters for the journey up the Zemu glacier. Lachen was strategically situated at the junction of a number of trade routes and there had previously been many demands for porters. Negotiations were conducted through their headman. He and the porters were expert at them and insisted on a high price. The same headman consulted me, complaining that when he drank too much brandy his eyes watered. He added that he had previously consulted an English doctor who had made the foolish suggestion that he should drink less brandy. He hoped that I was not equally silly. While at Lachen, a wedding took place. The bride and bridegroom, dressed in rich silk and flanked by near-relatives, sat in a row backed by an ornate brocade screen. The rest of the village watched the proceedings from a short distance away.

After a few days' rest, we set up off the Zemu river towards the glacier and the green lake. The snow was thick and it was hard work. Freddy went ahead to make a trail for the porters and paid for his efforts with a severe attack of altitude sickness. He recovered the following day, with rest. The vegetation was now mostly conifers and giant rhododendrons. There was no defined path and at intervals we came to small rivers whose bridges had been destroyed by snowfall in the winter. The porters cut down a tree trunk and crossed fearlessly although carrying heavy loads. It would have been a very serious accident if one had slipped and we were much more cautious. As expected, the men from Lachen gave continuous trouble, sitting down and saying that there was no possible camping place for several miles. Marco managed them very well, anticipating what they would do and jollying the more amenable to go a bit further; then the rest would follow.

After a couple of days we decided to make our base camp just short of the green lake and on the northern side of the valley. To the south there were magnificent views of Siniolchu and Simvu; to the west the five great peaks of Kangchenjunga towered above the rest. Although warm in the daytime, it was still very cold at night. We made a number of preliminary climbs. Marco and Freddy crossed the glacier to make a reconnaissance of approaches to Simvu. Richard, Jake and I set out to climb the Lagerburg (18,977ft). After about two hours, I felt that my poor alpine technique was holding them back and stupidly suggested that I would stop and they should go on without me. Foolishly they agreed.

At that time, the sun was shining and it was warm. Within half an hour the weather changed, mist descended and I became cold. Worse, they had not returned by the agreed hour. One hour, two hours passed. I became panicky. Had they had an accident? Worse still, had they come down and passed me in the mist? It was doubtful if I could safely manage the very steep snow slope by which we had ascended, roped. Even if I succeeded, would their lives be endangered if they spent several hours looking for me? In the end, they arrived back. They had climbed their peak, but found that it had previously been climbed by the Bavarian team which had tried to climb Kangchenjunga. It was dark before we reached base camp but there had been no accidents and I had learned an important lesson. Never be by yourself on a mountain.

Meantime, Marco and Freddy had been reconnoitring the base of Simvu and decided that, if it was possible to climb onto the north-west ridge, which appeared to lead to the summit, there was a good chance of success. When we had all returned to base camp, there were two important letters. The Political Officer had written to Freddy confirming his appointment and asking him to come to Gangtok as soon as possible. He had also written to Marco asking him to release Freddy. This could have been awkward. Although there was no question of a legally-binding contract, Marco had provided most of the finance. Our individual contributions would not have covered the total costs of the expedition. I felt that there was an implied bond of loyalty to the welfare of the other members and if Freddy went, Jake would be left without a climbing companion. Marco solved this problem with magnanimity. He decided that Richard would join Jake for post-monsoon climbing in the Lhonak region while he and I would hope to go to Tibet. Outwardly, there was harmony. I do not know what Marco really thought. Possibly, he was slightly relieved.

After a couple of days' rest, we crossed the glacier and set out for the first camp, together with three porters. The lower slopes of Simvu were covered with snow. On our skis we made good progress; skiing was far less tiring than plunging through thigh-deep snow. We also made a good firm path which the porters could follow on their short skis. Making kick-turns on a steep slope at 19,000ft was exhausting. After two days we established an advanced camp on the Upper Simvu saddle. These two days were most delightful but the nights were a different matter. When the sun went, one had to erect a tent quickly and creep into it. I was in a small bivouac tent in which I could not sit up. Even wearing all my clothes and in two sleeping bags I was still cold. The only insulation from the underlying ice and snow were the climbing ropes. There was also the problem of boots, which usually froze in bizarre shapes and became very hard to put on. Marco had wisely forbidden the use of a primus in the porter's tent since the fire risk was too great. As a result we cooked for them; a curious reversal of roles.

In spite of the night-miseries with 12 hours of darkness, Freddy and I enjoyed some recreational skiing at 20,000ft. Clearly by now we were well acclimatised. I also had a very curious experience. Standing on the Simvu saddle and looking south-west and down, all one could see was mist. Yet I had the overwhelming impression that I could see through the mist and perceive the teeming multitude of the plains, and simultaneously knew that in some mysterious way I would be linked with them in the future. And so it happened, from 1952 to 1998.

The climbing party found a steep ice face which appeared to lead to the crest of the ridge. Marco skilfully, if slowly, cut steps in the ice. He told me later that this was a very exhilarating experience. Finally, he reached firm snow in which he could fix his ice axe, attach a rope and thus let the others come up onto the ridge. Naturally, they were optimistic, but half an hour later they found that the ridge was broken by a wide and deep crevasse which extended down each side of it. With their limited resources they had to admit defeat. It is interesting that climbing in Sikkim was far harder than their previous climbs in the Spiti valley. Spiti is a very dry area, with virtually no rain and very little snow. As a result, the stages up to the advanced camp were relatively easy. Rimo Pargyal, which they climbed in 1933, is roughly the same height as Simvu at 22,000ft. In the Zemu valley we had constant mist and snow, even in the non-monsoon period. We met snow and ice at low altitude and the snow was often unstable. Setting up depots and advanced camps was much harder here than in the Spiti valley.

My job was to return to base camp with the porters, taking with us all the surplus luggage and equipment apart from tents and sleeping bags for the returning climbers. Skiing down fairly steep snow slopes was exciting, though I must admit that I was unbalanced by my heavy rucksack and fell frequently.

On my return to camp, I was faced with an unforeseen crisis. There had always been some friction between the Darjeeling porters and the two Garhwalis. They tolerated Ishwar Singh because he was older, but hated Jun Singh who was younger than many of them, yet claimed to be superior. While we were away, a number of the porters conspired, and persuaded the rest, that we were certain to be killed on the mountain and that then they could kill Jun Singh and divide our possessions among themselves. When I returned alone this convinced them that the others had been killed. My Tibetan was not good enough to sort this out and it was clear that things might be awkward. Fortunately, providence intervened. We saw coming up the valley one of the porters whom we had discharged after base camp was established. He told us that two sahibs – army officers – had been intending to climb in the area but one of them had been taken seriously ill and was being carried down to Gangtok. The other, Lt Harrison, would arrive soon. His presence was a double blessing since he helped to calm things down and also provide Jake with a partner to climb in the Lhonak valley which they did with some success.

The day after the climbers returned, we started to clear the camp. This is inevitably a sad business but it was important not to leave any rubbish. Some articles were given to the porters on a lucky dip basis. Freddy had at once left for Gangtok, the rest of us with Lt Harrison trekked to Lachen. The countryside had been transformed. Instead of snow, there were wild flowers. I have never ceased to be amazed at the way flower buds can form under the snow so that once the snow melts a fully formed flower emerges. At Lachen, Jake and Harrison departed for the Lhonak valley and achieved some excellent climbing. The abbot of Lachen had left for his summer retreat at Thangu, a small hamlet some miles north of Lachen and not far from the Tibetan border. Marco wanted to have another lesson from him, so we trekked up to Thangu. On the way we met many Tibetans mostly returning from pilgrimages to the holy Buddhist sites in India. I was struck by their stoicism. Several had malaria but I only had enough quinine for palliation. Indeed, even if I had had plenty it is doubtful if they would have followed the instructions for a long cure. Two men had advanced heart failure –

swollen legs and abdomens, congested lungs and so on – but in spite of this they battled on slowly even though a 12,000ft pass had to be crossed. Their overwhelming desire was to return to Tibet to die.

At Thangu we witnessed a remarkable ceremony. In Tibet and Ladakh, most villages are approached via a mani wall, the broad structure made of stones which are inscribed with the traditional prayer – *Om mani padme, hum.* At Thangu a new wall had just been built by an itinerant Tibetan, who possessed only the clothes he wore, an eating bowl and the tools of his trade. He spent his life travelling from village to village, building mani walls. The only reward he received was his food while he was working; a remarkable example of apostolic poverty combined with usefulness. The Abbot, arriving on a white mule, conducted a moving ceremony. Afterwards he asked Marco why he climbed mountains. Marco said that it was for peace and solitude. The Abbot rebuked him: 'You should be able to find those in yourself without artificial aids'.

The return trek to Kalimpong was unpleasant, the monsoon being in full spate. We were never dry, and the leeches were more active than ever.

ANDERS LUNDAHL

Strandåtind

Climbing in Arctic Norway

(Plates 21–25)

In the summer of 1732, Carl von Linné, then only 25 years old, undertook his famous journey through Lapland. By the middle of July he had reached the Norwegian coast at Sørfold (*see map*) where he went ashore by boat at Rørstad. His host was the Reverend Johan Rask, but Linné is most fascinated by 'the daughter of the house, Sara, 18 years old, extraordinarily beautiful'.

For a couple of fine summer days Linné lives a life free of care in the old northern Norwegian vicarage. Around him a defiant alpine landscape rises up out of the deeply-carved arms of the fjords: Husbyviktind, Skeistind, Strandåtind and all the others. In Linné's day there were some thirty families residing here, reduced by 1960 to thirteen, and in 1980 I visited the last permanent household: three grey-headed siblings who treated me to cold cuts of salmon, and proudly showed off the remarkable church with its twelfth-century crucifix.

Another famous scientist, the geologist Leopold von Buch, spent 1806-1808 in Scandinavia. He visited Kjerringøy in Sørfold in 1807 and remarked of Strandåtind 'that its high mountain ridge is so sharp that it barely offers a resting place for a bird, and reminds one of the most impossible peaks in the Habcherental by the Brientzersee'. (*Reise durch Norwegen und Lappland*, 1810).

In 1851 Kjerringøy was again visited by a prominent scholar, the Scottish glaciologist James Forbes. In his excellent book *Norway and its Glaciers* (1853) he depicted the Strandåtind massif magnificently. 'A few miles more brought us to a scene of desolate grandeur, rendered more striking by the contrast. The headland which divides the north and south Folden fjords may vie with the Aiguilles of Mont Blanc in the fantastic singularity of its forms. I have nowhere seen summits more perfectly acuminated.' (See the lithographic view in *Norway and its Glaciers* by James Forbes, page 58, 1853.)

Unclimbable or not? The first to raise the question in earnest was the pioneer Danish climber Carl Hall (1848-1908). Hall was the son of the famous statesman Carl Christian Hall, Denmark's prime minister from 1858 to 1863. Between 1880 and 1900 Carl Hall made no fewer than 50 first ascents of Norwegian summits. On 21 August 1889 he made an attempt on Strandåtind, reaching the top of the western low peak and getting up to an insurmountable 15-metre step in the col between the peaks – 'Halls hammare' [The Hall Step]. In his diary Hall remarked that the step is 'absolutely impossible without a 30 or 40-foot ladder'. With his faithful companion Mathias Soggemoen he also made an attempt on the NE Ridge, but had to give up at about halfway. When they got down the renowned merchant Erasmus Benedikt Zahl held a lavish farewell party for the gallant pair. 'I, Zahl of Kjerringøy, ask all those present to bear witness to my promise that if a Norwegian is the first to climb Strandåtind, I will give him a thousand crowns, cash on the table. A man is as good as his word!' But Hall never returned to Nordland, and Zahl himself passed away in 1900. Prior to that he had generously provided the promising writer Knut Hamsun, who had sought a travel grant from the master of Kjerringøy, with both economic and literary support. The character Mack who figures in the works *Pan*, *Benoni* and *Rosa* is none other than Zahl himself. Hamsun has borrowed the settings and gallery of characters for several of his books from his stay at 'Sirilund' – the Kjerringøy trading-post.

On 29 July 1912 the new master of the Kjerringøy trading-post, Gerhard Kristiansen, welcomed a group of travelling climbers comprising Carl Wilhelm Rubenson, Ferdinand Schjelderup, Harald Jentoft and William Cecil Slingsby. Rubenson and Schjelderup were founding members of Norsk Tindeklub – the Norwegian Alpine Club – in 1908. Slingsby, the father of Norwegian alpine sports, was quickly made the club's first Honorary Member. The year before, Rubenson had set a new world height record on Kabru at 7280 metres.

The following day a 'reconnaissance' of the peak was on the programme. The Norwegian trio were soon squatting below the vertical step. There is no easy way past it, the walls fall away into the abyss on both sides. Rubenson, as the birthday boy, was given the honour of leading. It was a victory for courage and determination. Thirty-six years later he admits: 'I don't recall anything about hand or footholds on the last part; I just scrabbled and dragged myself up in a wild panic.' The expedition took all of 27 hours; they reached the top, but it was a drowsy band that stumbled into the courtyard the next morning.

The broad-minded Rubenson refused to approve Schjelderup's judgement in the printed account in the Norwegian Tourist Society's Journal of 1913 that 'Strandåtind's first step will be a hard nut to crack for most others'. A new text had to be glued into all 5000 copies. 'The Step,' it now read, 'will be a hard nut to crack even for most others.' That Rubenson's efforts, both here and elsewhere, were on a level with the top European standard of the time is indisputable: The Hall Step is still graded 5 minus (VS) today.

Ten days later the same team, plus the 63-year-old Slingsby, was ready to tackle the North Ridge. The gusts of a storm almost lifted them up the very exposed ridge. A gloomy and overhanging chimney – *Jentoft's Chimney* – constituted the climax of the ascent. On the summit Slingsby was able to celebrate the 40th anniversary of his campaigns amongst Norwegian peaks.

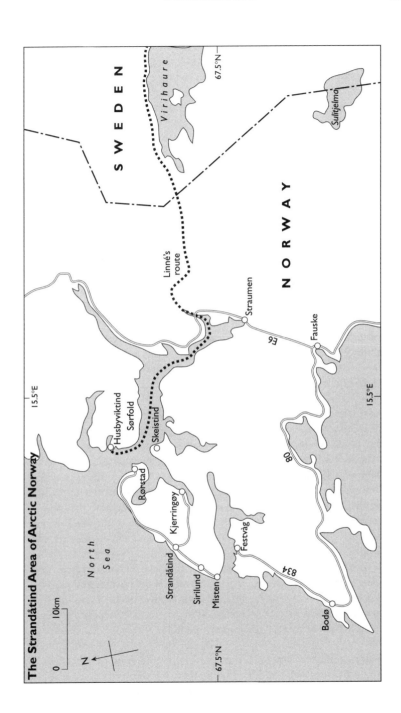

Nowadays the North Ridge is possibly the most climbed route, and forms the natural descent route with several fixed abseil anchors.

In 1924 Ferdinand Schjelderup returned to Strandåtind, and together with Ketil Motzfeldt and Fridtjof Lorentzen made the first continuous traverse of the peak from west to east: one of Norway's finest alpine excursions. Schjelderup was the most enthusiastic and active Norwegian mountaineer of his time. During his most ambitious period, up to 1924, he accomplished some 27 first ascents. It wasn't until 1955 that he hung up his climbing boots for good.

Arne Naess, still going strong and rightly dubbed 'the father of modern big wall climbing in Scandinavia', was particularly active in Arctic Norway during the years 1935 to 1937. His magnificent route on the South Buttress of Stetind did not receive a second ascent until 1966. It is felt that Naess's creation from 1935 outdoes another of the great granite climbs of the thirties: the North-East Face of the Piz Badile. In 1936 Naess visited Kjerringøy with his female climbing partner, Else Hertzberg, and they made the first ascent of the South-East Ridge of Strandåtind. The route is actually a little easier than the climbs done in 1912, but longer and more sustained.

The following year the mountain was visited by a British team from Manchester's Rucksack Club led by Harry Spilsbury. Spilsbury climbed in the Norwegian mountains for six seasons, including four summers in Lofoten. Spilsbury tells of his experiences in the north in a witty article written for the Norwegian Alpine Club's 50th jubilee book in 1958. Let's hear what he has to say about The Hall Step on Strandåtind:

> The rest of us approached the 20-metre wall, almost vertical, which barred the approach to the main peak. My second ensconced himself behind a large block, while I started to move diagonally upward to the right on a flake which seemed to protrude a bare 5cm from the mass of the mountain. There was virtually nothing for the hands; it was one thing to stand motionless on the flake, but quite another to move upward, and my second had to lift my rear foot to enable me to change my weight to the other. I was reminded of a Norwegian climber's description of the place as one where a well-directed push with a straw would send a man dangling into eternity. Cautiously I edged upwards and reached a crack where I found the first real handhold, and a piton. Here the flake had broken away, and a long step had to be made. I continued diagonally upward and reached a corner, where I found the most awkward move of all. I had to use a knee, but managed to surmount the difficulty, and soon reached a stance where I could belay and bring up my second.

Spilsbury confesses, however, that the senior members of the team, two unnamed 64-year-olds, had at least as hard a battle with their task – the first descent of the vast slabs on the south side of the mountain. 'When we reached the boat, we rather derided the senior members' stories of huge boiler-plates and other difficulties which they had encountered and overcome on their route.'

More recently the question arose of whether the vertical walls from the south and the north offered any possibilities. 'The walls are indeed terrible,' wrote Slingsby in his classic book on Norway, 'that of the higher being fully 2,000 feet of smooth rock, but the lines of the mountain are exceedingly beautiful' – a viewpoint that was agreed with as recently as last summer by an environmental expert from the Norwegian State Administration who proclaimed that Strandåtind is Norway's most perfect mountain.

Some attempts to climb the fine direct line on the South Face in the early 1970s came to a halt after only one pitch. The wide crack rapidly steepens to overhanging, and the sparsity of protection possibilities is hardly encouraging. Nonetheless, in 1985 Eva Selin and Anders Lundahl managed to overcome this obvious *direttissima*, which in its lower part offers exposed and committing grade 7 climbing. The upper part is considerably more accommodating and includes unique chimneying in some fantastic positions. With a height of 500 metres, the wall is one of the more imposing in northern Norway.

The North Face fell in 1988 to the same team; an elegant crack system with varied climbing on rough granite. Here the height of the wall is a little less, not quite 300 metres. Moreover the approach march is pleasant, since you follow a well-trampled path from Laater to the little lake at 270 metres above sea level, and from there, still on a track, you continue up to the pass at 500 metres, where you are standing in front of the almost kilometre-long northern facade of the mountain. You can comfortably reach this point in an hour and a half carrying a pack. There is water, of course, but not so many camping spots. Incidentally a couple of Bodö climbers attempted the north face a couple of years after the first ascent in the belief that they were first. They backed off the top section, and one can only hope that they didn't leave any bolts behind, as has been done on *Unnarennet*, a route which was free-climbed in 1992.

In 1990 attention turned once again to the southern side of the peak, where a couple of shorter new routes were put up at the left-hand end of the wall. *Landsstrykere* follows the obvious left-hand chimney and crack, and contains rather pleasant climbing in fairly wide formations. *Mysterier* starts further left again, directly below a massive roof. One follows cracks to the right of the roof, where excellent hand-jams prove useful. The crux pitch is strenuous, the rest is very entertaining. The approach to these routes follows the juniper and moss-clad slabs of the southern flank, and is not recommended in wet or misty weather.

At the end of the '90s the north face once again became the focus of attention. Torgeir Kjus and Björn Arntzen put up four routes of sheer aid. Among other things they had to contend with awkward cleaning in overgrown cracks. All of these lines, however, seemed ideally suited for pure free climbing, as was proved true last summer.

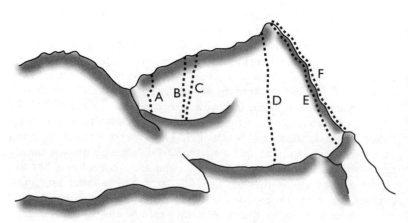

Strandåtind from the South

A   *Mysterier*   D   *Direttissima*
B   *Landsstrykere*   E   South Buttress
C   *Sult*   F   South-East Buttress

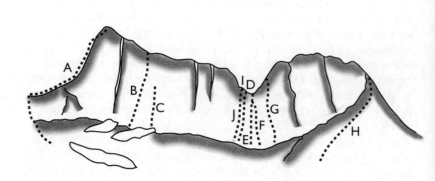

Strandåtind from the North

A   North Ridge   F   *Cuculus Noroculus*
B   North Face   G   *Lille Peder Edderkopp*
C   *Unnarennet*   H   West Ridge
D   *Jumarus Maximus*   I   The Hall Step
E   *Livet inni hodet mitt*   J   *Schlaraffenland*

During a couple of superb weeks in the height of the summer Eva and Anders devoted themselves to tackling what would prove to be some of northern Norway's finest free routes. Sensationally good friction allows one to dance like a drunken fly over the richly-varied crack formations. Several overhangs have to be won over, but surprise holds where one least expects them keep one's spirits up. It would be hard to find climbing as entertaining as this anywhere else. There are good anchors on most of the belays, but on *Livet inni i hodet mitt* ('Life inside my head') there are also two completely unnecessary bolts. There are also bolts on *Cuculus Noroculus*. Otherwise a wide range of Friends and nuts is required, which doesn't prevent some sections from including long run-outs. The routes are five pitches long and the rock is consistently good. But give the routes a few days after rain to dry out.

They also took the opportunity to do a seven-pitch new route on the south face, namely the righthand of the two obvious chimney cracks. The approach includes a succulent alpine meadow, the lushness of which is beyond compare. Here grow tall violet-blue *Cicerbita alpina*. Cascades of *Saxifraga cotelydon* decorate the cliffs, and in the gloom of the chimneys can be glimpsed the winter-green *Polystichum lonchitis*. The section round a dreadfully large roof about halfway up looks terrifying, but is more psychologically than physically challenging. Here one really is confronted by large formations.

A few words about the peninsula's other facilities: excellent camping and bathing spots, opportunities for freshwater fishing, a well-stocked grocery store which doubles as post office, tasty cloudberry meadows, opportunities to eat out and to visit the Kjerringøy trading-post. One can also hire canoes, even motor boats. By the end of May there is already midnight sun, and thereafter there is 24-hour daylight until the start of August. It is quite possible to climb in September, and many of the neighbouring peaks have so far only been climbed from their least difficult sides. For pioneers there are still things to be done.

A final visit to Linné's Rørstad can be warmly recommended. Here tranquillity prevails, and up on the church hill one feels transported to the days of Sara and the Reverend Rask. Time is reborn forever young.

STRANDÅTIND, 863m

Timeline

1889   First ascent of West Summit (712 m). C Hall and M Soggemoen.

1912   First ascent of Strandåtind: West Ridge by The Hall Step (5–).
C W Rubenson, F Schjelderup and H Jentoft.

1912   North-East Ridge (5–). W C Slingsby, H Jentoft, F Schjelderup,
C W Rubenson.

1924   First west-east traverse. F Schjelderup, K Motzfeldt and
F Lorentzen.

1936   South-East Buttress (4+). A Naess and E Hertzberg.

1937   South Flank (2-3). Descended by British team.

1971   South Buttress (5, A1). H Hellstrøm & E Holmgren

1975   First winter ascent. A Meyer and B Schmidt

1980   First free ascent of crack on front of The Hall Step (5+).
A Lundahl and E Selin.

1982   First free ascent of South Buttress (6). K E Andersen and E Vike.

1985   South Face *direttissima* (7–/7). E Selin and A Lundahl.

1988   North Face (7–). E Selin and A Lundahl.

1990   *Landsstrykere* (6). A Lundahl and E Selin.

1990   *Mysterier* (7). A Lundahl and E Selin.

1990   *Unnarennet* (6, A1). O R Jespersen and T Kjus.

1992   First free ascent of *Unnarennet* (7–). E Selin and A Lundahl.

1997   *Livet inni hodet mitt* (A1+). B Arntzen and T Kjus.

1998   *Jumarus Maximus* (A2). B Arntzen and T Kjus.

1998   *Cuculus Noroculus* (A2+). B Arntzen nd T Kjus.

1998   *Lille Peder Edderkopp* (A2–). M P Mosti and T Kjus.

2000   First free ascent of *Livet inni hodet mitt* (7–/7).
E Selin and A Lundahl.

2000   First free ascent of *Jumarus Maximus* (7–).
A Lundahl and E Selin.

2000   *Sult* (6/6+). E Selin and A Lundahl.

2000   First free ascent of *Lille Peder Edderkopp* (7+/8–).
A Lundahl and E Selin.

2001   *Schlaraffenland* (7+) E Selin and A Lundahl.

2001   First free ascent of *Cuculus Noroculus* (7+).
A Lundahl and E Selin.

ATTEMPTED BUT UNFINISHED PROJECTS

North Face
West Summit subsidiary peak: In 1997 B Arntzen and T Kjus climbed the obvious cornerline (A3), but retreated just one or two pitches from the top.

South Face
Approx. 125 metres to the right of the *direttissima*: In 1994 O R Wiik and A Aastorp climbed 2½ rope lengths (6, A2+), before smooth rock stopped them.

Grading comparison:
The Norwegian grading system is only apparently related to the UIAA system. In fact, the grading in both Sweden and Norway is harder than for instance in Germany. Present limit: 9+.

Scandinavia	England
5–	4c HS
5	5a VS
5+	5a/b HVS
6–	5b HVS
6	5b/c E1
6+	5c E2
7–	5c/6a E3
7	6a E3/E4
7+	6a/b E4
8–	6b E5

MICHAEL WARD

Early Exploration of Kangchenjunga and South Tibet

by the pundits Rinzin Namgyal, Sarat Chandra Das and Lama Ugyen Gyatso

(*Plates 54–56*)

The initial exploration of Kangchenjunga and of South Tibet, together with an understanding of the political and cultural trends in Lhasa, was carried out by three pundits, each of whom was associated with the Bhutia boarding school at Darjeeling in the latter part of the 19th century.

This school, which was independent of the Survey of India, was opened in April 1874 with Sarat Chandra Das (Pundit S.C.D.) as headmaster. Its declared aim was to provide a good education for young Tibetan and Sikkimese boys resident in the Darjeeling area, but its less obvious role, according to Sir Andrew Croft, the Director of Public Instruction in Calcutta, was to 'train interpreters, geographers, and explorers who may be useful if at any future time Tibet is opened to the British.'

Between 1848 and 1851 Joseph Hooker, later Director of the Royal Botanic Gardens, Kew, and President of the Royal Society, made the first botanical and topographical exploration of Sikkim. In his *Himalayan Journeys* he comments that 'It was not known that Kangchenjunga [Peak IX] and the loftiest mountain in the world was on my itinerary.' Hooker explored the south and west side of the mountain but it was pundit Rinzin Namgyal who made the largest initial contribution to our knowledge of this peak and the surrounding area.

Rinzin Namgyal (Pundit R.N.) was born in 1850 into a Sikkimese lama family whose family name was Kunlay Gyatso Laden La. He was the brother-in-law of Lama Ugyen Gyatso (Pundit U.G.). Educated at the Bhutia boarding school, he started survey work in 1879, and was in the team that met Sarat Chandra Das on his return from his first visit to Tibet. In 1883 R.N. explored the then unknown Talung valley in Sikkim and, a year later, accompanied H C B Tanner of the Survey of India on a journey to South Tibet by way of the Lipu Lek Pass, in the area where Kumaon, Tibet and western Nepal meet. Returning to Darjeeling, he was put on the payroll of trans-Himalayan native explorers, and his first independent mission was to survey the unexplored north and west sides of Kangchenjunga. This he did

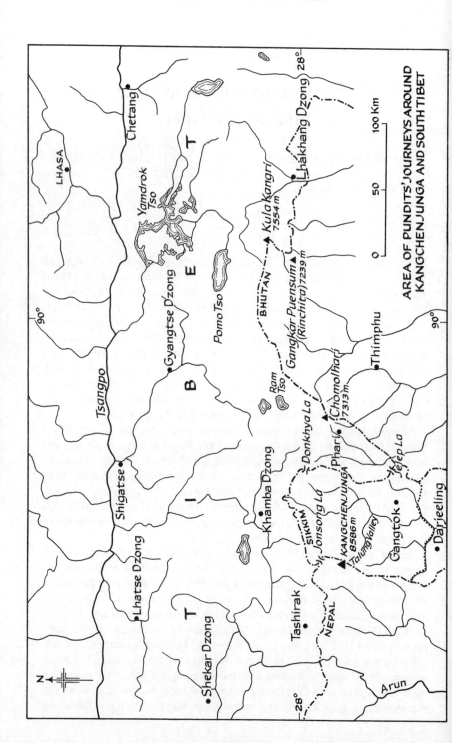

AREA OF PUNDITS' JOURNEYS AROUND
KANGCHENJUNGA AND SOUTH TIBET

between October 1884 and January 1885, making the first complete circuit of the mountain, and providing sketches of each side of the peak and the adjoining valleys; he also pointed out that there were many glaciers on the Nepalese side of the peak, which contradicted reports of 1880. He also defined the frontiers of Nepal, Tibet and Sikkim in this area.

In 1885-86 he was sent to explore east and west Bhutan, and in 1886 he tried, unsuccessfully, to determine the course of the Tsangpo river. In 1887 he worked with H C B Tanner again, surveying 26,000 miles of west and central Nepal from survey towers on the frontier. It was not until 1924-27 that the Survey of India was allowed to send native surveyors (though not Europeans) into Nepal. In 1888-89 R.N. worked with Needham around Sadiya on the Brahmaputra. J F Needham, Political Officer at Sadiya in Upper Assam in 1885, was one of the people who helped to prove that the Tsangpo and Dihang were one and the same river and that it flowed into the Brahmaputra.

In 1899 Rinzing Namgyal accompanied Douglas Freshfield on the first European circuit of Kangchenjunga, which confirmed its extensive glaciation. One area of contention was the Jonsong Pass on the north-west side of the mountain. Crossing the pass himself, Freshfield decided that R.N. had indeed crossed it in 1884, but that in 1879 Sarat Chandra Das and Lama Ugyen Gyatso had crossed a different pass further west.

The Freshfield party included the geologist Professor E J Garwood, the Sella brothers Emilio and Vittorio, an Alpine guide Angelo Maquignaz and Rinzin Namgyal. Garwood made the first modern map of the Kangchenjunga region, which showed the full extent of the glaciers and satellite peaks and superseded the previous map made by the pundit Sarat Chandra Das. Vittorio Sella took what may have been the first photograph of Mount Everest, from a spur on Jannu.

R.N. was the only pundit to visit England, where he met Queen Victoria and was presented with a gold watch. His last official work was probably in 1902, when he helped J Claude White to delineate the Sikkim–Tibet border.

Both Sarat Chandra Das and Lama Ugyen Gyatso came from a more cultured background than Rinzin Namgyal. Das was born in Chittagong in East Bengal, and studied civil engineering in Calcutta. After a bout of malaria, he was recommended, at the age of 25, for the position of headmaster of the newly-established Bhutia boarding school in Darjeeling. In 1876 Das read the newly-published *Narratives of the Mission of George Manning to Tibet and of the Journey of Thomas Manning to Lhasa* by Clements Markham. This book changed his life and kindled in him a love of exploration and a burning desire to visit Lhasa. As a result, he studied Tibetan energetically and confided in his friend Lama Ugyen Gyatso, who taught Tibetan at the school, that visiting Tibet was uppermost in his mind. Getting permission was extremely difficult but Das conceived the idea that his friend Lama U.G. could travel to monasteries in Lhasa and Shigatse carrying tributes from his family monastery at Pemionchi in Sikkim. Whilst there, he would obtain permission from the Tibetans for Das to enter Tibet. Lama U.G. agreed to this plan and British permission to cross the frontier followed rapidly. To maximise their visit, each received instructions from the Survey of India, and Das received permission from his wife by telling her that Shigatse and Tibet were only a few miles from Darjeeling and therefore he would not be away for too long!

Lama U.G. and Sarat Chandra Das left Darjeeling in June 1879 and crossed into Tibet west of Kangchenjunga. Das, who suffered severely from mountain sickness, had to be partially carried over the Jonsong La by a porter, Phurchung. He wrote: 'In this miserable fashion did I cross the famous Chathang La [Jonsong La].' U.G., despite his corpulence, crossed the pass by his own efforts. They reached Shigatse on 7 July and saw Tashilumpo monastery for the first time, 'a dazzling hill of polished gold'.

In the Panchen Lama's absence, the Prime Minister, who had secured the passport for Das, received them warmly and started the study of Hindi and Sanskrit. He was also taught how to use a camera, develop photographs, and use a telescope. On his return, the Panchen Lama became suspicious, believing that the two pundits might be British agents. However, he allowed them a silent audience and permission to leave for Darjeeling in late September with passports and forty volumes of Tibetan manuscripts. They were promised a visit to Lhasa on their return the following year.

In 1881 they returned along the same route, west of Kangchenjunga. After crossing into Tibet, this route followed an eastern tributary of the Arun valley and Tashirak village. The same route was used in a reverse direction by J B L Noel in 1913 on his unsuccessful attempt to reach Everest from the east. After meeting the Prime Minister again at his home at Dongtse, they left for Lhasa on 20 April. Unfortunately, Das became ill and had to rest for some time near the Yamdrok Tso lake, a famous geographical feature which, because of its shape, was known as the 'Signet Ring' or 'Scorpion Lake'.

After crossing the Tsangpo by the iron bridge described by the pundit Nain Singh in 1866, Das reached Lhasa, the city of his dreams, on 30 May 1882. Owing to a smallpox epidemic, so common in Lhasa, he was forced to cut short his stay, but he had time to map the streets, visit the temples, take part in religious festivals, buy many Tibetan books and observe religious and medical practices. Finally, he had an audience with the Dalai Lama, a child of eight with 'a bright and fair complexion with rosy cheeks'. On leaving Lhasa he visited Samye, the first monastery to be built in Tibet in AD 775, and visited Chetang on the Tsangpo; finally he returned to Shigatse, where he learned that the Panchen Lama had died. He reached Darjeeling on 27 December 1882 after an absence of fourteen months. Unfortunately the Tibetans eventually discovered the true nature of Das's mission and punished those involved by imprisonment, execution or beating.

Sarat Chandra Das's book *A Journey to Lhasa and Central Tibet*, published in 1902, was the first detailed account of Lhasa and South Tibet and is a veritable mine of information.

In 1885 Das accompanied Colman Macauley to Peking, where his tact, learning and diplomacy were much appreciated. Returning to Darjeeling, he settled down to a life of scholarship, producing a Tibetan–English dictionary in 1902. For many years he was involved in intelligence work. He died in 1917, probably in Japan. Truly he was 'a hardy son of soft Bengal'.

Das's companion on his two journeys, Lama Ugyen Gyatso, was born in 1851 into a distinguished Sikkimese-Tibetan family whose ancestors had founded the Tashi monastery near Sakhyong. He entered Pemionchi monastery at the age of ten to study for the priesthood, and remained there for twelve years. In 1872 he visited Tibet, obtaining the *Tongyur*, a complete set of 225 volumes of a famous Buddhist scripture, and a year later joined the Bhutia boarding school as a teacher of Tibetan. After his two explorations with Das, Lama U.G.'s third exploration, in 1883, was with his wife. He entered Tibet by the Donkhya La in NE Sikkim on 19 June. After visiting Kampa Dzong and Gyantse, he surveyed the surrounding country and then continued to Shigatse where he visited Tachi Lumpo monastery, and returned to the Yamdrok Tso lake previously visited, with Das, in 1882. From here he went south and east by the Lhobra valley to the Bhutan border. At Lhakhang, he, his wife and brother-in-law were imprisoned, but a few bribes secured their release and they made for Lhasa. It was during this period that Lama Ugyen Gyatso discovered the highest peak in Bhutan, Gangkar Puensum (Rinchita) at 7239m.

The party entered Lhasa secretly at night and sheltered with a friend at Drepung monastery. He surveyed Lhasa 'under the cover of an umbrella ... sufficient to disguise his proceedings'. Unluckily, he was recognised by a beggar who knew he came from Darjeeling and demanded money to keep quiet. U.G. paid up but left Lhasa immediately, riding on a pony but still taking bearings under the cover of his umbrella. Crossing the Tsangpo river, he completed the survey of the Yamdrok Tso lake and, travelling inconspicuously, crossed into Sikkim by the Chumbi valley. Resting at his own monastery at Pemionchi, he reached Darjeeling on 15 December 1883.

The account of his journey, given to Col. T H Holditch, was later described as 'one of the best records of Tibetan travel that has been achieved by any agent of the Survey of India'. On his expeditions with Sarat Chandra Das, it was Lama U.G. who obtained most of the geographical information, and he was described as 'the harassed and hard-working surveyor' whilst Das was portrayed as 'the light-hearted observer'. Lama U.G. continued to be of considerable assistance to the Government of India, and it was he who helped to take down an account from Kintup (who was illiterate) of his exploration of the Tsangpo. He also helped Das with his Tibetan–English dictionary and acted as an interpreter for various frontier missions. Finally, he was made Assistant Manager and then Manager of Government Estates. He died around 1915, leaving two widows but no children.

BIBLIOGRAPHY

Joseph Hooker, Himalayan Journals. Murray, 1854. 2 volumes.

Michael Ward, 'Exploration of the Bhutan Himalaya' in *Alpine Journal 102*, 219-229, 1997.

Michael Ward, 'The Survey of India and the Pundits' in *Alpine Journal 103*, 59-79, 1998.

Michael Ward, 'The Exploration of the Tsangpo River and its Mountains' in *Alpine Journal 105*, 124-130, 2000.

Derek Waller, *The Pundits: British Exploration of Tibet and Central Asia.* The University Press of Kentucky, 1990.

Sarat Chandra Das, *Journey to Lhasa and Central Tibet.* Murray, 1902.

Clements R. Markham, *Narratives of the Mission of George Bogle to Tibet and the Journey of Thomas Manning to Lhasa.* Trubner and Co., 1876.

D W Freshfield, *Round Kangchenjunga.* Arnold, 1903.

E J Garwood, 'Notes on a map of "The Glaciers of Kangchenjunga" with remarks on some of the physical features of the district.' in *Geographical Journal 20*, 13-24, 1902.

RICHARD ANDERSON

Climbing with the Doon School

I was lucky enough to spend 1998 and 1999 on a teaching exchange at The Doon School in Northern Uttar Pradesh, India. The school is situated in the Doon valley, which rises in the Himalayan foothills, so it is perhaps hardly surprising that the school has been involved in mountaineering since its foundation in 1935. Indeed, the first headmaster, A E Foot, was a member of the Alpine Club, while other members on the early staff were J T M Gibson, J A K Martyn, later headmaster, and R L Holdsworth. 'Holdie', as he was known to generations of Doon School boys, held the high-altitude record for smoking a pipe, on the summit of Kamet after the first ascent in 1931. It was on the same expedition that Holdsworth established a ski-mountaineering record of 7162m by descending from Meade's Col.

The earliest recorded school mountaineering trip was in 1937 when Gibson, Martyn and Tenzing Norgay first visited Banderpunch (6316m) in Western Garhwal between the Tons and Ganges rivers. Holdsworth arrived at the school in 1940 and in 1942 he, Martyn and three boys – but without Gibson who had joined the Royal Navy – climbed in the Arwa Valley above Badrinath, reaching about 6000 metres. One of the boys was 'Nandu' Jyal, later to become Principal of the Himalayan Mountaineering Institute in Darjeeling, who died on Cho Oyu in 1958.

After the war, in June 1946, Holdsworth, Gibson, Tenzing Norgay and Dawa Thondup, with Nandu and another boy, reached 5900m on the SE Ridge of Banderpunch before the monsoon overtook them, forcing them to retreat. Banderpunch and the nearby Kalanag or Black Peak (6387m) became very much Doon School peaks. In 1950, a Doon School party, including boys who had, perhaps, 'stared enviously at the pictures so often displayed in Mr Gibson's classroom and gazed at maps where exciting contours reveal so much adventure', climbed the peak and also, possibly, Kalanag, although this may have been done later in the 1950s. The most recent visit by the school to Kalanag was in 1984. Dr S C Biala wrote:

June 9: Harshmani Nautiyal, the Nehru Institute of Mountaineering instructor, was guiding the summit party well. It was around 2.30pm, when everybody was very tired and standing in front of an overhang which seemed impossible to negotiate. Harshmani was planning something different. Immediately to the right was a small snow patch connecting the final ridge. But a little beyond that point was a hanging glacier and a drop of thousands of feet. Everybody was asked to make an anchor. Harshmani moved forward, I was second in line followed by Arjun Mahey, Sunil, Divya and Kalu Singh, the Sherpa. After a pause, every individual moved one position ahead. After Harshmani reached the top, I was asked to move, while the first and third members were belaying. In this way everybody slowly reached the top of this hanging glacier, nervous and quite exhausted. But the peak itself was not very far, one simply had to follow the knee-deep snow ridge for another hour or so.

By 1950, Gurdial Singh, another Doon School master, was becoming active on the scene. In 1951, accompanied by Roy Greenwood, he led a school party which made a very rapid ascent of Trisul (7120m) in 16 days from Dehra Dun, which is pretty good going. That year also saw an ascent of the Matterhorn, by Doon School boys, in cricket boots, which prompted some raised eyebrows. A few years later Gurdial also led parties which attempted Kamet and were successful on Abi Gamin (7355m).

Jaonli (6632m) was another Garhwal peak that the school got to know well in the 1960s. Hari Dang, the leader, wrote:

It was while sleeping out on the small lawns of R V Singh's Landour house above Mussoorie on the ridge that we started taking an interest in Jaonli, an unclimbed 6600-metre mountain, which looked formidable from the south and was declared unclimbable by Gurdial. He advised against it, though we all toyed with the idea of climbing it. Looking at the map, the north face seemed gentler, and so in 1964 I got a group of boys together, took the Headmaster's [Martyn at that time] permission, and planned the first of the Jaonli expeditions. That attempt failed and so did the second, but they made it in 1966.

There seems to have been a lull in the 1970s, but with the arrival in the 1980s of Dr S C Biala, who claims to have written the only mountaineering textbook in Hindi, *Himalaya ki aur* ('towards the Himalaya') – near-annual expeditions restarted to Kalanag in 1984, Saife (6166m) and Koteshwar (6080m) in 1987, Kokthang (6279m) in Sikkim in 1988, Bhagirathi II (6512m) in 1991 when Dr Biala's daughter Suchi was one of the summit party, perhaps making a first female ascent. In 1992 they went to Ladakh and climbed Stok Kangri (6254m) before returning to the Garhwal in 1995 and 1996 to attempt Trisul and climb Kedar Dome (6831m). In 1998 they climbed the popular trekking peak Island Peak, near Everest. In 1999, the objective chosen was a return to Bhagirathi II, first climbed by an Austrian party in 1938 and forming part of the Bhagirathi massif lying between the Gangotri and Chaturangi glaciers. It does not have an extensive glacier approach and is close to the roadhead at Gangotri. The party assembled at the school at the end of the summer term in May. Dr Biala had decided to hand over the leader's role to a younger member of staff, Dr Aravindanabha Shukla, Aravind for short, who had been with Dr Biala on many school expeditions. Apart from myself, there was a young member of staff, Pankaj Joshi, who had some trekking but no mountaineering experience, and five boys, 17 or 18 years old. We also had two high-altitude porters, Vasudev Rawat and Mansingh, both very experienced, who came as guides. The school were a little wary of taking me on, because I was a good bit older than the rest of the party, but I managed to pass a step test run by the school doctor, which reassured them somewhat. Then there was the problem of the 'Inner Line'. Bhagirathi II was thought to be inside the Inner Line, so as a foreigner the school arranged to get me special clearance, but, it turned out, on the all-important map in Uttarkashi, the mountain fell outside the Line and the problem was solved.

We finally got away from school on 30 May. It was at about this stage that I realised I was part of a very old-fashioned expedition. We had porters, high-altitude porters, cooks and guides. The contrast with my last trip to the Himalaya, with Andrew Russell in 1977 on Sisne Himal in western Nepal, where we had no assistance above base camp, could not have been greater. But I was a guest on an Indian expedition, and one, moreover, with boys. The Himalaya with boys would be a rather different experience to being with them on British hills, or even the Alps.

We occupied Advanced Base Camp (ABC) on 4 June after a more or less straightforward approach. It became apparent at this stage, by comparing photographs from the 1991 expedition, that there was much less snow around this year. We were worried about the effect such a lack of snow could have on the route higher up. The 1938 route went up a subsidiary spur, then up the east face to the summit, a snow and icefield in gradient 45-55°. I am not clear exactly what the school party did in 1991. There is mention of a route to the south, via a col between Bhagirathi II and III, but this may have been rejected because of stonefall, in which case they followed the 1938 route and in the conditions that year both the spur and east face seemed well covered in snow. Aravind had not been on the 1991 climb, though Vasudev had, but before we left Dehra Dun he sketched out two possibilities, saying that the col route might be easier but more dangerous and sensibly leaving the decision until we could see for ourselves.

We could not see the east face clearly until we got to Camp 1 which was established at the base of the spur at 5200m on 6 June. This and the spur were largely free from snow and at first the face above seemed so too. However, through binoculars the grey aspect, which we thought was ice or rocks underlying a thin covering of snow, was in fact *penitentes* which I had not seen since the Hindu Kush in 1971. This was much more reassuring than rock. We occupied Camp 1 on 8 June after two more body-numbing carries and that evening two boys, Karn and Rohit, and I went glissading on the edge of a snow bowl just above Camp 1. It all helped acclimatisation.

Camp 2 was placed at the top of the spur at 5600m and we made our first carry there on 9 June. Karn, Sushant and I had got away first and at the top of the boulder field we were faced with climbing the spur or *penitente* field to the left. The spur looked unlikely, but we were halfway up the *penitentes* when we head shouts from Vasudev on the spur; he knew a cunning way through the difficulties and rapidly overhauled us as we were dodging round the now man-sized towers. Camp 2 was clear of snow when we reached it and we waited for the others to arrive in fine weather. Descent was by Vasudev's route.

It was now decision time about routes and the summit party. There didn't seem to be much discussion about the col route; attention centred on following the 1938 route from Camp 2. Nine hundred metres of *penitentes*, then hopefully more snow than ice, and finally breaking through the rocks at the top. As well as the two guides, Aravind and a high-altitude porter, the summit party would include Sushant, Karn and Rohit. I decided I wouldn't go. One summit more or less wouldn't make much difference and I had a feeling about the mountain – lack of bottle if you like – but too many of my friends haven't come back. I calculated that four adults would be enough for three boys, but I would see them off from Camp 2 and wait for them to descend.

I persuaded Aravind that the boys really ought to get some practice with crampons and ropes before the summit attempt, as it became clear that, for some, it was the first time that they had worn crampons. So we went to a slope above Camp 1 and had a happy afternoon falling about in the snow. It seemed that above Camp 2 the guides would fix ropes, then the boys would jumar up behind. I wasn't quite sure how they were going to descend; there was no mention of abseiling and we didn't practise it.

We reached Camp 2 on 11 June in reasonable weather. I had two boys in my tent, which was probably one of the few in the Garhwal to have guys and pegs. Jinbahadur the cook also came to Camp 2 and I was hoping we might be going for the chapati altitude record, but over-indulgence the night before rather restricted his culinary skills. The plan was that the summit party would get up for a 3am start. However, in the night a huge gale blew up with driving snow – one of those where the gusts feel as if an express train is coming into the tent. Three o'clock came and went without much movement. We crawled out at dawn to fresh snow and wind-driven cloud. The flysheet to Aravind's tent had blown off and was now probably in Tibet.

We squeezed into what remained and discussed what to do. Aravind was desperately disappointed as we talked over the options. The summit was certainly too dangerous for the boys in these conditions; as well as the wind, there was spindrift blowing all over the place. But we could not stay at Camp 2 because soon there might not be any tents to stay in. Perhaps I could take the boys down, while Aravind and the guides went up? I was happy, but the guides weren't keen. We reached the decision that the party would stay together. We must go down, even though time and food would be against making another ascent. Rather than adorn the summit with Doon School and Indian flags, an abandoned Doon School sock marked our high point.

Gagan Bhatia and I had to get back to Dehra Dun. Karn had already gone, but could something be salvaged from the party's failure on Bhagirathi? We studied the map. Thelu (6000m), on the spur above Bhujbasa leading up to the popular but not-so-straightforward Sudarshan Parbat (6507m), looked a possibility. Without losing too much height, it could be reached by diverting up the side of the Thelu glacier on the way down to Gaumukh. Aravind and Vasudev calculated that there was just enough food left for a rapid ascent. Gagan and I waved the Thelu party goodbye as our paths diverged on the descent. The next day, 15 June, they made a successful ascent of Thelu while we returned to the heat of Dehra Dun. Two days later we were reunited with them in Dehra and the smiles on their faces told of their success and another chapter in the story of the Doon School and the Himalaya.

Further reading:
Much of the historical information comes from *The Doon School Sixty Years On*, New Delhi, 1996. See also Jan Baibicz's *Guide to the Peaks and Passes of the Garhwal Himalaya*, Alpinistyczny Klub Eksploracyjny, Sopot, 1990.

DAVID SEDDON

Queen Victoria in Switzerland

Queen Victoria died on 22 January 1901. In 1868, at a low point in her life, she made a little-known visit to Switzerland. Prince Albert had died of typhoid on December 14th 1861 but for many years the Queen was haunted by his death. By 1865 she '... longed to spend four weeks in some completely quiet part of Switzerland where she could refuse all visitors ...' She had much to concern her, not least the strain of a succession of short-lived administrations and the amorous escapades of her two eldest sons, the Prince of Wales and Prince Alfred. During the summer of 1868 Disraeli, who had assumed office only in February of that year, was only just holding onto the reins of power. Gladstone was acknowledged to be the Prime Minister in waiting and his relationship with the Sovereign was already strained. In private, Gladstone lamented that the memory of Albert was not just sacred to the Queen: it was frozen in time. Finally, although the Fenian Brotherhood had ceased to be a political threat, it remained a personal one. Colonel Henry Ponsonby, the Queen's long-suffering Private Secretary, had considered the Tyrol as a possible destination but the distance and the war of 1866 between Austria and Prussia weighed against such a choice. Prince Albert had visited Switzerland in 1837, and so to Switzerland Queen Victoria was to go.

On August 5th 1868, with her fourth daughter Princess Louise, aged twenty, she embarked on the royal yacht *Victoria and Albert* before joining the train provided for her by Emperor Napoleon III. In Paris, she was greeted by the Empress Eugénie before travelling incognito to Lucerne as the Countess of Kent. There she stayed in the Pension Wallace where she lived in relative simplicity. Princes Arthur and Leopold and Princess Beatrice (aged 18, 15 and 11 respectively) were also present. Princess Louise mischievously signed her name as Lady Louise Kent. Sir Thomas Biddulph, Master of the Household, remarked to one of the Ladies in Waiting, 'It won't do for you to have Marchioness of Ely on your luggage. You will be grander than her.' She replied 'No dear, I shall put plain Lady Ely on my boxes.' John Brown won a place in the Queen's carriage while wearing a kilt. His insistence on treating Switzerland as part of Britain irritated everyone. 'J.B, of course, asks for everything as if he were in Windsor Castle,' wrote Ponsonby to his wife. 'If anything cannot be got, he says it *must* – and it is.'

Sir William Jenner, Court Physician, was not familiar with foreign sanitation, and rushed around looking for smells. Jenner, later to become President of the Royal College of Physicians, had been the first to distinguish between typhoid and typhus fever and had attended Albert during his final illness. Perhaps surprisingly, he had retained his position as the Queen's physician.

Victoria made expeditions to the Rigi and Pilatus. John Brown attended her assiduously with her favourite carriage 'the Balmoral sociable', as well as her favourite ponies, Sultan and Flora. A particular expedition was made to the Teufelsbrücke in the sombre defile of the Schollenen. Here flanks of jagged rock plunged down into an abyss. Turner had painted this scene following his first visit to Switzerland in 1802. At the Furka Pass, the Queen and her entourage took over a small inn for three days, much to the irritation of other travellers, one of whom later complained to the Berne newspaper *Der Bund*. As the mist cleared, the Queen and her party made their way to the Rhone Glacier, then much more extensive than it is today, and would have seen into the heart of the Oberland. Other less strenuous expeditions took her to Engelberg where she visited the monastery and was received by the Abbot. She was sometimes carried in a *chaise à porteur*, a sort of sedan chair, an experience she later described as humiliating. A local guide instructed her on the names of the surrounding mountains.

The Queen and Princess Louise sketched and painted as they went, and Victoria painted both the Rigi and Pilatus. Perhaps she had seen some of Turner's watercolours of Switzerland. He had painted a number of views of the Rigi; the *Dark Rigi* and the *Red Rigi* are among his finest late water-colours.

The Queen's departure from Switzerland threatened to develop into a diplomatic incident. While under pressure from the Foreign Office to return the visit of the Empress Eugénie in Paris, Victoria had already agreed to receive the Dowager Queen of Prussia who was also about to visit Lucerne. What could have been a tiresome impasse was averted, as the Empress was at Fontainebleu and could not come to Paris. Queen Victoria could therefore chat with the Prussian Queen before she left for London, where she arrived on September 11th. The Queen left Windsor for Balmoral a few days later to find the skyline of her 'ain dear hieland home' distinctly flat.

And was she cheered by her travels? Lord Jenkins records in his biography of Gladstone that, on his accession to power later that year, Gladstone found the Queen ' ... kind, cheerful, even playful ... .'

During her sojourn in the Alps, she had begun to sketch and draw people again, something she had rarely done since the death of Albert. Perhaps, at last she was a little better.

BIBLIOGRAPHY

Peter Arengo-Jones, *Queen Victoria in Switzerland*. Robert Hale,
     London(1995).
Elizabeth Longford, *Victoria RI*. Weidenfeld and Nicolson(1964).
Roy Jenkins, *Gladstone*. Macmillan(1995)

C A RUSSELL

One Hundred Years Ago
(with extracts from the *Alpine Journal*)

(Plates 57–61)

The first attempt to ascend Mont Blanc in the twentieth century[1] was made on Thursday, but without success. Even before the Pierre Pointue was reached the snow was found to be so deep that racquettes had to be used, while at the Grand Junction of the Glacier de Taconna progress was rendered very difficult from the same cause.

On reaching Grands Mulets (10,007 feet), it was decided to give up the task of reaching the actual summit owing to the great depth of the snow and the intense cold, and signs of wind.

Moreover, one of the guides was suffering from frostbite. The party, consisting of Mr. Crofts and the guides Joseph Demarchi, François Mugnier and Jules Monard spent the night at the Grands Mulets, and descended to Chamonix next morning.

The severe conditions experienced by Mr Crofts' party on 17 January 1901 were prolonged by exceptionally cold winds which persisted for several weeks in many Alpine regions. Although little mountaineering was possible the first ski ascents of two peaks were completed: on 30 March Henry Hoek and Ernst Schottelius climbed the Dammastock; and on 28 May Schottelius, accompanied by Friedrich Reichert, reached the summit of the Oberaarhorn.

A period of fine weather which commenced in May prompted an early start to the climbing season and by the end of the first week in June a number of successful expeditions had been completed.

Throughout Switzerland glorious, warm weather is being experienced, and with it Alpine climbing has begun in real earnest. Already the Jungfrau, the Matterhorn and Mont Blanc have been ascended, and daily large parties essay various climbs. The first expedition up the Jungfrau was made, appropriately enough, on Ascension-day, and it was immediately followed by a rather comprehensive scramble over the Dents du Midi.

The fine weather did not last and in the event conditions were bad for much of the climbing season. Frederick Gardiner, who arrived at Thusis on 6 June, later wrote that

The mountaineering season of 1901, taking it as a whole, was, in point of weather, one of the most unsettled and variable of recent years, for, excepting about ten days in July and a similar period towards the end of August, there was really no consecutive fine weather. As I spent June, July, and August in active mountaineering I had, in consequence, a long uphill battle with the elements almost throughout.

Although conditions were unfavourable for much of the summer many parties were active in the principal regions and a surprising number of new ascents was completed. In the Mont Blanc range on 16 July Emile Fontaine with Jean and Joseph Ravanel made the first ascent of the Aiguille du Fou after climbing the NNE ridge. On 20 July a new route on Mont Blanc was followed by the brothers G B and G F Gugliermina, accompanied by Joseph Brocherel. After reaching the summit of the unclimbed Picco Luigi Amedeo[2] from the Mont Blanc glacier by way of the NW face and making the first ascent of the SW, Brouillard ridge to Mont Blanc de Courmayeur the party continued in deteriorating weather to the observatory[3] which then stood on the summit of Mont Blanc before descending to Chamonix. A few days later, on 24 and 25 July, the same party completed the first traverse of the Col de l'Aiguille Verte, between the Aiguille du Jardin and Les Droites.

On 6 August the Duke of the Abruzzi, accompanied by four guides and five porters, bivouacked below Les Dames Anglaises, the group of rock pinnacles on the Peuterey ridge. On the following day after attempting without success to pass a rope over the top of the highest point – Punta Castelnuovo – with the aid of a rocket the Duke, with Laurent Croux and Ciprien Savoye, made the first ascent of Punta Jolanda,[4] the second highest pinnacle in the group. Other notable climbs in the range included the eighth ascent of the Brenva ridge route on Mont Blanc, by Ettore Allegra with Croux and Alexis Brocherel on 9 July and, on 21 August, the first ascent of the E ridge of Mont Dolent by Julien Gallet, accompanied by Abraham Müller senior and Jules Balleys.

In the Pennine Alps on 21 August the first complete traverse of the ridge between the Zinalrothorn and the Schalihorn was achieved by Hans Pfann and Emanuel Christa, who made the first recorded ascent of the Pointe Nord de Moming during the expedition. Another fine climb during August was the first ascent of the SW ridge, or Rothorngrat, of the Zinalrothorn by C R Gross with Rudolf Taugwalder.

Above the Susten Pass the first ascent of the E ridge of the Sustenhorn was completed by Otto Fischer and Fritz Weber on 13 July. In the Bernese Alps on 13 May Gustav Hasler, accompanied by Peter Bernet and Christian Jossi, made the first ascent of the Scheideggwetterhorn, the conspicuous shoulder of the Wetterhorn above the Grindelwald valley. On 12 July another new ascent was completed when the NE ridge of the Balmhorn was climbed by Hans Biehly and Hermann Seiler with Abraham Müller and his son.

In the Bernina Alps on 1 September J T Burton-Alexander and Dr Ernest Kingscote with Martin Schocher and Sebastian Platz made the first ascent of the steep S ridge of Piz Prievlus, the peak between Piz Bernina and Piz Morteratsch. To the east a notable climb was completed on 27 July when Eduard Pichl, Eduard Gams and Franz Zimmer followed a new and difficult line on the S face of the Dachstein.[5] In the Dolomites on 1 July Beatrice Tomasson with Michele Bettega and Bortolo Zagonel made the first ascent of the S face of the Marmolada, an outstanding achievement for the period.

In November Henry Hoek, accompanied by Alexander Tännler and K Moor, completed a traverse on ski in the Bernese Alps, making the first ski ascent of the Finsteraarhorn and reaching a point near the summit of the Mönch. On 31 December in the Pennine Alps Hoek and Ernst Schottelius with Tännler and Moor made the first winter and ski ascent of the Strahlhorn, spending an hour on the summit in perfect weather.

During the early part of the year a major railway project was completed, the line being officially opened to the public in July.

> The first trial of the new mountain electric railway from Fayet-St. Gervais to Chamonix took place successfully yesterday.
>
> This is the only railway of its kind in Europe, and although only twenty miles in length, has taken over two years to construct, on account of the formidable engineering difficulties.
>
> It requires only one man to manage the whole train, which travels at the rate of fifty miles an hour. Visitors will now be able to reach Chamonix from St. Gervais in twenty-five minutes, instead of the two hours hitherto taken by the diligence.
>
> The panorama from the train, which passes over numerous precipices and skirts many forests, is one of the most beautiful to be seen in the Alps.

Several expeditions of note were undertaken in other mountain regions during the year. In Norway J N Collie and Hermann Woolley visited the Lofoten Islands where they were joined on the island of Austvågøy by Geoffrey Hastings and Howard Priestman. Accompanied by Elias Høgrenning the party completed a number of climbs including, on 7 August, the first ascent of Store Higrafstind (1161m), the highest peak on the island.

In the Punjab Himalaya Dr Ernest Neve continued his exploration of the Kolahoi group in the Srinagar district, making another attempt to reach the highest peak (5425m). Climbing with the Rev C E Barton and two porters Neve had reached a height of some 5030m when, late in the day, he was forced to retreat. On 9 August Neve and Barton made the first ascent of Tatakuti, another peak in the district, to which they ascribed a height of 4731m. In the autumn a 'snow-capped cliff-sided peak, Rajdain' some 4690m in height to the east of the Kolahoi group was climbed by Neve's brother, Dr Arthur Neve accompanied by Dr Lefroy the Bishop of Lahore and the Rev Foss Westcott.

At the beginning of the year Oscar Eckenstein spent several weeks in Mexico where he made a number of ascents with Aleister Crowley. After establishing a camp at a height of nearly 4200m on the W slopes of Ixtaccihuatl Eckenstein scaled a difficult rock tower (4740m) on 22 January and both climbers explored the route to the summit (5286m) which they reached with the aid of crampons six days later.

On 9 June Edward Whymper, accompanied by the guides Christian Klucker, Josef Pollinger, Christian Kaufmann and Joseph Bossonay, arrived at Banff to commence his first and principal expedition to the Canadian Rockies. Following a visit to Canada during the previous year Whymper had contracted with officials of the Canadian Pacific Railway Company to undertake exploration, make ascents and take photographs in the vicinity of the railway where it passed through the range. In return for these services the Company agreed to pay his expenses incurred during the expedition, which was arranged with a view to future tourist development.

On 18 June Whymper and the guides set out from Banff, accompanied by W G Francklyn as photographer and eleven pack-horses managed by Bill Peyto, a local man, assisted by Jack Sinclair. No porters were engaged and relations between Whymper and the guides, who were obliged to carry heavy loads over difficult terrain, soon deteriorated. The situation was exacerbated by Whymper's refusal to consider the guides' advice to attempt major peaks such as Mount Columbia and Mount Assiniboine which at that time were still unclimbed. Klucker, who acted as Whymper's personal guide, later wrote[6] that

> Our expectations were far from being fulfilled. The whole enterprise remained a riddle, so far as we four guides were concerned. Our proposals were never carried out, but were rejected from the start. It became gradually apparent to us that Whymper was merely there by way of propaganda for the Canadian Pacific Railway, because we were never more than two good days' march from the railway line.

Although relations between Whymper and the guides did not improve the party explored a large area of difficult country, crossing a number of passes and making many first ascents. Whymper climbed several peaks, including Mount Whymper[7] (2845m) and Mount Marpole (2997m) with the guides and was accompanied also during his ascents of other mountains, including Isolated Peak (2845m) and Mount Collie (3116m), by the Rev James Outram who joined the party at Field on 23 July. Other peaks climbed included The President, or Emerald Mountain, (3138m) and The Vice President (3066m) by Outram with Kaufmann and Pollinger and, on 13 July, the Mitre (2889m), between Mount Lefroy and Mount Aberdeen, by Kaufmann and Pollinger.

On 1 September Outram, with the guides Christian Häsler senior and Christian Bohren and accompanied by Peyto, Sinclair and four pack-horses arrived at the base of Mount Assiniboine (3618m), the famous peak known as 'the Matterhorn of the Rockies' which had been attempted by determined parties on several occasions. Two days later Outram and the guides made the first ascent of Mount Assiniboine, climbing diagonally across the SW face and emerging, as Outram later recalled

> ... upon the S. arête barely 300ft. below the summit, which rose grandly before us, with only an easy slope of snow between us and victory.
> ... In twenty minutes more, at half-past 12, we stood at last upon the apex of the noble pyramid. The summit is a double one, crowned with ice and snow, the two points rising from the extremities of an almost level and narrow ridge, some forty yards in length. On the western side snow slopes tilt downward at an abrupt angle, whilst on the east a stupendous wall is overhung by a magnificent succession of enormous cornices, from which a fringe of giant icicles depended.
> ... The guides were now content and anxious to return immediately by the same route; but I had other wilder schemes simmering in my brain. The main ridge northward, after a sharp descent of 50ft., falls gently for a hundred yards or so, and then takes a wild plunge down to the glaciers at the mountain's base. Desirous of at least looking at the splendid northern face from above, I insisted on going to the rocky brow commanding this most imposing and characteristic feature of Mt. Assiniboine's grand mass.
> ... Scarcely had we gazed a minute ere the question came, 'Could we not manage to get down this way?' and the hope of crowning our triumph by a traverse of the mountain and conquering the reputedly inaccessible front (and that, too, in the descent), together with the certainty of getting an absolutely first-class bit of climbing, decided us to try.

The party then descended by way of the N face and NE ridge[8] to complete the first traverse of the peak – a notable achievement for the period.

To the west in the Selkirk range several expeditions of note were undertaken by ladies who were staying at Glacier House.[9] On 3 August Mrs Evelyn Berens and her husband, with Charles Clarke and Karl Schlunegger, climbed Mount Sir Donald (3297m) to make the seventh ascent of the peak and the first ascent by a lady. Some weeks later, on 18 September, Miss Henrietta Tuzo, accompanied by Eduard Feuz senior, became the first lady to reach the summit of the neighbouring Eagle Peak (2854m).

In Britain, where the death of Queen Victoria occurred on 22 January, exploration was continued by determined parties and several new routes were completed. In the Lake District two ascents of note were made on Pillar Rock: *New West Climb* on 26 May by G D and A P Abraham, C W Barton and J H Wigner; and the ascent[10] of *Savage Gully*, by C W and G D Barton and L F Meryon, on 27 August. The Barton brothers also climbed on Dow Crag, making the first ascent of the *Ordinary Route* in

North Gully on 25 August. In Scotland a famous climb was established on 22 June when Harold Raeburn, exploring alone on Ben Nevis, made the first ascent of the *Original Route* on Observatory Ridge.

A welcome event during the year was the publication, in two volumes, of *Aus den Hochregionen des Kaukasus*[11] by Gottfried Merzbacher – the second comprehensive record of exploration in the range.[12] This detailed account, illustrated with reproductions of drawings by E T Compton, Ernst Platz, M Z Diemer and R Reschreiter from photographs by the author and by other contributors including Vittorio Sella and Maurice de Déchy, was reviewed in the *Alpine Journal* where it was described as a 'valuable work – a model of methodical arrangement – a remarkable record of earnest and conscientious achievement.' Other books published during the year included *The Bolivian Andes*, Sir Martin Conway's record of climbing and exploration in the Cordillera Real.

On 5 September the death occurred of William Mathews, an original member and a former President of the Alpine Club. In a notice which appeared in the *Alpine Journal* T G Bonney recalled that Mathews was one of the founders of the Alpine Club and that '... The idea, in fact, of the formation of the Club was originated by him in a letter written to the Rev F J A Hort dated February 1, 1857.' Mathews, one of the outstanding climbers of his day, took part in many notable expeditions including the first ascent of Monte Viso.[13]

In conclusion it is appropriate to note the following extracts from 'The Future of the Alpine Club', a paper[14] by Sir Martin Conway which was published in the *Alpine Journal*.

> Though the Alpine Club arose during the struggle for the conquest of the Alps, and took its name from the great European range, there is evidence enough that, in the mind of its founders, mountains in general, and not only the peaks of Central Europe, were objects of interest. The title page of the 'Alpine Journal' and many of the papers in its early volumes are proof sufficient of this statement, if proof be needed.
>
> ... As a matter of fact the exploration, above the snow-level, of the mountain ranges of the world outside the Alps has thus far been made chiefly by our members. By accident, not by design, the Exploration of the Mountains of the World has become a characteristic work of our Club, and the first record of such explorations is the noteworthy feature of our 'Journal'.

Exploration which was continued by members of the Alpine Club throughout the twentieth century.

REFERENCES

1   The first climbers to ascend Mont Blanc in the twentieth century were
    Dr Jules Jacot-Guillarmod and his brother, of Neuchâtel, who reached
    the summit without guides on 28 May 1901.
2   Pointe Louis Amédée. Named by the Gugliermina brothers in honour
    of H R H Prince Luigi Amedeo di Savoia-Aosta, Duke of the Abruzzi.
3   See *A J 98*, 225-226, 1993.
4   Pointe Yolande. Named by the Duke of the Abruzzi in honour of H R H
    Princess Jolanda Margherita di Savoia – the eldest daughter of King
    Vittorio Emanuele III and Queen Elena of Italy – who had been born
    on 1 June 1901.
5   The *Pichlweg* – the first route on the S face of the Dachstein group to
    be established on the Dachstein itself; a route on another part of the
    face, under the Mitterspitze, had been completed by Robert Hans
    Schmitt and Fritz Drasch on 15 July 1889.
6   Christian Klucker, *Adventures of an Alpine Guide*, London, John Murray,
    1932.
7   Named after Edward Whymper who at the time of his first expedition
    to the Canadian Rockies was 61 years of age.
8   Known as the N ridge.
9   See *A J 104*, 208-209, 1999.
10 Earlier in the year, on 3 June, P A Thompson had climbed the gully on
    his own with the moral support of a rope from above for the last two
    pitches.
11 Gottfried Merzbacher, *Aus den Hochregionen des Kaukasus. Wanderungen,
    Erlebnisse, Beobachtungen.*, Leipzig, Duncker & Humblot, 1901.
12 *The Exploration of the Caucasus* by D W Freshfield had been published
    in 1896.
13 With F W Jacomb and the guides Michel and Jean-Baptiste Croz on
    30 August 1861.
14 Read before the Alpine Club on 17 December 1900.

Area Notes 2000

EDITED BY JOSÉ LUIS BERMÚDEZ

Alps and Pyrenees	*Lindsay Griffin*
Russia and Central Asia	*Paul Knott*
Greenland	*Derek Fordham*
Scottish Winter	*Simon Richardson*
India	*Harish Kapadia*
Pakistan	*Lindsay Griffin*
Nepal	*Bill O'Connor*
North America	*Kelly Cordes /*
	American Alpine Journal
Bolivia	*Javier Sanchez*

LINDSAY GRIFFIN

Alps and Pyrenees 2000

This report looks at selected activity during the year 2000, not only in terms of exploration and high technical performance but also in the wider Alpine world. In preparing these notes Lindsay Griffin would like to acknowledge the assistance of Jules Cartwright, Mikhail Davy, Ed Douglas, Martin Gillie, Mireille Lazarevitch, Valdo Linek, Igor Koller, Andy Parkin, Michel Piola, Hilary Sharp, Blaz Stres, Erik Svab, Thomas Tivadar, Paolo Vitali, and Adam Wainwright.

The *Alpine Journal* particularly welcomes details of new routes and information on members' activities in the Alps, as well as changes to established routes. These should be sent to the Club or directly to 2 Top Sling, Tregarth, Bangor, Gwynedd, LL57 4RL.

WINTER 2000

Introduction

After the tragedies of 1999, with over 100 killed in avalanches, including 12 people at Montroc above Argentière, 39 in an avalanche at the Austrian village of Galtür, 49 in two major tunnel fires (one of which kept the Mont Blanc Tunnel closed for the whole of 2000) and several well-publicised fatal climbing accidents, it would be nice to report that 2000 marked a return to normal. Alas, the terrible funicular disaster at Kaprun in Austria in

November, in which 152 skiers died, was just one of several catastrophes in the Alps last year, continuing a sense of gloom that the region is overcrowded and unsafe. Earlier in the year the Valle d'Aosta/Gran Paradiso region was swept by violent floods and mudslides, which killed more than 35 people and completely isolated villages. As if that wasn't enough, scientists at Cardiff University announced that the permafrost beneath the Alps was melting due to the process of global warming, which almost all experts now agree is occurring as a consequence of human activity.

Dr Charles Harris at Cardiff said: 'It is now clear that rises in atmospheric temperature are producing significant changes in permafrost levels. Global warming is changing the nature of weather systems and this is having disproportionate effects on temperatures underground.' In the last decade underground temperatures have risen by 1.2°C, according to tests done in Switzerland, five times the air temperature increase for the same period.

The European Union has now launched an intensive study across the Continent's mountainous areas. Named PACE (Permafrost and Climate in Europe), this will attempt to evaluate the future impact of this change. There are already predictions of collapsing rock faces, crumbling foundations under cable car stations and mountain huts, and more mud slides. 'There is no doubt that there is a real danger to human life, thanks to permafrost warming,' Harris added. 'We want to minimise the destruction.'

Weather patterns were also erratic, although there were long periods of settled weather in the summer allowing plenty of activity. But as the Italian climber Cesare Maestri said in December 2000, the day after nine climbers and one skier were killed in the Italian Alps in freak conditions, this is 'a strange, nonsensical winter'.

Legislation covering rescue services in the French Alps faced reform in the Senate, as Jean Faure, Senator for the Isère region and Mayor of Autrans, introduced legislation to make climbers, skiers and snowboarders more responsible for the charges incurred during rescues. The move was opposed by the then President of the Groupe de Haute Montagne, Yves Peysson, who warned that it was wrong to promote adventure sports and then remove the principle of free rescue.

Pyrenees

Long periods of fine warm weather, especially during January and early February, led to well-consolidated snow, and straightforward gullies were often in excellent condition. However, only a modest number of worthwhile new routes were recorded. Tragically, the disappearance is reported of Francis Mousel, best known as the author of *Pyrénés – Courses Mixtes, Neige et Glace*, probably the most useful and up-to-date guide to selected winter climbing in the Pyrenees (November 1997: in French). Mousel, who was also a notable soloist, was thought to have been going to try a route, alone, on the North Face of the Zermatt Breithorn but went missing on the 16 January.

26. An unclimbed granite peak in the Jarjinjabo massif, Sichuan Province. (*Tamotsu Nakamura*) (p65)

27. Another unclimbed peak in the Jarjinjabo massif, Sichuan Province, seen from the Zhopu pasture, north of the Sichuan-Tibet Highway (South). The peak on the right is 5382m. Nakamura describes the region as being particularly beautiful. The Nyingma-pa monastery at Zhopu was founded in the 1260s. (*Tamotsu Nakamura*) (p65)

28. Xianre Ri (6032m), Gongga Xueshan, Sichuan, reflected in a nearby lake.
This mountain is unclimbed. (*Tamotsu Nakamura*) (p65)

29. The unclimbed North Face of Xiashe (5833m), Shaluli Shan, photographed from the Zhopu Gompa. (*Tamotsu Nakamura*) (p65)

30. Mt Siguniang (6250m) in the Qiolangai was first climbed by a Japanese expedition in 1981 via the East Ridge, but the Japanese have also climbed the South Face, in 1992. To the north, Nakamura reports a number of granite towers up to 5500m. (*Tamotsu Nakamura*) (p65)

31. The highest peak in the Dangche Zhengla massif, photographed from the south-west. This peak is unclimbed. (*Tamotsu Nakamura*) (p65)

32. Lengo Gomba and rock peaks, Sichuan Province. The monastery was founded 600 years ago. (*Tamotsu Nakamura*) (p65)

33. Climbing Mount Korakas, Central Greece. (*J G R Harding*) (p89)

34. Skiing down Korakas. (*J G R Harding*) (p89)

35. The Cordillera de Santa Vera Cruz, Bolivia. The leftmost peak is Pico de la Fortuna (5493m), that second from right is Cerro Santa Vera Cruz, at 5560m the highest in the massif. (*Javier Sánchez*) (*see* Area Notes: Bolivia)

36. and 37. *Left and Above*
The tin and card of Joseph Prem, left in 1939 on the summit of Cerro Santa Vera Cruz, and the archaeological remains – offerings from the Tiwanaku culture – discovered near the same place. (*Javier Sánchez*) (*see* Area Notes: Bolivia)

38. The SE Face of la Fortuna (5493m). The line of the first ascent, *Khespiqala*, goes up the middle of the snowy face at Difficile, 70°, reaching the ridge on the left just below the summit. (*Javier Sánchez*) (*see* Area Notes: Bolivia)

Western Pyrenees

Peña Pequeña o Collaradeta In the Far West Laureano Gômez and Isidoro Sanchez climbed a new 400m route on the N Face of this subsidiary summit of the 2883m Peña Collarada. *El Túnel* was climbed in February and graded IV/3+. There is a short vertical section on pitch two but straightforward 50-60° névé above.

Pala de Ip On the NE Face of this 2783m peak, a little east of the Peña Collarada and above the Ip Reservoir, Oscar Cacho and Isidoro Sanchez spent one day in February climbing Cafetu (300m: IV/4). Three pitches of difficult climbing, with the first a 80-85° icefall, led to an easier upper snow fan at 55°.

Central Pyrenees

Vignemale One of the most notable events in the Pyrenees during the season was the long awaited first winter ascent of the *North Face Direct* on **Pointe Chausenque** (3204m). From 20-22 August 1961 J Bescos, R Montaner and J Vicente climbed the lower wall of the N Face, finishing up the *Diagonale*. On 23 and 24 September in the following year the great Pyrenean activist of the time, Patrice de Bellefon, with P Mirabal, H Paradis and S Sarthou, repeated the difficult lower section, then continued above the *Diagonale* to finish up the prominent pillar on the left side of the upper face. The 700m route was graded ED2 (A3 and 6a) and it appears that until this year no one had made a second ascent, the route almost gaining 'mythical' status.

The well-known French activist, Remi Thivel, first attempted to solo the Direct last winter, fixing the first two pitches before descending and recruiting a partner. He returned on 13 March with Cyrille Dupouy and completed the route with one bivouac, climbing a total of 20 pitches up to 6a and A2+ but still considering the overall grade of ED2 to be appropriate after a lapse of 28 years. The route was well-ahead of its time

El Turbón On the NW Flank of the N Ridge of the Castillo in the Aneto-Maledetta region J Marmolejo and J Sáex climbed *De Excursión por El Turbón* (400m: 55° and IV mixed). The climbers approached from the Margalida Hut and ascended the previously unclimbed and prominent gully in the middle of the rocky face to the left of the Couloir de las Vacas.

Tuca de Literola On this 2745m point, which forms the first summit in the long crest dividing the Literola and Remuñe valleys, Daniel Ascaso and Jordi Marmolejo have put up *El Ultimo Maciello* (250m: TD). The new route climbs the rock buttress immediately left of the Arlaud Couloir on the NE Face to gain the prominent leftward slanting snow ramp below the summit. Two difficult mixed pitches (M5 and M5+) led to this ramp, which was followed left (55°) to the final tower. Here, a 40m chimney (M4) led to the summit. The climb was completed on 10 January and would appear to offer a useful addition to the growing number of worthwhile winter routes easily accessible from Benasque.

Gavarnie In the famous Cirque Richard Dupont, Rémi Laborde and Jérôme Thinières completed an impressive *enchaînement*. On 29 February these three linked *Freezante* (200m: IV/4+) on the lower tier, *L'Alpe Julienne* (150m: V/5+) in the Atico sector and then continued above to complete *Arana* (100m: V/5), all in a rapid 6½ hours' sprint

Eastern Pyrenees

Gra de Fajol Petit On 19 April, outside the official winter season, Albert Marcau and Marc Serradel climbed *El Martell de Lucifer* up the mixed ground immediately left of the classic Central Couloir Direct. The difficulties were hard to protect and the route probably only feasible when exceptionally well-iced. The 70m line is direct to the summit and was graded III/3 (70/80° and M4+).

The twin summits of Gran and Petit Gra de Fajol lie in the south-west corner of the Ull de Ter cirque, only 30 minutes walk above the hut of the same name. The many routes and variations on the north faces (up to TD) make this one of the most popular venues for winter climbing on this side of the Pyrenees.

Andorra

Pic Negra d'Envalira On the North Top of this easily accessible 2816m summit, reached in 2½ hours from the popular ski resort of Grau Roig, Pako Sánchez soloed Magna Solitudo on 5 March. The new 230m line climbs a 50-60° snow couloir towards the left side of the W Face, finishing with two difficult mixed pitches (M4 on mediocre granite) on to the NW Ridge.

Mont Blanc Massif

The hot summer of 1999 stripped a lot of the ice from north faces and nearly all of it from more marginal lines. Together with the heavy early winter snow, this put paid to attempts on routes at higher altitudes. One AC member with a number of winter seasons described it as 'not disastrous, but certainly not vintage'.

The north faces in the Argentière basin – Les Droites and Les Courtes especially – were quite grey. However, this didn't stop Slovenian climber Marko Prezelj and friends from making a four-hour sprint up the *Shea-Jackson* on Les Droites. For mere mortals, other routes at slightly lower altitudes were climbable; the *Carrington-Rouse Route* on Les Pélerins received a number of ascents, and ice routes on the Pré du Bar, like the neo-classic *Madness Très Mince* and the easier *Petit Viking*, were also climbed regularly.

Mont Blanc From 10-13 March Patrice Glairon-Rappaz, climbing with Paul Robach, followed his success on the Grandes Jorasses (reported below)

with a winter ascent of 1984 Gabarrou/Marsigny route, *Divine Providence* (possibly the third complete overall winter ascent to the summit of Mont Blanc). The lower section of the route was reported as icy, slow-going but safe and the pair were able to climb free in rock shoes up to 6b, aiding the harder sections. As they were settling into their third bivouac, they picked up a bad weather forecast and so moved quickly on, reaching the summit at 4am in the teeth of a ferocious gale. They subsequently sat out the storm in a crevasse before returning to Chamonix by midnight.

Chandelle du Tacul From 2-4 January Martial Dumas and Fred Mathieu created a fine little aid route on the SE Face, left of *Les Pets*. The 200m line, christened *Cocaine,* gives six pitches of steady A1 and A2. With the current focus on big-wall climbing around the world, this will no doubt prove a welcome addition for those wishing to gain experience at non-desparate aid climbing in the mountains; that is, until it gets climbed free.

Grandes Jorasses Stéphane Benoist and Patrice Glairon-Rappaz made the second winter ascent of *Serge Gousseault Route* (1150m: ED3) on the NE Flank of the Walker Spur. The route was first climbed by Bertone, Claret and Desmaison in January 1973, two years after the death of Serge Gousseault on an earlier attempt with Desmaison. The two young French guides started up the route on 13 January with nine days' food, reaching the summit on 18 January at 1am in worsening weather. Benoist, who made the third ascent of *No Siesta*, said the technical difficulty of the routes was comparable. They faced a lot of difficult mixed climbing, some pure rock of around V+/A1 and stretches of steep ice. Neither climber carried a heavy pack, preferring to haul their bivouac equipment.

In February, the Slovenian climbers Urban Azman and Andrej Markovic made a winter ascent of the 1977 *Slovenian Route* (Knez/Matijevec/Vidmar/Zupan: 850m: ED1/2: V/5 or 5+ with some F4+ and A2) which climbs the N Face right of the Croz Spur.

During the ENSA meet, held in February and disrupted by heavy snow, two British parties at different times (Richard Cross with Al Powell and Jules Cartwright with Sam Chinnery) attempted *Alexis* (Gabarrou/Robert, 1993: 1100m: ED3/4: 90/95°), a route up the Central Couloir, finishing to the summit of Pointe Whymper. The pairs bivouacked halfway up the face after 18 hours, just below the climb's main difficulties, but retreated next day in worsening weather. This route still awaits a winter ascent and possibly a second complete ascent.

Previously unreported from the end of September 1999 was a new line, *La Belle Hélène* (V/5+M, 85°) on the N Face of Pointe Hélène (4045m) by Chamonix resident Andy Parkin. Parkin soloed the route, which takes an ephemeral line between the 1970 *Polish Route* (Chrobak/Poreba/Wroz, July 1970: V+ and 55-60°) and the 1997 Aubert/Lafaille route *Michto*, in one day, descending along the W Ridge over Pointes Marguerite and Young to the Col des Grandes Jorasses, then down the Mont Mallet Glacier to the foot of the face. Rarely self-belaying, he took a fall high on the route and was held by an equalised Friend and poor ice screw. Technical difficulties were comparable with the *Carrington-Rouse* on the Pélérins. Parkin's light and fast style contrasted strongly with that of the Russian climber, Valeri Babanov, who was attempting a new route on Pointe Marguerite at the same time, carrying bolts and using both fixed ropes and a portaledge.

Pointe Centrale de Frébouze In late February Andy Parkin and Adam Wainwright climbed a new route on this rarely-visited peak. *La Face Perdue* – an apt name for a line on the forgotten NW Face – lies to the right of the 1979 *Charlet Route*, climbing 400m of original ground before joining it for the upper section. Excellent conditions are required for this climb to be in condition and the pair graded it TD+: IV/5+.

Aiguille du Midi In one long day, 8 March, Andy Parkin and Adam Wainwright climbed a hard new eliminate line on the N Face to the right of the Eguster Couloir. The crux section proved to be the 300m corner in the steep rock buttress separating the *Eguster* from the *Carli-Chassagne Goulotte*. (Both these routes are TD, the former offering excellent winter ice when in condition.) The new climb is called the *Voie Ferroviaire*, a reference to the need for a new rail link to ease freight traffic that would otherwise use the reopened Mont Blanc Tunnel. Parkin and Wainwright graded their 1000m route ED2 V/6.

Rognon du Plan In mid-January Jules Cartwright made a first solo winter ascent of *Sylchris* (Profit/Radigue/Tavernier, June 1985: 700m: ED2: IV/ 5+) on the W Face. On the second day Cartwright spent four hours climbing the route's crux: 120 metres of Scottish 6. During this section he discovered his rope had been badly cut, so he needed to separate the two pieces and tie them together with a knot, after which progress was understandably much slower. He bivouacked for a second time on the snow ridge between the two gullies and on the third day climbed the upper section (Scottish 5) to the Col Supérieur du Plan. Wearing leather boots, Cartwright sustained slight frostbite, a situation made worse by running out of gas. He spent a short spell in hospital on reaching Chamonix but was happily soon climbing again within a month.

Petit Dru From 22-26 February Russian climbers Mikhail Davy and Alexander Klenov climbed a hard new route on the NW Face. Starting at more or less the same point as the *American Direct*, they took a line between *Passage Cardiac* and *C'est Arrivé Demain*. Two attempts were made, the first barely reaching a quarter of the way up the wall after five days' effort, when bad weather slowed progress to a near halt. On their second attempt they continued past their previous high point to reach the Niche then climbed variation pitches to the Classic 1935 *Allain/Leininger Route* above. Christened *Dream of Summer*, the route involved sustained climbing of around 6b/A2 with two pitches graded 7a and A3 and the possibly understated adjectival grade of ED2. However, this was very much an eliminate line and somewhat illogical in the upper section, where it climbed cracks either just left or right of the 1935 route in an attempt to avoid touching it.

Aiguille Sans Nom From 17-21 March Alain Ghersen made an inspired first solo winter ascent of the highly regarded 1978 *Gabarrou-Silvy Directissima* (ED2: 950m) on the mountain's N Face. Only climbed in winter for the first time in 1998 by Slovenian ace Marko Prezelj and Swiss Thierry Schmitter, the route has 300m of hard rock-climbing before giving way to an ice field and very technical mixed climbing above. It was the third time Ghersen had tried to make a winter solo, bad weather in early March putting paid to his second attempt. He reached the Sans Nom Ridge in perfect weather, continued over the Verte and was able to descend the Whymper Couloir in just 45 minutes.

Valais

Breithorn. On 21 June, Italians Claudio Bastrentaz and Jimmy Sesana made an impressive ski descent of the classic *Welzenbach Route* on the NNW Face of the Breithorn's West Summit (4165m). Although subject to some objective danger, the *Welzenbach* or *Bethmann-Hollweg Route* (Bethmann-Hollweg/Supersaxo/Supersaxo, 1919: Bachschmidt/Rigele/Welzenbach, 1926 via a variation start to the left: 1100m: TD) is probably the route least exposed to falling ice on the face. The crux is the leftward slanting couloir to leave the lower snow/ice field and this gave the greatest difficulty to the skiers with sections of 60°.

A little later, on 2 July, Slovenians Blaz Stres and Tomaz Tisler made the probable second ascent of *Karantanska* on the NNW Face, a route first climbed in 1994 by fellow countrymen Peter Meznar and Bojan Pockar. This route actually climbs little new ground. It follows a more direct line up the rock buttress immediately right of the 1964 *Arnold/Etter/Mader Route*, continues up the latter and, when that joins the classic *Welzenbach Route*, slants up right to finish via the 1974 *Arnold/Ineichen Direct Route*.

Stres and Tisler did this route in a weekend, driving seven hours to Cervinia on Friday 1 July, then taking the téléphérique to Testa Grigia and descending in 20 minutes to the Theodule Hut where they bivouacked. The next day they made a nine-hour ascent, finding rock at F5, water ice to 4+ and a mixed pitch of M4. *Karantanska* (meaning Corinthian, after the once independent state of Corinthia formed around 900 AD and formerly inhabited by Slovenians) is threatened by icefall but not too seriously in the conditions encountered last July. The pair roped up for seven pitches only and felt a grade of ED1 was appropriate.

The next weekend Stres returned with Matija Klanjscek and this time climbed the large snow/ice slope taken by the initial sections of the classic *Welzenbach Route* and *Arnold/Ineichen Direct Route*, slanting right to the shoulder of the *Prothero Route* at 3696m. This line had probably first been followed as long ago as 1974 and involved 50-60° slopes with short sérac walls up to 80°. Above, the pair continued up left on 50° slopes to cut through the final rock barrier via the *Barmasse-De Tuoni Route* (1989: D+: accessed from the Breithorn Plateau to the south), which follows a leftward-slanting gully that steepens to 80° and narrows to two metres (WI3+). The climb took only seven hours, as the Slovenian pair roped, but generally moved together (placing intermediate protection) for much of this 1000m route, which was seriously threatened by sérac fall especially in the final gully.

Bregaglia–Masino

Long periods of fine stable weather during the early part of the year gave local activists the chance to make several first winter ascents.

Punta Allievi After fixing the first three pitches on 26 February, Dante Barlascini, Marco Colombo and Paola Pazzini made the first winter ascent of *Inshallah* on the following day. Climbed by Maspes, Motto and Olcelli in 1998, *Inshallah* (500m: 17 pitches: 6b/6b+, 6a obl) climbs smooth friction slabs right of the 1937 *Boga Route* to reach the central basin, then climbs a steep wall close to the upper section of *Cosi È Se Vi Pare*. It is the longest route on the wall.

Pizzo Cengalo On exactly the same day that the winter ascent of *Inshallah* was being completed, the Lecco trio of Silvano Arrigoni, Adriano Selva and Andrea Spandri made a nine-hour winter ascent (the first?) of the magnificent *Gran Diedro* (Maspes/Merizzi/Pasqualotto, 1992: c500m/13 pitches: 6b)) on the E Face of the Cengalo.

Cima del Cavalcorte On the East Pillar of this well-known watchtower overlooking the lower Ferro Valley, Gualtiero Colzada and Mario Sertori have made the first winter ascent of *La Rossa* (D'Alessio and friends, 1997: c350m 6b and A1: a subsequent variant to the fourth pitch allows the route to be climbed entirely free at 6c). The winter ascent appears to have been completed in just one day on 10 March.

Punta della Sfinge On 13 March Marco Beltramini and Mario Sertori made a possible first winter ascent of the naturally-protected, six-pitch *Amicizia Route* (Oggioni/Rogantini/Sinapi, 1987: 230m: 6b) on the SE Face of the Sphinx (2802m) close to the Omio Hut.

Pizzo Torrone Occidentale – Punta 2987m On this popular playground close to the Allievi-Bonacossa huts, Mario Sertori made a solo winter ascent of *Ciota Cicoz* (160m: six pitches: strenuous 6b) on 20 March. This curious route on the SE Face, first climbed by Maspes and Perlini in July 1993, ascends the now established line of the rappel descent traditionally used by parties completing the ultra-classic *South Pillar* (Merrizi/Miotti, 1975: V and perhaps the most frequented route in the entire Zocca Valley).

Bernina

Piz Bernina The approach to the classic *Biancograt* (N Ridge), on this most easterly of the 4000m peaks, traditionally involves climbing a steep ice slope/couloir of c130m to gain the Fuorcla Prievlusa at the base of the ridge. In recent summers and especially towards the end of the season, this ice slope has all but disappeared, leaving unpleasant rubble with associated stonefall danger. For this reason local guides and hut wardens have created a new approach through the area of rock left of the couloir.

The route is rather convoluted, first reaching the base of the upper couloir, then making a long traverse left to circumvent a steep rock barrier before slanting back right over slabby terrain to reach the col. This rocky section is reported to be waymarked and well equipped with iron spikes, but the Swiss guides point out that this in no way detracts from the ambience of the route, which remains a superb high mountain expedition reserved for experienced alpinists.

SUMMER 2000

Mont Blanc Massif

The weather during the season was chaotic, keeping alpinists on their toes the whole time, ready to adapt to each day's uncertain forecast. There were numerous accidents with six climbers killed on 15 August alone, the day of the Guides Festival in Chamonix. Two of these fell down the Whymper Couloir after an ascent of the N Face of the Verte, the other four being unfortunate victims of a huge rock fall whilst descending the *Normal Route* on the Tour Ronde. On the Italian side of the range it would appear the continued closure of the Mont Blanc Tunnel has stifled a lot of activity, while at accessible venues on the French side Michel Piola and various other regular activists continue with their project to re-equip a number of quality rock climbs. Some of the best ascents of the 'summer' were actually achieved in the spring and are reported below.

Since 1997, when a project under the title of 'Mont Blanc 2000 – Safe Granite' was initiated to re-equip routes in the Massif, a number of great classics on popular venues such as the Grand Capucin, Pilier des Trois Pointes, Aiguille Pierre-Alain and Tour Rouge, have been re-bolted. This has involved replacing old and now dubious 8mm bolts with 10mm stainless steel (generally 12mm on the main belays). In order to preserve the spirit of the first ascent, no additional bolts have been introduced except in rare cases when a particular passage has been thought highly dangerous in its original form (for instance where a fall would result in hitting a terrace) or where new variations have been added. Last summer those involved in the re-equipping process turned their attention to a number of fine routes in rather more remote surroundings. Although these offer superb climbing, they have completely failed to gain the popularity they deserve. The main work has centred on climbs close to the Chapoua Hut (Flammes de Pierre and Pointes below the Aiguille Moine), the Leschaux Hut and in the Aiguilles Rouges - Brévent region.

Aiguille Noire de Peuterey Proving that it is still very possible to make a major high-quality first ascent in the Mont Blanc Range, August 2000 saw the completion of *Nero su Bianco*, a 19-pitch rock climb on the SE Face of Punta Brendel (3499m). The 700m high SE Face of the Brendel, the fourth tower on the S Ridge, was only previously climbed by the possibly unrepeated 1981 *Manera-Meneghin Route* (ED1: VI and A3). On 23 August, 37-year-old Maurizio Oviglia, well known for his development and subsequent guide-books to many of the important crags in both Sardinia and the Gran Paradiso, plus the 29-year-old Slovenian-born Erik Svab, resident in Trieste, started up the face left of the 1981 route, crossed it at the end of pitch five, rejoined it on pitch nine, then climbed three pitches up the slanting crack and wall graded V+ and A3 by the original ascensionists. The pair then rappeled and after a day's rest re-climbed these 12 pitches, placing gear on lead and free-ing the hardest pitches (7, 11 and 12); then, where the 1981 route escapes out left, they continued more or less directly to exit just left of the summit. The 19-pitch route gave 940m of climbing with obligatory difficulties of 6b+ and a crux of 7b. Two other pitches rated 7a. The most commendable and notable aspect of this ascent was that natural gear (nuts, Friends and conventional pegs) was used throughout. The only gear left in place apart from the rappel anchors (pegs, nuts and slings) was a single peg on pitch 12.

Peuterey Integral A notable ascent of the classic *Peuterey Integral* (ED1) was made in an incredible 20 hours from the Val Veni to the summit of Mont Blanc by the Courmayeur guides Armand Clavel and Matteo Pellin. The pair made the climb to celebrate the 150th anniversary of the creation of the Courmayeur Guides Association and were filmed from the air throughout their ascent (*Una Ciliegina sulla Torta – l'Integrale del Peuterey*).

Grand Capucin An new independent line on the Grand Cap seems an unlikely possibility in this era, but *La Tête dans les Nuages,* put up solo over 15-16 May by Dominique Brau-Mouret, climbs previously virgin rock right of the *Swiss Route* for eight long pitches before finishing up the last two rope lengths of *Le Sourire de l'Eté*. An overall grade of ED2 (6a and A3) was reported

Grandes Jorasses Starting on 27 June and finishing at 1.00am on the 30 June, Patrice Glairon-Rappaz made the first uncontested solo ascent of the celebrated *No Siesta* (Gledjura/Porvaznik, 1986: 1000m: 90°: 6b and A2). Glairon-Rappaz backroped almost all the climb, finding the ice on the lower section in very poor condition and the rock often mediocre, much worse in fact than that encountered on the *Serge Gousseault Route*, which he climbed the previous winter (*see above*), which appears to have gained an unjust reputation. Carried out in less-than-perfect weather with heavy snow showers at frequent intervals, this was an impressive effort from the 29-year-old French alpinist, for which he received a Piolet d'Or nomination. It will of course be remembered that a second ascent of this fabled route was claimed just one year after its first by the Slovenian, Tomo Cesen, who in 1987 announced that he had soloed the line in just 14 hours.

Pointe à Daniel Apart from the great routes on the Petites Jorasses, rock climbing in the vicinity of the Leschaux Hut has failed to gain popularity. Last summer Michel Piola attempted to address the problem by re-equipping his own 1991 route *Tonton Daniel* (230m: seven pitches: 6b, 6a obl) on the Pointe du Daniel, then adding two fine new routes alongside.

At the beginning of August, with Hervé Bouvard and Benoît Robert, he climbed the left edge of the huge slab that characterises this face, stopping after seven pitches at the foresummit. *Dark Cristal* was sustained, with the first six pitches either 6b or 6b+ and the last 6a+. A few days later and further to the right, cutting through *L'Esprit d'Escalier* on its third pitch, the same three climbers created *Cristal Palace*. This nine-pitch route (6c+ or 6b with two points of aid) continues up to the crest of the ridge over a series of stark, jagged towers.

Rognon du Plan On the N Face between the ultra classic *Fil a Plomb* and the Col du Plan Couloir, Philippe Batoux and Fabien Peyonnet climbed an independent line christened *Ice Tooling*. Completed in one day, 23 May, this route branches left just below the crux pitch of the Col du Plan Couloir to climb a conspicuous dièdre and mixed terrain above (c300m: III/4: 80°, M5), entirely left of Andy Parkin's December 1994 solo variation finish to the Col du Plan Couloir.

Tour Verte Parallel to but just left of the ultra classic *Le Piège* is a new offering, *Pasang, de retour d'Everest*, from Fanny Bellucci, Thierry Franc, Michel Piola and Benoît Robert. The route was completed in two sessions, on 16 August 1998 and 7 August 2000, and has six pitches with one of 6b+ and one of 6b (6a obl). Although harder than *Le Piège* it could potentially become the second classic of the Tour Verte.

Aiguille du Roc The 500m S Face offers a number of ultra classic climbs that are protected entirely by natural gear. However, nearly all parties will descend from the top of the routes by rappel, generally via the much-less-than-perfect anchors of the route *Tout va Mal*. Last summer Thierry Franc, Benoît Robert and Piola made things much less stressful by climbing and re-equipping *Tout va Mal*. They discovered the climb to be long, of great quality and quite strenuous, and during the ascent decided to equip several new variants. On pitch two they made a slanting traverse to reach the stance at the top of the original first pitch (6a+: glacier recession has affected this and many other routes in the neighbourhood). On the 8th pitch they followed the crest of the pillar at 6b and on the 10th pitch climbed direct at 6c+ (or 6b with three points of aid) in order to avoid the pendulum of the original line. Variants to the 12th and 13th pitches were both graded 6a.

Aiguille du Moine – Pointe 3064m Didier Gumy, Karen and François Pallandre have added another route to this fine granite pyramid on the SW Ridge of the Moine. *La Voix du Druide* (280m: ED1: eight sustained pitches with cruxes of 6c, 6b obl) climbs up the centre of the NW Face, right of the 1988 *Ratheaux/Renault Route* and is reported to be excellent.

Aiguilles Rouges

In the last few years a number of excellent routes have been created in the Aiguilles Rouges close to the Brévent and Flegère télépherique stations. Although the rock here is solid gneiss, it is extremely compact and very difficult to protect with natural gear. Hence these modern routes have been entirely equipped with bolts. Situated at a moderate altitude and receiving considerable amounts of sunshine, they dry very quickly. Add easy accessibility and a magnificent panorama and you have all the ingredients to appeal to a large sector of today's modern crag climbers. Around five new routes were recorded last summer.

The popularity of the Aigulles Rouges, and indeed many rock-climbing venues on the north side of the Chamonix Valley, is set to increase further with the publication of a new topo guide, *Les Aiguilles Rouges - Escalade au Soleil*. Written by Thomas Dulac and Godefroy Perroux, the 272-page guide, with many colour photos, describes the climbing to be found at Les Houches, Le Brévent, La Flégère, Lac Blanc, Poya-Chéserys, Praz Torrent, Rénard-Barberine-Passet, Emosson and Grand Perron. The book can be bought in the usual Chamonix shops at a cost of 187 Francs but is also available direct from Perroux at DP Editions, 182 Route du Pont, 74310 Les Houches, France.

Clocher du Brévent Julie Balmat, Patrice Hanrard and Emanuel Méot have created *Krakoukasson* on one of the buttresses that descend south from the Clocher du Brévent (2398m). The 250m route sports eight pitches with a crux of 6a (5+ obl) and the descent is via an easy walk off the back.

Clochers de Planpraz Famous for its delightful little traverse above the Plan Praz téléphérique station, the Clochers now have another line put up on 19 August by Jérémy and Morgane Franc, Emmanuel Méot and Christophe Mussat. *Cocher-Cochon* climbs two successive buttresses in a total on nine pitches with difficulties of 5+/6a (5 obl).

Contrefort de l'Index At the start of the season Michel Piola completed his route *Mani Pulliti* on the East Spur of the Contrefort. This is the spur right of the descent couloir from the Index. Piola climbed this six-pitch route (4 to 5) in 1999 but returned last year to give it a thorough cleaning and add some equipment. Natural protection is still useful, notably at the start of the fourth pitch, and the route could potentially become a classic of the Aiguilles Rouges.

Grande Floria In September Laurent Collignon and Michel Fontès put up the four-pitch *Robin Wood* (6a, 5 obl) on the buttress to the right of the one on which the modern classic Piola route *Asia* is situated. The same pair also climbed the E Ridge of the same buttress to give a longer climb christened *A Isa*. This eight-pitch route has unavoidable difficulties of 5.

The Traverse of the Alps

Since the British alpinist Sir Martin Conway made the first really great traverse of the Alps in 1894 (from the Col de Tende in the Maritime Alps to the Ankogel in Austria) and celebrated it with his book *The Alps from End to End*, there have been many variations on this theme. The latest and almost certainly the most widely publicised took place from 26 August 2000 to 9 February 2001, when the well-known French alpinist, Patrick Bérhault, travelled by foot (walking, skiing or snow-shoeing) from Mojstrana in Slovenia's Julian Alps to Menton on the Mediterranean, south of the Maritime Alps, a distance as the crow flies of more than 1200km. Bérhault wanted to complete a traverse with a difference, linking together ascents of historic climbs that to him truly represented the evolution of alpinism. He eventually climbed 22 high-standard routes, often in demanding wintry conditions with a number of different partners. Several of these ascents were outstanding.

Starting on 27 August with the N Face of Triglav, he progressed to the Dolomites and a succession of nine climbs, which included the *Brandler-Haase* on the Cima Grande in seven-and-a-half hours, the *Phillip-Flamm* on Punta Tissi in eight hours and *The Fish* on the S Face of the Marmolada in seven hours.

With conditions far too snowy for the Badile, he climbed instead the classic N Face of the Cengalo and then moved on to the Oberland for an attempt on the *Harlin Route* on the N Face of the Eiger. However, with conditions again too bad, he decided to continue straight to Chamonix, where he arrived on 22 October. The weather was now fantastic and over 23-25 October he completed his most significant ascent of the entire journey when, with Philippe Magnin, he made the fourth ascent of the *Serge Gousseault Route* on the left flank of the Walker Spur. This was three days faster than the previous winter ascent, completed the preceding January (*see above*), and a day faster than the only summer ascent (the second overall ascent) by the talented duo of Gordon Smith (UK) and Tobin Sorenson (USA) in 1977. On 28 October he made an eight-hour ascent of the *Hypercouloir* on the Brouillard Face of Mont Blanc.

Three weeks now elapsed before the weather was good enough for him to return (by bike) to the Valais for an ascent of the Matterhorn by the *Schmid Route* and then onwards to the Oberland for an ascent of the Eiger by the *1938 Route*. Then it was on south via the difficult *Boivin Route* on the N Face of the Grande Casse, the Meije, the Ecrins, a solo winter traverse of Monte Viso and several hard routes in the Maritime Alps before he finally reached the Mediterranean coast on 9 February. He had spent 167 days completing his Alpine Voyage and ascended a total of 141,863m, 22,280 of these on the 22 climbs. Inevitably, the book will follow.

Huts

The **Tête Rousse Hut** on the *Normal Route* to the summit of Mont Blanc via the Gouter Ridge is being reconstructed. A new building, almost 3½ times the size of the present, is being built close to the existing hut. Costing an estimated 10 million francs, it should be ready by the summer of 2003.

The Saint Gervais Guides have improved access from the Col de Tricot to the **Durier Hut** (3,69m). From the 2120m Col a signpost indicates the path, which runs along steep alpine pastures to the Refuge du Plan glacier. From this hut cables lead to a system of ledges allowing parties to join the Miage glacier, from which an ascent, similar to that to the Aiguille du Gouter on Mont Blanc's *Normal Route*, leads to the Durier Hut. This now forms the best escape route from the hut in the event of bad weather.

A small reminder to alpinists visiting the **Gervasutti Hut** below the E Face of the Petites Jorasses. The final section of the approach from the Val Ferret is threatened by a band of séracs invisible from below. A British climber reports seeing his tracks completely obliterated by a large ice avalanche just five minutes after he had passed. In the early 1990s the well-known French climber, Alexis Long, was killed by sérac fall in just this vicinity.

Bregaglia–Masino

The summer season does not appear to have been too productive in the creation of new routes. However, it was notable for three extremely impressive first solo ascents on some of the most technically demanding alpine rock walls in the range.

Pizzo Trubinasca In June, Lecco climbers, Adriano Selva and Andrea Spandri, climbed *Dixon* on the sombre N Face. Put up over two days in 1989 by Paolo, Crippa and Dario Spreafico, this 14-pitch ED2 involves bold, thin and delicate friction work that should appeal to the devotees of the harder slab routes in the Mello Valley. With an obligatory crux of VIII–, it is considered to be one of the hardest routes in the Bregaglia and has today received no more than 10 ascents. Early the following month Selva returned for the first solo ascent, climbing the route in only five hours, backroping all but the first four pitches.

Cima Scingino In late July Adriano Selva made the first solo ascent of the rarely repeated *Delta Minox* above Bagni del Masino. This 12-pitch route on the steep compact S Face of the SW Pillar was first climbed by the legendary Tarcisio Fazzini (with Gianola and Riva) in September 1988. It is widely considered to be one of the finest and most difficult climbs of its type in the entire range and a lasting tribute to the late Fazzini. The route is sustained at a high level of difficulty, with unavoidable moves of VIII– and a crux of VIII+. Fixed gear is reported to be rather spaced, especially on the first and fourth pitch (both VII–/VII with only several points in 40-45m). It is not known whether Selva had previous knowledge of the route but he did take an enormous fall on the penultimate pitch (graded VII).

New Routes close to the Gianetti Hut Luca Maspes and Manlio Motto are reported to have put up a new route on the Torre Vecchia (aka Dente della Vecchia, 2913m), which is home to the old classic 1954 *Fiorelli Route* (150m: V) and the splendid, more modern 1987 Fazzini offering, *Champignon Merveilleux* (110m: VI–), and another on the Avancorpo del Porcellizzo, home to the classic *1968 Route* on the E Face by Isherwood and Kosterlitz (VII).

Precipizio degli Asteroidi Over the Easter Weekend, Gabor Berecz and Thomas Tivadar added another big-wall route to the SE Face of the Precipizio. *Dirty Dancing* lies in the Pejonasa Wall area close to Tivadar's existing aid lines such as *Kartykiraly* and *Mama Mia* and was climbed over four days with three nights spent on the wall in a portaledge. The route joins *Carretera de la Cocia* (Fazzini/Fazzini/Gianola, 1987: 750m: VII– and A2) after nine new pitches, at which point the pair were hit by a big rainstorm, which stopped further progress. *Dirty Dancing* (5.10 and A3), was reported as not particularly difficult and did not require the use of any bolts, making it the first route on the wall to be climbed without them. However, the crux, a roof on pitch five, required successive Bathook moves in drilled holes.

Monte Qualido On 16 August Palo Duris and Brano Hinca from Slovakia repeated *Qualifalaise* (Brambati/Carnati/Vitali, 1997: 120m of slab and crack climbing up to 7a+, 6b+ obl), a four-pitch route immediately left of *Mediterraneo* and right of *Il Paradiso può Attendere*. Then on 17, 18 and 20-23 they climbed *Melodramma* (Covelli/Covelli/Fieschi/Spatola, 1989: 500m: VII and A3). The two Slovaks repeated the original line (probably the fourth ascent), which finished after 13 pitches at the junction with *Il Paradiso può Attendere*. However, from 24-27 August, Czechs, Vojtech Dvorak and Radek Leinerth repeated the 1991 ascent, which continues for a further four pitches, finishing up the 1993 route *Melat*. This was probably the second ascent of *Melodramma* climbed in this fashion.

One day prior to this ascent the Czech pair had climbed the modern bolted route *Stargate* (Caloni/Pizzagalli/Soldarini, 1996: 700m: 17 pitches: VII/ VII+ obl and A1) at 7b and prior to this had created a new variation to *Il Paradiso*. *Time to Leave,* a 22-pitch line climbed on the 18, 19 and 21 August, follows the first 12 pitches of *Il Paradiso* (Boscacci/Masa/Merizzi, 1982: 950m of climbing: originally VII and A3 but all free at IX– by Beránek, Koller and Machaj in 1995), then breaks out right to create a new two-pitch link with *Mediterraneo* (Brambati/Carnati/Vitali, 1997: 6c+ and A0, 6b+ obl), which is then climbed to join *Melat* (Brambati/Carnati/Vitali, 1993: 700m: VII+ obl and A2) five pitches below the top. Dvorak and Leinerth completed this route all free at IX–.

Picco Luigi Amedeo On the 'Grand Capucin' of the Bregaglia-Masino Group, local activist Luca Maspes made the first solo ascent of the celebrated Fazzini/Gianola/Riva route *Electroshock*. This 12-pitch route on the c400m high SE Face above the Torrone Valley was first climbed in 1989 at VIII+ and A0 and featured obligatory moves of VIII–. It was still considered one of the hardest lines in the Central Alps in 1994, when Slovakians, Oto Bajana and Martin Heuger, spent two weeks on the route during July, finally making the first free ascent at IX (F7c) and thereby creating probably the hardest alpine rock route in the range. To date it has only received around 10 ascents and features very technical and strenuous overhanging sections, cracks and some slabby sections protected by a combination of natural gear, pegs and bolts. Maspes, a 29-year-old alpine guide from Sondrio, now living in the Mello Valley and arguably the foremost modern activist in the region, fixed the first three pitches on 1 July, then returned the following day to finish the route in a total climbing time of 14 hours. He backroped using a modified Grigri and climbed the route at F7a and A1, with two moves on skyhooks.

Punta Meridionale del Cameraccio It is still possible to put up long rock routes of a relatively accessible standard on the Italian flanks of the range. In June Lorenzo Lanfranchi and Luca Maspes put up a new 600m line on the SW Pillar left of the esoteric 1978 Guerini/Merizzi/Villa route, *Il Pilastro degli Dei*. The pair climbed their route fast using minimal protection and recorded maximum difficulties of only V+/VI.

PAUL KNOTT

Russia and Central Asia 2000

Thanks are due to the growing network of correspondents in the region, in particular Vladimir Birukov, Nikolai Chetnikov, Risk Online, Zoya Kondratieva, Vladimir Komissarov, Sergei Kurgin, Kasbek Valiev, Victor Vasyanin and Ivan Yarovai. News and information is gratefully received from expeditions of any nationality visiting these mountains.

Although climbing is being inhibited by conflicts and instability in some parts of this vast region, in others infrastructure and service improvements are making access easier for visiting climbers. Maps and route details for several climbing areas can be found at <http://mountains.tos.ru/kopylov>.

The Caucasus
Despite popular concern over security in this area, 2000 saw noteworthy climbs in many parts of the range. Unfortunately February saw a tragic incident on **Ushba (4710m)**. Mark Richard, Vincent Diamond, Marc Payne and four Russian climbers were camping at about 4000m on the Shkhelda Glacier when their camp was buried by an avalanche.

In the summer season several routes were climbed as part of the Russian Mountaineering Championship for high altitude technical ascents. The St Petersburg team of A Andreev, D Kirsanov, D Krivitski and I Potankin climbed a new route taking the centre right of the W Face of **Kiukiurtliu (4639m)**. The route, climbed from 26 June to 6 July, was awarded second place in the Championships and given the grade of 6B. Also awarded were two hard repeats, both at 6A, on **Mt. Dalar (3979m)** above the Uzuncol Valley. From 27-29 July a team from Shelkovo near Moscow led by Y. Dzhaparidze climbed the N Face of the tower on the L of the N Face (first climbed in 1976 by Michael Warburton and Valentin Grakovich). From 29 July to 1 August a Perm team led by A Shavrovich climbed the 1962 *Snesarev Route*, also on the L side of the face. In the same area from 8-9 August **Kirpich (3800m)** was climbed by the *Rhombus* on its W Face by Moscow climbers led by V Volodin.

Local climbers keen to stimulate climbing interest in the range have launched the project 'Open Caucasus', which has inspired two new winter routes in early 2001. From January 4-8 Yuri Koshelenko and Viktor Bobok from Rostov on Don made the first ascent of the N Face of **2nd-W Shkhelda Peak (4310m)**. Access to the face was gained via first ascents of two ice falls. In March 2001 Koshelenko was joined by Andrey Andreev,

227

Alexei Krivitsky and Sergey Voronin on the first ascent of *Northern Edge* (1200m, VI, 5.10, A2+) on **Erydag (3925m)**, a mountain in the Eastern Caucasus well known for technical rock climbing. The route took six days to the summit, with strong winds battering the climbers throughout.

The Pamir

Exploratory activity in 2000 was concentrated in the **Zaalaiskiy Range** east of the Kyzyl Art Pass. In July the area was visited by an Anglo-Russian expedition led by Tom Avery and Anatoli Moshnikov. After making ascents of **Golova Orla (5440m)** and **Kenelda (5439m)** they attempted **Khurumdy (6613m)**, retreating at 5900m due to poor conditions. Shortly afterwards a team from Kyrgyz Republic led by Alexander Novik made two first ascents in the area. From 4-9 August they made a traverse of **Zarya Vostoka (Eastern Sunrise, 6349m)**, then on 14 August they climbed **Pik Chorku (6283m)** from the Alexander Zotova Col to its NW. A trip organised by Andrew Wielochowski and Sergei Semiletkin was active in the same area, also in August, using a base camp at 3500m on the Kyzyl-Su River accessed from the Taunmurun Pass. An attempt on the NW Ridge of **Zarya Vostoka** was curtailed by poor weather, but first ascents were made of various peaks just under 5000m closer to base camp. The group experienced no major access problems, but did find tighter security than usual. In December a group from Tashkent including Victor Vasyanin made a winter attempt on **Khurumdy**. The climbers retreated from 5600m due to prolonged high winds and heavy snowfall.

Prior to their visit to the Eastern Zaalaiskiy the Wielochovski/Semiletkin-led team made an attempt on **Zartosh (6106m)** in the **Muzkol Range**. They climbed above the col between Zartosh and its W summit **White Pyramid**, but retreated short of the summit due to fresh snow.

The Pamir Alai

Concern continues about the threat of armed extremists operating in this area. There are widespread expectations that the underlying conflict will intensify. During the summer season American climbers Tommy Caldwell, Beth Rodden, Jason Smith and John Dickey had an alarming brush with terrorists, who forced them to descend from their portaledge camp and held them hostage. Eventually, feeling their lives were threatened, they managed to escape and after an 18-hour run were fortunate to meet the Kyrgyz Army. There were also other similar incidents during 2000 involving visiting climbers.

Previously unreported from summer 1999 was a British expedition visiting the Lialiak and Karavshin areas. In late July in the Lialiak area Mark Pretty and Ian Parnell climbed the new route *The Kyrgyz Way* at E4 5c 1150m (700m technical) taking the central spur of the W Face of **House Peak (3800m)**. Moving to the Karavshin area in August the pair first investigated **Central Pyramid (3809m)**, climbing new routes including

Smetana Moon at E5 6a 820m, 520m technical (200m L of *Black Magic*), and *The Big Joke* at E5 6a 1000m, 700m technical (100m L of *Smetana Moon*), both on the Upper Tier. On the Wall of Dykes on the **Russian Tower (Pik Slesov, 4240m)** they made the first ascent of *The Last Laugh* at E5 6A 680m, 100m R of a prominent waterfall. Parnell then teamed with Pete Scott from New Zealand to climb the new route *Albino Boys*, 100m L of the start of *Black Magic*, on the lower tier of **Central Pyramid** at E4 6a. Finally he made the solo first ascent of *The Isolationist* on the central spur of the E Face of **Kotin (4509m)** at E2 5c and 1300m.

Meanwhile Anne Arran and John Arran climbed new routes *The Hostage*, E5 6a 550m, joining *Missing Mountain* on the **Pamir Pyramid (3700m)**, and *The Philosopher's Stone*, E6 6b 1300m on Wall of Dykes (pitch 9 shared with *The Great Game* climbed by Dave Green and Paul Pritchard in 1997 (*see AJ103 p.260*).

The routes described above were all climbed in lightweight style using little in the way of fixed rope, bolts or pegs, in contrast to the approach taken by other climbers in the area. The team noted the potential of the alpine rock faces lying beyond the immediate rock towers, many of which are unclimbed or have had only one ascent. (*See also AJ105 pp. 68-70, 275.*)

The Tien Shan

The Tien Shan continues to attract considerable interest from British teams. Pat Littlejohn's activities here over the past few years have been recognised by his election as Honorary President of the Kyrgyz Alpine Club. Recent exploratory activity has encompassed both hard new routes in popular areas and ascents in lesser known parts of this extensive range.

A major event in the **Central Tien Shan** was the 'Festival Khan Tengri 2000', which appears to have enjoyed high level support in Kazakhstan with visits from government officials and various international diplomats. Of over 500 participants from almost 30 countries, many were helicoptered to the N Inylchek Glacier and 280 attempted **Khan Tengri** (approximately 79 were successful). As part of the festival a speed ascent was organised on **Khan Tengri**, the first from the N side. The winner was Denis Urubco of the Kazakh Military Sport Club, with times of 7 hours 40 minutes to the summit and 12 hours 21 minutes return trip from base camp.

Due to unusually deep snow, high winds and cold temperatures there were no successful ascents of **Pobeda (7439m)** during the 2000 summer season. The furthest point reached was by a Kazakh team, which turned back 400m from the summit.

Climbers from Central Asia and Russia have been active during recent winters in the Ala-Archa area of the **Kyrgyz Range**. In January 2000 the Kyrgyz team of Alexander Ruchkin, Dmitriy Grekov and Andrey Puchinin climbed a new route on the N Face of the **1st Tower of Korona (4810m)** which they named *The Mobiles Route*. Climbing lightweight, they completed the 900m mixed route in 9 hours at 5B, 5.10/A1, descending by moonlight.

In late November Kyrgyz climbers Mikhail Mikhailov, Andrey Puchinin, Alexander Gubayev and Vitaly Akimov climbed a new route on the central N Face of **Free Korea (4740m)**. Claimed to be harder than all previous routes on the face, *Grey Rocks Girdle* often exceeded 90° and was climbed using a portaledge over 11 days. Later in the season a team from Krasnoyarsk climbed a further new route on the face, taking an ice couloir on the L of the face at the 5th category of difficulty. In addition the 1997 Ruchkin-Puchinin route *North Wall Direct* (6A/A3+) was climbed both by a team from the Kazakhstan Army and by climbers Gutnik and Novoseltsev.

The range also attracted popular interest amongst local alpinists during 2000, which included a mass ascent of **Komsomolets (4140m)** involving more than 100 people. There was also a ski and snowboard descent from **Pik Adygene (4404m)**, and a ski trip to the confluence of the Manas, Toktogul and Ala-Archinsky Glaciers. Europeans David Gerrard and Hilda Grooters visited the area in August, making the traverse of Towers 3-5 on **Korona (4860m)**.

In September a team guided by Pat Littlejohn, Victor Saunders and Vladimir Komissarov made the first recorded climbing visit to the W part of the **Kuilu Range** S of Lake Issyk Kul, approaching by 4wd vehicle along the Kuilu Valley. From a base camp in the Karator Valley at c.3300m teams led by Komissarov and Littlejohn made ascents of seven moderate summits of which the highest was **Tsarevich (4920m)**, while Saunders' team climbed **Pik Humani (4800m)** at AD– and **Pik Karator (5203m)** via a snow route at PD. Littlejohn, Ingrid Crossland and Diarmid Hearns then made an attempt on **Pik 5088m**, gaining its N Ridge but unable to complete it due to poor conditions. Later they summited via the S Ridge and named the peak **Matarshinitsa**. Following this three peaks were climbed above the nearby Ashutor Valley including **Krenintor (4732m)**.

In July-August a group led by Rob Johnson with members from Queen Elizabeth and Milton Abbey Schools made first ascents in the nearby **Ak-Shiirak Range**. Of the five peaks climbed the highest was **Tsunami (4750m)**, which was ascended via the SW Arete at PD–.

Exploration continued in the **Western Kokshaal-Too** range on the border between Kyrgyz Republic and China. In late July the UK/Netherlands team of David Gerrard, Hilda Grooters, Danny Boothman and Louise McParland visited the Itali Glacier area, attempting **Pik c.5000m** from a base camp accessed by 4wd vehicle at c.3800m.

Previous teams visiting the Western Kokshaal-Too have observed the potential on the Chinese side of the border, and this previously unvisited area was explored during July-September by the US team of Mike Libecki, Jerry Dodril, Jed and brother Doug Workman. Having obtained permission with considerable difficulty, the team travelled by road via Ak-su and Karabulak, then with animal support beyond the road end. They attempted **Pik 5697m** on the border with Kyrgyz Republic, but were turned back by a storm close to the summit. The climbing was on steep granite, snow and ice. Following this attempt they climbed on crags in the area which were steep, clean and solid with strong natural lines. Overall, they report almost limitless climbing potential on impressive towers, walls, spires, and ridges.

Previously unreported from 1999 was the visit of a large Moscow team to the Grigoriev and Palgov Valleys near the E end of the Western Kokshaal-Too. The team, led by Boris Starostin, Fedor Akhmatov, Valerii Boiko, Victor Efimov and Eugeny Monaenkov, used a base camp at the confluence of the two rivers at c.3500m reached by some adventurous driving. A group led by Akhmatov made the first ascent of **Chon-Turasu (Dzholdash, 5780m)**, from the S at 5B. A group led by Boiko climbed a new route on **Dankova (5982m)**, taking the NNE Ridge at 5B. A team led by Manaenko made the first traverse of **Krylya Sovetov (5450m)** at 5B. Also climbed were **Piks 5200m** at 4B, **4825m** at 5A, and other smaller summits. On 12 August on the ascent of the N Face of **Pik Cosmos (5940m)** falling ice caused the death of Igor Korsun, after which the expedition was called off.

In the **Ugamskiy Range** of the Western Tien Shan an ascent was made of the 6A *Rafikov Route* taking the L side of the NE Face of **Kyzylbash (4200m)**. The Norilsk team, headed by A Paveljev, climbed the route over three days to 22 August.

In July a Royal Engineers expedition led by Stuart Batey visited the **Dzungarskiy Alatau** on the Kazakh-China border. The team made the second ascent (first British ascent) of the highest peak **Semyonov Tien Shansky (4622m)**, and made ascents of seven further peaks in this little-explored range.

Siberia and the Russian Far East

Reports from the Altai suggest an increasing level of interest in the range by Russian alpine skiers and snowboarders. There have also been reports that Siberian alpine climbers have put up a number of hard new routes in a spectacular gorge in the Kara-Kabak area of the Northern Chuiskiy.

The tradition of extended wilderness traverses in Russia was continued during 2000 by a team of six from Mezdurechensk led by Sergey Kosin, which completed an extended ski and raft tour of the **Putorana Plateau** in Central Siberia. At a total of 2548km this tour was more than twice the length of that made by the same group in 1997 (*see AJ103 p.263*). Leaving Norilsk on 23 March they went by ski via the Melkoye, Lama, and Ayan lakes and the Amnundakata, Dulismar, Yaktali and Kureyka rivers to make ascents of mountains **1312m**, **1701m** and **Kamen**. They also made an ascent of plateau **Talabaiski Greben (1040m)** by a new route. After covering 1018km on ski they completed the trip by rafting down the Vivi and Niznaya Tunguska Rivers to finish on 12 July.

Ice-climbing potential has been reported in the same region, around Norilsk. An outdoor tower provides training from October to June, and within skiing distance there are 30m waterfalls at the edge of the Putorana Plateau as well as further climbing interest accessible by helicopter. The city also provides unique 'mixed climbing' on the icicles that form on its high-rise buildings.

In Kamchatka, local climbers celebrated the Millennium (2000-2001) at the top of the volcano **Avachinskaya (2741m)**. In the $-25C$ temperatures the champagne froze in the bottle, but fortunately could be warmed in a convenient fumarole. Interest in ice-climbing also continues in the area, with reports of January ascents of the 70m frozen waterfall at the base of **Vilyuchinskiy (2173m)** by local club 'Kutkh'.

DEREK FORDHAM
Greenland 2000

(Plates 16, 17)

As in previous years the majority of so-called 'sports' expeditions to Greenland were to cross the ice cap, almost without exception by the east-west trade route from the Ammassalik area to Kangerdlugssuaq. In contrast to previous years, however, all expeditions have been remarkably reluctant to respond to requests for information! These notes represent the acquired knowledge of the author and the 10 responses to more than 39 separate enquiries.

Inland Ice

The first party to start across the Inland Ice from east to west was a three-man group led by Clive Woodman (UK). They left the Hahn Glacier on 20 April and reached Kangerdlugssuaq 35 days later having encountered lower temperatures and higher precipitation than expected. The party came across the road onto the Inland Ice being built by VW as access to a vehicle test track and expressed the same concerns over this grotesque intrusion into a wilderness area as were expressed in these notes in AJ 2000.

Also in April a four-person group led by Michele Pontrandolfo (Italy) left Isortok equipped for a 60-day crossing to Kangerdlugssuaq which they managed in 32 days. The group experienced delays caused by the high winds and poor weather encountered on the Inland Ice with temperatures dropping to –35°C.

A rather more brisk crossing was made in May by Marek Kaminski and Wojtek Ostrowski (Poland) who were helicoptered onto the edge of the Inland Ice on 2 May and, using parachutes as sails, reached Pt.660 near Kangerdlugssuaq 13 days later. They also reported weather conditions less than perfect with much deep fresh snow.

Starting from Apuserserpia on 1 August a three-man group led by Audun Hedland (Norway) took 23 days to reach Kangerdlugssuaq. This expedition made particular efforts to keep their loads as light as possible and had pulks weighing 60kg at the start of a journey for which they had allowed 33 days. They experienced a rather warm 'summer' crossing with mixed weather including wind and falling snow but chose such a good route through the coastal areas that their decision to save weight and not take a rope was not regretted. However the final four days of negotiating half-metre-deep melt water lakes on the West Coast may have suggested that a dinghy would not have gone amiss! This group also encountered the awful VW test road and were reprimanded for photographing a car – on the Inland Ice of Greenland!

These expeditions across the Inland Ice seem to reflect the pattern noticed over past years; that they are taking longer than traverses made 20 years ago, perhaps as a result of the poor and changeable weather encountered these days. The jury is out on climate change but on the Inland Ice it certainly seems to be happening.

West Coast

The only reported activity on the West Coast was Greenland 2000, a sloop-based expedition led by Bob Shepton (UK) which involved a total of nine persons as crew or climbing members.

The expedition was the first part of what is intended to be a two-year project to climb among the coastal mountains of West Greenland. From Kangerdluarssugssuaq Fjord the group made ascents of **Pt.1510** and **Pt.1230** before moving on to climb directly from the boat onto the first pitch of a sieged first ascent of the N Face of **Sandersons Hope, 1045m**, rashly claiming it to be the biggest sea cliff north of the Arctic Circle (see below).

South Greenland

This increasingly popular area which is relatively easy of access saw several expeditions in the field with the aim of making hard rock-climbing ascents of the big walls and spires with which the area is well endowed.

The first was the six-man 'Thumbnail 2000' led by Ian Parnell (UK) which in July/August made a 31-pitch six-day free ascent of the 1300m **East Face** of **Agdlerussakasit**, claimed to be, 'one of the world's biggest sea cliffs'. Sadly, while the climb was in progress Matthew Bransby was killed in an abseiling accident near to the base camp in Torssuqatoq Sound.

The eight-person British Eastern Torssuqatoq Spires Expedition led by Jonathan Bracey (UK) was in the field during July to September and made first ascents of **Whaleback Peak 1200m, Pt.1303, Flatiron 1120m, The Great White 1050m** and **The Crest 1180m**. The rock in the area was not good and took its toll when Ian Renshaw fell and broke his heel, necessitating helicopter evacuation to Nanortalik.

The eight-man British American South Greenland Expedition led by Jim Lowther (UK and USA) operating in strictly national groups during July and August made 13 first ascents between 1112m and 1948m in the areas to the north of Kangikitsoq Fjord and east of Kangersuneq Qingordleq Fjord.

'*Non c'è due senza tre*' ('If it's happened twice, it will happen again.') was climbed by an Italian-French team on the West Face of the Third Pillar on **Nalumasortoq**, the impressive wall that rises out of Tasermiut Fjord. On 25 May, Mario Manica (Italy), Giancarlo Ruffino (Italy), Francesco Vaudo (Italy) and Jerome Arpin (France) established base camp on the shore of Tasermiut, at the foot of Ulamertorsuaq. Without spending a night there, they immediately started work on Nalumasortoq to take advantage of the good weather. Climbing in pairs, one team fixed ropes on the route while the other stocked the foot of the wall with equipment and supplies. On the first section, the climbers found belays left by the British team of Nigel Shepherd and Ian Wilson in 1996. After the first few pitches which lead rightwards to the prow, the route follows the huge dihedral that leads directly to the summit. The route was 19 pitches with difficulties of 6c and A3. The team placed one bolt. On 31 May Ruffino was forced to withdraw with a knee injury. Next day, the remaining climbers reached the summit.

East Coast

Peter Darmady and Mark Huxham (UK) made several summer ski ascents in the mountains between the Knud Rasmussens Glacier and Femstjernen. Oliver Beihammer and Wolfgang Freinberger (Austria) used the Knud Rasmussens Glacier as the starting point for a journey to Mont Forel which, owing to various problems, had to be abandoned.

In the Lemon Mountains Richard Pash (UK) returned with seven companions during June and July to climb and explore the regions adjacent to the area visited by his expedition in 1999. The group made 32 new routes and carried out a ski tour into the **Lindbergh Fjelde** to the north.

In May Christine Watkins led a three-woman international group (UK, Germany, Holland) to the **Watkins Mountains**. The party was delayed by weather in Iceland and Greenland but managed to make ascents of six peaks between 2992m and 3609m from the upper Woolley Glacier, four of them first ascents.

Further north in the **Staunings Alps** in July, Hans Laptun led a four-man Norwegian/French party into the hills behind Mestersvig and on to the Sorte Hjørne hut, Mellompass and Malmbjerg. They report that all the huts at Malmbjerg have been removed and the site is now covered by the debris of a large rockfall. The Arcturus Glacier has also changed and large lateral moraines now make access to the glacier much more difficult than a few years ago.

The Scottish Suess Land Expedition composed of the four members of the Anderson family took two inflatables to Kirschdalen in July. After a weather delay at Ella island they enjoyed 30 days of flawless 'Arctic Riviera' weather during which they travelled into Antarctic Sund and Kejser Franz Joseph's Fjord and made the first ascent of a peak on the east side of Engdalen. They returned to Mestersvig via **Alpefjord** reporting good climbing rock on the north side of the fjord and good char fishing in Forsblad fjord.

Another Scottish family group, The Forsblad Fjord Expedition formed of John, Clare and Michael Throgood boated in and explored the Alpefjord and Forsblad fjord areas during August.

The eight-strong North East Greenland Project led by Mike Lea (UK) also used inflatable boats to complete a circumnavigation of **Clavering Island** at 74°N. They reported that marine life was abundant including bowhead whales, narwhals, killer whales and walrus. Ascents were made of several peaks on Clavering Island and above the neighbouring fjords.

The Nanok company has continued its programme of restoring the old trapper's huts in the area north of Mestersvig and in 2000 the group completed the restoration of Hoelsbu and established an historical collection of artifacts from the trapping era in a hut near Sandodden.

In the farthest north area of Greenland, known as **Avanarsuasua**, Dennis Schmitt (USA) was back again with seven companions. From Bliss Bugt on the north coast they penetrated the **Daly Bjerge** and from an advanced base camp overlooking the unexplored **Bertelsen Glacier** made a number of ascents of peaks rising above the glacier.

Even in this ultimately high latitude part of the High Arctic desert a significantly increased rate of summer snowfall is reported.

SIMON RICHARDSON

Scottish Winter 1999-2000

The 1999/2000 Scottish winter season was dominated by the ascents of three high standard mixed routes. The first winter ascents of *The Steeple* on the Shelter Stone, and Rolling Thunder and Mort on Lochnagar all demon-strated a leap in technical standards and are milestones in the evolution of Scottish winter climbing. In contrast to many top level mixed climbs on the Continent and in North America, where protection is pre-placed by abseiling the route beforehand, these advances were all achieved by preserving the Scottish ethic of attempting routes ground-up. To illustrate the skills, persistence and tactics required to succeed on today's cutting edge Scottish winter climbs, these three routes are described in detail below before highlighting a selection of noteworthy ascents in other areas. Route descriptions of all the routes described in this review can be found in the 2000 Scottish Mountaineering Club Journal.

The Steeple – The Ultimate Last Great Problem

The season started with a bang in November when Alan Mullin and Steve Paget made the first winter ascent of *The Steeple* (IX,9) on the **Shelter Stone**. A winter ascent of *The Steeple* had been considered the ultimate last great Scottish winter climbing problem for over 20 years, but it was felt to be so futuristic that few people thought it a real possibility. The 250m route is graded E2 in summer and has seven pitches of sustained 5a and 5b climbing with one pitch of 5c. Clearly a winter ascent was not only going to involve very technical snowed-up rock climbing, it was also going to take a long time.

Having gained a good working knowledge of the cliff from two previous attempts over the last two seasons, Mullin and Paget calculated that an ascent would require at least 24 hours' climbing time. This would involve two bivouacs if the route were to be climbed in daylight. Clearly this was not an enticing prospect given the unpredictability of Scottish weather, so the pair decided the best tactic was to climb the route in a single push. Rather than lose two nights' sleep by starting very early in the morning, they deliberately chose to start in the middle of the day and climb through the night.

Alan Mullin set off up the first Steeple corner pitch at 1 pm on Saturday afternoon, and by the time Steve Paget had led the second corner pitch it was dark. They circumvented the summer 5c crux by following the slanting crack of *Postern* and the difficult *Bad Karma Variation* to *Winter Needle* which they had climbed the previous season. *The Steeple* layback cracks then led to the foot of the main 40m Steeple Corner – a prominent feature of the route. The corner was climbed in two pitches and took nine hours. Two nuts were used for aid to start the second section of the corner, and by the time Paget had reached the good ledges at the top of the corner the pair had spent 15 hours climbing in darkness, and it was now becoming light. Unfortunately a warm front moved in early in the morning and the difficult final pitch was led in thawing conditions with bare walls and wet snow in the cracks. As planned they finished the route in just over 24 hours of climbing, and were back home that afternoon.

The overall statistics of the climb are impressive. The 250m route had three pitches graded 9, two of 8 and the remaining four graded 6 and 7. The route was given an overall grade of IX, 9 and Alan Mullin commented afterwards that it was equivalent to making ascents of four of the hardest Northern Corries test-pieces one after another. Without question it is the most sustained technical winter route climbed in Scotland to date.

Rolling Thunder - An Unprecedented Solo Ascent

After *The Steeple* ascent a fierce debate raged about whether the Shelter Stone was in acceptable winter condition, but Mullin upped the ante a few weeks later by making an incredible on-sight solo first winter ascent of *Rolling Thunder* on **Lochnagar**. The rock climbs on the steep and vegetated overlapping slabs of the Tough-Brown Face are often wet and infrequently climbed. *Rolling Thunder*, a sustained four-pitch E1 5b between *Mort* and *Tough-Guy* was first climbed in the summer of 1982, and it is doubtful whether it has ever been repeated. The steep and vegetated nature of the cliff fascinated Mullin, and after a summer visit viewing the climbs from the below, he was convinced that *Rolling Thunder* was a winter possibility.

Mullin left the Loch Muick car park at 6am and broke trail through deep drifts for four hours to reach the North-East Corrie. Two other teams made it into the main coire that day, but they wisely chose to climb on the more accessible Central Buttress. The cliff was covered in fresh snow, piled high on ledges and the cracks were verglassed. Mullin back-roped the first 25m pitch, pulled up his 60m rope and then ran the next three pitches together, making a more direct version of the summer route in the process. It snowed so hard during the afternoon that *Parallel B* and *Raeburn's Gully* avalanched to either side of the Tough-Brown Face. He reached easy ground in a fierce storm, roped down in the dark and was back in his car driving home by 9pm.

The precarious nature of the climbing which involved long reaches for turf tufts and small moss clumps meant he took five falls. *Rolling Thunder* with the *Death by Misadventure Variation* was graded VIII, 8 and must be considered one of the most serious mixed routes in the country. Alan Mullin's ascent of *Rolling Thunder* was without precedent. For good reason, very few Scottish winter first ascents have been climbed solo. The most notable example is Tom Patey's *Crab Crawl* traverse across the cliffs of Creag

Meagaidh, and in a similar vein, Martin Moran traversed the three central Beinn Bhan coires in 1989. Both routes were outstanding achievements, but their length and Grade IV climbing meant they were logical solo undertakings. No one had ever climbed a Scottish grade VIII alone before, let alone make a solo first ascent of one.

Mort - A Challenge for the Next Generation?

A month later, all eyes were once again on **Lochnagar** when Brian Davison, Andy Nisbet and Dave McGimpsey made the first winter ascent of *Mort* (IX, 9). The current SMC guide book to the cliff describes *Mort* as a challenge for the next generation, but it was the old guard in the shape of Davison and Nisbet who claimed the mountain's greatest winter prize.

Mort, which takes a prominent line through the centre of the damp and vegetated overlapping boiler-plate walls of the Tough-Brown Face, was first climbed in 1967 and is graded E1. Nowadays it sees no more than one or two ascents each summer and is thought to be at the upper end of its grade. As the most prominent line through the Tough-Brown Face it was an obvious, if futuristic winter challenge, and was first tried by Colin MacLean, Nisbet and Davison in January 1985. The date is significant as the only route of comparable difficulty at the time was *Guerdon Grooves* on Buachaille Etive Mor which had been climbed by Arthur Paul and Dave Cuthbertson the previous winter. MacLean led the first hard pitch, using two rest points above the big roof which is the summer crux, and reached the belay ledge after five hours. Nisbet and Davison were too cold to lead through, so MacLean continued in the lead but he reached a blank section about 15m from easy ground and retreated. Although they had failed, the attempt was an eye-opener and Nisbet and MacLean were quick to capitalise on their experience. Over the following weeks they made the first winter ascents of *Unicorn* in Glen Coe and *Winter Needle* on the Shelter Stone.

All three climbers returned to *Mort* during the following winters. Davison estimates that he visited Lochnagar 18 times with MacLean to try the route, but it was rarely in condition. In March 1992 Davison and Nisbet made an attempt which ended after Davison took a 20m fall over the crux roof, which he had just free climbed, landing at Nisbet's feet. As the number of people climbing high standard mixed routes has risen over recent years, it became clear that the route was not going to hold out forever. In December, just after his *Rolling Thunder* solo, Alan Mullin made a spirited attempt with Guy Robertson. Climbing on sight in difficult powder conditions, Mullin regained MacLean's 1985 highpoint, but was again stopped by the blank nature of the rock.

Just after New Year, Lochnagar was in superb condition. Most importantly for an ascent of *Mort*, there was a thin smear of ice above the blank section which had stopped MacLean and Mullin on their previous attempts. Early on Saturday 15 January, Nisbet climbed up to the first stance and

Davison led through on the critical second pitch. Onlookers were highly impressed as Davison pulled swiftly through the roof, and stepped left around a rib into a vertical groove. The only protection on this section was a warthog and a poor tied-off blade peg and Davison reached the belay ledge after two hours in the lead. On the third pitch, Nisbet took a couple of 5m falls at the blank section, before handing the lead to Davison who managed to place a poor peg and reach a small turf placement and the ice smear above. The ice was thin and almost vertical, but after 15m Davison reached the belay ledge. Nisbet and McGimpsey came up in the dark, and it was then a formality for Nisbet to lead the final pitch to easy ground.

Nisbet rated *Mort* as the most difficult Scottish winter route he has ever done. This is a significant assessment as Nisbet has been at the forefront of the sport for 20 years and has made first ascents of a quarter of Scotland's Grade V routes.

The Cairngorms

It was the rapid succession of snow storms and freeze-thaws over the New Year period that brought Lochnagar into exceptional condition in January. Guy Robertson and Tim Rankin were first to appreciate the quality of the ice on the mountain when they made an ascent of *Pinnacle Grooves* just after New Year. Normally this route is a VII, 7 icy mixed climb, but it had been transformed into a continuous runnel of ice and was a straightforward grade V. A few days later Pete Benson and Finlay Bennet made the second ascent of *Trail of Tears* (VII, 8) on the Tough-Brown Face. This was one of the most sought-after repeats on the mountain and had seen a number of near misses over the last two seasons. Benson and Bennet found it in superb icy condition and continued up the Tough-Brown Ridge to the plateau. Nearby on the Douglas-Gibson Face of Shadow Buttress B, Simon Richardson and Chris Cartwright climbed the steep open corner to the left of *Eclipse*. This had been attempted by Aberdeen climbers in summer and winter since the 1950s, but the compact nature of the rock and total lack of protection had deterred all comers. On this occasion the exceptional conditions allowed *The Dark Side of the Moon* (VI, 6) to be climbed on thin ice all the way.

Another freeze-thaw cycle brought the cliff into even finer condition the following weekend. Whilst Davison, Nisbet and McGimpsey were climbing *Mort*, Benson and Bennet returned to the Tough-Brown Face to attempt the second ascent of *Diedre of Sorrows* (VIII, 8). First climbed by Dougie Dinwoodie and Andy Nisbet after a number of attempts in 1986, this route was considered to be the hardest mixed route in the country. The pair made good progress until the crux third pitch when Benson took a fall onto an in-place peg. This pulled out and he fell onto Bennet cutting his neck and breaking his helmet. Benson re-climbed to his highpoint and replaced the peg, but unsure of where the route went above, they decided to retreat.

The following day Andy Cave and Dave Hesleden started up the route, somewhat intrigued to see that a party had been on it the day before. As Cave led the third pitch, he clipped Benson's new peg but was surprised to see that there was no sign of further progress. Another couple of moves and Cave was on easier ground that led to the stance. On the final pitch, Hesleden was unable to find sufficient ice to climb the original finish, so he climbed the final 5b pitch of the summer route *Dirge* to reach easier ground. This new Direct Finish turned out to be the hardest pitch on the climb.

In the Northern Cairngorms Alasdair Coull and Sam Chinnery made the second complete ascent of *Winter Needle* (VIII, 8) on the Shelter Stone. *Winter Needle* was first climbed in winter by Andy Nisbet and Colin MacLean over two days in February 1985. They avoided the first two slab pitches by climbing the big left-facing corner left of *Clach Dhian Chimney*, and climbed the *Steeple* Layback Cracks to bypass the Crack for Thin Fingers pitch. Last season Alan Mullin and Steve Paget climbed *Bad Karma* (IX, 8), a series of variations on the Nisbet-MacLean line, in a single 17-hour push. Coull and Chinnery took the 1985 winter start and then followed the summer line in its entirety. They had a bivouac on the big ledge below the Steeple Corner and finished the route the next day. No aid was used and the overall grade was thought to be VIII, 8. Coull and Chinnery's superb ascent is unlikely to be the final chapter in the *Winter Needle* story however, as several teams now consider a one-day ascent of their line to be the next logical step.

Central Highlands

In Glen Coe, Malcolm Bass and Simon Yearsley added the imposing *Dark Mass* (VI, 6) to Church Door Buttress on **Bidean**. This starts up the spur of *West Face Route*, crosses the traverse of *West Chimney Route*, continues up the imposing cracked wall above and swings round the right edge of the buttress in a sensational position to finish up a series of corners. Big news on **Buachaille Etive Mor** was the second complete ascent of *Raven's Edge* (VIII, 7) by Alasdair Coull and Sam Chinnery. This exposed line of hanging grooves and corners on the right edge of Raven's Gully was first climbed in winter by Brian Sprunt and Rick Allen in 1984. One of the highlights of the climb, the open-book corner on the third pitch, was avoided on the right, and Rab Anderson and Rob Milne climbed the complete route in March 1996. Chinnery and Coull made a smooth ascent and confirmed the route as one of the finest winter expeditions in Glen Coe.

On **Ben Nevis**, Simon Richardson and Chris Cartwright took advantage of a cold and snowy spell in mid-February to make the first winter ascent of *The Crack* (VIII, 8). This difficult eleven-pitch route takes the imposing series of offwidth cracks and chimneys up the vertical wall to the right of *The Shroud* and continues up the crest of Raeburn's and Baird's Buttress to reach the summit of Carn Dearg. The North Face of **Aonach Beag** was particularly icy and at times there were queues to tick the modern classics of *King's Ransom* (VI, 6) and *Royal Pardon* (VI, 6). Roger Webb brought the cliff bang up to date by climbing the steep buttress to the left of *Royal Pardon* with Martin Hind. *Mean Streak* (VII, 6) takes a very steep and narrow ice runnel to gain easier ground and the final section of *King's Ransom*.

On **Creag Meagaidh** there was an early repeat of *Postman Pat* (VII, 7) on Great Buttress by Dave McGimpsey and Paul Thorburn. A few days later Andy Clarke and Nick Kekus climbed the shallow ice and mixed groove system to the left. *Born Slippy* (VII, 6) is the most significant addition to the mountain since *Postman Pat* was climbed by Mal Duff and Andy Perkins in February 1991.

Northern Highlands

The finest addition to the Northern Highlands was the first ascent of *Genesis* (VII, 7) on **Beinn Bhan** by Andy Cave and Dave Hesleden. This prominent eight-pitch line which had been eyed by several North-West regulars in recent years, takes the overhanging fault to the left of *Die Riesenwand* on the huge Giant's Wall of Coire nan Fhamhair. The route avoids the lower overhanging section of the fault by traversing first left, then back right along exposed narrow turf ledges to reach the main chimney line. A steep hanging icicle was passed on the right, and a through-route was taken below a huge chockstone to gain a series of steep bulges which led to the end of the major difficulties on the fifth pitch. The climb weaves through some unlikely ground and is a worthy companion to the other three-star adventures on the wall such as *Gully of the Gods* and *Great Overhanging Gully*.

Nearby on **Beinn Eighe**, Guy Robertson and Jason Currie made the second ascent of *Blood, Sweat and Frozen Tears* (VII, 8). This was Robertson's third attempt on the route and its reputation as one of the finest technical mixed routes in the North-West was confirmed. Andy Nisbet and Dave McGimpsey made several good additions to An Teallach, but their best route was *Haystack* (VI, 7) which climbs the impressive left wall of *Hayfork Gully*. Nisbet had discovered this very steep 170m face several years ago but thought it impossible. Each time he returned it looked a little more hopeful, and in early January the pair plucked up the courage to try it. They were delighted to find it was possible to link together an unlikely line of zigzag ramps and hidden chimneys up the centre of the wall.

It would be a mistake to think that Scottish winter pioneering is all about climbing the hardest routes. Of the 150 new routes added during the season, the majority were in the middle grades. A good example of the adventurous nature of the climbing on offer was the enterprising visit by Roger Webb and Martin Hind to **A'Mhaighdean** near Carnmore where they climbed *A Ridge Too Far* (IV, 4) to the right of *Pillar Buttress*. Winter climbing in the Great Wilderness is not something to be undertaken lightly – after topping out on the most remote Munro in Scotland, the pair were then faced with a ten-hour walk back to their car.

HARISH KAPADIA

India 2000

This year was marked by several good expeditions and ascents of new peaks in the Indian Himalaya. Amongst the leading climbs in the Garhwal were ascents of **Nilkanth**, a new line of ascent on **Shivling** by the Germans and the Korean ascents of **Mukut Parvat East** and **Abi Gamin**. A British team visited the Arwa valley again and made a fine ascent of **Arwa Spire**. Indian teams climbed **Sudarshan Parvat**, **Chaturangi** and **Sri Kailash**.

The Indian Mountaineering Foundation organised two small-budget expeditions to **Burphu Dhura**. The second expedition made the first ascent of the main peak.

In Himachal the first ascent of **Kangla Tarbo** was achieved by an Irish team. **Gepang Goh** was attempted by an Indian team while Japanese teams made excellent exploratory climbs in Spiti.

In the higher ranges, **Kangchenjunga** sent back an Austrian team from a height of only 6200m. The exploration of Rimo Glacier and the ascent of **Rimo IV** by an Indo-French team was another highlight of the season. The team also reached Karakoram Pass and Col Italia, one of the rare civilian teams to do so, creating a history of sorts.

On 'common' peaks, apart from those covered here, the following was the tally:

Expeditions in the Indian Himalaya, 2000

Peak	Expeditions
Kun	3
Kedar Dome	2
Stok Kangri	6
Jogin Group	4
Thelu	7
Kalanag	2
Manali / Ladakhi	5
Kalindi	1
Bauljuri	1
Bhagirathi II	2
Baby Shivling	1
Rudugaira	1
TOTAL	35

Sikkim

Kangchenjunga (8586m)
Expedition :　　Austrian
Leader :　　　Willi Bauer
Period :　　　April-May 2000
Result : The ten-member team set up base camp at Green Lake (4700m) on the Zemu Glacier in mid-April. They proceeded slowly up the E Ridge route with ABC at 5250m, Camp 1 at 5625m and Camp 2 at 6200m. The route ahead was full of soft snow due to fresh snowfall and they found the route too dangerous, abandoning the attempt at 6200m on 8 May.

Garhwal

New Route on Nilkanth
On 1 June a British expedition led by Martin Moran made the first ascent of the W Ridge of **Nilkanth** (6596m). This ice spire rising directly above Badrinath temple is one of the most beautiful summits of the Indian Himalaya and has maintained an enigmatic reputation with only a few known ascents in 50 years of attempts from all sides.

After a five-day climb John Leedale, Andy Nisbet and Jonathan Preston (UK) and Casper Venter (SA) made it to the top with Moran. The route involved an initial danger of sérac fall on the climb from base camp, but thereafter was relatively safe with rock pitches up to IV+, some sustained Scottish grade II and III mixed climbing and a fine corniced summit ridge at an overall grade of D+/TD–. The team fixed 200m of rope around pinnacles at the foot of the ridge but thereafter climbed in alpine style in a six-day round trip from base camp.

First inspected by Edmund Hillary during his first visit to the Himalaya in 1951 the W Ridge was most recently attempted by British climbers Chris Pasteur and Duncan Tunstall in 1993, who had to retreat from 5850m owing to altitude sickness.

During the Nilkanth ascent other groups from the party explored the unclimbed Panpatia range of peaks to the south, known as Vishnu Ghar Dhar (Vishnu's Fortress), making the first ascent of **Pt 5919m** (for which the name **Lakshmi's Peak** is proposed) at PD+/AD– standard , followed by the first recorded crossing of the 5200m Panpatia Col to Madhyamaheshwar temple and Kalimath.

The party was lucky to enjoy excellent weather during the climbing period from 17 May to 2 June, 2000. On the day of return to base camp after the Nilkanth climb the weather broke and a week of heavy rains commenced.

A wealth of other exploration remains to be tackled on the other peaks of the Panpatia range, notably 6257m **Parvati Parvat** and **Pt 5968m**. However, the glacier approaches to many of the peaks are difficult. More details can be found on Martin Moran's web site: www.moran-mountain.co.uk.

Abi Gamin (7355m) and Mukut Parvat East (7130 m)

Expedition: Korean
Leader: Nam-il Kim
Period: July-August

This Korean team of 15 members established their base camp on 3 August with the help of 150 porters. This was the team which had climbed **Mukut Parvat East II** (the lower peak) two years before. They approached the mountain from Badrinath. Common camps were set up for both peaks. Finally, on 11 August, they established Camp 3 at around 6600m. **Mukut Parvat East** was climbed by three members on 22 August and four members reached the summit on 26 August. **Abi Gamin** was climbed by three members on 27 August.

Arwa Spire (6193m)

Expedition: British
Leader: Kenton Cool
Period: September-October

This shapely peak in the remote Arwa valley was first noticed by an Indian expedition in 1997. In 1999, a British team climbed **Arwa Tower** (6352m) for the first time. This year a six-member British team with Kenton Cool as their leader attempted Arwa Spire in the post-monsoon season. Their initial attempt on the mountain via the N Face was not successful. They changed their route and succeeded via the E Ridge. On 11 October, Peter and Andrew Benson reached the virgin summit and they were followed by Alan Powell, Kenton Cool and Ian Parnell on 16 October. This was one of the finest climbs in the Garhwal this season.

Bhagirathi III (6454m)

Expedition: Swedish
Leader: Hendrik Kuiper.
Period: August - September

Unsuccessful. The two-member team attempted the peak via the W pillar. On 11 September they retreated due to bad weather and extreme cold.

Expedition: German
Leader: Walter Hoelzler.
Period: September - October

Unsuccessful. This German team of four members reached 5800m but heavy snowfall and ice on the route stopped their attempt.

Gangotri (6672m)

Expedition: Italian
Leader: Massiuo Pagani
Period: September - October

Unsuccessful. The Italian team consisting of eight members reached around 5800m from where they had to retreat because of heavy snowfall and bad weather.

Jogin I (6465 m)

Expedition: British
Leader: Paul Farmer.
Period: September - October

Unsuccessful. The team of six members attempted this peak in the Kedarganga valley in the post-monsoon season. On 2 October they had to turn back from 5900m due to too much unconsolidated snow.

Satopanth (7075 m)

This is one of the most frequently attempted 7000ers of the Gangotri region.

Expedition: Spanish
Leader: Edurado Cuber Cabrera
Period: June

Unsuccessful. The team of eight climbers attempted the peak on 6 June and on 13 June. Both the attempts were foiled by bad weather.

Expedition :   Indian (Pune)
Leader :   Patade Rajesh (five members)
Period :   August

On 21 August the team set up Base Camp on the Nandanvan Plateau on the Gangotri glacier. They passed Vasuki Tal and reached Camp 1 on the 29th. On 1 September they left at 8.30 a.m. to attempt the summit directly from Camp 1 at about 6000m. Nikrant Shinde fell and his fall was arrested by Rajesh Patade. However Nikrant had broken a finger and suffered bruises and the expedition was called off.

Satopanth was also attempted unsuccessfully by a Swiss team. No details are available.

Shivling (6543 m)

This famous peak in the Gangotri area received its fair share of attempts and ascents. The details of some of them are as follows:

Expedition: French
Leader: E Ratouis and B Hassler
Period: May - June

On 30 May, Irma Wolf and Bruno Hassler reached the summit of Shivling by the W Ridge. Earlier the same pair had climbed **Bhagirathi II** (6512 m) on 10 May by the E Face. On 22 May Bhagirathi II was also climbed by B Laubert, F Gendarme and I Retat.

Expedition:	German
Period:	May-June

This was a two-member team comprising Thomas and Alexander Huber, but when, early in the expedition, Alexander fell ill, Thomas Huber teamed up with Ivan Wolf, a member from the Swiss expedition, and they made an ascent via the N Ridge direct on 31 May. This was one of the finest climbs on Shivling in several years and they called it *Shiva's Line*.
Both climbers received the French award of *Le Piolet d'Or* for this climb.

Expedition:	American - Canadian
Leader:	Karen McNeil
Period:	September-October

This American-Canadian ladies' team of four members initially made an unsuccessful attempt on the E Ridge from 22 to 28 September. Afterwards they attempted the peak by the W Ridge and after establishing two camps en route, the leader with Sue Nott reached the summit on 3 October.

Expedition:	Swiss
Period:	October

Unsuccessful. This two-member team of F Markus and B Romen reached 6000m where too much snow prevented further progress.

Expedition:	French
Leader:	M François
Period:	September

Unsuccessful. This seven-member team attempted Shivling via the N Face. They had to stop 150m below the top owing to bad weather.

Expedition:	French
Leader:	Emmanuel Pozzera
Period:	August

Unsuccessful. This seven-member team attempted Shivling via the W Ridge but the attempt was called off owing to bad weather.

Expedition:	Indian
Leader:	Dilip Naskar
Period:	August / September

Unsuccessful. This six-member team attempted the normal route. However, a bad storm on 23 September forced them to retreat.

Nanda Kot (6861m)

Expedition :   Indian
Leader :   Basanta Singha Roy
Period :   October

A famous peak on the Milam Valley trail. After proceeding along the Gori
Ganga, base was established at 4140 m in the Lwan valley. After two more
camps they reached 6100m on 19 October when they found the terrain too
difficult and returned.

Thalay Sagar (6904 m)

Expedition: Korean
Leader: Hwang Won Chel
Period: August - September

Successful. This Korean team of eight members established their Base Camp
on 15 August. They faced occasional bad weather. They chose the NW
Ridge for their attempt. On 10 September Jeong Il Oong and Kim Jun Mo
reached the summit.

Rataban (616 6m)

Rataban has two approaches. One is via the Valley of Flowers and Bhuidhar
Pass. The other route approaches from the N, reaching the same pass. This
year the peak saw three attempts.

Expedition :   Indian (Bengal)
Leader :   Suman Guhaneogi
Period :   June

This team approached the peak from Kosa valley near Malari. Three camps
were set up on the Kosa Kunar glacier. They attempted the top on 18 June
but were stopped at 6010m by a large crevasse.

Expedition :   Indian (Calcutta)
Leader :   Amulya Sen
Period :   June

This team approached the peak from Bhuidhar valley (Valley of Flowers)
and set up their Camp 3 at 5150m near the pass. On 3 July they stopped
about 60 metres below the summit as a hail storm caught up with them.

Expedition :   Indian (Howrah)
Leader :   Kaushik Bhattacharya
Period :   August

This team approached the peak from Bhuidhar valley (Valley of Flowers)
setting up three camps, the last one on the pass at about 5490m. They faced
bad weather but finally on 27 August the leader with five members and
three HAPs reached the summit. The summiters were Soneh Lahiri,
Baidyanath Santra, Binod Kr. Ram, Rakhal Ghosh and Amit Patra.

Sudarshan Parvat (6507m)

Expedition :   Indian (Jamshedpur)
Leader :   Rajendra Singh Pal (9 members)
Period :   June

This team followed the same approach as above. They followed the route of first ascent (1981) and the summit was reached on 9 July via the E Ridge. Summiters were N S Panwar, R S Pal and R Bhat.

Expedition :   Indian (Calcutta)
Leader :   Bivujit B Mukhoty (12 members)
Period :   August

They followed the now popular E Ridge approach. Base Camp was set up at Thelu-Raktavarna glaciers' junction on 28 August and three more camps were set on the Swetvarna glacier up to 6000m. However owing to persistent bad weather and lack of time they gave up the attempt at 6000m.

Chandra Parvat (6728m)

Expedition :   Indian (Durgapur, Bengal)
Leader :   P C Nath (13 members)
Period :   May-June

This beautiful peak has two summits and stands on the Suralaya Bamak. The team proceeded along the Gangotri glacier to Suralaya Bamak setting up ABC and two more camps on the mountain. Finally on 30 May the ridge which rises from the Suralaya Bamak was climbed to the summit. Summiters were P C Nath, Monotosh Majumdar, Bahadur and Thapa.

Peak 5242 m (East of Panch Chuli V)

Expedition :   Indian (Calcutta)
Leader :   Pradeep Kr Kar (16 members)
Period :   May

The main intention of the team was to attempt the virgin peak of **Panch Chuli III** from the eastern approaches. They approached from Son Duktu village and through the Meola glacier. However, considering the difficulties of Peak III they decided to climb the peak which rises on the ridge falling from the long ridge of **Panch Chuli V**, to the south of the Meola glacier. This gentle peak was climbed on 22 May by Pradeep Kr Kar, S Majumdar, Arup Saha and Moloy Kanti Halder.

Deoban (6855m)

Expedition :   Indian (Nawabgunj, Bengal)
Leader :   Pallab Das (16 members)
Period :   July

This is a high peak situated near **Kamet**. The team set up a Base Camp at Vasuki Tal and followed the long ridge falling from **Bidhan Parvat**. On 18 July Camp 4 was set up at 6400m. However bad weather forced them to wait at this camp for 2 days and as there was no improvement in the weather, the attempt was given up.

Chaturangi (6407m)

Expedition :   Indian Ladies (Calcutta)
Leader :   Ms Rupa Santra (14 members)
Period :   September-October

A well known peak in the Gangotri glacier group. The ladies' expedition followed the route from along the glacier to set up series of three camps on the mountain. The summit was reached on 1 October by Ms Rupa Santra, Ms Barnail Mukherjee and Ms Angibi Devi.

Two IMF expeditions to peak Burphu Dhura in 2000

The Indian Mountaineering Foundation organised two expeditions to **Burphu Dhura** (6414m) during the year, in addition to the expedition in 1999. The first expedition followed the route pioneered by the previous expedition and climbed the S Peak. The second expedition reached the main summit – a worthy first ascent in eastern Kumaon.

The first expedition, consisting of eight members, was led by R C Bhardwaj. Other members were Roshan Ghatraj, Amresh Jha, Sadique Ali Khan, Rushad Nanavatty, Naresh Bhardwaj, Nagendra Sahi and Balwant Singh Kapkoti. They left Delhi on 8 June and travelled via Munsiari to make a base camp on the Sankalpa glacier at 3630m on 16 June. Advance Base Camp was established on the Kalabaland glacier on the 18 June at 4565m. 150m of rope was then fixed to reach the foot of the S side of **Burphu** main. Camp I was established here at 5430m on 23 June. Passing through several crevasses they fixed 450m of rope and established Camp II on the rocky route leading to a snow plateau at 5760m. This was on 26 June.

Ascent of Burphu South

On the same day, 26 June, four members of the team started from Camp I at 5.45am and repeated the ascent of Burphu South via the NE Ridge (first climbed in 1999 by the same route). Summiters were R C Bhardwaj, Amresh Jha and Nagendra Sahi. The other team on the 27th occupied Camp II and fixed 150m rope towards the main summit. However, the weather remained bad for the next three days and they were forced to return on 30 June. The highest point was reached by Roshan Ghatraj, Sadique Ali and Nagendra Sahi. An avalanche swept down Rushad Nanavatty on 27 June between ABC and Camp I. Member Balwant Singh Kapkoti was escorted down towards ABC when an avalanche rolled down between the gully and the slopes of **South Burphu Dhura**. He was carried down 150m and escaped with slight injuries. He was saved by a good helmet and a strong British rucksack given to him by his father. On 1 July they returned to Base Camp and came back to Munsiari.

The second expedition to Burphu Dhura, which was successful in making the first ascent of the peak, was led by Wing Cdr S S Puri. It followed the same route to ABC as the first two expeditions. A Base Camp (3830m) was set up on 22 September 2000 at the junction of the Kalabaland and Sankalpa glaciers. ABC (4400m) was at the foot of the Kalabaland icefall. Two further camps were established at 5200m and 5800m. On 26 September a party of three occupied the last camp. The summit was climbed on 27 September 2000 by Loveraj Dharmashaktu, Balwant Singh Kapkoti and Ramesh. They left camp at 5am and proceeded along the route which had been fixed a day earlier. They reached 'Shark's Fin', a prominent feature on the ridge, at 6am. Proceeding carefully, they reached the two-humped summit, climbing both the humps to make sure there was no mistake. The summit was reached at 9.50am. This was the first ascent of the peak. Another challenging peak in the Kumaon had been climbed.

Himachal Pradesh

Kangla Tarbo I (6315 m)
Expedition: Irish
Leader: Patrick O'Leary.
Period: August - September
Kangla Tarbo so far remained a major unclimbed peak in the Khamengar area. The 65-year-old veteran, Patrick O'Leary, who is one of the prime explorers of the Spiti Himalaya led his team of five climbers and they were successful in reaching the virgin summit of **Kangla Tarbo I**. On 9 September, G Brian, D Colin and R Hugh reached the top via the S Face. They explored the nearby valleys after their climb.

Menthosa (6443 m)
Expedition: Japanese
Leaders: Kazuto Obata and Kazuto Yamamoto.
Period: July - August
Result: The team trekked from Udaipur to their base camp via Karpat village. Their route followed the SE Ridge. Two members reached the summit on 12 August. On 13 and 14 August the ascent was repeated by three different members each day.

Snow Cone (6311 m)
Expedition :   Indian
Leader :   Biplab Sengupta
Period :   June
This peak is situated at the head of the Bara Shigri glacier in Lahul. It is to the N of **Shigri Parvat**. This was an eight-member team from Calcutta. Base camp was established at Concordia on 25 June 2000. After establishing

two more camps the summit was climbed on 29 June. The summiters were: leader, Protush Sau, Subrata Majumdar and Raju Kumar with three High Altitude Supporters.

Mulkila IV (6517 m)
Expedition: Japanese
Leader: Minoru Yanagi
Period: July - August
Unsuccessful. The leader along with Kiyoshi Ishi and M. Zazala reached around 5700m on 13 August where huge crevasses in the upper section stopped them.

South Parbati (6128 m)
Expedition: British
Leader: Oliver Sanders
Period: September
Unsuccessful. Oliver Sanders with Martin Chester and Iain Peter attempted the SW Ridge. They had to face bad weather with heavy snowfall almost every day. Constant rockfall was another hurdle. This is a high pyramid peak in the Parbati river valley approached from Kullu and Bhuntar.

Unnamed Peaks (6222m) and (6140m)
Expedition: Japanese
Leader: Takako Kato
Period: July - August
This Japanese team consisting of 12 members successfully climbed both the peaks. Peak 6140 m was climbed on 5 August via its N Face by 7 members. Peak 6222m was climbed by 7 members on 7 August via its NE Ridge. Both these peaks are situated on the border of Lahul and Spiti, northwest of Lagbhorche peak. This is situated north of Kunzum La and approach is via Lungbar Topko and Karcha nala.

Unnamed Peak (6250m) H.P.
Expedition: British
Leader: Graham Boswell
Period: July - August
This peak is situated towards the north of **Chandra Tal**. They turned E from Topko Gogma. The peak is near point Tagne (5870m) marked on the map. The team of 11 members reached the E Col and then followed the E Ridge to the summit. On 5 and 6 August 6 members and then 3 reached the top respectively.

Peak 6127m (Lahul)

Expedition :   Indian (Calcutta)
Leader :   Prasanta Roy
Period :   October

The eight-member team travelled on Manali-Leh highway to Darcha and trekked on the popular Shingo La route to Palamo and Chuminako where a BC was set up. This peak is situated west of Shingo La and is approached by a nala in the west as the final climb to the Shingo La begins. The team set up Camp 1 on 7 October. On the 8th they reached a col at 5900m and as they were approaching the summit a storm hit them. They stopped about 350m below the summit.

Peak 6111m (Lahul)

Expedition :   Indian (Bengal)
Leader :   Jyotrimay Dutta
Period :   August

This peak is situated near Baralacha La. It is to the north of Suraj Tal. The team set up BC on 20 August at 4870m and Camp 1 at 5330m near a glacial lake. On 25 the summit was climbed by the leader with Prasant Mandal, Subir Mandal, Jayanta Kr. Dutta and Sanjay Kr. Barman.

Shiva (6142m) (Lahul)

Expedition :   Indian (Bengal)
Leader :   Gautam Bamik
Period :   August

A big 16-member team reached BC at 3600m near Runsun Tal from Manali. The attempt was given up at 5800m due to large crevasses which they could not cross.

Gepang Goh (6053m) (Lahul)

Expedition :   Indian (Calcutta)
Leader :   Sanat Kr. Paul
Period :   August

The team travelled from Manali across Rohtang Pass to Sissu nala. They set up two camps but faced heavy snowfall on 23 August. However they attempted the peak on the 26 but gave up due to further snowfall. This was an eight-member team.

Expedition :   Japanese
Leader :   Takashi Iazawa (six members)
Period :   August

The team followed the same route as the Indian team and attempted the N Face. Two camps were established and a final attempt was made on 10 August. However continuing bad weather and lack of time forced them to return.

Ladakh – Zanskar

Dzo Jongp (6150m) (Zanskar)

Expedition :   German
Leader :   Hermann Wihlem George
Period :   August

A 15-member team from Germany climbed the E Face of this peak situated in the Markha valley. The peak is to the S of Thiksay monastery. Nine members reached the summit on 26 August.

Eastern Karakoram

Saser Kangri (7672m)

Expedition :   Indian (Chandigadh)
Leader :   Rakesh Kumar (eight members)
Period :   August-September 2000.

The team approached this high peak in the East Karakoram via the Nubra valley. They followed the South Phukpoche Glacier and established three camps by 25 September. They had intended to follow the normal route from this side, across the peak IV. However, a long spell of bad weather stopped their climbing and the team returned.

Peak 6230m (on Samar Lungpa)

An 18-member expedition from the Indo-Tibet Border Police led by M P Singh left the remote military base of Daulat Beg Oldi (4848m), N of the Chip Chap River, towards the end of August and summited P. 6230m, a peak on Samar Lungpa, close to the Karakoram Pass, on the 11 September. The pass itself is at 5569m, a desolate spot on the old silk route from Leh to Yarkand. Peaks in the vicinity have a relatively small altitude gain above the surrounding plateau and are normally technically straightforward scree mountains with a little snow cover. However, due to obvious strategic reasons very few have ever been climbed.

Rimo 2000 Karakoram Expedition

An Indo-French Expedition was organised to the East Karakoram in July-August 2000. The expedition climbed two peaks, **Rimo IV** (7169m) and **Migpa** (5935m). They reached two historic passes, the Karakoram Pass and the Col Italia. Two new cols, Lharimo and Dzomsa, were explored. Three Rimo glaciers were explored after several decades. And other points in the area were observed and reached.

Karakoram Pass

Starting from Leh on 31 July 2000, the team followed the trail to the Karakoram Pass. On this historic Central Asian Trade Route caravans passed until 1959. The India-China war of 1962 put the area under restriction. In the past 40 years this was perhaps only the third civilian party to visit the Karakoram Pass.

On 12 August the team reached Gapshan. From here two separate base camps were established, on the South Rimo glacier (on its R bank) and on the Central Rimo glacier (at the foot of the central moraine).

South Rimo Glacier

Two camps were established on the way to the peak. After a day of bad weather, Rimo IV (7169m) was climbed (third ascent) on 23 August by Dr Jeff and Sherpa Pema Tsering. Lt Cdr S Dam reached an altitude of c.6800m before descending to help the ailing liaison officer down to ABC. The route to the summit followed the West Face, approached from the cwm between peaks **Rimo III** and **IV**. Two cols, Lharimo Col, on the southern rim of the glacier, and Dzomsa Col, on the northern rim of the south Rimo glacier, were reached on 24 and 25 August respectively, each by three French members .

Central Rimo Glacier

The area of the Central Rimo glacier had been visited only twice before. In 1913 an expedition led by Filippi de Filippi spent some weeks on the South, as well as the Central Rimo glaciers, mapping the area, though the party did not reach Col Italia. Their photographs and panoramas are a complete record of these glaciers. In 1930 a party of Italians led by Prof G Dainelli was climbing on the Siachen glacier. The Nubra river, which drains the Siachen glacier, was flooded and blocked their exit beyond Warshi. As an alternative escape route they climbed on the Teram Shehr glacier and crossed a high col at its head and descended the Central Rimo glacier. They named this col 'Col Italia'. Their party then returned to civilisation by the caravan route from the Depsang La. No other party had visited this glacier in the last 70 years.

Three Indian members and four Sherpas proceeded on the Central Rimo glacier. After initial difficulties they opened the route which led to 'Lake Filippi', at the centre of the bifurcation of the Central and the South Rimo glaciers. The party followed the right bank of the Central Rimo glacier to set up, in all, four camps up to the foot of 'Col Italia'. En route were seen 'Lake Dainelli' and the snout of the North Rimo glacier (the international boundary). After a day of bad weather, 'Col Italia' was reached on 23 August by three Indian members and two Sherpas. It is a 7 x 7 kilometre plateau and they overlooked the legendary 'Raider's Cols 1 and 2' towards the Shaksgam pass.

They returned to Camp 1 on 25 August. The next day the Sherpas Huzefa, Nima and Karma made the first ascent of **Migpa** (5935m) and obtained a view of both the glaciers. The expedition returned by the same route to Sasoma on 2 September and to Leh on 4 September.

Death of Kaivan Mistry

Kaivan Mistry, an enthusiastic mountaineer from Bombay, died while crossing the Shyok river while returning from the Rimo Expedition.

On 27 August, as the teams were returning as planned, tragedy struck while the Central Rimo team was crossing a branch of the Shyok river. Suddenly, Dan Singh fell and three other members tumbled with him. All four were swept away by the Shyok river, even though the water was only knee-deep. But huge chunks of ice were floating rapidly down the river and the cold was intense. Three members, Huzefa Electricwala, Harish Kapadia and Kumaoni Dan Singh managed to reach different banks. Dan Singh was reached first and rescued by Sherpas. Meanwhile, injured, wet and shivering, Harish and Huzefa spent almost three hours sheltering under a small rock on the opposite bank before help arrived. Kaivan Mistry, who was unable to throw off his heavy rucksack, may have hit his head against a rock as he fell. He was carried 2-3kms downstream, where he was found dead by the South Rimo team that was crossing the Shyok river at the same time. Kaivan's body was carried to Gapshan and, on 29 August, flown to Leh by an Indian Air Force helicopter; it was sent to Mumbai on the 30th after a post-mortem at Leh.

Kaivan Mistry (32 years) was an experienced mountaineer on his 9th trip to the Himalaya and Karakoram. He was a lighting-engineer-designer for the theatre world in Mumbai. He was well known in mountaineering and art circles. Very enthusiastic about the outdoors, Mistry loved the trans-Himalayan barrenness. On many Himalayan nights he regaled his friends with his typical Parsi humour. He was unmarried and has left behind elderly parents. Kaivan will be sorely missed.

Death of S P Godrej

Another Parsi who passed away was S P Godrej. He was a unique person with varied interests in mountains, conservation, wildlife and nature. He was the Chairman of Godrej Industries in India and could have passed a comfortable corporate life. But his commitment to life brought him in contact with various issues and he devoted time (and many times offered sponsorships) to worthy causes. S P Godrej passed away at the age of 88, and his humour and vitality was still maintained in his last days. He was the doyen of all activities related to nature. An Hon Member of the Himalayan Club since 1978, he was President of the Indian branch of the World Wide Fund for Nature and was associated with the Bombay Natural History Society and many other organisations. He worked actively for the Indian Heritage Society which fought against the destruction of many old heritage buildings in Bombay.

LINDSAY GRIFFIN

Pakistan 2000

Thanks are due to Asem Mustafa Awan, BMC, Bernard Domenech, Xavier Eguskitza, David Hamilton, Sean Isaac, Walter Keller, Klettern, Yuri Koshelenko, Jamie McGuinness, MEF, Pakistan Ministry of Tourism, Emanuele Pellizzari, Simon Perritaz, Marko Prezelj, Alexander Ruchkin, Adam Thomas, UIAA Expeditions Commission, Dave Wilkinson and Simon Woods for help with providing information.

It was a mixed season on Pakistan's mountains, not least on the 8000m peaks. While not a single climber reached the top of Gasherbrum I, a total of 25 summited K2 and were the first to do so since July 1997. June's fine weather was rather too early for most expeditions to mount a summit bid, and by the next suitable period towards the end of July a significant number of teams had already run out of time and left for home. Inevitably, there were several near misses but fortunately only one death. Sadly, this occurred to one of Spain's best-known mountaineers, Félix Iñurrategi.

The weather in the Karakoram was good throughout most of June and excellent in the latter part of the month. After this, however, the only clear weather window occurred briefly towards the end of July, with August generally bad owing to the influence of a heavy monsoon, and early September only marginally better. Access to Concordia for the 8000m peak base camps was easy early in the season owing to the low winter snowfall, but dry conditions on lower peaks and glaciers presented problems for numerous expeditions.

The Baltoro 8000-metre peaks

Gasherbrum II (8035m) A total of 45 climbers representing 10 expeditions reached the 8035m summit of **Gasherbrum II**, all between 20 and 30 July. These included many French and Swiss (three Swiss expeditions under the overall direction of the guide, Kari Kobler), 12 Austrian and German climbers from a very successful commercial expedition led by Ralf Dujmovits (climbing his seventh 8000m peak), the first Venezuelans, Carlos Casillio and José Delgado (who spent the previous month unsuccessfully attempting Gasherbrum I), and the Latvian, Ilgvars Pauls (who is also a Seven Summiter). There were several veterans such as the Austrians, Albert Hausler (59) and Jurgen Spescha (57), and a number of women such as Martine Maurette (France), Barbara Hirchbichler (Germany), Michele Mirat and Madaleine Pasche (Switzerland), and the Austrian, Paula Hub, who has a couple of 8000m peaks to her name and whose husband made one of the very early ascents of the peak back in July 1979.

An increasing number of local high-altitude porters are also reaching the summits of 8000m peaks and last year saw Whad Ali Shah, Amin Ullah Baig and Sajed Ullah Baig, Qadrat Ali, Rasul, Subz Ali and Ghulam Rasool all reach the top of Gasherbrum II.

There were three Spanish teams on the mountain, one of which, a group of Catalans, included the well-known Iñurrategi brothers, Alberto (31) and Félix (33), who were attempting to add both Gasherbrum I and II to their long list of 8000m peaks. Starting with Makalu in 1991 the two brothers had climbed to the summits of 11 of the giants, all without the use of supplementary oxygen, before coming to Pakistan in June. Like everybody else in the field, they were prevented by poor weather and snow conditions from seriously attempting Gasherbrum I, but both reached the summit of II on 28 July. Later the same day, as the pair were descending from Camp II (c6500m) using in-situ fixed ropes, Alberto remembers arriving at an anchor point with two ropes. He clipped in to one and slid down to the next belay station. Just a few minutes later his older brother, Félix, was beginning his descent of the other rope, when either it snapped or the individual anchor failed. Félix fell more than 400m to his death.

Broad Peak (8047m) The very unsettled July weather prevented most expeditions from reaching the summit of Broad Peak. Only those who were able to remain at base camp until the end of July, stood any chance of success. Fifteen climbers reached the top, a remarkably low number compared with the normal tally. All were on the *Normal Route*.

Five Japanese and two Pakistanis summited between 26 and 30 July. These included: Hideji Nazuka, making his eighth ascent of an 8000er, and Ali Musa from Shimshal, who both reached the foresummit on an earlier attempt that season; 58-years-old Kazuyoshi Kondo, making his fifth ascent of an 8000er, and Muhammad Hussain from Machulu; Hideto Kurahashi and Masahide Matsumito, who, due to deep snow, were forced to make an unplanned bivouac just below the foresummit during the ascent. A Korean expedition was also successful; five Koreans and one Pakistani (Nizir Hussain), including Park Young-Seok (his 12th 8000m peak). There were also two Hungarians, Zoltan Acs and Laszlo Mecs, from an expedition led by David Klein, making the first Hungarian ascent of the mountain.

K2 (8611m) Twenty-five climbers reached the summit of **K2**, more than in any single year since 1996. All expeditions tackling the mountain from Pakistan last year did so via the Abruzzi Ridge or the SSE Spur (aka the *Basque Route*). Some attempted both. The first to summit were four Koreans on 26 June via the SSE Spur. Four more from this 11-member team summited three days later. The Koreans fixed 3000m of rope and all but one member used oxygen on the summit day. The one Korean climber not using supplementary oxygen was the accomplished Park Jung-Hun, who had already climbed the SW Face of Everest and the South Face of Annapurna. However, he appears to have suffered very severe frostbite in one foot.

It was exactly one month before any other climbers were able to summit, but from 29-31 July a total of 19 people reached the top. Most of these climbed via the Abruzzi Ridge and included the first Brazilian, Waldemar Niclevicz, the first Turkish climber, Nasuh Mahruki, the first Ecuadorian, Ivan Vallejo, the fifth Nepalese, Shera Jangbu Sherpa from the Khumbu and the sixth British climber, Andy Collins, from a predominantly American expedition led by Gary Pfisterer, husband of the late Ginette Harrison. Summiters also included the Italian guide from the Aosta Valley, Abele Blanc, completing his 11th 8000m peak. Blanc and Niclevicz were the first to break trail above the Shoulder on 29 July and did not make the highest point until 6.00pm. They descended through the night, with Blanc reaching the top camp on the Shoulder at 4.00am, while Niclevicz decided to seek refuge in a crevasse and finally returned at 7.00am.

Another well-known but controversial figure in Korean mountaineering also made the summit. Um Hong-Gil (39) was making his first attempt on the mountain as part of a well-equipped and strong Korean team. The story of Um reaching the summit on the 31st, having abandoned the Hushe porter, Ali Mohammed, on the Shoulder when the Pakistani became seriously ill (to be later helped down the mountain by the American, Fabrizio Zangrilli, from Pfisterer's expedition) and the furore at Base Camp has been well documented. Pfisterer's group wish to emphasise that the Korean team that first opened the route and summited in June displayed the opposite character, giving oxygen for one-and-a-half hours from their own sets to a Pakistani porter high on the mountain when he became sick.

Um Hong-Gil's claim to have climbed all the fourteen 8000ers is widely disputed, as there appears to be very strong evidence from his companions on Lhotse (1995) that he stopped well short of the summit and it is known for certain that his two ascents of Shisha Pangma (in 1993 and 1994) were only to the Central Summit.

All this somewhat overshadowed the greatest performance on the mountain during the season. Two very well-known and respected mountaineers, Yasushi Yamanoi from Japan and Wojciech Kurtyka from Poland, who were part of a five-member team that included Yamanoi's wife, the very accomplished high-altitude climber Taeko Yamanoi (formally Nagao), were planning to attempt the unclimbed East Face in alpine style. However, after three sorties, each defeated by bad weather, and a subsequent attempt on the SSE Spur, only Yamanoi felt motivated to continue.

Leaving base camp at midday on 28 July, Yamanoi climbed alone up the SSE Spur to reach the Shoulder by 4.00pm the following day. After a short night's rest he reached the summit at noon on the 30th and was back in base camp on the evening of the 31st. This is probably the fastest time (48 hours) in which this route has been climbed, but in 1986 Benoît Chamoux reached the summit via the Abruzzi Ridge in just 23 hours from Base Camp.

One climber who did not make the top was 43-years-old Hans Kammerlander, who was trying for the second year in succession to ski from the summit. He reached the Shoulder at the end of June's good weather period but was not sufficiently acclimatised to go much further. Kammerlander feels that K2 is completely skiable via the SSE Spur, except for a 50m rock section in the Bottleneck, and is coming back for another attempt in 2001. However, on 14 June, prior to the attempt mentioned above, Kammerlander led a large party of 'clients' to the top of an unnamed peak, c6000m, located west of Broad Peak Base Camp. This appears to have been a first ascent and an application to name it has been made to the appropriate authorities.

There were five expeditions attempting the North Ridge from the Chinese side: Samdruk's powerful Tibetan team attempting all the 8000m peaks; an American-led group; a Japanese and a Mexican expedition, plus two German climbers. Reports suggest only a few of the climbers were prepared to put in the work fixing ropes etc, while the rest sat back and waited for the job to be completed.

The Americans, who included well-known mountaineers, Paul Teare and cameraman Jeff Rhoads, as well as the female high-altitude climber, Heidi Howkins, were at base camp for several months and made repeated attempts on the Ridge but were never able to get above c7500m. Howkins and the Spanish climber, Araceli Segarra, were both attempting to become not only the sixth female but also the only living woman to have climbed K2. However, all expeditions failed.

Central Karakoram

Kondus Valley – Tahir Tower Americans, Dave Anderson, Jimmy Chin, Steph Davis and Brady Robinson, managed to gain permission to visit the Kondus Valley, close to the war zone on the disputed Indo-Pakistan border. The four Americans chose an impressive, virgin, c1000m-high rock spire in the lower valley, which they named **Tahir Tower**, reaching the summit on 20 July after 10 days on the face and 35 pitches with maximum difficulties of 5.11 and A3. The route was christened *All Quiet on the Eastern Front*. The team reported good relationships with the Pakistan military met in the valley during their stay.

Hushe Region

The Nangma Valley This valley is rapidly establishing itself as one of the premier rock-climbing venues in the Karakoram-Himalayan chain and several major new routes were added last summer. Unfortunately, it is also reported that last summer a huge mudslide wiped out Kande, the village at the entrance to the valley from where all expeditions recruit their porters.

Shingu Charpa (The Great Tower) Koreans, Shin Dong-Chul, Bang Jung-Ho and Hwang Young-Soon, made the first ascent of **Shingu Charpa, 5600m** (aka The Great Tower) in the Nangma Valley. The three Koreans reached the summit on 23 July after overcoming difficulties rated at 5.11 and A2.

Amin Brakk Adolfo Madinabeitia, with his partner Jua Miranda, returned to the West Face of **Amin Brakk (c5850m)** last summer to create *Namkor*, a 1550m line between the two routes completed in 1999; *Sol Solet* to the left and *Czech Express* towards the right side of the face. The new route has 31 pitches with approximately half free up to 6b+ and half aid. *Namkor* (Balti for 'bad weather') becomes the second route on Amin Brakk to be awarded the A5 rating.

Brakk Zang A Korean team made two new routes on the South Face of this 4800m rock spire west of Amin Brakk in the Nangma Valley. One, *Anjong Neonj* (5.9 and A4–), was immediately to the right of the pillar taken by the *1998 British Route*, and one, *Moon Sung Wook* (5.9 and A3+), a little to the right again but still left of the *Spanish SE Pillar* climbed in 1998.

Kharidas Valley The North American trio of Nils Davis (USA), Sean Isaac (Canada) and Todd Offenbacher (USA) made the first ascent of a previously unnamed granite spire in the Kharidas Valley, the next valley north of the increasingly popular Nangma Valley in the Hushe region. The three were only the second party to climb in this valley. On 18 July they made the first ascent of a spire, which they named **Ibrahim Brakk (c5200m)** after their Balti cook. On the last pitch, which nearly defeated the team, Davis was able to pull out a fine lead, overcoming loose ground and crumbling flakes with only marginal gear, to complete a pitch of 5.10+ and arrive on the summit one hour before dark. The climbers, who were carrrying no bivouac equipment, made a rappel descent through the night, leaving behind half their rack. No bolts or pegs were used and the route was christened *Azad Kashmir* ('free Kashmir'), 700m: V 5.10+R.

Chogolisa (7665m) In a significant relaxation of security around the war zone on the Indo-Pakistan border, Spanish film maker, Sebastian Alvaro, gained permission to attempt **Chogolisa** via the East Ridge in order to portray early Karakoram explorations of the Duke of Abruzzi. Well-known Spanish climbers such as José Carlos Tamayo played characters, dressed in period costume. Unfortunately, the attempt failed.

Baltoro and Panmah Muztagh
Trango Group
Great Trango, SW Ridge Americans, Miles Smart and Tim O'Neill, made a spirited attempt on the unclimbed SW Ridge, which bounds the right side of the great NW Face climbed by Russian and American teams in 1999. The pair adopted a lightweight approach and in late August reached a point just a few pitches below the summit ridge after a 4½-day push. Technical difficulties have been quoted as 5.10 and A2. At their high point a storm intervened and the pair were forced to make a difficult 1½-day retreat down the ridge, making nearly 2000m of rappels. This monster ridge has seen only one previous attempt, by Spanish climbers in 1990, and the two Americans believe they climbed to much the same high point.

Trango Tower A six-member German team made the third ascent, probably all-free, of the 1989 Albert-Güllich route, *Eternal Flame*, on the South Face, right of the *1976 British Route*. The team fixed ropes above a high camp on the Sun Terrace and finally reached the summit in two groups on 22 and 27 July. *Eternal Flame* was also the venue for a 'speed attempt'. Smart and O'Neill tried the route twice. On the second attempt they had reached a point nine pitches from the summit after only nine hours of climbing, when O'Neill took a massive 35-metre fall. He was badly bruised but otherwise surprisingly uninjured. The pair retreated.

Three very experienced Mexican big-wall climbers hoped to make the first Latin-American ascent of the tower via a capsule-style ascent of the *Slovenian Route* but they gave up sometime during August.

Little Trango Tower Americans, Brian McMahon and Josh Warton, made a possible first ascent of the small spire on the ridge between Trango and Great Trango Towers. The pair reached the tower from the Trango Glacier to the west and climbed the seven-pitch *PM Wall* at 5.10.

The Hainabrkk Group
Hainabrakk East Tower Americans Heather Baer, Roxanna Brock, Brian McCray and Steve Schneider made the first ascent of Hainabrakk East Tower via an all-free 1100m route on the SW Face christened *For Better or For Worse*. Operating as two male-female couples, the team first fixed ropes to approximately one-third height, then spent two weeks on the wall, climbing every pitch except five on sight. The five were first worked then redpointed and had difficulties up to 5.12a. The middle part of the route offered less than perfect rock but the upper section was beautiful golden granite with fine jamming cracks and the occasional chimney.

The four Americans reached the summit only one day in front of a second American team, Jonathan Copp and Michael Pennings, who were making their own new route on the tower during their first visit to Pakistan. These two climbed the East Face in a continuous push of just 2½ days, naming their line *Tague it to the Top* (after the late Cameron Tague, who was killed in a fall on Longs Peak last summer). Most of the route went free with crux sections of 5.11 but there were two pitches of aid (C2) and a difficult tension traverse. This impressive granite tower stands south of the more famous Shipton Spire (or more properly Hainabrakk).

Prior to this, Copp and Pennings had made the first ascent of the adjacent **Cat's Ears Spire**. The pair took one small tent and a single sleeping bag, climbing the 1200m route completely free except for three pendulums. Their first foray was blocked by bad weather but on the second attempt they took one day to return to their high point, sat out a storm on the second day and then made the summit in a continuous 24-hour push on the third. The final pitch was a 10m-high 5.9 monolith with only one point of protection and no summit belay, which forced both climbers to lead and then climb back down the pitch. The 23-pitch *Freebird* was rated 5.11+ and A0.

There was considerable activity on the increasingly famous 5852m tower north-west of Uli Biaho commonly known as **Shipton Spire**. Three Basque climbers, José Eskibel, Jokin Larrañaga and Tasio Ortiz, tried to complete the line of the original attempt on the spire, by Americans, in 1992. But by mid-August, after 21 days on the ascent, they chose to retreat after climbing 1150m with difficulties up to A4 and 6b.

Two other Spanish climbers tried to make the second ascent of *Inshallah* (Davis/Harvey/Shaw, 1998: 1,350m: 5.12a and two moves of A1) up the middle of the South Face in late July/early August but retreated after climbing only 500m of the route at 6a and A2.

The second ascent of *Inshallah* was made in a very fast three days by the dynamic partnership of Copp and Pennings, shortly after their ascents of both the East Tower and Cat's Ears Spire. The two rated the climb highly and compared the quality of the rock to anything found on El Capitan. They went for speed rather than a pure free ascent and used aid when the climbing got hard but it is reported that during all three ascents (and descents) in the region, they only placed five pegs and took four of them back home.

Hainabrakk (West) Tower Finally, after their ascent of Little Trango Tower, Brian McMahon and Josh Warton appear to have climbed a multi-day rock route on one of several lower buttresses that rise to the summit ridge of **Hainabrakk (West) Tower**. *Unfinished Symphony* went at 5.10 and A1 but the climbers did not continue up the long summit ridge.

Latok III (6949m) The Russian big-wall team of Sergey Efimov, Yuri Koshelenko, Alexander Ruchkin and leader, Alexander Odintsov, had their eyes set on the unclimbed West Face of **Latok III**, but their attempt nearly ended in disaster. The face is 2000m high with the first section a snow/ice slope and the upper 1300m an impressively steep rock wall at relatively high altitude.

Latok III was to be the fourth summit of the on-going project entitled 'Russian Way – Big Walls of the World'. Koshelenko had hoped the team would attempt the face in alpine style but he was out-voted on his choice of line and the four went for a *direttissima* towards the left side of the face that would require a capsule-style approach and much aid. They started their ascent on 19 July, hauling an initial load of 100kg up the broad couloir on the left side of the face. The four took two days and climbed around 25 pitches to get established at the start of the rock wall (c5700m). A heavy snow covering on the 45°-60° ice slope had made the ascent to this point hard work. Above, the team progressed slowly, climbing only 2½ pitches over the next two days (6 and A3+) to reach an altitude of c5835m. The corner they were trying to ascend was composed of poor rock and Koshelenko's suggestion to descend and outflank the obstacle by climbing the buttress on the left appears to have been ignored. If further proof were needed, while lying on their portaledge at the end of a day in which Koshelenko had already received a cut to the head from a falling stone, a large rock burst through the tent fly and completely shattered Koshelenko's helmet. It snowed heavily for two days, confining the Russians to their ledge. However on the 25th the weather seemed to be on the mend and the team set off up the wall, only to get caught in more stonefall. This time Koshelenko, who was jumaring back up the fixed ropes, was hit on the hands. The result was two broken thumbs and a decision to retreat.

On the 26th they started down. The sky was cloudless and the ice slopes now heavily laden with snow. Koshelenko was lowered, Ruchkin came next setting up the rappel anchors, then Efimov and finally Odintsov. At around 3.30pm the team were on the lower section of the face and only five rope lengths above the glacier, when they were pummelled by an avalanche that left a two-metre groove in the slope above. At that point Efimov and Ruchkin were together. They set up a belay on ice screws out of the fall line, then proceeded to lower Koshelenko while Odintsov waited one pitch above. Suddenly, another big avalanche hit. When Ruchkin finally emerged from the debris, badly battered with three broken ribs and a damaged neck, he found himself alone apart from two ice axes. Efimov, the rucksacks and the remaining ice tools had been swept away.

Odintsov came down and the three descended painfully to the foot of the face, where to their surprise they found Efimov sitting to one side of the base of the avalanche cone and all their equipment scattered close by. While his companions thought he had been killed in the avalanche, Efimov was convinced he was the only survivor after his 350m fall and at around 4.00pm had radioed Michail Bakin, a Russian doctor in base camp, to that effect. Bakin, Odintsov, plus the injured Klenov and Koshelenko, managed to transport Efimov, who had broken a leg and ribs, down to a safe point on the glacier but not before they had another lucky escape when a huge rock fall from the face above stopped in the avalanche cone just 20m away. The path out from base camp was too narrow and precariously positioned to carry an invalid, so the Russian's Laision Officer made a rapid descent to Skardu to order a helicopter. There appears to have been a lengthy administrative delay before one could be released but on 30 July and after the intervention of the Russian Embassy, Bakin and Efimov were successfully flown to Skardu hospital and the others were able to walk out, arriving on the 3 August.

Ogre III (6960m) Maurizio Giordani's five-member team of high-standard Italian rock climbers was defeated by a combination of high technical difficulties, lack of time and bad weather on the SE Ridge of what they refer to as the 'unclimbed Ogre III'. This is the name given by the Italians to the West Summit of Ogre II (6960m), which in their opinion is a distinct top separated by two or three days' climbing from the Main or Central Summit ascended in 1983 from the NW by a Korean expedition.

Arriving at their 4400m base camp on the Uzun Brakk Glacier in June, the Italian team acclimatised and by the 17th had fixed 1000m of rope up the approach couloir to a col at the start of the steep rocky section.

Maurizio Girardi and Emanuele Pellizzari reached a similar high point to the Japanese in 1981 before being forced down in a storm. They removed all their equipment from the mountain except for 15 rappel anchors (each a single bolt plus karabiner) in the gully.

Later this same pair attempted a new route on the nearby **Ogre's Thumb** but retreated after five pitches (VII maximum) in a snowstorm. The expedition cleaned the lower glacier of all sorts of rubbish, from abandoned wrapping to shovels and tents, then hired two extra porters to take it all back to Skardu. The SE Ridge is a very serious and technically difficult climb, which will prove a challenging objective to future parties.

Western Karakoram

Solu and Sokha Glaciers Dave Wilkinson continued his exploration of the largely unknown glacier basins accessed from the Arandu Valley with a small expedition to the Solu Glacier immediately south of the Hispar. With fellow British climbers Ken Findlay, Paul Hudson and Karl Zientek, Wilkinson established base camp on 22 July at c3850m, a little way above the herdsmen's encampment of Sugulu and three days' march from the jeep road at Bizil. Although briefly visited and mapped during Shipton's 1939 expedition, there were no known reports of previous mountaineering activities from the Solu Glacier. However, en route to base camp the British party heard from locals that an expedition had visited the valley several years before and climbed peaks from the glacier basin west of Singulu.

The British team chose to reconnoitre the unnamed side glacier rising north from their base camp but found the abnormally dry winter and spring had made approaches to many of the peaks both difficult and dangerous.

The team was also bugged by the generally very unsettled weather but managed to climb one peak on the Hispar watershed ridge. They named this **Sekha Brakk, c5450m** ('Dragonfly Peak'). Attempts on other peaks in the region were thwarted by bad weather and although the team note considerable potential for future parties, there is little that would give easy climbing and approaches would be far from straightforward.

At the same time two British climbers, Ian Arnold and Dave Millman, were visiting the adjacent **Sokha Glacier** to the south, where they managed to climb one small peak. Arnold had visited the glacier twice before and in 1992 climbed the South Face of **Pt. 5495m** (IV+) and made a spirited attempt on the difficult and serious North Face of **Pt. 5956m**, an unclimbed peak on the main ridge SW of Sosbun Brakk, subsequently christened **Sokha Brakk**. Little climbing has ever been attempted on the Sokha's dramatic peaks, though the glacier was visited as early as the first part of last century by the indefatigable Bullock-Workmans and then again in the late 1930s first by Tilman then by Scott Russell.

A small and primarily female group of British mountaineers planned to spend the second half of July exploring the glacier north of Arandu. Base camp was reached but as a result of the previous lean winter and almost continuous rain, feasible lines on accessible peaks were threatened either by stonefall or avalanche. No climbs were completed but the team did find evidence of a camp, which they surmised must have originated from the Bullock-Workman expedition in the early 1900s. This glacier system was also visited in 1959 by Tony Streather's British Army expedition, which climbed a peak (provisionally named Gloster Peak) on the Hispar watershed.

Pumari Chhish (c7350m) After an unsuccessful attempt in 1999, which reached 6200m on the South Face of the unclimbed South Summit of **Pumari Chhish**, Julie-Ann Clyma and Roger Payne returned in May for a second attempt. However, this time the weather was considerably and consistently worse and the pair could do no more than reach 5300m on the same line.

Lupghar West II (7010m) A Frenchman, Nicolas Sieger, is thought to have made what is possibly the first official ascent of **Lupghar West II** in the Hispar Muztagh. In early August Sieger's four-member team accessed the mountain from Shiskat Village near to Gulmit on the Karakoram Highway, but after the other three team members left for home when their time ran out, Sieger is reported to have left base camp (4400m) at 7.00am on 21 August, bivouacked at 5500m and then climbed all the way to the summit to arrive at 9.00pm on the 22nd. The difficulties were sustained above 6000m with sections of front-pointing to 70°. Sieger descended through the night to regain his base camp at 7.00am the following morning. The Frenchman has applied to name the peak **La Rochelle** after his home town.

Lupghar Sar is a collection of three summits of almost equal height on an east-west axis above the Gharesa Glacier north of the Hispar River. The West Summit was climbed in June 1979 via the SW Ridge by Austrians and again in early August the same year by Japanese, who continued to traverse the 1½ kilometre ridge to the Central Summit. The East Summit is believed to have received an unauthorised ascent in the 1980s. All three summits are quoted as c7200m, though not surprisingly the Japanese felt the Central Summit to be fractionally higher. However, distant photographs and the report made by the Italian expedition that climbed neighbouring Dut Sar in 1993, imply that the East Summit is the highest.

Lupghar West II lies approximately two kilometres NW of Lupghar Sar West and has long appeared an obvious target, being clearly visible from the Highway. In 1986 two Spanish climbers explored an approach up the Baltbar Glacier and discovered that the SW Spur of the mountain offered a magnificent line.

Spantik (7028m) Two of the most significant ascents of the year occurred early in the season in the Western Karakoram, when two parties climbed different lines on the fabled NW Face of the **Golden Pillar of Spantik (7028m)**. These were a repeat, with two variations, of the *1987 British Route*, and a new line on the upper buttress left of the *British Route*, towards the true crest of the pillar. The experienced multinational team responsible for the two ascents comprised Mikhail Davy and Alexander Klenov from Russia, Emmanuel Guy and Emmanuel Pellissier from France, Attila Ozsvath from Hungary and Marko Prezelj from Slovenia. The team established base camp (4600m) opposite the face during the fourth week of May. In unsettled weather the two French and Prezelj first made an acclimatisation ascent of **Melangush Chish (5348m)**.

Following this, the four non-Russian members reached the Girgindal Pass, from where the two French climbed a possibly virgin summit, **P. 6070m**, which they christened **Ha Chish**.

Climbing in two independent groups, both teams set off together on 7 June for the foot of the initial tower. At the end of the day Guy, Ozsvath, Pellissier and Prezelj were bivouacked at c5600m in a rimaye on the hanging glacier below the upper pillar, having reached this point in only eight hours. Following in their tracks, the two Russians reached the same point on the following day, then continued slowly upward in poor weather while the four-man team first tried to sit it out, then decided to retreat.

On the 12th the four started again and regained their former bivouac site in just six hours, and early on the 13th they started on the upper pillar as a rope of four, one person leading without a sack and the rest jumaring and sack hauling. Prezelj remarked that his previous experience of difficult mixed climbing in Scotland stood him in good stead. After 12 pitches the party was able to install two bivouac tents on small ledges.

The next day they climbed a further 12 pitches in deteriorating weather and in darkness reached a point just two pitches below the top of the pillar. The following day, after leaving their precariously-positioned bivouac sites, Prezelj led the final 'open-book corner' and a subsequent ice pitch to the top. After a final bivouac (c6500m) near the top of the descent route, the four down-climbed and rappeled the spur to reach base camp in one day.

The team were able to confirm that most of the climbing was between Scottish 4 and 6. They did not consider the route to hold any exceptional difficulties by today's mixed-climbing standards but they were full of praise for the British first ascent by Mick Fowler and Victor Saunders which, at the time, was a truly outstanding achievement and possibly the hardest mixed route then climbed on a 7000m peak in the Himalaya/Karakoram.

Meanwhile the Russian pair had been forcing a difficult line towards the left edge of the upper pillar. Davy and Klenov eventually made nine portaledge bivouacs on the pillar, overcoming sustained and difficult terrain involving pure rock climbing, mixed and aid climbing, and on occasions climbing no more than three pitches a day. They finally traversed right to join the final few pitches of the *British Route*, up which they finished to place their 12th bivouac of the route beneath a cornice on the summit plateau. The next day they reached the top in two hours and began a long descent, following the tracks of the previous four climbers.

The Russians quoted technical grades of F7a, A3 and 95° for their ascent which was the product of characteristic determination and perseverance, and won the two protagonists First Prize in the High Altitude Technical Ascents class of the 2000 Russian Mountaineering Championships and a nomination for the prestigious French award of the Piolet d'Or.

On the opposite side of the mountain four expeditions attempted the increasingly popular SE Ridge from the head of the Chogolungma Glacier. A joint French-Pakistan team were unable to make full use of the short periods of fine weather but three members of Lev Ioffe's American-Russian team, seven members of Iwazaki Hiroshi's Japanese expedition and nine members from a Jagged Globe multi-national commercial expedition led by David Hamilton all reached the summit. Despite the length of the route, technical difficulties are relatively low and much of the ridge still negotiable in poor weather, making it a much safer proposition than Diran for those wishing to climb a non-technical, low 7000m peak in Pakistan.

Diran (7257m) Four expeditions had permits for this 7257m peak south of Hunza that has become a popular objective for commercial expeditions. All were on the mountain at the end of July or throughout August and all failed, one with tragic consequences. The *Normal Route* via the North Face and West Ridge is relatively gentle in angle, cut by crevasses and séracs, and quickly becomes avalanche-prone after snowfall. In the unsettled conditions of early August, as an Italian team led by the guide Nicolas Berzi was high on the mountain, two members, Domenico Palandri and Omar Vecchio, were avalanched and killed.

Diran has a long history of fatalities. A safe and successful ascent relies on tackling the climb only in stable snow conditions.

Phuparash (6824m) In the much neglected Phuparash Group between Spantik and Diran, Hideki Nakayama's three-member team failed in August on the unclimbed **Main Summit (6824m)** of **Phuparash**. A similarly small Japanese expedition attempted this peak in 1997. The lower **Central Summit (6785m)** was climbed in 1977 by a British team.

Rakaposhi (7788m) The three-man team of Andrew Barker, Adrian Burgess and Paul Moores planned to attempt the unexplored East Face of Rakaposhi (7788m) from the upper Bagrot Glacier. However, the very dry conditions above made the glacier approach to the foot of the face extremely dangerous and the mountain was not attempted.

Ultar (7388m) A four-member French expedition comprising Jérôme Blanc-Gras, Erwan le Lann, Christophe Profit and Hervé Quallizza were unsuccessful during May/June on their project to ascend the giant c3600m-high **South East Pillar of Ultar (7388m)**. This pillar, similar to but three times the height of the Walker Spur, has been attempted only once previously (by Japanese).

Nico Sar (c5800m) Americans, Walter Keller and Amy Rice, made the first ascent of **Nico Sar**, a peak off the Borth Glacier at 36° 33.917'N, 74° 09.399' E. After establishing base camp at c4750m on the Nercherkin

Glacier, a subsidiary glacier branching steeply north from the Borth, the pair placed two camps, at 5300m and 5650m, climbed almost 1000m of excellent ice up to 70° and reached the summit on 12 August. They down climbed and rappeled the same route.

WESTERN HIMALAYA

Nanga Parbat (8125m) All but two expeditions to Nanga Parbat were attempting the *Standard Diamir Face Route* and of these only one was successful. On the 9 July Lee Hong-Kil, Lee Hwa-Hyeung and Kwan Oh-Soo reached the 8125m summit at 1.00pm.

The Swiss climber, Erhard Loretan (41), with life-long climbing partner Jean Troillet (52), was unsuccessful in his attempt on the massively long and unclimbed **Mazeno Ridge**. Since 1995, when he finally completed all fourteen 8000m peaks (the third man to do so) Loretan's two forays to 8000ers have both been on the Mazeno Ridge. The first, in 1997 with Wojciech Kurtyka, failed about one-third of the way along this 15km crest, which rises from the Mazeno Pass.

An even better-known name in world mountaineering, and one which is very much associated with Nanga Parbat, is Reinhold Messner. Messner first reached the summit in 1970 via a new route on the Rupal Face and again in 1978 via another new route from the Diamir side. Last summer, with Hans Peter Eisendle and Wolfgang Thomaseth, the 56-year-old Messner made a surprise return to what could easily be termed *his* mountain and on 29 July completed a new line up the NW Face.

The three mountaineers from the Süd-Tirol climbed the prominent, easy-angled snow face at the far left side of the Diamir Face, right of the long NW Ridge that falls towards Ganalo Peak. The face rises from the upper reaches of the Diamir Glacier and is guarded by a big sérac barrier. The three established a high camp below the face at around 6000m, then climbed alpine style (of course) through the centre of the barrier and on up snow slopes above to bivouac at 7200m. The following day they reached c7500m, more or less joining the *1978 Slovak Route* below the North Summit (7816m). Above this point the team felt there was too much fresh snow to continue to the North Summit or onwards towards the Main Summit via the Bazhin Gap, and retreated back down their route. Other members of the expedition included Reinhold's younger brother, 46-year-old Hubert.

It was during his epic descent of the Diamir face in 1970 that Reinhold lost another younger brother, Gunther, in an avalanche. Reinhold himself reached the valley more dead than alive and was cared for by the villagers of Diamir. Now, as a token of his appreciation, Messner plans to build a small school for the 50 or so children of the area and finance a teacher for the first five years of its operation.

HINDU RAJ

Ishkoman

Kampur (5499m) The American Carlos Buhler and Russian Ivan Durashin travelled to the Hindu Raj and made the first ascent of **Kampur** via the 1500m NW Face. After a bivouac at the bottom of the wall, the pair climbed the face right of the central rock rib to exit on the NW Ridge. They reached the summit in 19 hours from the foot of the face, enjoying many pitches of fine mixed climbing.

This previously virgin peak lies north of Ishkoman overlooking the Mathantir Valley. It was photographed by Schomberg as long ago as the 1930s and appears in the 1935 *Alpine Journal*. Buhler and Durashin are also reported to have made ascents of several other small peaks in the area.

Pt. 6189m At the same time an Italian expedition under the leadership of Franco Brunello was operating in the region, largely climbing and mapping in the Chiantar Valley. The expedition climbed several routes, notably the first ascent of the SW Face of **Pt. 6189m**, a 1400m line with sections up to 70°, which was achieved in just six hours by Tarcisio Bello. The peak overlooks the Suj Glacier north of Mathantir. (*See* http://www.intraisass.it/news.htm)

Khan Sar (5708m) In August Tom Gleeson and Graham Rowbotham (Canadian), Bryan Godfrey and Jock Jeffery (New Zealanders) and Peter Ford and Simon Woods (British) visited an unnamed glacier basin above the village of Borth in the Ishkoman Valley. Access via the Ishkoman Valley proved problematic owing to widespread seasonal flooding, but eventually the party was able to establish a c3600m base camp at a summer pasture named Doaw Jrabe. The party first attempted an unnamed 5708m peak but was forced to retreat when a tent at their 4800m camp was hit by a large boulder, resulting in a fractured arm for the occupant, Tom Gleeson.

Following Gleeson's evacuation to Gilgit, the team made another attempt and on the 24th were successful in reaching the summit via an ascent of the East Face. Three camps were made above base and although the upper section of the face was found to be badly avalanche-prone, a stable line was eventually discovered leading directly to the summit. The peak was christened Khan Sar after the expedition cook.

Shan Sar (c5500m) The five climbers mentioned above then attempted a second peak, west of Khan Sar. Two camps were made, the highest at 5000m, and the summit was reached via the accommodating slopes of the North Face leading to a final, heavily corniced ridge. This peak was christened **Shan Sar** after the expedition's second cook and estimated to have an altitude of c5500m. A subsequent attempt on a peak in an adjacent valley, approached by crossing the East Flank of Shan Sar at a height of around 5200m, had to be abandoned.

Dhuli Chish (6531m) A French expedition (Delevaux, Gervaise and Laurent) were unsuccessful on the 2000m high mixed North Face of Dhuli

Chish. The team was one of the last to arrive in Pakistan, only starting for their mountain in early September. **Dhuli Chish** lies west of the Darkot Valley north of Yasin and was first climbed in 1973 via the West Face and South Ridge by three Italians.

Uddin Zom (6010m) A four-man Anglo-New Zealand team comprising Phil Amos, Adam Thomas, Simon Woods (all UK) and Jock Jeffery (NZ) made the first ascent of 6010m Uddin Zom in the Matkesh/Ochiri Valley (South Western Hindu Raj). In all, three attempts were made on the West Face to North Ridge; a 1200m route of alpine D– (80°). The team was defeated on its first two attempts by heavy snowfall at the 5430m-high camp but the final attempt took place in good conditions from the 27-31 July, after a week spent at base camp in almost constant rain.

The four were almost certainly the first climbers to explore the Matkesh/ Ochiri Valley. They named their peak after a local goatherd, on whose summer pasture they pitched base camp. More information on this, the Khan Sar expedition reported above, and one or two other exploratory forays can be found on the website http://www.virginsummits.org

HINDU KUSH

Istor-O-Nal NE Summit (7276m) During July and August ten members of the Neuchatel section of the Swiss Alpine Club made a spirited attempt on the unclimbed 7276m NE Summit of Istor-O-Nal. The only previously known attempt on this peak occurred in 1977, when Japanese climbers approached from the South Atrak Glacier to the north but they failed at 6500m owing to technically difficult rock and ice formations. Also attempting the peak from the north, the Swiss, led by Simon Perritaz, established base camp on the glacier at c4700m and Camp 1 on the upper section of the glacier some five kilometres distant. The Swiss chose the steep West Rib of **Pt. 6241m**, and after fixing 1200m of rope, established Camp 2 below this summit. They then rappeled 70m into the upper section of the Japanese Couloir and followed it to the col at 6000m.

The ridge above proved narrow and difficult, with steep rock towers, ice walls and large cornices. The expedition fixed a further 500m of rope and placed Camp 3 at 6300m, above which the difficulties began to ease. Camp 4 (6800m) was established on 19 August. However, on the previous day a huge rock fall cut the fixed ropes on the rib below Camp 2, leaving Antoine Brenzikofer, Christian Meillard, Yan Smith and Jean-Micheal Zweiacker the only climbers at Camp 3. With no hope of more supplies from below, these four decided to try a summit dash from Camp 4 on the 21st. The temperature that morning was – 30°C as the four left the tent and climbed a couloir to the summit slopes. Unfortunately, these slopes proved steeper and harder than expected. Progress slowed and feet became frozen. At 4.00pm the climbers had reached an altitude of 7170m. Although they knew the summit was in their grasp, they also knew it would need another two hours to reach, followed by a difficult and cold descent. Wisely they elected to retreat and with time running out no more attempts could be made.

Tirich Mir (7706m) To celebrate the 50th anniversary of the first ascent of Tirich Mir (the highest peak in the Hindu Kush), Arne Naess's Norwegian team held an anniversary reunion in the Hurrungane region of Norway in July. All four summiters (Per Kvernberg, Henry Berg, Naess and Tony Streather) were happily able to attend the celebrations.

Dir Gol Zom (6778m) Three members, including the leader, of Hidehiro Minami's mature five-person Japanese team were successful on **Dir Gol Zom**, a shapely peak which rises a short distance from the Upper Tirich Glacier.

Noshaq (7492m) In June and July, Jamie McGuinness (New Zealand), Murray Macpherson (Canada) and Martin Nielson (Denmark) from a five-member multi-national team made what is probably the first serious attempt on this peak since 1978. Noshaq, which lies on the Afghan border north of Tirich Mir, is both the second highest mountain in the Hindu Kush and the highest peak in Afghanistan. The *Normal Route* climbs the long and gentle West Ridge, which, were it not for the fact that it lies entirely in Afghanistan, would now almost certainly be one of the most popular objectives for commercially organised expeditions aiming to climb a high but non-technical peak. Up to its last ascent in 1978 before the Russian invasion the following year, Noshaq had been climbed around 32 times and was the first 7000m peak to receive a winter ascent.

The three climbers first followed a medial moraine between two unstable ice falls, then climbed scree slopes to reach a rib on the SE Flank of the South Ridge. Camp 1 was placed on the rib at 5850m and Camp 2 close to the crest of the South Ridge at 6450m. Here the three had a lucky escape. They decided to position their camp in the lee of a large sérac, but during the night the region experienced a significant earthquake, a common occurrence in this part of the Hindu Kush and subsequently found to register 5+ on the Richter Scale. The next morning the sérac was discovered to have several large and ominous cracks. The tents were hurriedly moved and during the following day the sérac collapsed. The three climbers continued up the South Ridge to approximately 6500m but a combination of altitude and the apparent length and difficulty of the mixed section above led to a retreat.

ADMINISTRATION

The Ministry of Tourism has been forced to change premises owing to the expiry of the lease on its former office. However, the Ministry now promises full computerisation and it is thought that in the near future e-mail enquiries and bookings will be possible. There was also an increased use of helicopter services due to the current trend towards semi-privatisation of helicopters. The provision of helicopter services for commercial and rescue purposes is now in the hands of Askari Aviation. Contact askaria@isb.paknet.com.pk. More air rescues took place last year not only due to the much greater availability of helicopters but also because of an increased use of satellite phones at base camps. However, permits are required for these and applications must be made up to a month before the expedition arrives in Pakistan.

In a very positive step, the Ministry of Tourism has announced a reduction in the Additional Member Fee and is rumoured to be seriously considering further royalty reduction. In the table below the Royalty quoted is that currently required from expeditions with up to seven members. The old and new fees for each additional member are shown.

Altitude of Peak	Royalty (US$)	Additional Members	($ per person)
		OLD	NEW
K-2	12000	3000	2000
8001-8500	9000	3000	1500
7501-8000	4000	1000	500
7001-7000	2500	500	300
6000-7000	1500	300	200

BILL O'CONNOR

Nepal 2000

Mountaineering in the new millennium was heralded by little that was innovative – most mountaineers were content to go where others had gone before. What was missing in quality, however, was countered in quantity. At Everest's Khumbu base camp, during the pre-monsoon season, tent space was particularly hard to find, with over 500 climbers and Sherpas looking for a slot in which to rest their heads.

A new cleaner image for high-altitude climbing was given a boost by Bob Hoffman's American Environmental Expedition. Apart from putting 13 climbers on the summit (10 Sherpas) on 24 May they succeeded in bringing down 509 oxygen bottles, plus 122 of their own. They also removed 168kg of burnable rubbish plus 12kg of batteries and 35kg of non-biodegradable rubbish from the mountain! Of this, the glass and tins went to Kathmandu for recycling, whilst the gas cylinders, bottles and batteries went to America for disposal. As well as all this, another 832kg of human excrement and 750kg of waste food went to Gorak Shep for burial at a prepared site. Incidentally, the human waste is being transported specifically by Tibetans rather than Khumbu Sherpas.

Distinguished Italian mountaineer Alessandro Gogna, sponsored by an Italian Mineral Water company, was reported to have led a similar clean-up operation on the north side of the mountain below the North Col. Reports, however, suggest that this has been less than successful and that expeditions operating on the Tibetan side last spring continued to abandon large amounts of rubbish. The Sagarmatha Pollution Control Committee has made it a requirement of expeditions to dump their human waste somewhere other than base camp. Reports suggest that the Khumbu base-camp is now in pretty good order – long may it last.

PRE-MONSOON 2000

Annapurna 8091m
Fifty years on from its first ascent by Maurice Herzog's French expedition, four teams attempted to repeat the route. All failed low down because of dangerous avalanche conditions on a route that is recognised as being normally objectively dangerous. The first ascent of Annapurna on 3 June 1950 by Maurice Herzog and mountain guide Louis Lachenal was a landmark in Himalayan climbing. Not only was it the first 8000er to be climbed, but it was also notable in that it was climbed without prior reconnaissance.

Cho Oyu 8201m

A busy time on this popular, commercial 8000er, which statistically is the safest of the World's 14 highest peaks to climb. There were 17 expeditions active on the Normal Route and 70 climbers, including 20 Sherpas, reached the summit. By the end of the pre-monsoon season Cho Oyu had had a total of 1160 ascents. No significant mountaineering records were set, although in reaching the summit on the 8 May 2000, Koreans, Bae Gin-Soek and Ha Chan-Soon, along with Sherpa Pasang Gombu, were the first to climb an 8000er in Y2K.

Everest 8850m

Although not really disputed, the height of Everest is agreed on by most climbers, plus or minus a metre or two. According to Bradford Washburn, given that its top is always snow and that cornices come and go, the predominantly west-south-west winds will result in little variation in the mountain's actual height. So the actual height of Everest is 8850m – or thereabouts! For those with an interest in these matters the height of the South Col, on the other hand, can be calculated with pin-point precision, since a steel bolt, set in solid rock, marks the actual spot at a height of 7890.816m.

Cleaning Up In The Khumbu

The Sagarmatha Pollution Control Committee took control of the icefall this year and opened and maintained the route into the Western Cwm. Using the services of experienced Sherpas from Arun Treks, the route was found, ropes were fixed and ladders placed. Expeditions were then charged $2100 (up to 7 members) for using the route and $275 for additional members going through the icefall.

MORE RECORDS ON EVEREST

Most Ever

As predicted Y2K saw a record number of people on the mountain and a record number of ascents. On the Tibet side 30 expedition groups attempted the mountain, whilst from the south there were 26 groups. In total, the 56 groups put 133 (134) climbers on the summit.

First in the new millennium were four Russians who climbed via the North Ridge. Of the 133 only two climbers, both Sherpas, reached the summit without bottled oxygen. There is some debate as to whether Ram Krishna Newar actually reached the summit as claimed – if proven true 134 climbers reached the summit.

There was little activity on any other than the 'Standard Routes' from the north and south, although two expeditions attempted the South Pillar. The Danes were successful in their attempt, with five members reaching the summit in the middle of May. They followed the original Polish Route to circa 8040m, at which point they broke out right to reach the South-East Ridge at circa 8150m from where they followed the normal route via the Balcony to the summit. A Spanish team retreated from 8740m.

Fastest
Impressive indeed was the ascent by well-known Babu Chiri, a 33-year-old Sherpa. Having bivouacked on the summit in 1999 he went on in spring 2000 to climb from base camp to summit in only 16 hours and 56 minutes, reaching the summit on the 21 May at 10 am. After leaving base camp at 5pm he climbed through the night, met up with his brother Dawa on the South Col, from where together they reached the summit at 10am. He only used oxygen between 8500m and the summit. On descent, they spent the night on the South Col before returning safely to base camp. This was Babu Chiri's 10th ascent of Everest and his brother's fifth ascent.

Sadly, Babu Chiri Sherpa died on Everest on 29 April 2001, after falling into a crevasse at Camp II in the Western Cwm.

Most
Three days after Babu Chiri's ascent, which equalled those of Ang Rita and Appa Sherpa, the 39 year old Appa went on to make his eleventh ascent of the mountain and so regain the record.

Oldest
On 12 May 1999 Georgian climber, Lev Sarkisov at 60 years and 161 days became the oldest man to climb the mountain. On 19 May 2000, the record fell to Toshio Yamamoto aged 63 years and 311 days old when he reached the summit via the North Ridge. This was almost surpassed when Alan Hana, who is older still had to retreat from the South Summit. Polish woman Anna Czerwinska, aged 50, became the oldest woman to summit when she reached the top on 22 May.

Youngest – almost
A 15-year-old Sherpa schoolboy, with no previous climbing experience, attempted the mountain but retreated from the Hillary Step with frostbite on 21 May. He later had five fingers amputated.

British Ascents
Several well-known British climbers, Rick Allen, John Barry and Andy Salter reached the summit. Mountain Guide John Barry, born in Strabane, Northern Ireland, could possibly claim to be the first Irishman to climb the mountain from the south. Polly Murray became the fourth British woman to climb Everest when she reached the summit on 16 May. On the north

side Paul Walters reached the summit on 17 May, whilst Mark James and Dan White summited on the 18 May. All three were members of a military expedition.

The well-known and liked Pakistani mountaineer Nazir Sabir, the first from his country to climb K2, became the first Pakistani to climb Everest.

Everest star Peter Habeler, now aged 56, also returned to the mountain. In 1978, with Reinhold Messner, he became the first person to climb the mountain without oxygen. Still without bottled oxygen for this attempt, he climbed above the South Col but retreated when things became too difficult.

With so many people on the mountain there were, thankfully, few fatalities. Two climbers died during the spring season, both on the North side, both from falls. Since both climbers were descending alone, the cause of these accidents is not known.

Lhotse 8516m

There was a lot of spring activity on Lhotse. 15 climbers reached the main summit and a further two the slightly lower, more difficult, west summit.

Five Georgians and four Russians reached the summit on 15 and 21 May. This was a strong team with some distinguished high-altitude climbers including Valeri Pershin, Gleb Sokolov and Eugeni Vinogradski. They had originally hoped to traverse to the unclimbed Lhotse Middle from a high camp at circa 8000m near the West Face Couloir. However their attempt was halted by an avalanche and unsettled weather.

The efforts of Italian mountaineer Sergio Martini must surely be applauded. Now aged 50, Martini summited Everest via the North Ridge in 1999, to become, at the age of 49, the oldest man to claim all 8000ers. However, his ascent of Lhotse in poor visibility was disputed when Korean Park Young-Seok, climbing the mountain a few days later, reported that his tracks stopped short of the summit. Martini returned this year and without Sherpa support climbed the mountain on 19 May. He reached the summit with Slovenian climbers Milan Romih and Franc Pepevnik and can most certainly now claim to be the oldest man to climb all fourteen 8000ers. Perhaps more impressive is that this schoolmaster from the Dolomites is essentially unsponsored and paid for his own trips.

Lhotse West Summit

At 9.45am on 26 May, British Mountain Guide Sandy Allen and South African Cathy O'Dowd reached the West Top of Lhotse. Although this was not a first ascent, the summit has had few visitors. The route follows the West Face Couloir to a point 100-200m below the col. At this point Pemba Tenji Sherpa who was accompanying them went for the true East Summit whilst Allen and O'Dowd climbed a rock chimney adorned with fixed ropes (UIAA 111), followed by exposed scrambling and a final corniced fin leading to the exposed summit.

Pumori 7161m
Four expeditions attempted this attractive peak. All were engaged in the Standard route. Two members of an American Expedition reached the summit on 14 May.

Manaslu 8163m
Four expeditions attempted and succeeded in climbing this difficult mountain. Alberto Inurrategi, his brother Felix and Antonio Garces climbed the normal route, reaching the summit on 25 April. A week later they attempted Annapurna but failed. Jean Christophe Lafaille, on an Italian expedition's permit but climbing independently, made a solo attempt on a line up the North East Face that failed. He then rejoined the Normal Route as far as Camp 2, where he had a gear cache. His route then continued up a couloir line left of the Normal Route before breaking left to climb easy snow slopes and make camp at circa 7400m. On the following day, after leaving camp at 5am, his route went right of the foresummit to reach the main summit at 9am.

Franco Brunello's seven-man Italian AC team and a seven-man Korean group led by Han Wang-Yong were both successful. Four Italians and one Korean reached the summit on 12, 14 and 15 May.

Nilgiri North East 6750m
A French group – members of the Groupe de Haute Montagne – having failed in their attempt on the North Face of Annapurna, went on to attempt Nilgiri North 7061m. They eventually climbed the the South Spur to a point they christened Nilgiri North East on the East Ridge of Nilgiri North. The point had most certainly been climbed before. The route is said to offer good climbing, similar to the *Swiss Route* on Les Courtes or *Route Major* on Mont Blanc and was graded Alpine D+/TD–.

North America 2000

ALASKA

Perhaps the epicentre of North American alpine climbing, Alaska continued to receive world-class ascents on big, difficult routes as well as repeats in blazing alpine style. On **Denali**, the 9000ft *Czech Direct* (initially climbed as a siege effort in 1986) received its second and third ascents, and quantum leaps in the definition of 'alpine style'. In May, Ben Gilmore and Kevin Mahoney repeated the massive route in alpine style in seven days, a fine feat of its own. Less than a month later, Steve House, Scott Backes and Mark Twight blitzed the route in 60 hours of climbing, sans bivvy gear. House claims 'It was my first world-class route' – a powerful statement from one of North America's top alpinists. They simul-climbed and soloed considerable amounts of the 5.9 WI6 route, belaying thirty-one 60-metre pitches in their remarkable ascent.

Also on **Denali**, *Reality Ridge* received its first solo from Robert Shonerd. Bart Paull and Fred Wilkinson, each a mere 20-years old, blazed the *Cassin* in 56 hours – a route requiring up to a week for many seasoned alpinists.

An adventurous Canadian couple, Sacha Friedlin and Marie-Diane Cyr, hiked into the Alaska Range, climbed **Foraker** and **Hunter**, and Friedlin soloed **Denali**, before the pair hiked back out after approximately two hearty months.

The profound *Infinite Spur* on **Mt Foraker** received its third and fourth ascents at more or less the same time over about one week in late May. The first team was veteran Alaska hardman Carl Tobin and the timeless alpine superhero Barry Blanchard, with 'the lads' close on their heels: Gren Hinton and Glen Deal, both in their early 20s.

On **Mt. Huntington** persistence paid off for Brad Grohusky and Rod Willard who, with Mike Gruber and Mark Thompson, finally succeeded on their new wall route. *Golden Granite West Face*, 1200ft of climbing between the *Colton-Leach* and *Polarchrome* routes, is the big gash gully starting on the left side of the face.

Mt. Hunter's North Buttress continued to receive attention, with its undeniable allure. Jeff Hollenbaugh and Bruce Miller, both from Colorado, arrived in hopes of the *Moonflower Buttress*. However, with the route practically becoming one to queue-up for, and the need to battle parties with haulbags and portaledges, their light and fast ideals would be problematic on the popular route. Instead, they climbed Twight and Backes' unrepeated *Deprivation* to the big zigzag where they logically finished on the Moonflower's *Bibler Come Again* exit. The pair were forced to retreat in bad weather just shy of the buttress' top.

Brits Jules Cartwright and Ian Parnell climbed a stellar new route, *The Knowledge* (Alaska Grade 6), to the right of the *Moonflower* in late May and early June. The difficult mixed route shares some pitches with the *Moonflower* but is primarily an independent line and a very impressive one.

Jim Donini had better luck this year on the impressive **Thunder Mountain** than in the previous year (nail-biting epic with Malcolm Daly), climbing a new rock route on the prominent *Central Spur* with John Bragg. The two hadn't climbed together since their historic first ascent of **Torre Egger** nearly 25 years ago. Their initial attempt on the buttress ended in stormy retreat, but they left a gear cache. They returned to their high-point via a couloir entering from the right, gaining their point rapidly on moderate snow, before continuing on steep rock to the top of the buttress.

Exploration and climbing, primarily on excellent granite, continued in the Little Switzerland area, with many fine routes established.

In the Ruth Gorge, Scott DeCapio and Kelly Cordes emerged from their base-camp laziness to try several routes, and surprisingly climbed some, including a difficult new route on **London Tower**. *The Trailer Park* climbs the left couloir for 3200ft, with many difficult mixed sections. The pair climbed the route in 12 hours, base to summit. Also in the Ruth, Tim Wagner and Seth Shaw climbed a 4000ft-plus new route, *The Escalator*, on **Mt. Johnson**. Their route, climbed in a 31-hour round-trip push through intermittently stormy weather, climbs what could be called the *SE Couloir*, left of the prominent unclimbed East Buttress. Tragically, the highly-respected Shaw was killed a week later by a massive sérac collapse while ice bouldering near Johnson.

Opposite the Ruth, the Buckskin Glacier saw action in the fall – a rare time for parties to visit Alaska. Gilmore, Mahoney, and House climbed a 5000ft new mixed route on the **Moose's Tooth**. The route begins in the deep gully between the Moose's and **Bear's Tooth** before finding a corner system giving passage to the upper slopes and the summit. Also on the trip, DeCapio soloed the probable first ascent of **Peak 9160** via the 3160ft South Face. For it's likeness to **Mt. Assiniboine**, DeCapio informally named it 'Canadian Rockies Peak'.

The lesser known, but impressive **Chugach** and **Wrangell** mountains received many new routes as well, primarily by Alaskans with local knowledge of the gems, establishing fine routes on scarcely-known peaks.

Mt. St. Elias's *Mira Face* received its second ascent, and the first ski descent (an often-attempted feat) by the Colorado team of Doug Byerly, Lorne Glick, Andy Ward and James Bracken. On St. Elias, another impressive ascent was a three-day blast (including one day pinned down by weather!) of the *Homberger Route* by Alaska climbing veterans Dave Nettle and Bean Bowers.

In the Coast Range, the spectacular South Ridge of **Mt. Oasis** was finally climbed, the first time the peak's summit had been reached. The route climbs granite with some snow, following a glacier climb to a col, about 4000ft base to summit. The project was planned by the venerable Fred Beckey, who remained at the col while Kelvin Vail and Jon Walsh completed the first ascent.

CANADA

The big-wall hotspot Baffin Island saw many new routes. Kurt Albert and party redpointed *Odyssey 2000* (5.12b, 12 pitches) on the E Face of **Polar Bear Spire**. The route was comprehensively bolted. On **The Fin**, *Earth, Wind, and Choss* was established by Russel Mitrovich, Mike Libecki, and Josh Helling plus expedition camera crew Peter Mallamo and John Middendorf. The route, conservatively graded VI 5.10 A2+, was filmed by American Adventure Productions, and will be broadcast on the Outdoor Life Network Channel.

A handful of Norwegian climbers, Bjarte Bo, Halvor Hagen, Torkel Roisli and Odd-Roar Wiik visited the **Sam Ford Fjord** and couldn't keep still! On the North Face of **Polar Sun Spire**, *The Norwegian Route* was established (VII 5.10 A4). After the ascent, Bo quickly got bored and freesoloed the South Ridge of **The Beak**, perhaps a new route. Soon afterwards, Hagen and Wiik climbed a 10-pitch new route to the previously (probably) unclimbed S summit of **The Turret**. Then Bo and Roisli started a new pillar line on **Great Cross Pillar**, climbing 18 pitches, mostly free up to 5.11, in rock boots. They called the route *Helluland Revisited* (V 5.11 A1). The pair relaxed for a few hours during the night, but finished the round trip in about 36 hours.

Canadians Jason Methot and Jason Robinson climbed a steep new 3400ft line on the **Cat's Eye Wall**, calling it *Pillar of Fire* (VII A4 5.10 WI 3). At one point, a sound above made them fear rockfall, but it was a solo BASE jumper roaring past them! Also on Baffin Island, Canadians Ben Demencech, Matt Maddaloni,and John Millar climbed a 2800ft wall on the south bank of Gibbs Fjord, calling it *Midnight Watch*.

In the St Elias Range **Mt. Logan** was the main target, as always. Aside from the standard attention given to the *E Ridge* and *King Trench* routes, Swiss climbers Werner Stucki and Christian Zinsli repeated (second ascent) the *Hummingbird Ridge-Thunderbird Variation* in impeccable style. After warming up by making the first ascent of **Mt. Teddy**, 3960 metres, via the 1300-metre-high East Face, they blazed the route on Logan in a mind-boggling 26 hours. The route ascends about 3600 vertical metres, and they climbed it mostly unroped. Conditions dictated an unplanned descent of the East Ridge, almost a repeat of the FA party's epic, but fortunately pilot Paul Claus happened to fly overhead and pick them up!

Mt. Kennedy's proud 6000ft *N Buttress* saw its first alpine-style ascent, by Andy Cave and Mick Fowler. (*See article 'Mount Kennedy – North Buttress' in this volume.*)

Rock climbing near the **Cirque of the Unclimbables** continued, with Chris Van Leuven and Matt Childers climbing a new route on the **Minotaur** in a spectacular and rarely-visited cirque in the Ragged Range.

BC's impressive Waddington Range of the Coast Mountains saw action, with **Mt. Monarch's** *N Ridge* getting its first ascent by Bill Durtler, Bruce Fairley and Don Serl. On neighbouring **Mt. Combatant**, a new route *Perseverance* was made on the last major unclimbed buttress on Combatant, left of Child and Foweraker's 1995 route *Belligerence*, by Brendan Cusick and Alan Kearney. In the same group, Brits Simon Richardson and Dore Green made the first ascent of the impressive 800m rock pillar directly beneath the summit on the 1400m South Face of **Mount Tiedemann** (3848m). On the *Cataract Buttress* of **Mt Shand**, an impressive line was established by Mark Hartley and Lorne Hoover.

Impressive free routes were established at **Squamish**, with the Grand Wall on Squamish Chief freed by Scott Cosgrove; and on the Sherrif's Badge formation of the Chief, Peter Croft and Hamish Fraser freed a new line, *The Fortress*. It was the last of the three main walls to be freed. Also on the Chief, Conny Amelunxen and Adam Diamond established a new wall route, *Bald Egos*.

In the Selkirks, new routes established on **Mt. Dag** were *Ankles as Far as the Eye Can See* and *Ankles Me Boy*, by Jason Magness, Sam Price, Mike Brown, George Ortiz, Craig Clarence, and Andy Magness, operating in two teams.

Topher and Patience Donahue put up *Cameron's Pillar* (1500' 5.11+), a stellar line on the South Face of the **South Howser Tower** named after their friend Cameron Tague, whose spirit they felt 'during every perfect jam'. The duo established other shorter routes on the trip, and made the first free ascent of *Tower Arête* (1000' 5.12–) on **Snowpatch Spire**.

In the loose, massive, and impressive Canadian Rockies, Raphael Slawinski and Jim Sevigny established *Leftover Rib* on the stunning East Face of **Mt. Chephren**, the route ascending an obvious rib left of the *Gran Route*.

CONTINENTAL UNITED STATES

While **Yosemite** didn't see lightning-fast speed records in 2000, free action, and free solos, were indeed impressive. Dean Potter became the second person, after Peter Croft, to free solo *Astroman*. While Potter used an easier variation on the crux of pitch three, the ascent was indeed awesome and admirable. El Cap was freed by two new routes, *Lurking Fear* and *Golden*

Gate. The former was freed by the young duo of Tommy Caldwell and Beth Rodden, with the latter by the inimitable Huber brothers.

On **Lower Cathedral Rock**'s North Face, Steve Gerberding and Dave Griffith made a new wall route, *Children of the Corn.* Eric George soloed a new/variant line, *The Long Walk* on **Half Dome.**

New action in **Red Rocks** was had by Roxanna Brock and Gary Fike, as well as Brian McCray and Mike Lewis – not to mention the reticent local crew establishing routes nobody knows of!

Paul Ross kept busy in the desert of the Colorado Plateau and Utah, establishing a plethora of new routes, many of shaky towers that most people of sound mind would steer clear of. Busy in Zion and throughout Utah, firing scores of new routes, were Nate Brown, Troy Anderson, Jason Stevens, Jared Nielson, Douglas Heinrich, Boulos Ayad, Eric Draper, Bryan Bird, Dave Littman, Joe French, Fly'n Brian McCray, and Burt Arend.

The Black Canyon of the **Gunnison** in Colorado had a new solo variation to *Black Planet* by Brent Armstrong, and the fast and furious team of Mike Pennings and Jonny Copp fired a new line, *No Pig Left*, descending to the base of the new line carrying one rope and no pitons.

Rolando Garibotti, whose impressive ascents belie his refreshing reluctance to talk about his climbing, repeated the *Grand Traverse* in under seven hours. Many parties bivvy on the traverse, and to do it in a day is a worthy goal for most climbers. The late Alex Lowe's 8.5 hours on the traverse was thought to be inhuman and impossible to match!

The hardcore local Montana crew continued to get after it on the big remote ice and mixed lines of **Glacier National Park**, as well as other areas of the remote state. In Glacier, Chris Gibisch, Kevin McCracken, Patrick Knoll, Jeff Shapiro, Ryan Hokanson, Patrick Knoll, Gabe Boisseau, Chris Gibbish and Blase Reardon led the charge. In the **Bitterroot** mountains, pioneering activity on impressive rock faces continued, led recently by a crew including Brad Stevens, Jim Crossland, Jimmy Pinjuv, Chris Trimble, Rafael Graña, Kevin McCracken, Jeff Shapiro, Jim Earl, Stephen Porcella, Ben Osburn and Eric Roberts.

MEXICO

In **Basaseachi Falls**, a new wall, which has been called 'Cascada', received two impressive new lines. Lucas Laeser, Dierk Sittner and Pete Daumeister established *Subiendo el Arcoiris* (IV 5.12c A0 or 5.13b?, ten pitches), which ascends a prow left of a huge waterfall for 900ft. Cecilia Buil also opened a new route, solo, on the wall and named the route *Lluvia de Plata.*

JAVIER SANCHEZ

Bolivia 2000

(*Plates 35–38*)

Santa Vera Cruz is the smallest chain of mountains in Bolivia, contained within a distance of 20km between Huañacota in the north and Ichoco in the south. There are several glaciers, which are located in the southernmost point in Bolivia.

In 1904, Henry Hoek wrote a chapter on the Santa Vera Cruz in his book *Bolivia's Mountains*, but he only traversed the range walking towards Quimsa Cruz, and climbed nothing significant. Thirty-five years later, the German Joseph Prem, one of the most important originators of alpinism in Bolivia, climbed **Santa Vera Cruz (5560m)** itself on his own. His 1939 expedition was repeated some years later by another German, Frederic Alfed.

Forty years on, the Chilean Andean expert Evelio Echevarría, who knows this land better than anyone, climbed the small hill called **Cala Cala (4600m)** which is located to the north of the small lake Huariananta. He went back twice to climb the 'Chupica' – which means 'red blood' in Aymara – without success, thus leaving four of five significant summits in this area unclimbed.

In May 1999, we three friends, Javier Navarro, Isidro Gonzalez and Javier Sanchez, decided to climb the region's second-highest summit, **Fortuna Peak (5493m)** in an attempt to generate new interest in climbing here. On 8 May we set out for the summit, taking 17 hours to climb a slope of between 50° and 70°. We called the route *Khespiqala*, which translates as 'precious stone' in Aymara. We were helped by unusually heavy snow conditions. Normally our route would be a mixed climb.

Two days later, we climbed Santa Vera Cruz itself by a new route on the crevassed western snow slopes that Prem avoided. The route was called *Jenecheru*, or 'the first is always burning'. On the summit we made two interesting discoveries: a small cairn containing a tin with Prem's card from 60 years before, and also a number of artefacts from the late period of the Tiwanaku culture. According to Oswaldo Rivera, the Bolivian archaeologist, these date back 800 years.

The items were offerings to Pachamama, or Mother Earth, and included some silver brooches, called Tupus, which were used to fasten clothes, a small wooden receptacle, two ceremonial wooden cups with geometric patterns, a hawthorn needle and a human collar bone, used as a spoon. All these things were covered in fabric. The purpose of these early climbers may have been different to ours, but we felt we shared a community of spirit with them, searching for peace and calmness. The Achachilas, or spirits of the mountains, gave us good luck in finding that treasure. It is amazing that these mountains, only four hours by bus from La Paz, had not seen more ascents.

Mount Everest Foundation Expedition Reports 2000

SUMMARISED BY BILL RUTHVEN

E ach year the Mount Everest Foundation supports a number of expeditions undertaking exploration in one form or another amongst the high mountains of the world. As well as 'Approval' – which in itself sometimes has the effect of opening other purses – most expeditions which are not already well funded also receive a grant, typically ranging between £200 and £1500. Whilst this only represents a small proportion of the overall cost of an expedition, the moral support and the promise of a few hundred pounds during the preparatory stages of an expedition can sometimes make the difference between it going and not going.

All that the MEF asks in return is a comprehensive report. Once received, copies are lodged in the Alpine Club Library, the Royal Geographical Society and the British Mountaineering Council where they are available for consultation by future expeditioners. In addition, some reports – up to and including 1999 expeditions – have recently been given to the Alan Rouse Memorial Collection in Sheffield Central Library.

The following notes are based on reports that have been received during 2000-01, and are divided into geographical areas.

NORTH AMERICA

00/10 Sea to the Sky, St Elias 2000 Dr Alun Hubbard (with John Millar from UK and Jay Burbee & Dave Hildes from Canada). July-August 2000
This team's 'purist' plan to start climbing from Icy Bay after sailing from Vancouver had to be shelved when their boat was damaged by another vessel, and the approach was completed by hire car with an air drop at the base of the Seward Glacier. Poor weather gave the impression that they were too late in the season, first delaying the establishment of a camp at 1600m and then making navigation impossible through the maze of séracs and chasms higher up. This meant that their planned high-level traverse linking seven peaks could not be achieved, but they were successful in making the first ascent of Mt Baird, 3550m, via its E Ridge, descending by its E Face.

00/23 British Yukon 2000 Mick Fowler (with Andy Cave, Chris Pasteur and Duncan Tunstall). May-June 2000
Mt Kennedy, 4200m, lies in the Kluane National Park on the border between Canada and Alaska, and its 'inspirational' 1800m NW Face (in Canada)

remains unclimbed. On arrival at its foot, this team realised why, judging the avalanche risk too great in the prevailing weather conditions. Shifting their attention to the North Buttress which had previously had 2 fixed rope 'siege-type' ascents, in a 6-day push Cave and Fowler made the first alpine-style ascent which they graded TD Sup, and 'serious'! Pasteur and Tunstall attempted the NE Face/E Ridge of the mountain, but were stopped by a huge crevasse spanning the whole glacier. However, they made probable first ascents of two nearby peaks of 2850m and 3325m. (*See article 'Mount Kennedy – North Buttress' in this volume.*)

00/29 British Denali/Hunter Experience 2000 Jules Cartwright (with Ian Parnell). May-June 2000
The plans of this team to put up contrasting new routes on Mount Hunter, 4442m, and Denali, 6194m, were hampered by heavy snowfall. Despite this and two fractured ribs sustained by Parnell when hit by a snow mushroom, they climbed a 1200m ED4 (Alaskan Grade 6) new route *The Knowledge* on Hunter's N Buttress. Snow conditions were considered too dangerous to continue to the summit, so they abseiled down the nearby Moonflower Buttress. Their later attempt on Denali was abandoned at 4900m, whilst an intended reconnaissance of a new line of Kahiltna West failed to reach the base of the mountain. (*See front cover photo.*)

00/30 Crown Jewel 2000 Dr Brian Davison (with Lindsay Griffin and Brian Griffiths). April-June 2000
This team set out to explore the previously unvisited cirques S of the Pika Glacier in the 'Little Switzerland' area of Alaska, making first ascents of as many peaks as possible. A base camp was set up where they were dropped off by their ski-plane on the East Fork of the Crown Glacier at c.1800m, and a second camp some 5km down the glacier to the SE. Despite widely varying temperatures and unconsolidated snow conditions, they succeeded in climbing two new routes on The Crown Jewel, 2362m (second highest peak in the Pika Glacier cirque) together with first ascents of a dozen other mountains.

00/34 British Mt Russell 2000 Geoff Hornby (with Mike Smith from the USA). May-June 2000
When his original partner dropped out at the eleventh hour, the future of this expedition seemed in jeopardy, but then the leader – already in Alaska – met up with a worthy replacement. However, that was not the end of his problems as, with continuous high winds (which prevented anyone from summiting the W Buttress on Denali), the local pilots were unwilling to fly to the remote Chedotlothna Glacier from where he planned to attempt a traverse of Mount Russell, 3557m. A flight to Ruth Glacier was substituted, and from here two first ascents were achieved – Mt Sholes, 1905m, and Mt Tassles, 2091m.

SOUTH AMERICA & ANTARCTICA

00/1 British Cape Renard Tower 2000 Julian Freeman-Attwood (with Crag Jones and Skip Novak). February-March 2000
The ascent of the N Face of this 747m tower (actually a separate island) on the edge of Antarctica has become something of an obsession for this three-man team, despite the major logistical problems entailed in even reaching the area. This year, after climbing some 20 pitches of E 1/2 rock and Scottish III to V, they reached, some 100 metres below the summit, a blank wall which would not be climbable without bolts, which they were not prepared to use. They were more successful on nearby Wiencke Island, where they made probably the second ascent of Monte Italia, 1097m.

00/3 Cochamo 2000 Seb Grieve (with Leo Houlding). Feb-March 2000
Although originally planned as a four-man team, this expedition to the Cochamo valley in Central Chile (some two hours inland from Puerto Monte) eventually went ahead with only two. Their aim was to free-climb existing routes on Mt Trinidad, c.2300m, and investigate the scope for new routes on hitherto unknown rock walls. The approach through jungle proved to be considerably easier than anticipated, having been cut and clearly marked by previous climbers, including some Brazilians who were still in the area. Although the weather was initially good, it rapidly deteriorated, and the pair only managed to repeat a route called *The Eides of March* (E5 A3) before they had to leave.

00/7A British 2000 Western Patagonia Dr David Hillebrandt (with Nick Banks, Chris Smith and Niall Washington-Jones). October-November 2000
Despite previous experience of the horrendous Patagonia weather, this team must have short memories, as they keep going back. Their original objective, La Dama Blanca, the highest peak in the Cordillera Sarmiento of Chile, was climbed by a Spanish team early in the year, so they turned their attention to the second highest, Angels Wings, c.1800m. Their intended approach from the east proved to be impossible owing to avalanches, séracs and a steep valley with wet slabs reaching sea level. By hitching a lift on a passing French yacht, they moved their base camp further south, initially finding access easier – but then the weather caught up with them. One storm lasted 11 days, so that they were lucky to be able to retrieve their equipment.

00/13 Quimsa Cruz/Illimani 2000 Dr Adele Pennington (with Di Gilbert, Sarah Nuttall, Sue Savage, Catrin Thomas and Claire Waddingham). July-August 2000
Until a few years ago, the MEF had received few applications from expeditions planning to visit the Cordillera Quimsa Cruz of Bolivia: now it is one of the most popular areas on the continent. From a base camp at

4500m, this all-female party explored the Immaculado Region, achieving 16 new routes and five first ascents of peaks c.4900-5500m. At the end of the expedition, an attempt on the Khoya Khoyu route on Illimani N Summit, c.6300m, was defeated by crevasses, 'concrete' ice and an amphitheatre of overhanging séracs, but honour was restored by a successful ascent of the normal route on Pequena Alpamayo in the Cordillera Condoriri. This expedition was awarded the MEF Alison Chadwick Memorial Grant for 2000

00/26 Cerro Torre in Winter 2000 Andy Parkin. July-September 2000
Although intended to be a two-man team, the 'leader', David Hesleden, injured his back early in the year so, although departure was delayed in the hope that he would recover sufficiently, eventually Parkin went on his own. It was assumed that the winter season would provide more stable weather than other times of the year, and thus make the second ascent of the *Maestri/ Egger Route* on the NE Face of Cerro Torre, 3102m, a feasible proposition. However, this was not to be, climbing being very slow and dangerous owing to strong winds and large amounts of verglas, and his attempt on the *Compressor Route* was abandoned 300m below the summit. Bad weather conditions were also experienced on the *Super Couloir Route* on the NW Face of Fitzroy, 3444m (where lack of ice stopped him just below the jammed block) and on the East Face of Cerro Doblado, 2675m (abandoned owing to excessive snow). As a consolation, Parkin teamed up with local Argentinean climbers to make first ascents of a number of icefalls in the El Chalten valley.

00/27 Cymru/Bolivia Quimsa Cruz 2000 Mike Rosser (with Sharon Abbott, Brian Cummins, Wayne Gladwin, John James and Paul Westwood). August 2000
This team succeeded in putting up 10 new rock routes (50 to 200m and 4B to 5C) on Cerro Taruca Umana, 4900m, and making first ascents of three peaks, c.5000m, in the Cerro Achuma range. Their plans to explore the Cerro Jankho Willichi range were thwarted by ground conditions.

00/36 Patagonia Winter 2000 Crazy Gringos Andy Kirkpatrick (with Richard Cross). July-August 2000
This team hoped to make several first winter ascents, particularly of Torre Egger, c.2850m, probably via a new route on its E Face. However, once in the field, deep snow made them realise that more man-power would be required if they were to succeed, so they attempted a repeat of the *Compressor Route* instead. Bad weather on this forced a retreat from the Col of Patience. Attempts on the *Parkin Route* on Aguja Mermoz, 2732m, and the *French Couloir* on Cerro Pollone, 2579m, were also abandoned owing to bad weather but, undeterred, these optimistic gringos still feel that winter is a good season for climbing in Patagonia.

GREENLAND AND ARCTIC AREAS

00/9 Greenland 2000. Tilman in a New Millennium Rev Bob Shepton (with Laurie Haynes, Steve Holland, James Jackson & Dudley Smith as 'First Crew' and Graham Austick, Angelica Heisel, Paolo Paglino & Alberto Zuchetti as 'Second Crew'. June-September 2000
This was the first part of a two-year project to explore and climb the mountains along the west coast of Greenland, using the leader's 10m sloop *Dodo's Delight* as a mobile base camp, after sailing it from Scotland. From Kangerdluarssugssuaq Fjord, Shepton, Haynes and Holland made first ascents of Pt. 1510 and Pt. 1230, which in view of their nationalities they named 'Scotland the Brave' and 'Aussie Peak'. (Inuit translations are still awaited!) Sailing further north to the Upernavik area and climbing directly from the boat onto the first pitch, Austick, with Italians Paglino and Zuchetti (supported by Shepton and Heisel) used siege tactics over 14 days of mixed weather (6 climbing) to make the first ascent of the N Face of Sandersons Hope, at 1045m the country's biggest sea cliff north of the Arctic Circle. They called the route *Arctic First Born*.

00/11 British Eastern Torssuqatoq Spires 2000 Jonathan Bracey (with Vicky Barratt, Virginia Cooper, Matt Goode, Charlotte Mainwaring, Steve Powell, Alex Messenger and Ian Renshaw). July-September 2000
Despite delays at the start of this expedition due to prolonged periods of rain, and assisting 00/35 (see below), this expedition achieved not only its primary aim of the first ascent of Whaleback Peak, c.1200m, but also of Pt. 1303 (aka Whaleback), Flatiron, c.1120m, The Great White, c.1050m and The Crest, c.1180m. Routes were up to 700 metres in length and were graded up to TD and E3. The fragile nature of the rock was emphasised when a hold on another peak broke and Renshaw took a 15-metre leader fall, breaking his heel in the process. He was evacuated to hospital in Nanortalik by helicopter.

00/15 British Lemon Mountains 2000 Richard Pash (with Nicola Faulks, Rupert Finn, Danny Heywood, Lucy Pash, Tom Spreyer, Jim Thacker and Pippa Whitehouse). June-July 2000
During his very successful expedition in 1999 (99/15, reported in AJ 105), this leader became aware of the large number of peaks in the Lemon Mountains still awaiting first ascents. On this return visit, which also included an exploration on ski of the Lindbergh Mountains to the north, the team reduced the number considerably, by climbing 32 new routes, including first ascents of 20 mountains. (*See article 'The Lemon Mountains of East Greenland' in this volume.*)

00/20 British American South Greenland 2000 Jim Lowther (with Chris Bonington, Rob Ferguson and John Porter from England, Graham Little and Scott Muir from Scotland and Mark Richey and Mark Wilford from USA). July-August 2000
Climbing in strictly national parties, between them this team achieved 13 first ascents on 12 unclimbed peaks between 1112m and 1948m in areas to the north of Kangikitsoq Fjord and to the east of Kangersuneq Qingordleq (Fjord). The rock (granite) varied from 'astounding' to 'horrendous'. The great success of the expedition was largely due to the swarms of mosquito and black fly which shared their base camp, giving little incentive for hanging around.

00/31 Watkins Mountains 2000 Christine Watkins (with Anne Picard from Holland and Charlotte Steinmeir from Germany). May 2000
Bad weather prevented this international team of women flying from Iceland for over a week, thus severely reducing the time available for climbing and exploring in Greenland. Things were no better when they did arrive, so they joined up with a three-man Tangent expedition to make the best of the time available. Ascents were made of six peaks between 2992m and 3609m from the Upper Woolley Glacier, four of them being first ascents.

00/35 Thumbnail 2000 Ian Parnell (with Ben Bransby, Matt Dickinson and Gareth Parry, plus Matthew Bransby and Sandy Ogilvie in support). July-August 2000
The 1300m E Face of Agdlerussakasit, 1763m – aka 'The Thumbnail' – rises straight out of Torssuqatoq Sound with no foreshore, and has been described as 'the world's biggest sea-cliff'. This team achieved its first free ascent in 6 days with 31 pitches up to E6 6b. Sadly, whilst they were descending, they heard on their radio that Matthew Bransby had been killed in an abseil accident on a one-day climb near Base Camp. The MEF extends its deepest sympathy to his family and friends.

HIMALAYA – INDIA

00/18 British Arwa Spires Al Powell (with Andy Benson, Pete Benson, Kenton Cool, Ian Parnell and Dave Wills). October 2000
In 1999, an expedition (99/19, reported in AJ105) to the Arwa area of the Garhwal succeeded in climbing the Tower but failed on the Spire, 6193m. Using knowledge gained on that earlier trip by Kenton Cool, this team first made unsuccessful attempts at routes on the N Face and the Central Buttress before turning their attention to the E Ridge. Here they were more fortunate, and all but Wills (who was unwell) reached the summit by an 800m TD route.

00/25 Parbati South West Ridge Olly Sanders (with Martin Chester and Iain Peter). August-September 2000
At least three previous expeditions have attempted the SW Ridge of Parbati South (aka Pt. 6128) in the Kullu without success. This team researched the 800m route carefully and felt that – given reasonable weather – three weeks in the area should give them sufficient time to climb it. Initially the weather was relatively kind, and they were encouraged to find that the rock was good granite with pitches of VS and HVS. Then all this changed, with daily snowfalls and a band of very rotten unstable rock at 5600m putting paid to their attempt. A dam project may mean that the beautiful approach via the Parbati Valley could be impassable within a few years.

HIMALAYA – CHINA AND TIBET

00/22 British Tibet 2000 Dr Charles Clarke (with Pasang Choephel, Sesum Dhargye and Gyatso Tsultrem from Tibet). July-August 2000
Having already explored the northern, eastern and western approaches to Sepu Kangri in the Eastern Nyenchen Tanglha as part of 96/17, 97/31 and 98/44, Clarke was keen to explore the southern side, and thus complete a circumnavigation, hopefully climbing some sub-6000m peaks en route. With permit problems and rumours of blocked roads, they eventually travelled by Land Cruiser from Lhasa to Diru, and then, as pillion passengers on motorcycles, to Khinda. Further on, they hired horses to cross Dhakim La, 5402m, and Tam La, 5254m, previously crossed in 1998. The furthest extent of the journey was a village called Pa, from which they saw – but did not have time to attempt – a tantalising range of peaks up to 6500m. Return to Lhasa was by a different route over two more 5000m passes. Although no peaks were climbed, the expedition provided valuable information about a little-visited area.

00/38 Guangxi Caves 2000 Ged Campion (with Bruce Bensley, Pascale Battazi, Arthur Clarke, Alan Fletcher, Wiliam Hawkins, Harry Lomas, Stewart Muir, Anthony Penny, Shaun Penny, Mike Pitt, Alister Renton, John Riley, Graham Salmon, Arthur Salmon and John Whalley). September-October 2000
A reconnaissance trip to the Lingyun area of Guangxi Province by members of the Yorkshire Ramblers' Club in 1998 indicated potential for much undiscovered cave passage, so this was a return visit to see if the area lived up to expectations. In an extensive exploration of the area they surveyed 12km of new passage, and carried out biological and chemical studies of the water in the caves.

HIMALAYA – NEPAL

00/24 British Chamar 2000 Tony Barton (with John Allot, Tim Riley and Tom Wiggans plus Peter Berggren from Sweden). September-November 2000

Despite having a valid permit from the Nepalese Ministry of Tourism & Civil Aviation to climb the West Face of Chamar, 7187m, on arrival in the Sringi Khola, where they planned to establish a base camp, the local Lama would not allow this team to attempt it. Learning that if they continued they might be stoned to death, discretion deemed it advisable to try approaching the mountain from a different side. Unfortunately, the E side turned out to be in the same high-avalanche-risk condition reported by a British expedition six years earlier (MEF Ref 94/20). As a result the attempt was aborted at 5900m.

00/37 Danga Sir Chris Bonington (with Dr Rupert Bennet, Daniel Bonington and Gerald Bonington with Furtenjee Sherpa, plus James Bonington, Jude Bonington and Dave Hummerstone in support). April-May 2000

Although the area around Lhonak, WNW of Kangchenjunga, has been closed for some time, a permit was granted allowing exploration and attempts to be made on any peaks in the Danga area. Once there, it was discovered that the range was quite complex, and what had been thought of as the main peak of Danga, 6359m – and an appropriate objective for the team – was actually Danga II, 6194m. They decided to attempt this peak anyway, and succeeded in making its first ascent on the only totally clear day of the trip. James Bonington joined the summit team in place of Rupert Bennet who was suffering from pleurisy.

KARAKORAM – PAKISTAN

00/8 Hucho Alchori 2000 Mary Twomey (with Penny Clay, Christine Goulding, Colin Wells and Elly Whiteford). July-August 2000

The Hucho Alchori Glacier lies off the Keralungma, South of Hispar, and a team member who had visited the area previously felt it offered plenty of scope for exploration and first ascents of sub-6000m peaks. However, lean conditions in the previous winter resulted in the proposed routes being incomplete and threatened by stonefall. Persistent rain meant that all other peaks had a high avalanche risk. Exploration of the area revealed traces of Fanny Bullock-Workman's camp from the early 1900s. Hopefully, climbers in the next century will not find evidence of any MEF-supported expeditions in this one!

00/14 Anglo-New Zealand Hindu Raj 2000 Adam Thomas (with Phil Amos and Simon Woods from UK and Jock Jeffery from NZ). June-August 2000

Following a self-funded expedition in 1999, this team made a successful application to the MEF for this trip, which planned to explore the Ochiri (Chonuk) and Matkesh valleys, SE of the Hindu Kush range, approaching from Chitral. Despite weather described as 'poor but never terrible' and Customs confiscating part of their food shipment because it contained pork, they made the first ascent of a 5995m peak by its SW Face at an alpine grade of D–/D. They named the peak 'Uddin Zom', Uddin being the family name of a local goat-herder whom they befriended, and who provided much assistance and hospitality whilst they were in the area.

Following the ascent of Uddin Zom, Woods and Jeffery joined another international expedition (not MEF-supported) which made the first ascents of Khan Sar, 5708m, and Sahan Sar, c.5500m from the Ishkoman Valley on the other side of the Hindu Raj.

00/21 2000 Pumari Chhish Julie-Ann Clyma (with Roger Payne). May-June 2000

Despite being close to the Hispar-Biafo Glacier trekking route, only one of the summits of Pumari Chhish – the North, 7492m – has been climbed, the ascent using 2300m of fixed rope. With experience gained on their previous attempt (99/33A reported in AJ105), this duo hoped to make the first ascent of the 7350m South Summit. Base camp was situated at c.4250m on the Yutmaru Glacier, and with an intermediate ABC they reached their old Camp 1 on a col at c.5100m, continuous snowfall supporting their decision to take skis. After both climbers had been hit by avalanches – fortunately without injury – they decided it was too dangerous to continue, and spent the rest of their time exploring the inaccurately mapped area.

00/33 British Solu 2000 Dave Wilkinson (with Ken Findlay, Paul Hudson and Karl Zientek). July-August 2000

Although this team had originally planned to explore the Sokhu Glacier, when they learned that the nearby Solu was totally unvisited, they decided to explore that instead. Poor weather foiled their attempts on several mountains, but they did manage to achieve what they assumed to be the first ascent of Sekha Brakk (Dragonfly Peak), c.5200m.

CENTRAL ASIA AND THE FAR EAST

00/16A Kazakh Apogee 2000 Stuart Batey (with Alan Beeton, Carl Burks, Catherine Clare, Allan Gransden, Andrew Grubb, Mick Jenkins, Frank McCorriston, Carl Morrish, John Owens, Darran Weller and John Wharry). July-August 2000

In previous years the Royal Engineers Military Survey Department had organised major exploratory mountaineering expeditions to Ecuador, India and Chile; but for their Millennium Expedition they selected the Dzungarian Alatau of Southern Kazakhstan. Despite the collapse of a bridge under their 4x4 bus during the approach, a base camp was established in the Abay Glacier Valley, from which team members climbed 15 peaks between 3330m and 4622m, 7 being first ascents. They also explored an area covering 600 sq km, collecting data to populate a Geographic Information System (GIS) which will eventually be accessible via their website.

OTHER AREAS

00/5 Poi North Face John Barry (with Pat Littlejohn, Jan Rowe and Steve Sustad). February 2000
This team attempted the Yosemite-like unclimbed 760m N Face of Mount Poi (the 'Ayers Rock' of Kenya, situated in the Ndoto Mountains several hundred kilometres N of Nairobi) in February 1999, but injuries sustained by the leader when a large boulder came away caused that expedition to be curtailed. Maintaining their strict 'no-bolt' policy despite few obvious cracklines, this return visit was considerably more successful, and after 17 pitches of climbing up to 6A and E6 (plus an 'ungradeable lasso pitch which would have been the envy of the Pampas') the summit was achieved after four fantastic days of climbing and two hammock bivouacs. They have called the route *Dark Safari*. (*See article 'Big Walls in Kenya' in this volume.*)

00/17 Welsh Low's Gully 2000 Jerry Gore (with Steve Long, Louise Thomas and Mike Turner). March-April 2000
Although Low's Gully on Mount Kinabalu, 4101m, received its first complete descent a few years ago, all attempts to climb the 750m E face had so far failed. However when this team arrived, they found that a group of Spanish climbers were just completing a 40-day first ascent of a route which they called *The Alchemist*. Lacking the luxury of such a time scale, the Brits set off to reduce this considerably, and at the same time to climb a new route. Compact granite at the base of the wall forced them to follow the Spanish route for the first 100m, but above this they branched off onto their own, and despite rain varying from heavy to torrential they topped out in 15 days on a 19-pitch route which they called *The Crucible* (A4 E4 6A).

00/39 Benerat 2000 (caving) Dick Willis (with Tim Allen, Colin Boothroyd, Andy Eavis, Pam Fogg, Tim Fogg, Pete Hall, Martin Holroyd, Pete O'Neil and Tony White plus three local cavers). November 2000
This was the tenth in a series of joint Anglo-Sarawak caving expeditions to Mulu National Park. New discoveries in Cobweb Cave in Gunong Benerat extended the mapped length from 15.1 km to 26.7 km, making it the second longest cave in the Park, and the fifth longest in SE Asia. Several 'new' caves were found and surveyed, but with increasing activity by illegal birds-nesters, it has become necessary to conceal information about new discoveries.

Book Reviews

COMPILED BY GEOFFREY TEMPLEMAN

Snow in the Kingdom. My Storm Years on Everest
Ed Webster
Mountain Imagery, Boulder, Colorado, 2000. pp 589, $29.95

Snow in the Kingdom is a love story, a personal record of the author's infatuation with Mount Everest. His passion began in 1986, took him close to the summit twice, and finally up the most difficult face and nearly to his death. It is a moving and intimate diary of a great adventure.

Webster began climbing in New England as a teenager and soon went on to difficult climbs in the United States, Europe, Britain and Canada. The death of his beloved girl-friend on a climb – for which he held himself responsible – clouded his life for a year but he went back to full-time climbing and at age 30 was ready for the Himalaya. As a boy he had been stirred by a lecture on Mount Everest, and when an invitation came he eagerly accepted.

In the next two years he went with world-class mountaineers to two difficult and dangerous routes on the Tibetan side, but they were turned back by the notorious Everest weather and rifts in the party. This apprenticeship in harsh reality, sweetened by a solo ascent of Changtse, only increased his infatuation. He quickly joined three others and decided to attempt the fearsome Kangshung face which had been climbed only once, in 1983, by a very dangerous route. Webster studied their photographs and persuaded his companions to try a safer though more difficult route.

The four would climb without bottled oxygen and without Sherpas, calling it a 'pure' climb. The story of will, strength and undaunted courage on this awesome route occupies more than a third of the book, magnificently illustrated by 64 colour plates distributed in six sections throughout the book, plus black and white photographs on almost every page.

Three of the party got close to the summit, but only Venables, the British member, made it to the top. One chilling chapter describes the exhaustion, hallucinations and terror which flooded over them during the harrowing three days of descent to safety. They had been too long above 24,000ft, without adequate food, water or rest; all would pay a price, but especially Webster, who lost all his fingertips on one hand and several toes. He feared he would never climb again but a year later he began to regain some of his skills, though he knew the hypoxia and cold would make Everest impossible for him.

Webster is one of the few who have been on all three of the great faces of Everest and his descriptions and insight are excellent. The conversations throughout the book ring true because he recorded them each night in his diary, and even when disabled, he dictated the record. It has taken twelve years to complete the book, which he then published himself.

This is a big book, printed on high quality paper, with superb illustrations and very well hardbound. The personal informal style, the real conversations, the candour and self-scrutiny make this a refreshing change from the standard Himalayan fare today. There's enough but not too much self-examination and philosophy – though only a little about Tibetan or Chinese culture and socio-economics. A few of Odell's original photographs appear here for the first time, and Webster speculates about Tenzing Norgay's childhood and possible meeting with George Mallory in 1924. There's a good bibliography and an unusually good index.

All in all, a splendid and important book.

Charles Houston

The Wildest Dream
Mallory: His Life and Conflicting Passions
Peter and Leni Gillman
Headline, 2000, pp.xiv+306, £18.99

The question is not why there have been so many books about George Mallory, but why there haven't been more. He was and remains a compelling figure, not least because of the cinematographic last glimpse of him on the slopes of Everest, but also because of his apparently effortless connections and his physical beauty. Lytton Strachey wrote of him: 'Oh heavens! His body!' His tutor at Cambridge, the highly strung Arthur Benson, described Mallory as 'one of the most ingenuous and purest-minded creatures I know. . . very beautiful, too, to look at, and finely proportioned, so that it is a pleasure to me to see him move, or do anything.' Of course both men were keen on getting George into bed, but even the senior master in his house at Winchester was struck by his physical appeal. 'He had a strikingly beautiful face,' wrote Graham Irving. 'Its shape, its delicately cut features, especially the rather large, heavily lashed, thoughtful eyes, were extraordinarily suggestive of a Boticelli Madonna, even when he had ceased to be a boy – though [and here you can imagine Irving's voice dropping an octave] any suspicion of effeminacy was completely banished by obvious proofs of physical energy and strength.'

And if his friends were overwhelmed by his mixture of long lashes and butch physique, then Mallory's character was no less admired. After his death, Howard Somervell described him as one of his few real friends, 'loved as one of the most delightful and splendid of men'. Robert Graves, whom Mallory had taught at Charterhouse, described him as 'his first real friend' who showed Graves that marriage could 'after all be made a decent relationship'. To Geoffrey Young, whose affection one assumes was touched by erotic desire as well as love and friendship, Mallory was his 'mountain sunlight, the light of almost passionate hope and reassurance'.

Leaving aside the man himself, there were his friendships and connections with several of the most influential movements and thinkers of the early twentieth century. With *entrées* into the Bloomsbury Group and leading Liberal circles, with friends like Arnold Toynbee, Maynard Keynes and Duncan Grant, it's difficult to see how Mallory *couldn't* have been an interesting man. And yet, in some ways, the picture of him is a little hazy. So many extraordinary people wanted something from Mallory that their desires seem to blur the edges of the man himself: the waspish, cynical Stracheys wanted his body; Benson wanted to find a 'kindred spirit'; Young wanted his leg and his youth back. (People still want things from Mallory, of course. A reputation, perhaps, or the contents of his pockets.)

One of the great strengths of this new biography by Peter and Leni Gillman, is the generous good sense it exhibits in analysing Mallory's personal life. He had homosexual experiences, it's true, but so what? It would be difficult to leave public school and Cambridge behind *now* without something of the kind happening. But at Cambridge in the 1900s? And if he had been gay, then his life would have been more complicated but no less admirable. As it happens, the Gillmans tell us, he was straight, and happily married, except for the inevitable tensions that arose from his long absences during the Great War and afterwards on Everest.

Mallory's marriage forms the central plank of their view of him, and it's a valid foundation. In that sphere, as in others, Mallory's life is like the prototype of the modern climber, torn between a successful career doing something 'worthwhile' as so many of his friends did, while at the same time mesmerised by the mountains and the knowledge that there he could live intensely, the master of his own fate. You could, cynically, argue that there have been plenty whose intellects have not had sufficient edge to match their ambition and who have consequently turned to the mountains as the arena in which to leave their mark.

But the Gillmans suggest that Mallory's career, far from being stalled, was showing new growth and that his participation in the 1924 Everest expedition sprung not from desperation but more from an inability to leave the damn thing alone. The most affecting passages centre on the correspondence between Ruth and George, especially the final letters from base camp, which show Mallory aching for home and the arms of his children even as he turned to face the mountain for a final attempt. Simply put, and this may sound familiar to an awful lot of mountaineers, he wanted to have his cake and eat it. (Although few of us can afford the kind of childcare the Mallorys enjoyed.)

The Gillmans also squash a lot of ill-considered theories, like Walt Unsworth's suggestion that Mallory took Irvine along on that fateful day because he fancied him. It's true Irvine was not in as good condition as Odell, but then neither was Mallory. The young man's technical expertise was reason enough. The Gillmans also puncture some of the imperial froth that surrounded and still surrounds the early Everest expeditions, quoting Mallory's cynical appraisal, to Rupert Thompson, of the reasons he was on the mountain in 1921: 'I sometimes think of this expedition as a fraud from beginning to end, invented by the wild enthusiasm of one man, Younghusband; puffed up by the would-be wisdom of certain pundits in the AC; and imposed upon the youthful ardour of your humble servant. The prospect of ascent is almost nil, and our present job is to rub our noses against the impossible in such a way as to persuade mankind that some noble heroism has failed again.' Change the personnel, and he could have been talking about the war he'd so recently witnessed.

I especially enjoyed the Gillmans' demolition job of the secretary of the Mount Everest Committee, Arthur Hinks, a pernicious little man who habitually sent spiteful notes under the pretence that they came from his president and made withering assessments of Mallory's abilities from the security of his desk. George Finch was dropped from the 1924 expedition, to Mallory's horror, with clinical indifference in part because the man had the temerity to wear his hair long and to be a somewhat impoverished Australian. Imagine! The snobbery and prejudice of the upper echelons of the Alpine Club and, even worse, the Royal Geographical Society, are now – one assumes – a thing of the past.

Not that Mallory wasn't capable of his own brand of snobbery. He seems to have taken a dim view of North Americans, and indeed anyone outside his own circle who didn't sparkle in conversation. He had liberal instincts, but they carried the whiff of patrician smugness. In the rough and tumble of real politics, rather than the talking shops he experienced, Mallory's prejudices would have bubbled to the surface more obviously. But then, and this is the real tragedy, we shall never know. Perhaps with Everest out of the way and his naked ambition, his confidence that he would be someone of consequence tempered by experience, Mallory would have played a useful role in steering the nation's elite from its jingoistic and blinkered habits. Ruth Mallory, instinctively devoted, quite correctly didn't give a damn about the mountain. She wanted the man.

Perhaps this book's greatest achievement will be to redress the avalanche of cliché and self-justification that has surrounded the discovery of George Mallory's mortal remains. The bleached flesh and splintered bones of this gifted, forgetful, driven, privileged and generous man should not be the lasting image the public holds in its mind's eye. The Gillmans are partial to their subject, and at times a less generous view would have offered balance, but they show that at the core of himself George Mallory was a climber. And I'd sooner remember him for that.

Ed Douglas

Fearless on Everest
Julie Summers
Weidenfeld & Nicolson, 2000, xii+290, £20

'My face is perfect agony,' Andrew Irvine scribbled in his diary, close to the summit of Everest. 'Have prepared two oxygen apparatus for our start tomorrow morning.' They were the last words he would write. On 8 June 1924, he and his partner George Mallory climbed into the clouds and disappeared forever, creating one of mountaineering's most fundamental myths. Irvine was 22 years old.

One of the curious things about the discovery of George Mallory's body in 1999 was how long it took for the climbers who found him to realise just who it was lying half-buried in front of them. Of course, they had set out that morning looking for Irvine. They believed they had a rough fix on the body discovered by Chinese climber Wang Hong Bao which was thought to be Irvine's. But even when they found a name tag on one of the pieces of clothing which identified it as belonging to Mallory, the first instinct was to ask why Irvine was wearing something belonging to George. The mistake, I'm sure, was largely due to altitude. So often preconceptions get welded more firmly into place by hypoxia. But I'm sure that part of it is explained by the notion that finding Mallory was too good to be true; a little like going out to look for a treasure map and instead finding the treasure.

Irvine has almost always been described in relation to Mallory, a cipher for analysing Mallory's motivation, even his sexual orientation. Why should he have chosen to climb with an inexperienced Oxford student, when Noel Odell, fit and well acclimatised, was close at hand? Walt Unsworth, in his widely praised history of Everest says: 'One is forced to the conclusion that no recognizable logic played a part in Mallory's decision. Was it after all, as Duncan Grant has suggested, that Mallory chose Irvine partly on asethetic grounds? ...Was he an ageing Galahad making a last desperate bid to find his Holy Grail and choosing as companion a young man who embodied all he himself had once been?'

Well, no, actually, he wasn't – and he didn't. Unsworth's coded reference to a homosexual impulse in Mallory 'choosing' Irvine is simply wrong and if you want to know why, then I suggest you read Peter and Leni Gillman's biography of Mallory, *The Wildest Dream*, which won the Boardman-Tasker Award last year. But Unsworth's remark is also reductionist in its treatment of Irvine, as though he was entirely plastic, to be formed however the rest of the expedition chose. The obsession with Mallory – understandable given the richness of his life – among most climbing historians has only served to perpetuate this view.

Now this excellent new biography of Irvine, *Fearless on Everest,* written by his grand-niece Julie Summers, has revealed that far from being just an impressionable and inexperienced boy, there was so much more to Irvine than you might have imagined. While the handsome rowing blue's life was tragically short it was nevertheless action-packed, and included an illicit affair with his best friend's step-mother which prompted a divorce which wasn't settled until after Irvine's death. Summers has also produced new evidence for why Mallory chose to climb with Irvine which stops the gossipy imaginings of some historians in their tracks.

While Andrew Irvine was struggling towards the top of Everest, his erstwhile lover, a former chorus girl born Marjory Thomson, was being divorced by her husband, the steel magnate Harry Summers, Julie Summers' great-grandfather. Irvine met Marjory through her stepson Dick, a shy, dark-haired boy whom Irvine had befriended on the fives court at Shrewsbury School during their first week there. Dick Summers had been devastated by the premature death of his natural mother, and thrived on his friendship with Irvine, nicknamed 'Sandy' for his shock of blonde hair.

Irvine, who grew up in Birkenhead, spent summers with Dick at Cornist Hall in North Wales, massively extended by Harry Summers who added a swimming pool and kept a Rolls Royce in the garage. Harry's wealth had also impressed the 19-year-old Marjory Thomson, whose blue eyes and, according to Julie Summers, 'charming, sunny personality' completely bowled over Summers, then 52. They were married in 1917, but Marjory soon started seeking out company more her own age.

Irvine had gone up to Oxford in 1922, shoe-horned into Merton for his prodigious talent as a rower, one of the stars of the 1919 'Peace Regatta' at Henley, the first since the Great War. He won a place in the University Boat as a freshman and was part of the winning VIII in the 1923 Boat Race, which Oxford narrowly won – the only occasion they did so between 1913 and 1937. 'They were almost like gods,' one female spectator wrote of the Oxford crew, men who had just missed serving on the Western Front. 'We just stood and stared in awe and admiration.'

In response to those who argue that an ascent of Craig yr Ysfa's Great Gully, an exploratory trip to Spitsbergen and a winter's skiing at Mürren are hardly sufficient preparation for an attempt on Everest, Luke Hughes makes the point in the last edition of the *Alpine Journal* that 'anyone who has trained for and rowed in a Boat Race twice will have known about pushing the limits and urging his team-mates to do the same. Nor should his inexperience have been such a handicap; amateurs, not fearing to tread behind more seasoned partners, have a tradition for excelling on Everest.'

Although she had first known him as a boy, Sandy's burgeoning physique, charming manners and new celebrity made an impact on Marjory Summers. She made a determined effort to capture him and began an indiscrete affair, driving Irvine to the theatre in her husband's Rolls and taking him for intimate picnics in North Wales. When Irvine was invited on the Oxford University expedition to Spitsbergen, where he so impressed Odell, Marjory joined the team for the first leg to Tromsø, Irvine visiting her first-class cabin at night.

Harry Summers finally became aware of his wife's infidelity when a friend saw Irvine leaving her bedroom in the middle of the night, soon after he returned from Norway. Divorce proceedings were instigated by the millionaire, and a settlement reached in 1925, a year after Irvine's disappearance. Summers speculates that Irvine loved Marjory but was relieved to be out of the relationship, considering Marjory too poor a catch for marriage. Harry Summers gave her £3000 a year in the settlement, but after a string of marriages to wealthy husbands, Marjory returned the money to the Summers family in her will.

Dick Summers, after a brief liaison with a Danish heiress, proposed to Irvine's sister Evelyn, Julie Summers' grandmother. The proposal devastated Irvine, who, despite his own affair with Marjory, felt betrayed and jealous of Dick's intimacy with his beloved sister. Despite their friendship, Irvine thought Evelyn was wasted on Dick. 'You'll have to make a real man of him before I'll feel really happy about it,' he told her in a letter. Their friendship remained strained when Irvine left for Everest.

Irvine's other great relationship, with George Mallory, was perhaps the most unlikely of all. Mallory was 38 and hugely experienced. Irvine had barely climbed at all before leaving for Everest, but after their time together in Norway, Odell championed his inclusion in the Everest party of 1924. Irvine was practical, able to strip and repair machinery; that skill and his legendary strength were, to the Mount Everest Committee, more use on Everest than climbing prowess alone. The team relied on heavy and unpredictable oxygen sets, and Irvine was seen as the man to keep them functioning. Plans for modifications drawn up by Irvine and rediscovered during Julie Summers' research, show just how skilled Irvine was as an engineer. On the mountain itself, he showed himself full of the practical efficiency and common sense that are most useful on a big, technically straightforward mountain.

The expedition, or at least some of it, left Liverpool Docks at the start of March, 1924. Cruelly, as Irvine waved goodbye from the ship carrying him to India and Tibet, his younger brother Thurston announced to the rest of the family: 'Well, that's the last we'll see of him.' During the voyage, Mallory found his young partner likeable if dull-witted, telling his wife Ruth that Irvine was 'one to rely on, for everything except for conversation'. Both were Cheshire men; the local paper ran the headline 'Mount Everest Expedition – Two Birkenhead Men In The Party'. But if Irvine lacked intellectual depth, he shared Mallory's obsessive drive and saw the former schoolteacher as a role model.

He was popular with the other climbers, and worked hard on the mundane chores that make life at extreme altitudes so hard. Irvine sometimes comes across as being a bit too eager to please, but given his background, demeanour and age, this is hardly surprising. Where Summers did particularly well was hunting down Irvine's correspondence from the mountain, a bundle of eleven letters, in May 2000, which shed new light on the climbing decisions taken on the mountain, dispelling much of the speculation and controversy surrounding the last days of the 1924 expedition.

Mallory, who had briefly been James Strachey's lover, described Irvine as having 'a magnificent body for the job', a comment that added fuel to Duncan Grant's conclusion that Mallory was thinking 'on aesthetic grounds' when choosing Irvine. But, in a way, Mallory was underestimating Irvine. Because he lacked, or had not yet developed, Mallory's articulate explanation of mountaineering's appeal, it is tempting to consider him as just a body, honed by rowing and fearless, but just a body. The appeal of this book is that it fills that vacuum. The most poignant moment in *Fearless on Everest* is not the disappearance of Mallory and Irvine on Everest, but the letter Arnold Lunn's nine-year-old son Peter, whom Irvine had befriended at Mürren, writes to Irvine's mother:

'At Mürren in the skiing he was always so cheery. He explained to me all about compasses, barometers, oxygen etc. without showing any sign of getting bored of my questions. I especially loved that side of his modesty that enabled him to speak as though I am grown up. I am very sorry for you at having lost your son, for having a mother, I know what it would be like.'

Ed Douglas

Siegfried Herford: An Edwardian Rock-Climber
Keith Treacher
The Ernest Press, 2000, pp.168, £16.95

To anyone interested in the early days of rock climbing this must be an unusually interesting book, not only because it explores a singular and romantic personality but also because of the exceptional and diverse influences which touched him. His name probably reverberates in your mind with Botterill's Slab (second ascent; after nine years) and, of course, with the epic first ascent of Central Buttress on Scafell.

Treacher often gives us a somewhat jumbled story but the book remains a treasure house. Dozens of interesting personalities and topics are glancingly touched on: Ludwig Wittgenstein, Unitarian theology, Froebel education in the North West, the early days of aeronautical engineering, the invention of the 'roller' bicycle chain, to name a few. A particular focus of interest which ties some of these together and will be appreciated by many readers, concerns the early thinking which surrounded the beginnings of adventurous – eg 'Outward Bound' – educational experiments.

After a mercurial and almost absurd sequence of trial schools, young Siegfried went to the Herman Lietz school at Bieberstein – one of several German schools founded in the wake of ideas generated by Cecil Reddie of Abbotsholme. This experience tapped into a strain in Herford's make-up for heroic leadership and service and to his family's connections with

Germany. In his first week at Bieberstein, for example, he found himself helping to organise schoolboys to fight a major fire, which threatened to burn down the whole school. A little later, he played a big part in organising a school expedition to Iceland. In the summer of 1909 a party climbed to the summit of Mount Hecla and later made an adventurous and, as it turned out, dangerous crossing of one of the ice-sheets. This was, indeed, the kind of pioneering epic which Herford relished.

One intriguing development from all this came a few years later, partly through his friendship with Geoffrey Young, when Herford surprised some of his friends by taking a strongly pacifist position in the 1914-18 war. One thinks both of his namesake Siegfried Sassoon and, much later, of Menlove Edwards. But Herford's story ends, not in literary achievement but with a Flanders bomb.

The book contains a worthy collection of contemporary photographs and, on the jacket, a reproduction of Mark Scott's moving memorial window at Eskdale. A fine and fascinating book.

Robin A Hodgkin

Frank Smythe: The Six Alpine/Himalayan Climbing Books
*Bâton Wicks, 2000, pp.944, £18.99 **

I'll have to confess to always having had a slight prejudice against Frank Smythe, which I cannot quite put my finger on. His books have long since been out of print, and the few I read years ago failed to impress; the received wisdom was that they embodied a rather dated romantic mysticism. It was as if the undoubted prejudices against him in certain quarters of the Alpine Club in the fifties had somehow percolated all the way down to me. Or perhaps it was simply that the names of his books are generally so uninspiring: *Climbs and Ski Runs*, for example, must be one of the most humdrum titles ever to grace the front of a mountaineering book, giving no hint of the evocative writing that lies within. So it came as a complete revelation to me to reacquaint myself with Smythe's work in this superb new 944-page six-book omnibus of some of his best writing.

There are two main surprises. First, I had not previously grasped the full range of his climbing achievements. Although he was not an outstanding rock climber, I had forgotten about his contribution to the first ascent of the West Buttress of Cloggy (led by Jack Longland). But it was in the Alps and the Himalaya that he really left his mark. He made several very important first ascents in the Alps, including the Sentinelle Rouge and the

* The Publisher has asked us to note three small but important misprints in the Smythe/Graham Brown controversy. On p.927, line 6: 9 a.m. should read 9 p.m.; on p.929, line 12: 1933 should read 1928; on p.930, line 8: the first "my hopes" should be deleted.

justifiably named Route Major on the Brenva Face of Mont Blanc, and over a dozen first ascents in the Himalaya, including Kamet (the highest peak in the world to be climbed at that time), Nilgiri Parbat and Mana Peak – the final 800 feet of which he climbed solo when his companion was overcome with fatigue.

He also took part in several much bigger expeditions, attempting Kangchenjunga in 1930, and Everest in 1933, 1936 and 1938. On Everest in 1933 he reached 28,100 feet without bottled oxygen – again solo, when his companion (Shipton, this time) flaked out – a feat that was arguably one of the most impressive performances on Everest until Messner's solo ascent nearly fifty years later. He was determinedly opposed to the use of oxygen, as being both 'bad sportsmanship' and 'artificial, unnatural, and therefore dangerous'. He was certainly a bold climber, and on one occasion when he went for a summit the Sherpas decided that 'undoubtedly the Sahibs were mad and especially Ismay Sahib (the nearest the Tibetan can get to my name)'. Another contemporary wrote that although he was physically quite frail, when he was at great altitudes 'a new force seemed to enter him'.

But the biggest revelation is the quality of Smythe's writing. There are some quaintnesses of English, it is true – like 'benignantly' and 'rank bad mountaineering withal' – and not all the writing is of a consistently high standard, but at his best a no-nonsense Englishness is miraculously combined with the intensity of a poet. It is full of vivid vignettes – of people's faces being lit up by a gust of flame from a camp fire, of lightning storms, of boulders falling in the night and just missing his tent, and of towers of ice being illumined suddenly by the setting sun. His first trip to the Alps at the age of eight has all the evocativeness of Ruskin – but done with about one-tenth as many words. He can also be very amusing, as when Wood-Johnson had the 'brilliant idea' of trying to ride a yak – from 'a gentle, doormat-like creature it became possessed of seven devils' and sent him flying through the air, or on the subject of his skill at making 'hashes ... which Mrs. Beeton at her best could hardly hope to emulate. My record hash was compounded of eighteen ingredients; I remember it well because I was sick afterwards.' At times he is quite touching. When he buys a goat for camp food – which he dubs Montmorency, 'but why I cannot for the life of me recollect' – he finds that he has 'not known him above an hour before I regretted his fate; he was very intelligent, very affectionate, very fond of human society, very docile at the end of his lead, and he had the most pathetic expression, as much as to say, "Please don't kill me yet. Let me enjoy a little longer the sun, the air and the luscious grass."' Finally, Smythe is, if you'll forgive the pun, very frank – especially about the merits and weaknesses of his climbing partners and porters, for he disagrees with 'the hide-bound convention that your companion on a mountain shall remain only a name.'

What raises Smythe's writing well above most mountain literature is the sheer breadth and depth of his interests; as well as climbing – and many of the climbing descriptions here are among the most gripping I have ever read – he was interested in the whole mountain landscape, the mountain people and their culture, and he had a near-fanatical passion for botany. And he was multitalented: as well as being a prolific writer (27 books), he was a fine photographer, and a musician capable of listening to a Tibetan melody and writing it down in four-part harmony.

He is also something of a philosopher. And it is here, traditionally, particularly among his colleagues in the Alpine Club, that Smythe has been held to have come unstuck. Lord Schuster said his observations were 'neither as original nor as profound as he seems to think', while Sir Arnold Lunn condemned him for attempting to 'construct a religion out of his mountaineering experiences'. And very recently I have heard another critic describe his ideas as 'wacky'. Looking at his writings again, I think this is very harsh, indeed entirely unsustainable. Smythe's wackiest idea is that he believes in God, an idea that has never gone down well with the scientific reductionists. I think also the fact that he was – as he himself confessed – an 'incurable romantic', interested in flowers and sunsets, made some of his contemporaries regard him as a bit wet. Smythe tells us that Ruttledge called him a 'blooming sybarite, only he did not use the word "blooming"', and he admits that he runs the 'risk of being labelled "sentimental" – a red rag this word to the bull of materialism.'

I think the so-called 'philosophical' aspect of Smythe's work needs to be looked at a little more closely. While he was certainly a religious aesthete he was scarcely the mystic that some have branded him. God is mentioned extremely infrequently, and then only in a very abstract way. Fascinated by one particularly delicate mountain flower, he simply remarks: 'Heaven knows how it grows – and that I think is the correct answer.' There is nothing remotely intellectual or obscure about his beliefs. 'A clever friend once told me,' he says, 'that "the trouble with you is that you feel more than you think." If this is so, thank God for my disability ... I am content to accept with childlike faith and delight the infinite beauties and grandeurs of the universe.' If this is a philosophy at all, it is a very gentle philosophy. True, there are clichés – there is a chapter at the end of *Climbs and Ski Runs* that amounts to little more than a re-write of Whymper's famous reflections at the end of Scrambles – complete with platitudes like 'on [the hills] we approach a little nearer to the ends of the Earth and the beginnings of Heaven' – but there are also some sincerely held beliefs with which many modern climbers would undoubtedly concur.

So what are Smythe's main beliefs? First, that climbing is not about 'conquests' – despite the title of his early book, *Kamet Conquered*. A mountaineer's '"conquests" are within himself and over himself alone'. Second (in a splendid chapter entitled 'On Doing Nothing', in *The Valley of Flowers*), that 'to get a kick out of life, a man must sample the contrasts of life ... to appreciate the joys of activity it is necessary to practise passivity ... if he neglects inactivity, he neglects contemplation and we cannot appreciate Nature otherwise.' Third, against materialism and conflict, he advocates 'simple living in natural surroundings' as the means of freeing ourselves from 'the germs of unhappiness and frustration, which produce the particular fever of war'. (And for him the worst type of conquering attitudes were to be found in the 'foul plague of Nazism'.) Fourth, and very closely connected with this: that it is in the peacefulness of the mountain setting that we realise that 'we are part of a growth infinitely serene; why then should we not partake of serenity?' Thus he detests the noise of guided parties on the Dent du Géant who render 'the still morning ... hideous by triumphant catcalls and other offensive noises'. And, in the 'incredible silence' that he experiences alone on the summit of Mana Peak, he feels that 'to shout would be profane'. And, finally, on such occasions Smythe often becomes aware of what he calls a 'Presence ... some supreme Purpose', and senses that 'in some inexplicable manner' he has been brought 'into closer touch with the creative forces out of which we have been evolved'. That is Smythe's 'philosophy' in a nutshell.

Now, this is all a matter of taste, but I personally enjoy such 'old-fashioned' reflections – it is only the 'politically correct' who would cursorily dismiss such ideas as being past their 'sell-by date'. And his purist attitudes to climbing anticipate the likes of Messner or Fowler.

Perhaps the most successful book in this collection – in which all the main themes and strengths of Smythe's writing seem to come together in a perfectly balanced and beautiful way – is *The Valley of Flowers*. After his second unsuccessful Everest expedition, he returned the following year, 1937, to the Bhyundar Valley, in the Garhwal Himalaya, which he had already dubbed the 'Valley of Flowers' when he first discovered it in 1931. Here his great theme of living a life of contrasts finds its fullest expression. The merit of Garhwal, he says, is that the climber can 'spend the morning on the snows and the afternoon amid the flowers. In such contrast lies the spiritual essence of mountaineering. The fierce tussle with ice-slope and precipice and complete relaxation of taut muscles on a flower-clad pasture; the keen, biting air of the heights and the soft, scented air of the valleys. Everest, Kangchenjunga and Nanga Parbat are "duties", but mountaineering in Garhwal is a pleasure – thank God.' Here, in the peace and quiet of this mountain paradise, previously unvisited by Western man, Smythe not only makes a number of very impressive first ascents, but is also able to spend a lot of time collecting flowers. His enthusiasm is infectious. Of *P. candollii*, for example, he says ' ... you must see this plant on a misty day, when it seems to attract the distant sunlight to itself, so that its thin almost transparent petals glow as though illumined from behind. Even if you have little or no interest in flowers, it demands that you pause and pay tribute to its beauty and to the Divinity that raised it among the barren rocks.' Viewed from the Valley of Flowers, the 'distant combative world' that he reads about in the papers he receives by mail seems 'utterly fantastic ... it was as

39. Ginette Lesley Harrison (1958-1999) (*South-west News Service*) (p101)

SOME NOTABLE FEMALE CLIMBERS FROM THE 20TH CENTURY

40. to 45. *Clockwise from top left*: Alison Hargreaves on the S side of Everest in 1994; Catherine Destivelle in the Exit Cracks, North Face of the Eiger; Wanda Rutkiewicz, the first woman to climb K2, along with seven other 8000ers, before her death on Kangchenjunga in 1992; Jill Lawrence (*left*) the leading 1980s female rock climber, talking to the late Janet Adam Smith at the 1988 Festival of Mountaineering Literature at Bretton Hall; Chantal Mauduit who climbed six 8000ers before her death on Dhaulagiri in 1998; and Beatrice Tomasson, who kicked off the century with a futuristic guided ascent of the South Face of the Marmolada di Penia. The portrait is by the fashionable late 19th century artist John Singer Sargent.
(*Sprayway; Destivelle collection; Rutkiewicz collection; Ed Douglas; Mauduit collection.*) (p99)

46. Nicholson, Cooke, Roaf, Chapman, and Pallis, from the 1936 Zemu Valley expedition. (*R C Nicholson*) (p173)

47. *Right*
    Roaf writing his diary on
    the approach march.
    (*R C Nicholson*) (p173)

48. Sherpas wearing their Grenfell cloth windproofs. (*R C Nicholson*) (p173)

49. First camp on Simvu. (*R C Nicholson*) (p173)

These pictures of Richard Nicholson's are from his photo album of the expedition. They are now held by his great nephew Tim Mitchell, who is conserving the collection.

50. Repairing the bridge across the Zemu Chu during the approach. (*R C Nicholson*) (p173)

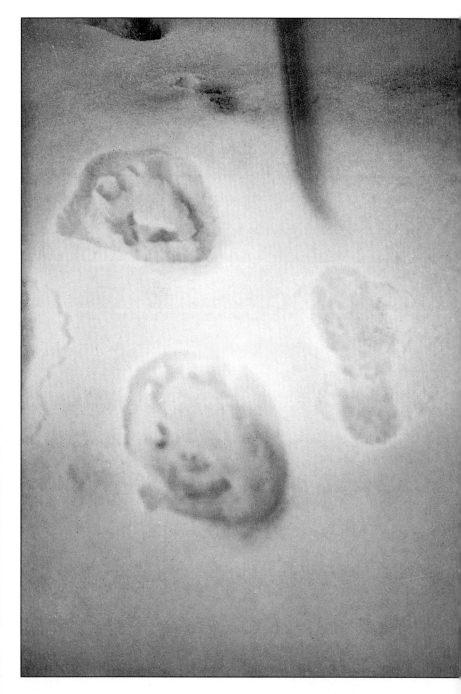

51. The photograph of 'yeti' tracks taken by Eric Shipton on the Rongbuk Glacier in 1935. (*Eric Shipton*) (p153)

2. The famous shot taken on the Menlung Glacier in 1951; Gillman points to the less definite impression of the creature's 'toes' bottom right. (*Eric Shipton*) (p143)

53. A giant Himalayan woolly flying squirrel. (*Mayoor Khan*) (p48)

though I were looking down on an ant-heap that had gone completely crazy.' He is deeply impressed by the Himalayan peoples who say: '"We don't want your civilisation ... for wherever it is established it brings unhappiness and war." It is a terrible indictment and it is true.'

It is fitting, then, that the last book in the collection features Smythe's last mountaineering trip before the Second World War, and that on the very last climb he makes before the outbreak of war – the Innominata Ridge on Mont Blanc with Jim Gavin – they are accompanied by four young Germans. There is a striking camaraderie between them as the two parties keep overtaking each other, with the Germans warning them of falling ice and later offering them 'candied fruit, which we accepted gratefully'. The Germans, 'all ardent Nazis', were 'fit, active young men, and their leader was of that strikingly handsome type that Germany so freely produces. ... it is one of the greatest tragedies the World has seen that a political ideology ... should imbue such men with its vicious principles.' But the ambience of the holiday had been one of 'such peacefulness' that 'the thought of war, which, had we but known it, was only a few days' distant, seemed so absurd, so fantastic, so completely and utterly inappropriate, as to be unbelievable.' Smythe does not labour the point; as they descend, the thunder begins to growl and 'a few days later Europe was at war'.

The book ends with some useful appendices, including an outline of the whole of Smythe's climbing career up to the War, a list of all his writings, a detailed account of his petty but unpleasant feud with the 'touchy' and 'disputatious' Graham Brown ('the only enemy I have ever made'), and several of Smythe's own articles, including a scathing attack on the use of mechanical aids in climbing.

If the book has any real weakness it is that, except for a very meagre and mean-spirited affair by Sir Arnold Lunn, who was clearly jealous of a rival's achievements, there is no brief biography of Smythe. We are not told how he came to die at the early age of 49, though there is a mysterious and minuscule footnote on the very last page intimating that there will be a 'later volume' covering the years up to his death. On the plus side, the book is very well illustrated with both archive and modern photographs, and it is peppered with useful maps and diagrams, which Smythe's original volumes lacked.

All in all, this adds up to a magic, monumental work that is astounding value at £18.99. Diadem and Bâton Wicks have done the mountaineering world a great service over the last 15 years in producing these omnibuses of out-of-print works by such luminaries as Shipton, Tilman and Muir, and this is perhaps the most attractive to date. I urge anyone interested in mountains, mountaineering, indeed the whole mountain landscape and culture, to read this exceptionally rewarding collection.

Gordon Stainforth

Military Mountaineering
A History of Services Mountaineering 1945-2000
Bronco Lane
Hayloft, 2000, pp.296, £25.95 (pb £17.95)

In the bad old days, if a Serviceman went off on an expedition he was regarded by his strait-laced superiors as something of a renegade. Having been on a string of polar and mountaineering expeditions, I was summoned by the Colonel and informed that my activities were giving the unfavourable impression that, somehow, I was being disloyal to the regiment. Another Colonel gave me lousy marks for 'Power of Communication' just after I had written a climbing book which got a Book Society Recommendation, put a half-hour Himalayan film on TV and appeared as the castaway on Desert Island Discs. Not to worry; as they say: 'if you can't take a joke, you shouldn't have joined!'

All is now changed, as Bronco Lane graphically reveals in *Military Mountaineering*, a record of Services mountaineering from 1945 to 2000. This same period, of course, saw a world-wide explosion in mountaineering. The three Services all founded their mountaineering clubs, which then provided the official infrastructure from which to mount ever more ambitious expeditions to the Greater Ranges. What started as a trickle soon became a torrent.

Three years of painstaking research have enabled Bronco to catalogue a staggering 700 or so Service expeditions to every far corner of the earth, varying from a small exploratory probe to some remote and neglected massif to a full-blooded Everest expedition. There are also interesting dissertations on the background and present roles of the Royal Marines Mountain and Arctic Warfare Cadre, the Army Mountain Troops and the RAF Mountain Rescue Teams.

Such a list could have been dull and repetitive. However, Bronco is a lively ex-SAS soldier with a robust sense of humour and a light literary touch. The book therefore reads remarkably well and is far more than a mere record or reference tome. It is amply illustrated but the standard of reproduction is not high. It is a must for all serving or retired Service mountaineers and a useful research tool for anyone planning a climbing expedition to almost anywhere. Finally, although there are plenty of accounts of Service women playing a full part in more recent expeditions, the story is told of Gwen Moffat being debarred by Whitehall officialdom from taking part in the 1959 Army Mountaineering Association Karakoram Expedition.

For older Service climbers, like myself, the book is a beguiling walk down memory lane.

Mike Banks

Legless but Smiling. An Autobiography
Norman Croucher
St Ives Printing and Publishing Co., 2000, pp.vi+368, £26.50

The title is apparently the slogan of Callestock Cider Farm in Cornwall, which is certainly appropriate. The story of how Croucher lost his legs at the age of 19 is well known – the planned bivouac in the Cornish countryside, the drunken night out, the stagger back to find the bivouac site, the tumble down the embankment onto a railway line, and the coming-to with no legs below the knees. A lot of the detail of what happened in the following years afterwards is not so well known, and this book puts that right.

Being a determined sort of character, Croucher soon started to get back into climbing, in a small way to start with, but even then his sights were set on one of the 8000-metre peaks. Work in his early years saw him running the crypt at St Martin-in-the-Fields, sorting out the problems of the homeless. Eventually he found this work depressing and exhausting and decided he needed a practical challenge that would also toughen his legs for more serious climbing, so he walked from John O'Groats to Lands End. Then it was off to the Alps. Guides were found to accompany him, and he soon saw off the Mönch, Jungfrau, Breithorn, Mont Blanc, the Eiger and the Matterhorn. Quite a bag!

From then on, Croucher's sights were set on the rest of the world, and the book details each of his major achievements. Peru came first, climbing Pisco and Huascaran with, amongst others, Julie and Terry Tullis, Dennis Kemp and Henry Moorhouse. In 1982 he climbed Aconcagua and, later the same year, Mustagh Ata with John Cleare's expedition. In the years that followed, Mount Kenya, Kilimanjaro, Illimani, Mt Assiniboine, Elbrus, Alpamayo and Cotopaxi were fitted in around numerous Alpine seasons. More trips to the Himalaya followed, with an ascent of Masherbrum II, attempts on Broad Peak, Everest, Shisha Pangma and, finally, the ascent of Cho Oyu, the coveted 8000-metre peak. The list of ascents at the back of the book runs to 80 peaks – quite a formidable list for any individual, let alone one with two artificial legs.

At nearly 400 pages, there is quite a lot of detail about these expeditions, and all except one are happy, if arduous, experiences. The Everest chapter describes a commercial expedition which left the author feeling bitter and frustrated, and he doesn't pull his punches here.

One cameo I liked came from the Huascaran trip. They were walking up the trail when they passed a group of smart Austrian climbers. Harry Curtis, a person of unkempt appearance, was in the lead. The Austrians looked at him aghast. Then came Julie Tullis. 'We don't climb with women,' commented the Austrians. Finally, around the corner came the third member, with his crutches quietly clicking at every movement. 'That's our leader,' said Harry.

Geoffrey Templeman

The Great Arc
John Keay
HarperCollins, 2000, pp.182, npq

'No scientific man ever had a greater monument to his memory than the Great Meridional Arc of India. It was one of the most stupendous works of science.' This comment, by Sir Clements Markham, President of the Royal Geographical Society, sums up the work of William Lambton and George Everest in the first half of the 19th century. They produced a gridiron system of triangulation, both horizontal for distance and vertical for height, which was the basis for the then quite exceptionally accurate maps of the Indian Subcontinent produced by the Survey of India.

This system of triangulation was started by Lambton in Madras and initially went south to the southern tip of India. It then continued north under Everest, his successor, through central and northern India until it was checked partly by the Himalaya and partly by the Independent Kingdoms that border Central Asia. In addition, it went east and west to Bombay and Calcutta, skirted the Himalaya and entered Kashmir. The obstacles were daunting, the mortality among surveyors was high, but the accuracy of observation and measurement was remarkable.

If genius can be defined as an infinite capacity for taking pains, with inspiration one per cent and perspiration 99 per cent, then both Lambton and Everest were geniuses. Obsessive to the point of monomania and physically exceptionally durable, Lambton was rarely ill, whilst Everest suffered a lot from ill health. For instance, he describes 'four successive attacks of fever in six months'. For treatment 'he was bled to fainting, had upward of a thousand leeches, 30-40 cupping glasses, 3 or 4 blisters besides daily doses of nauseous medicine, all of which produced such a degree of debility as to make it of small moment whether I lived or died.' Indeed, it seems fairly clear that this treatment of Everest did nothing to prolong his life and probably hastened his death.

The third genius of the Great Trigonometric Survey was an Indian named Radhanath Sickdar. He was a human computer, a number cruncher, whose skills and dedication were absolutely vital to the success of the project. Endless revisions and adjustments, of the highest mathematical complexity, had to be made in order to ensure that the Survey was as accurate as possible. It is he who is credited with the 'discovery' of the height of Mount Everest, and the fact that it was nearly a thousand feet higher than any other peak.

Whilst relatively little is known about Lambton, this book, together with a recent monograph by Professor J R Smith, have fleshed out the life of George Everest. John Keay likens him to a film-maker orchestrating a vast production where scientific probity was tantamount to artistic integrity. 'Creative genius was at work, enormous expense had to be justified, a perfectionist reputation upheld and a monumental ego sustained. If the Great Arc was the star of the production, all India was its set.' With an explosive temper and an obsessive personality, Everest's treatment of his assistants left much to be desired, though he did mellow with age.

Although a map was important to the Government of India, the fundamental drive of both Lambton and Everest was 'geodesy' or finding out the exact shape of the earth, and there were often official comments and complaints about the tardiness of map production. These maps were of great importance to the Government of India, for they demonstrated that the British had a better grasp of geographical features and centres of population than the local rulers, and the maps were the precursors of roads, railways and telegraph that connected and knit together the people of this vast, inchoate country of so many different cultures, religions, languages and topographical features.

At some stage the Survey hoped to connect up with the Russians in Central Asia, but this had to wait until the early part of the 20th century. The Survey also spawned the Pundits who clandestinely explored so much of the Himalaya and Central Asia in the 19th century. This book has a unique photograph showing Montgomerie, who initiated the Pundits, Waugh, who decided to name the world's highest peak after George Everest, his immediate predecessor, Walker who took over from Montgomerie, and Thuiller, an assistant superintendent. However, with the ghosts of the obsessive and meticulous Lambton and Everest peering over my shoulder, I must point out a photographic error. This is a black and white reproduction of a colour painting by Hermann Schlagintweit painted from a viewpoint at Phalut. The reproduction is laterally inverted and the mountain, despite Schlagintweit's original caption, is not Everest but Makalu – Peak XIII.

A book about the Survey of India could be dauntingly dull, but this is quite the opposite. It is witty, lucid, erudite, intelligently written and imparts a mass of information in a lighthearted manner. It has filled an enormous gap in my own knowledge of the exploration of Asia, and it contrasts the really enormous difficulty of carrying out accurate measurement and field work in the 19th century with the relative ease with which it is possible to do these things today.

Michael Ward

Killing Dragons. The Conquest of the Alps
Fergus Fleming
Granta Books, 2000, pp398, £20.

This history of mountaineering in the Alps has been given much publicity by the media, and it evidently has the ingredients for a best-seller in the present-day market. The author has a fluent style and has many a lively, if well-worn, tale to tell; the illustrations are well chosen, and there are plenty of apt quotations from the classic writings. All these factors combine to make the book a 'good read'.

And now for a few grumbles. The author tries to cover himself by saying at the outset that 'those who know the Alps like the back of their hands ... will doubtless smite me for a thousand heresies of omission or mis-description'. He also admits that his treatment is selective: he deals only with the Western Alps, and in the main only with the first ascent of major peaks: thus Mont Blanc and the Matterhorn inevitably have pride of place – but he cannot refrain from bending his own rules to include the Eigerwand. He also has much to say about the investigation of glacier flow and the attendant controversies. With these limitations some of the great names such as Owen Glynne Jones, Cecil Slingsby, Geoffrey Winthrop Young are mentioned barely or not at all.

A bit of further smiting cannot be resisted. Much is made in the early chapters of the terror inspired by the Alps in early times (hence the book's title) – this is a half-truth: the Alps served to connect as much as to separate, witness many pass routes used from ancient times. Eccentricities of characters such as W A B Coolidge are well described, but it does seem rather patronising to call Francis Fox Tuckett a madman (p208). There are too many simple errors of fact which could have been avoided with a bit more time and care: thus (p6) Mount Pilatus is not near Geneva, (p14) Geneva was not a member of the Swiss Confederation in Saussure's time, (p215) Horace Walker was not Lucy Walker's father, (p331) John Tyndall was not killed by an overdose of chloroform. On p350, where the ill-fated Eigerwand pair Sedlmayer and Mehringer are discussed, it is pointed out that the *Alpine Journal* misspelled the name of one, but the author misspells the name of the other.

After so much Coolidge-like nitpicking, let me end by quoting what the author says about the *Alpine Journal* in his bibliography:

'... It is still in publication [indeed!] and its many volumes are invaluable to anyone interested in the history of the Alps or mountain/glacier exploration.' We should no doubt forgive our author much for such a handsome acknowledgement.

Ernst Sondheimer

How the English Made the Alps
Jim Ring
John Murray, 2000, pp.287, £19.99

It is fitting that John Murray should publish this history of tourist development in the Alps, for during much of the nineteenth century it was Murray's own *Handbook* that was seen by many Victorians as *the* Alpine traveller's bible. Indeed, such was its success that between 1838 and 1892 the *Handbook* ran to no less than 18 editions and enjoyed sales of almost 50,000 copies. Although no mountaineer, Murray owed his election to the Alpine Club to the fact that his guidebook 'contributed so much to our knowledge of the Alps that he was ... almost the sole authority on the subject.'

The original *Handbook*, which is frequently quoted here, contained much of interest to the early alpinists. It is not clear, however, at whom this present book is aimed. Although an initial glance at *How the English Made the Alps* would suggest that a significant part of the book and most of the illustrations deal with alpinism, this is not the whole story. That is how it should be, for the pioneers of our sport may have been responsible for kick-starting Alpine tourism, but we delude ourselves if we think for one moment that mountaineering is anything but a bit-player in the economy of the Alps today. A study of the figures for winter sports soon puts alpinism into some sort of perspective.

Since he's bent upon telling the story of Alpine tourism in the form of popular history, Jim Ring's title smacks of inaccuracy, for a number of important characters in the story were not English, but Scots, Irish, Welsh. However, the first two paragraphs of his Preface are devoted to a defence of the title, in which Ring claims that since it was customary for the inhabitants of Alpine countries to refer to their early visitors as English, never British, he has decided to do the same.

Leslie Stephen once wrote that: 'Before the turning point of the eighteenth century, a civilized being might, if he pleased, regard the Alps with unmitigated horror.' And yet it took barely a generation to view those same Alps with a less than jaundiced eye. So how did the English 'discover' the Alps and create an industry out of their enjoyment? What was it that turned a general abhorrence of mountains into an obsession that borders upon idolatry?

The key, of course, was the Age of Enlightenment which was not the spontaneous product of one single nation, but the result of an intellectual climate that honoured no frontiers. It just so happened that a level of English society had sufficient leisure, financial security and the inspiration to explore and express new thinking. Their grand tours invariably included Alpine scenes which for the first time gave vent to ecstatic praise, and for many came to represent God's very own handiwork. Thomas Gray, for example: 'Not a precipice, not a torrent, not a cliff, but is pregnant with religion and piety.'

But it took a Genevese scientist, not an English poet, to replace pedestrian worship with adventure among the snowclad heights. With the words: 'What I really saw as never before, was the skeleton of all those great peaks whose connection and real structure I had so often wanted to comprehend', de Saussure gave legitimacy to mountain exploration and the activity (for purely scientific reasons, of course) of mountaineering. The rest, as they say, is history.

That history has been told and retold many times, perhaps never better than in the words of Ronald Clark. But *How the English Made the Alps* is not a history of alpinism, although it scans the subject as it also scans the history of skiing, and includes (as it must) a review of the Alps as a sanatorium. It also tells of the importance of roadbuilding and the coming of the railways that did much to make the mountains accessible to a class of traveller who of necessity had to work for a living.

Today tourism is the world's largest single business; in the mid-1990s some 700 million people were annually travelling abroad. A little over two hundred years ago just a handful of English strode among the Alps to improve their health or to receive almost divine inspiration for their poetry. Mountain-scientists took matters further. Not content with valley scenery they ventured onto mountain peaks, studied glaciers and took rock samples, until bit by bit, like a dancer with seven veils, they stripped away any pretence of scientific study and climbed simply because they enjoyed it.

Then, as the Golden Age of Mountaineering was being celebrated by the winning of summit after summit by (mostly) British climbers, a certain Midlands printer with a fervent Christian zeal was arranging outings to rallies and religious entertainments. These outings were so successful that in 1851 Thomas Cook took 165,000 visitors to the Great Exhibition, and twelve years later led his first tour to the Alps. From 26 June to 15 July 1863, a party of sixty visited Geneva and the Mont Blanc region. 'It really is a miracle,' wrote one of his customers, 'Everything is organized, everything catered for, one does not have to bother oneself with anything at all, neither timings, nor luggage, nor hotels.'

In 1897 *The Excursionist* reported: 'When Queen Victoria came to the throne ... a return trip by diligence to Switzerland via the Rhine had cost £36 and taken sixty-six days. It can now be accomplished in two weeks for £9. Since Thomas Cook's first excursion train it is as if a magician's wand had been passed over the face of the globe.'

The Alps were in the process of being 'Anglicized' before Cook's tourists arrived. That process now gathered pace, and the demands for what became known as the 'cardinal British institutions' of tea, tubs, sanitary appliances, lawn tennis and churches led to a boom in hotel building and the delight of the railway companies.

Cook's tours were to the summer Alps, but it was Henry Lunn, described by his son as 'a queer mixture of merchant adventurer and mystic', who developed winter tourism in the mountains, and effectively marked the end of exclusivity in the Alps that had been so long enjoyed by the worthies of the Alpine Club. Lunn's first trips were to Grindelwald where he organised religious winter conferences, but he had abandoned these by 1897 and turned his skills to running his own travel agency specialising in winter sports. In those days winter sports meant skating, curling, sleighing and tobogganing, but thanks to Henry's son Arnold, who fell in love with skiing at Adelboden in 1903, all that was about to change.

In the early years of the twentieth century the new sport of skiing spread rapidly with the founding of the Ski Club of Great Britain, then in 1908 the Alpine Ski Club, and the following year two books were published that helped introduce growing numbers of Englishmen to the sport – and to the

Alps in winter. In 1909 Lunn managed to persuade the authorities to open the rack-and-pinion railway to Mürren for the winter season, and within two years the village had become so popular that it was described as 'practically British territory'. Mürren was not alone in courting and being courted by the British, for all over Switzerland the winter season gave new life to former summer-only resorts, and there were those who concentrated on visitors from this side of the Channel by advertising in English newspapers.

The Great War was a catalyst for change in so many respects, not least in English (British) influence in the Alps. The old order had been swept away. Politics, society, and the cultural and economic stability that had enabled the English to patronise and develop the Alps to their taste for much of the nineteenth century had all been disrupted and there could be no more certainties. There was a brief resurgence, but while the number of tourists from these shores slowly regained momentum, their proportion never recovered. One need only look at our own Club's influence in the inter-war years to see how activists from the Continent were forging ahead with a different set of rules to those laid down by the founders of the sport. While Colonel Strutt blustered and frothed about the use of pitons on the Grandes Jorasses, his fellow club members were engaged in carrying the flag of Empire on the Tibetan slopes of Everest. In skiing the British continued to slide down the slopes for fun, while our neighbours across the water tended to take it rather more seriously. And their numbers were greater than ours.

How the English Made the Alps takes the story as far as the last war. 'In 1940,' concludes the author, 'even as Churchill came to power, it seemed to Arnold Lunn and other English alpinists of his generation that the story of the English in the Alps had come to an end.'

The idea behind this book is a fascinating one, for it unites the many factors that developed tourism, not only in the Alps, but into a worldwide phenomenon. But I'm afraid it is an uneven story that frustrated me at times – especially where errors crept in that could so easily have been checked. The young Douglas Hadow, for example, who died in the Matterhorn tragedy, is referred to as Roger; Armand Charlet as Arnold; William Mathews' name is misspelt, and the illustration of Leni Riefenstahl and camera crew on a rock peak was clearly not taken on the summit of Mont Blanc as the caption suggests. Minor errors, perhaps, but they undermine the authority of much else that the reader has to take on trust. A pity, because the amount of research required to tell this history must have been considerable. It deserved the eye of an editor familiar with that history – or at least with the characters who played in it. But don't let me put you off. This is a book that is worth reading and it will, if nothing else, remind you of what Zermatt, Grindelwald and Chamonix might have been had not the English 'made the Alps'. Should we hang our heads in shame – or feel proud and rejoice? I leave that to you to decide.

Kev Reynolds

Pyrenean High Route. A Ski Mountaineering Odyssey.
John Harding
Tiercel SB, *2000, pp325, £40*

In the last chapter of this book John Harding states his view that the quintessence of ski mountaineering is the concept of quest. In his case that quest has taken him to regions little visited by British ski-tourers, such as Turkey, Corsica and latterly Greece, but above all to the Pyrenees. This book is an account of nine skiing visits to the High Pyrenees, between 1975 and 1988, during which he achieved, in stages, a complete traverse of the range. After an initial guided tour, he decided this was not for him, so thereafter all his visits were guideless, with in all 18 different companions, including eight members of the Alpine Club.

Compared with ski touring in most parts of the Alps, Pyrenean ski-touring is in a different league. The summits are lower, so there are no large glaciers, but the terrain is steep and complex, and the avalanche risk is almost certainly higher than in the Alps. Maps are poor compared to those of the Alps. The huts are mostly unguarded in winter and spring, with the exception of those in Catalonia, and often the huts used were in a derelict state. So, in addition to the usual ski-touring equipment, the parties had to be fully self-sufficient, and sacks might weigh anything from 40 to 60 lb, if not more. Then there is the weather. In the Alps one can expect reasonable spells of settled weather, but here it seems to be completely unpredictable, and the book reads almost like a never-ending catalogue of forced retreats and desperate descents to the nearest village. However, there were many good days which clearly offered some memorable skiing. Overall, John reckons he had 43% good days, 21% indifferent and 36% really bad. There must be a certain fascination in this battling with the elements, for eight of John's companions travelled with him more than once, indeed five of them three or more times.

The book begins non-chronologically with an account of the 1979 tour, when the party encountered even worse than usual weather. During a retreat from the Baysallance hut they had the misfortune to be caught in a vast avalanche off the Petit Vignemale, in which four out of the five of them were trapped. Thanks to their transceivers all were located and dug out, but sadly John's cousin Alain was found to be dead. Many of us might have settled for something easier in future, but as a dedicated mountaineer John determined to push through with the Traverse, partly as a tribute to his cousin's memory. Other tours also suffered mishaps – a damaged back, a dislocated shoulder and broken arm, and John himself was evacuated with concussion.

John has settled for telling his story as it was, so he does not hesitate to tell us his feelings at the time, his uncertainties and frustrations, and disagreements with his companions, who might be less dedicated to the quest for the Traverse. It is this honesty which makes the book compulsive reading. We learn about his companions: the ever dependable Alan Wedgewood; the charming but irresponsible Jean-Pierre – 'c'est très classique' – always inviting friends and acquaintances to come along, without John's knowledge; Walter Good the Swiss avalanche expert – 'no time for that rubbish in a place like that' (referring to digging of snow profiles) – and devotee of steep slopes and couloirs; Roger Childs, linguist and Spanish landowner, working his magic on the hostesses in Spanish inns; David Williams, supreme skier and fast uphill; Rupert Hoare the irrepressible peak-bagger.

Anything written by John can be relied upon to give us an insight into the culture and history of the region, and so, among other things, we learn something of the little-known pioneers Anne Lister and Parrot, as well as the better known Packe and Russell. And I was disappointed to learn that Belloc's Miranda, of Tarantella, was not after all a captivating young lady, like Carmen, gardienne of the Ventosa hut.

The narrative is illustrated by 41 photographs, half of them in well reproduced black and white. A list of these would have been useful, as would an index. The maps printed are on much too small a scale to give anything more than an indication of the route taken. Anyone wishing to follow the route in detail would have to obtain something much better. Finally, the book does seem to be rather pricey.

Jeremy Whitehead

Travail So Gladly Spent
Tom Price
The Ernest Press, 2000, pp.280, £17.50

The mountaineer has little use for the 'level playing field' beyond commandeering it as a campsite. But it is, figuratively speaking, the presumed arena for the review of books by mountaineers. The reviewer is expected to be informed and informative, judicious rather than prejudiced, interesting yet disinterested, offering opinion without being opinionated.

Not in this case; I eschew both the worn turf of the playing field and the austere chill of the moral high ground. This book has too many resonances for me to be other than partisan. *Déjà vu* obscures my vision. The overlap was mainly in the decade following the Second World War. Tom's six years in the forces reduced a generation gap to a few years. We shared a similar social and academic background and essentially the same foreground – the people, the climbing clubs, the huts and the hills, but especially the attitudes and the equipment.

No 1 Nylon line, for example. This hybrid of string on steroids and (I am told) knicker elastic boasted a breaking strain of half a ton. Light, and its cost irresistibly modest, we saw it as the answer to alpine abseils. In those traditional days the reality was excruciating; it sliced into the shoulder like piano wire. The tangles it could generate were indescribable in a respectable journal. Ignorance of elementary physics hid the awful relationship of mass and velocity. Only good luck shielded us from the terrible consequences of hanging from a thin cord tensioned over a sharpish edge.

We shared (and still share) the Yorkshireman's genetic awareness of the value of money. A pound saved by bivouacking rather than using a hut represented another day in the hills. Unless there was a barn or cowshed or a boulder, the sleeping bag would be damp with dew if the night had been clear. Rain would be repelled to some degree by a plastic sheet and condensation would supplement the invading water. We even engaged in trade. While Tom sold coffee beans to the good people in the post-war Pyrenees, I hawked my nylon rope round Innsbruck at the end of the season.

We both, in similar circumstances, abused our acquaintance with the worthy G Graham Macphee, patron of our university club. Our respective parties found ourselves in the wrong valley in the wrong weather at the wrong time. We sought to evade the just consequences of our folly by bending the wrought-iron rules of the Fell and Rock. Hammering on the hut door after midnight loudly enough to be heard above the storm, we used the doctor's good name as the thin end of our wedge and grovelled our way in.

Tom's long affair with adventure has taken him to a wider world. A surveying expedition to South Georgia, man-hauling sledges like Scott half a century earlier; a canoe journey in the Canadian arctic; a horseback safari in the Lesotho hills; all physically demanding and, in their different ways, forcing him to dig deep into his mental resources.

This inner journey rather than anecdotal ephemera is the aspect of the book which could have lifted it above the ordinary. Doing risky things for fun sometimes exacts the ultimate penalty and imposes burdens on family and friends. The loss of several close friends on Batura Mustagh and his years with the Eskdale Mountain Rescue must have given the author cause for pondering the selfishness of climbers, and his employment in outdoor education, the opportunity for analysis. His suspicion of that industry combined with his involvement in it would have made his assessment of its value well worth reading.

John Temple

Pushing the Limits: The Story of Canadian Mountaineering
Chic Scott
Rocky Mountain Books, 2000, pp.440, £30

This marvellous large-format book is the result of five and a half years' full-time work, some of it spent writing in a tent when the money ran out, by a man who crossed Canada three times, recording 90 interviews and looking at tens of thousands of photographs. At one point he actually had to sell his collection of CAJs and AAJs to survive. The result is a triumph of comprehensive coverage, individual stories and picture-packed design. Both writer and publisher have built a book that will last well. Knowing that a history on this scale is likely to contain some small errors that will immediately be spotted by the first, keenest readers, I asked the author if he had received any corrections yet. 'Not one,' was his reply when he came over here six months after the book was published in Canada. Accuracy, as I had been told by people who knew him, would not be a weakness of this encyclopaedic labour of love.

The book begins with maps – and the only colour photographs in the book, which strongly evoke the variety of climbing in each area: the Rockies, the Coast Mountains and Vancouver Island, the Columbia Mountains, the East, the North and the Arctic Islands. These areas provide the structure for the coverage of each historical period chosen by the author. The story really begins in 1887 when the first peak over 10,000 feet was climbed by the Canadian surveyor J J McArthur, who made a technical ascent of Mount Stephen. Then came Norman Collie, George Baker and, in 1899, the first Swiss guides, brought over by the Canadian Pacific Railway. Scott ends his chapter of 'Glory Days' of first ascents in the Rockies and Selkirks with the ascent of Mount Alberta in 1925 by a Japanese party led by Swiss guides.

The section covering 1926-1950 is titled 'Canada drifts from the mainstream of world mountaineering', but it contains such stories as that of the Mundays, Don and Phyllis, who carried 60lb loads for 13 days of bushwacking in search of Mount Waddington, felling trees to cross glacial torrents (photo page 108). They were ultimately unsuccessful after a decade of such trips, reaching a slightly lower summit on two occasions. Such was Canadian mountaineering in an era given a negative title by an author building up to a section called 'Canadians make their mark overseas, 1955-1990' which coincides with the period 1951-1990 at home that is titled 'Canadian mountaineering comes of age'.

British climbers such as Brian Greenwood, who are largely unknown in the UK, have made a huge contribution to climbing in their adopted country, as is fully acknowledged by the author. But the issue of Canadian distinctiveness is revealed by such chapter titles as 'John Lauchlan - the first Canadian climbing star' and 'Canadians climb Mount Waddington at last'. Indeed, the final section, 'Into the future 1990-2000', indicates the variety of Canadian climbing: waterfalls, big walls, alpine, sport and competition climbing. Scott also lists 'gym climbing' which implies never going out into daylight as a Canadian climber. (Even Sheffield 7 climbers, who stay in their cellars during hot days, venture out as far as Burbage to go bouldering in winter!) How will these climbers understand the contents of this book? Or the photo on page 390 of a naked climber casting something called a 'shadow' on rock?

If the purpose of a history is to inform, contextualise and raise issues for the future, what questions does this book raise? Continuing in his reporting mode, the historian offers what he must think is a neutral title: 'Crag climbing evolves into sport climbing'. He reports that the debate in the Rockies in the '90s was about chipping rather than retrobolting. 'In the 1990s the search began for long, multi-pitch sport routes,' Scott writes. At Back of the Lake (Louise), he reports, 'traditional routes with minimal protection were retrobolted, making the crag one of the great sport climbing areas in North America'. So what happens when these activities get both more specialised and more overlapping? The prospect of the 'evolution' of bolted alpinism and top-down 'built' big-wall routes makes the story of the Mundays at the front end of this book look rather quaint.

On the issue of access Scott has more to offer in a statement that is somewhat ahead of much European and UK thinking: 'During the next decade climbers must band together and deal with access issues before the land managers and their lawyers do it for us. This is already happening in British Columbia ... ' Surely the terrific traditions of such a diversity of forms of climbing, on the wonderful richness of terrain in Canada celebrated by this book, deserve more imaginative forms of evolution than those dependent upon the drill and the helicopter.

There's more history waiting to be made, Scott suggests, in first winter ascents in the St Elias Range, on the SE face of Mount Logan and on remote big walls. His work lays down a challenge from the spirit and achievements of the past. This book is the finest tribute imaginable to human imagination and endeavour in a country that must present one of the greatest challenges to the historian of mountaineering.

Terry Gifford

The Lost Explorer. Finding Mallory on Mount Everest
Conrad Anker & David Roberts
Simon & Schuster, 1999, pp.192, $22.00

In last year's *Alpine Journal* Luke Hughes reviewed in detail three of the books on the finding of Mallory's body. Too late for a review to be included in that issue was the book by the American climber who actually found the body – Conrad Anker. *The Lost Explorer* is a dual effort with David Roberts, presented in alternating sections. Roberts gives a potted biography of Mallory, together with accounts of all three Everest expeditions in the twenties, plus some of his own thoughts on the ethical arguments that raged after the event in 1924.

Anker's writing does not have the literary quality to match that of Roberts, but makes up for this by his personal involvement and by the immediacy of his writing. Much has been made of the naïvety of the team in being surprised at the uproar created by the way they handled the subsequent publicity and, whilst Anker does his best to explain their actions, an unpleasant aftertaste still remains.

Anker describes his own first unaided ascent of the Second Step, from which he continued to the summit. In the book's final section, Anker gives the reasons why he has reluctantly come to the conclusion that Mallory and Irvine could not have reached the summit.

The book is well worth reading in order to share Anker's thoughts on what may have really happened during Mallory and Irvine's climb, together with his explanation of the events following his own expedition. The mystery is still there, however.

Geoffrey Templeman

Voices from the Summit:
The World's Great Mountaineers on the Future of Climbing
Ed. Bernadette McDonald and John Amatt
National Geographic Adventure Press, 2000, $30

Voices from the Summit celebrates 25 years of the Banff Mountain Festival by bringing together 31 climbers and mountaineers to consider the future of their sport. The contributors are diverse and the selection criteria intriguing, with the common ground a passion for mountains. Many of those included are legends who have become mentors for climbers wishing to follow in respected footsteps. There are glimpses of living history in Anderl Heckmair, Sir Edmund Hillary and Riccardo Cassin, evidence of received wisdom from those who have followed – Catherine Destivelle, Royal Robbins, Thomas Hornbein – and always the 'new breed' whose worlds – consciously or subconsciously – echo the sentiments expressed by earlier practitioners; the philosophical parallels in the essays by Doug Scott and Leo Houlding, for example, bear welcome witness to this.

Thus, a sense of tradition is created, built on shared values and common experiences: an unequivocal desire by climbers to protect their playgrounds – foolish, indeed, to bite the recreational hand which feeds so well – and an insistence on the need for challenge, adventure and routes in harmony with their surroundings, climbed solo, capsule or alpine style and leaving no trace.

The paradox of climbing is often articulated – it is only by going to dangerous and unforgiving environments that we find the rich spirituality lost within the artificial confines of society's materialistic rewards structure. As climbers look back to the beginning of the last century, it seems clear that society has always been the reason for escape for those who love to test themselves – nothing new there. In Doug Scott's words: ' ... the climber creates for himself heightened sensibilities and an awareness verging on the extraordinary, summoning up areas of his being that are normally hidden. These are times when a little light is let into our lives ... '

Another frequently discussed topic is debated within these pages – 'Making a buck out of climbing' by Greg Child. Here again, the whole spectrum of belief is explored, from Dr Charles Houston's firmly-stated view that professionalism is 'unseemly for mountaineering' to Greg Child's articulate and outspoken tenet that money can be ethically made out of climbing so long as the climber is not motivated solely by financial gain.

The American alpinist Kitty Calhoun points out that those who climb as hard and as simply as possible will never attract sponsors, since their climbs are so remote and personal that they will never generate high-profile publicity. This ideal – to embrace Krzysztof Wielicki's 'extremely hazardous lifestyle', to be driven by what is around the next corner, to climb for the joy of being in the mountains – sings out of many of these essays – reassuringly, in the bleak picture of a littered and debased Sagarmatha National Park painted by Junko Tabai.

And there are more delights: Audrey Salkeld's scholarly piece on Mallory and Irvine, exploring the current obsession with their place in history and our own continuing need to define and categorise – even at the price of conjecture. David Breashears revels in the role of mountaineering camera-man, seeking to create images which record and inspire, just as Sir Edmund Hillary's photograph of Tenzing Norgay on the summit of Everest led Breashears into a life of climbing.

The book ends with 25 pages devoted to the history of the Mountaineering Festival – anecdotal, informative and succinct. The whole volume is enhanced by the black and white photographs of each of the contributors: occasionally the props they have selected proving an amusing and no doubt intentional distraction.

For those outside the world of climbing, *Voices from the Summit* provides a richly detailed source of information and inspiration. Those who are already members of the climbing community will acknowledge their own motivations – and continue to debate and dissent in their quest for a better alternative to what society has to offer – in short, to quote Ed Douglas quoting John Ruskin: 'to believe that the only wealth is life'.

Val Randall

Feeling through the Eye
The New Landscape in Britain 1800-1830
Spink-Leger, London, 2000, £20

Feeling through the Eye is the catalogue of an exhibition of works for sale held at Spink-Leger in March/April 2000. All were landscapes or town-scapes dating from a highly significant moment in British art, the early decades of the nineteenth century. Several of the pictures were mountain landscapes. The catalogue illustrates all the works in colour. The introduction, by Timothy Wilcox, has much interesting and relevant information; but it is nevertheless not wholly satisfactory, as it fails to show the unity and development of the material.

Virtually all the great names of the landscapists of the period are represented and a variety of locations. The most distant mountain scene (with one exception) is an attractive watercolour of Ben Lomond by John Samuel Hayward. There are several works from the Lake District, including William Daniell's delightful *The Estuary of the River Leven*, near Ulverston, which shows Cartmell Fell. There are even more from North Wales, among them a number by John Linnell, very influential in the movement, and a fine series by Joshua Cristall – Snowdon from Plas Gwynant, a mountainous view near Snowdon, Beddgelert Church (with Lliwedd beyond) and Nant Guinion (Nant Gwynant?), all executed with much skill and care and showing an obvious attraction to the mountain landscape. A most forceful work comes from the hand of Thomas Girtin, at the height of his powers in 1799, *Mynydd Mawr*; the light on the mountain is sombre, apart from a flash of sunlight on a bridge and a little plain near the foreground. The picture strongly expresses the mood induced in the artist by the mountain scene.

But the 'jewel in the crown' of the exhibition is J M W Turner's *Mont Blanc from Fort Roche in the Val d'Aosta* which has all Turner's mastery of rock and trees and water, and a bottomless gorge to convey a feeling of height. As he commonly did, Turner includes some figures to humanise the scene. The glory of the picture is Mont Blanc. There are few works from his 1802 tour of the Alps where the mountains are unclouded, and this is certainly the most splendid. There are yet surprises, wonderful surprises, in mountain art.

James Bogle

The Enchanted Mountains. A Quest in the Pyrenees.
Robin Fedden
The Ernest Press, 2000, pp.142, £15.95

I remember when this book first came out in 1962 picking it up in a bookshop with interest, not only because it was a book about mountains, but also because it had a colour frontispiece by the artist John Piper, another passion of mine. The frontispiece is still there in this new edition, but minus the colour, which robs it of its beauty. Otherwise the book is the same, with the addition of some new photos. Robin Fedden's writing captivated me and has made me return to the book many times since. Slightly old-fashioned in some ways, it is a far cry from the modern expedition volume.

Fedden and his companions, including his wife and Basil Goodfellow – although they are never named – spent three summers walking and climbing in the Pyrenees, and the author has moulded these into one narrative. He says himself that 'this book is not primarily about mountaineering', but he gives a wonderful picture of wanderings in remote mountain country, and of encounters with local people and the history of the area. There is little detail in the book, and you certainly couldn't use it as a guide, but it is to be savoured slowly in quiet moments.

Climbing High. A Woman's Account of Surviving the Everest Tragedy
Lene Gammelgaard
Pan, 2000, pp.xvi+212, £6.99

Lene Gammelgaard climbed Everest in 1996 at the time of the tragic events in May of that year. She reached the summit as a member of the Sagarmatha Environmental Expedition, being the first Scandinavian woman to reach the summit. The expedition was led by Scott Fisher, who did not survive.

Climbing High was published in Denmark in 1997, but had to wait a further three years to find a publisher in English. The bulk of the book is concerned with the minutiae of expedition life and the author's ambitions, but only really comes alive after the summit, when describing the descent through the storm to the South Col and benightment in a snow hole. The writing, however, is sometimes a little hard to take: 'Mother Goddess of the World, Chomolungma, Sagarmatha, truly you are the grandest mountain, and I tread upon you with the profoundest respect and awe. Your summit is all I desire.' We'll put it down to the translation.

Facing Up. A Remarkable Journey to the Summit of Mount Everest
Bear Grylls
Macmillan, 2000, pp.xiv+290, £14.99

This is the book of one man's ascent of Everest – 'the youngest British climber to reach the summit and return alive', as the blurb puts it, although this record has been disputed since the book's publication. Everest had always been in the young Grylls' mind, but a parachuting accident while in the army seemed to put paid to that ambition. His recovery was good, however, and not long afterwards he reached the summit of Ama Dablam, making Everest a possibility again. He organised a small expedition, linked up with Henry Todd's larger one and, after surviving a crevasse fall, reached the summit after seventy days on the mountain.

On Top of the World. Climbing the World's 14 Highest Mountains
Richard Sale & John Cleare
Collins Willow, 2000, pp.228, £19.99

To mark the fiftieth anniversary of the ascent of Annapurna, the first 8000-metre peak to be climbed, the publishers have brought out this large-format book telling the stories behind each first ascent, commencing with Annapurna and culminating in Shisha Pangma. Having John Cleare as one of the authors, it goes without saying that there are copious excellent illustrations. Each section gives a summary of the exploration of the peak, plus details of the first ascent and interesting subsequent ascents, completed by diagrams of the various routes. An appendix gives names of ascensionists on all 14 peaks, and the book forms a very useful summary of the history of the eight-thousanders.

Everest. The Mountaineering History.
Walt Unsworth
The Mountaineers/Bâton Wicks, 2000, pp.xviii+790, £25.00

This is the third edition of Unsworth's monumental work. So much has happened on Everest since the second edition in 1989, including new routes on the NE ridge and North Face, the tragic events of 1996 and, more recently still, the discovery of Mallory's body, that interest in the mountain is at an all-time high. A new edition was almost inevitable. For almost anything you want to know about Everest, this book is indispensable.

Storms and Sunsets in the Himalaya
A compilation of Vignettes from the Experiences of a Mountaineer
Parash Moni Das
Lotus Publishers (Jalandhar City), 2000, pp.(4)+184, Rs.250,00

The author, a member of the Indian Police Service, the Indian Mountain-eering Foundation and the Himalayan Club, has walked and climbed in the Himalaya for many years. As Deputy Inspector General of Police in 1995 he led a team which reached the summit of Mana Peak in Garhwal via the difficult North Ridge, and in the next year he was Senior Deputy Leader of the ITBP Mount Everest Expedition which achieved the first Indian ascent from the north. The sub-title of the book describes exactly what it is – a compilation of vignettes based on all these experiences – but it is unusual in including a short story and a short play.

Hell of a Journey
On Foot Through the Scottish Highlands in Winter
Mike Cawthorne
Mercat Press, 2000, pp.xii+164, npq

Mike Cawthorne had already traversed all the Munros in 1986 when, after ten years of wanderings and climbs in many parts of the world, he decided that there was still great adventure to be had closer to home by climbing all 135 of the 1000m peaks in Scotland in one continuous push, in winter. This he did in 1997-98, solo with the exception of a few days with friends, starting at Sandwood Bay and zigzagging across the country to end at Glencoe. As might be expected, he encountered blizzards, swollen rivers, wind chill and all the adverse conditions you can think of, as well as those brilliant days which are only experienced in mid-winter. The book is well written, particularly the short passages of conversation, and well illustrated.

Rock Climbing in England and Wales
David Simmonite. Ed. Neil Champion
New Holland, 2000, pp.160, £24.99

Extreme Rock & Ice. 25 of the World's Great Climbs
Garth Hattingh
New Holland, 2000, pp.160, £29.99

New Holland seem set on cornering the market in large-format, glossy climbing picture-books. These are their two latest and they are both beautifully produced. Simmonite has covered the rock-climbing scene in England and Wales from far north to far south-west, from Bowden Doors to Sennen Cove, in a series of stunning action shots, mostly taken by himself, in 25 chapters/areas. I find the pictures excellent, as the majority feature the climb rather than the climber, which is the opposite of what seems to be the current fashion. Most, of course, are of climbs in the upper grades.

Hattingh's third book for New Holland keeps up the high standard of photographic reproduction seen in all their books, but it is best treated purely as a book of photos, as there are countless errors in the text and captions, showing a lack of knowledge of mountaineering and its participants. The selection of the 25 is also odd; whilst no one would argue with the Golden Pillar of Spantik or the south face of Lhotse being world class climbs, *Total Eclipse of the Sun* at Ogmore doesn't seem in quite the same class.

Across the Frozen Himalaya
The Epic Winter Ski Traverse from Karakoram to Lipu Lekh
Harish Kohli
Indus (New Delhi), 2000, pp.296, Rs.595 (£17.99)

It was in 1981-82 that Harish Kohli carried out his great traverse across the Himalaya, 8000km from the Karakoram to Bhutan, in a total of 475 days. As if this wasn't enough, he then decided to do a winter ski traverse of a section of the Himalaya, starting at the Karakoram Pass, and ending after 2000km at the Lipu Lekh Pass on the India/Tibet/Nepal border. The eight-member team kept as high as they could throughout the journey and were joined at various times by British, American and Australian supporters. They crossed a total of 20 passes, some previously unknown, and had their share of hazards and mishaps, getting lost on several occasions and suffering intensely from the adverse conditions.

Mount Everest Massif
Jan Kielkowski
Explo, 2000, pp.314, £18

I suppose it would have been almost unthinkable 50 years ago that anyone would produce a guidebook to Everest, detailing the many routes that find their way up the mountain, and also Lhotse, Nuptse and the other peaks that form the massif, but here it is, in a much enlarged and revised edition of Kielkowski's 1993 opus. It joins his volumes on Cho Oyu, K2 and Kangchenjunga as part of his plan to issue monographs on the highest mountain ranges on Earth. As the author says, he has 'tried to include all available information concerning the described region', and it is all here – geography, geology, expeditions, ascensionists, bibliography, place names, maps and so on. A marvel of research.

Shisha Pangma. The alpine-style first ascent of the South-West Face.
Doug Scott & Alex MacIntyre
Bâton Wicks / The Mountaineers, 2000, pp.322, £12.99

Bâton Wicks have reissued this book, originally published in 1984 as *The Shishapangma Expedition*, in a new standardised format and, in their usual way, with useful appendices bringing the climbs on the mountain up-to-date (1999), and with an extended bibliography and new additional photos. This was always one of the better expedition books and it is good to have it in print again.

The Alpine Club Library also received the following books during 2000:

Trekking and Climbing in Nepal Steve Razzetti, with Victor Saunders
New Holland, 2000, pp.176, £13.99

Lonely Hills and Wilderness Trails Richard Gilbert
David & Charles, 2000, pp.320, £16.99

The Stanford Alpine Club John Rawlings
CSLI Publications, Stanford University Libraries, 1999, pp.(10)+194, $39.95

The Deprat Affair. Ambition, Revenge and Deceit in French Indo-China Roger Osborne. *Pimlico, 2000, pp.244, £10.00*

Il Terreno di Gioco dell'Europa. Scalate di un Alpinista Vittoriano
Leslie Stephen. *Vivalda Editori, 1999, pp.288, L.35,000*. Italian edition of *The Playground of Europe* with new introduction and illustrations.

The ULGMC at 50. A Celebration of the University of London Graduate Mountaineering Club 1950–2000 Ed. Jill Bennett, *2000, pp.36*

Montagna Grigia. Catalogo della letteratura grigia e minore. Biblioteca Nazionale del Club Alpino Italiano, etc *2000, pp.350.*
Catalogue of all the 'lesser works' in the library of the CAI.

The Independent Hostel Guide, Britain and Europe Ed. Sam Dalley
The Backpackers Press, 2000, pp.336, £4.95

La Conquista de Los Tres Polos. Una Hazaña de al Filo de lo Imposible
Sebastián Álvaro & Javier Ortega
Temas de hoy, 2000, pp.262, npq

Barrow's Boys Fergus Fleming
Granta, 1999, pp.xx+490, £8.99

Das Edelweiss. XVII. Special Issue of the 80th Anniversary
Kwansei Gakuin University Alpine Club, 2000, pp.396, npq

Tremadog Dave Ferguson, Iwan Arfon Jones & Pat Littlejohn
CC, 2000, pp.286, £13.50

Winter Climbs in the Cairngorms Allen Fyffe
Cicerone, 2000, pp.186, £15.00

North Devon and Cornwall David Hope & Brian Wilkinson
CC, 2000, pp.368, £14.50

West Cornwall. Bosigran, Chair Ladder and The Lizard. Vols. 1 & 2
Ed. Nigel Coe. *CC, 2000, pp.344 & 328, £17.50*

Peak Limestone. Wye Valley Ed. Geoff Milburn
BMC, 1999, pp.192+illus. & 288 (two parts), £15.95

Queueing for Everest Judith Adams
Oberon Books (Oberon Modern Plays), 2000, pp.104, £6.99

Travel Medicine and Migrant Health Ed. Cameron Lockie et al.
Churchill Livingstone, 2000, pp.xvi+500, £39.95

Tourism and Development in Mountain Regions
Ed. Godde, Price & Zimmermann. *CABI Publishing, 2000, pp.viii+358*

Rother Walking Guides:
  Mallorca Rolf Goetz. *2000, pp.160, £7.99*
  Around Mont Blanc Hartmut Eberlein. *2000, pp.122, £7.99*
  Provence Thomas Rettstatt. *2000, pp.134, £7.99*
  Iceland Gebriele & Christian Handl. *2000, pp.134, £7.99*

Lonely Planet Guides:
  South Africa, Lesotho & Swaziland J. Murray & J. Williams.
    2000, pp.676, £13.99
  Mozambique Mary Fitzpatrick. *2000, pp.200, £11.99*
  Hiking in the USA *2000, pp.512, £14.99*
  Walking in France 2000, pp.400, £12.99

Extreme Expeditions. The Big Freeze C J Charley
Puffin Books, 2000, pp.vi+154, £3.99

Odle – Pùez. Dolomiti fra Gardena e Badia Lorenzo & Pietro Meciani
CAI/TCI, 2000, pp.400, L70,000

The Lycian Way. Turkey's First Long Distance Walk Kate Clow
Upcountry (Turkey), 2000, pp.128, £12.99

The Long Walk. The True Story of a Trek to Freedom Slavomir Rawicz
Robinson, 2000, pp.242, £6.99

Die Kleinen Dolomiten und Gino Soldà (1907-1989) Adriano Tomba
Città di Valdagno, 2000, pp.30

A Journey North. One Woman's Story of Hiking the Appalachian Trail
Adrienne Hall. *Appalachian Mountain Club Books, 2000, pp.xx+202, $22.95*

Life at the Extremes. The Science of Survival Francis Ashcroft
Harper Collins, 2000, pp.xxii+312, $22.95

Kidstuff. Poems to share with children Dave Wynne-Jones
CK Publishing, 2000, pp.58, £2.99

Kingdoms Beyond the Clouds. Journeys in Search of Himalayan Kings
Jonathan Gregson. *Macmillan, 2000, pp.xxvi+510, £14.99*

In Memoriam

COMPILED BY GEOFFREY TEMPLEMAN

The Alpine Club Obituary	Year of Election	
Andrzej Zawada	1987	Hon.
James Merricks Lewis Gavin	1936	
Malcolm John Cameron	1987	
Heather Larsen	1964	LAC
Paul Henry William Wallace	1963	
Michael Joseph Ball	1991	
Robin Cyril Hind	1961	
Montgomery Harrison Wadsworth Ritchie	1934	
Sir Eric Mensforth	1957	
John Michael Leigh	1991	
John Byam-Grounds	1938	
Michael Blayney Thomas	1960	
Harold Stanley Flook	1960	

First, I must apologise for a mistake which appeared last year in the obituary for Fred Jackson by J H Emlyn Jones. Mention was made of Jackson's friend 'Dr Aubrey Wentham'; this should have read 'Dr Aubrey Leatham'. This was my error and I apologise to both Emlyn Jones and Dr Leatham.

I have also been informed that Wing Commander N Ridley submitted an obituary for Fred Jackson which, by an oversight, never reached either the Editor or myself. In apologising to Wing Commander Ridley, I should mention that his tribute to Fred Jackson appears on page 335 of this volume.

Unfortunately, it has only been possible to obtain obituaries for just over half of those whose names appear in the In Memoriam list this year. As always, I would be happy to include any others next year.

Geoffrey Templeman

Andrzej Zawada, 1928 -2000

Andrzej Zawada was once described in *Mountain* magazine as 'the preeminent war lord of Polish mountaineering.' In today's post-communist Europe, the aptness of this rather curious description is none too obvious. In Poland in the 1970s and '80s, however, organising major expeditions required both huge personal effort and status. It was not just a matter of gaining permits and finding the right people (and Zawada helped launch many climbers, such as Kurtyka and Wielicki). The real fight was to gather enough food, equipment, cash and respect from the State to be able to leave the country with a real chance of success – essential if there was to be a 'next time'. To achieve this required both persuasiveness and perseverance. Zawada had both, making him to some degree a 'Lord' in the country he so loved.

But it was not all plain sailing. Andrzej Zawada had to play a dangerous game, balancing his 'official' image with his deeply held personal views, and a vision of an independent and free Poland. The knocks on the door in the early hours were a constant fear, as they were for most free-thinking Polish climbers of this period.

He once said, 'Poland is a nation without any fixed boundaries. We have been invaded from all directions, and what is happening now under the communists is only a time within another cycle. Poland will be free again.' Fortunately, he lived to see the start of a new period in Polish history.

Andrzej was a gentle man, charming and well known both as a mountaineer and a respected geophysicist. His climbing successes stand in the top rank of importance in mountaineering history. He was a winter specialist. He introduced this most cruel of seasons to the Himalaya. Perhaps his fascination with winter climbing reflected his own internal season under the communist regime. Starting in the winter of 1959, he completed a remarkable 19-day traverse of the entire 50-mile-long main ridge of the Tatra. Andrzej went on to lead first winter ascents of Noshaq (72/3), Everest (79/80), Cho Oyu (84/85), and Lhotse (88/89 – deputy leader). Inevitably, there were also failures: K2 (87/88), Nanga Parbat (twice, in 96/97 and 97/98) and Lhotse 79/80 when he personally came close to making the first winter ascent, reaching 8250m.

But not all his trips were in winter. He made the second ascent of the *Bonatti/Gobbi* on the Pilier d'Angle in 1965. He climbed Pik Lenin in 1970 (his first 7000er) and in the following year made the first ascent of Kunyang Chhish (7852m) in the Hispar. In 1997 he organised the first Anglo-Polish expedition. This remarkable trip to the Hindu Kush made five alpine-style big wall ascents, and displayed Zawada's remarkable creativity and persuasive talents. Starting without enough cash to fly to Kabul, Zawada decided to 'smuggle' the six-man British contingent across the Soviet Union by train – telling them to say nothing when spoken to by the Russians. Arriving at the military staging point on the Oxus just months before the invasion of

Afghanistan, he confronted the Russians with two choices – let the expedition cross or send it back and create an international incident. The Russians let the team pass.

His career was recognised by honorary membership of the Alpine Club in 1987 and by the Groupe de Haute Montagne in 1998. He wrote and lectured extensively about his exploits and contributed to a number of historical works, including Gillman's *Everest* (1993) and an authoritative six-volume history of Polish Mountaineering. Among his other passions were sailing, skiing, history, a large collection of maps and archives of world exploration and, most importantly, his wife Anna Milewska, a well-known film and theatre actress, who survives him.

Andrzej Zawada died of cancer on 21 August 2000, aged 72. He had fought the disease for some time, just as he struggled with or against so many other things that either inspired him or appalled him. On that train journey across the Soviet Union in 1977, he entered a compartment where Alex MacIntyre(ivich) lay sprawled with his Walkman and politely asked to 'see this new ice tool, this pterodactyl you told me about'. MacIntyre duly dug out the weapon from one of his sacks and passed it to Zawada. To everyone's amazement, Andrzej then stormed down the carriage and smashed each of the six speakers playing Soviet muzak of patriotic military tunes. 'Ah, I see this pterodactyl works perfectly. In Poland, we do not allow such tedious music.'

John Porter

Major-General J M L Gavin CB CBE, 1911-2000

Jim Gavin was born in Chile, but he was British to the core. He was educated in England, at Uppingham School, followed by a two-year course in engineering at Cambridge. Although our time at Cambridge overlapped and we were both members of the Cambridge University Mountaineering Club with whom he skied but did not climb, I did not meet him at Cambridge but in 1935 at Helyg in the Ogwen Valley, North Wales. From then until late 1941, when he went to Singapore, I climbed with him a lot in North Wales, Scotland and the Alps.

In 1935 his meeting and climbing with Frank Smythe led to him participating in the 1936 Everest expedition which, owing to the early onset of the monsoon, did not get above the North Col, and the party had a difficult descent from there in dangerous snow conditions.

In 1937 we met in Chamonix, and after climbing the Requin, made a memorable attempt at traversing the Drus. I was ahead with Edmund Wigram (doctor on two pre-war Everest expeditions) and Charles Rob, another doctor, when a shout from below brought us hurrying down to where we found that Jim's second on the rope, Charles Nicholls, another sapper officer, had dislocated his shoulder in swinging across a holdless slab on a short fixed rope (La Pendule). Edmund, as the senior doctor, rotated his shoulder back into place and improvised a sling to support his arm. This ended any hope of the traverse, but as the weather was hot and set fair, Edmund, Charles Rob and I completed the climb to the top of the Grand Dru, leaving Nicholls on a broad sunny ledge. Then we returned to help Nicholls down and reached Montenvers well before dark. This ended Nicholls' climbing career, as his shoulder kept on coming out.

Gavin, Rob and I then set out on a high-level route to Zermatt, traversing mountains rather than passes. When we reached the Col des Maisons Blanches at the foot of the Valsorey ridge of the Grand Combin there was a cold north wind blowing. We did not fancy climbing the exposed ridge, and the alternative, a long and difficult descent to the Corridor route, was equally unattractive. Having consulted our postcard, therefore, (our only guide) we set out hopefully on a level traverse, Gavin and I sharing the lead. This was at first threatened by séracs, and as we had no crampons and had to cut steps, the going was slow. But soon the going improved and we reached a point directly below the summit where our ledge ended. We were then able to climb up to the summit. This was a new route on this mountain, as I discovered from an article in *Die Alpen* in 1943, in which some Swiss climbers claimed it as a new route in 1943. (We had not made our ascent public.) By then, in mid-war, we were scattered far and wide and it was too difficult to put the record straight.

Jim had climbed with Frank Smythe in 1935, which led to his selection for the 1936 Everest expedition, and after our 1937 dramas he continued to climb with Frank Smythe until the outbreak of war. In early 1940 Jim had an unnerving experience when a submarine in which he was travelling to Norway hit an underwater obstruction – perhaps a mine which did not detonate; but they were able to limp back to England.

At the School of Mountain Warfare in Lochailort, where we were both instructors, Jim and I with others made climbing expeditions to the Cuillin of Skye and to the Cairngorms, where we stayed in Freddy (known as Spencer) Chapman's private hut in the Abernethy Forest. Jim was exceptionally fit and strong, but he was exhausted by Freddy on a traverse of the four highest peaks in the Cairngorms.

At the end of 1941 Jim went to Singapore to demolish guns and other installations as the Japanese approached. At that point he met crisis and romance. He had fallen in love with Barbara Murray, a journalist in Singapore, and when the Supremo there decreed that only selected personnel and their wives could be evacuated by air to Sumatra, he married Barbara and they flew to Sumatra where Jim found a derelict tug boat, and profiting from his engineering skill and pre-war ocean yacht racing, put it in order and sailed to Ceylon. From there they reached the mainland of India, where Jim had to deal with a mutiny on a northbound train. He had a heart attack, but reached Kashmir to recuperate, but it was six months before he was fit enough to re-cross the pass and return to England. Soon after his return, I visited him in Surrey where he was living, but he was a shadow of his former self.

The last time I saw Jim was in 1993 at the Royal Geographical Society where the 40th anniversary of the first ascent of Everest was celebrated. After Barbara died he went to live in Dorset with one of his daughters. In 1997 I rang him and suggested visiting him there. He said he was very frail but would like a visit and his daughter would send me directions; but she never did, and the next thing was that I saw his obituary in *The Times* and *Telegraph*.

Jim Gavin was a sparkling character, with enormous charisma and humour. He was a good climber, and though not an 'ace' like his contemporaries Smythe, Colin Kirkus and Menlove Edwards, he was a desirable participant on any expedition.

Ashley Greenwood

Mal Cameron, 1946-2000

I met Mal over 27 years ago in Cwm Cywarch at the Mountain Club Hut in Mid Wales. He was keen to climb in some of the remoter areas away from the crowds. We did quite a few of the second ascents of some of the classics, his knowledge and experience from other areas being invaluable for correcting grades and star ratings. We also did a few new routes together, such as, in 1974, *Nudging Groove*, a HVS on Table Buttress on Cyfrwy, Cader Idris; *Gorilla's Armpit*, a 2-star HVS route on Bird Rock in 1975; and in 1981 a route on Barmouth Quarry called *It's Looking Good Houston* – a typical cracking name that Mal came up with.

We climbed a lot in summer in the Alps. Our two families would usually meet up in Cham, suffer the appalling weather for a few days, then rush off to sunshine in the Verdon Gorge. *Eperon Sublime* was our finest route down there, which of course included the gripping *Luner Bong* abseil.

A trip to the Vanoise with Mal and Sue, where we did the North Face of the Grand Casse and had a close call with the large sérac barrier at two-thirds height. The whole front section peeled away just as we got level with it, sweeping down the section we had just ascended!

The family trip to the Bernina Alps in 1975 was one of our best. It started with a rush up Piz Morteratsch, which ended in major heave-ho problems. Then we did the *Biancograt* on the Bernina. The next route was the plum of the area: the *Klucker Neruda route* on the NE face of the Roseg – very scary climbing under huge sérac walls in the lower half.

A quick move of campsites to the beautiful valley beneath the Badile and the final route of the holiday, the *Cassin route* on the NE face. The weather was good to start with but in the upper section we got caught in the traditional storm. It was the famous Gaston Rebuffat tale all over again but the strong man of the team this time was Mal. A hideous night was spent on the summit (we couldn't find the bivvi hut) and then the endless abseils down the North Ridge.

Malcolm has climbed with many of the top-line climbers of the day and harder tales than the above could be told. For instance, Mal did the *Nant Blanc Face* of the Vert with Smiler Cuthbertson. Also, with Smiler, the *Rochers de Prelles* in the company of Patrick Cordier. With the Vagabond lads, the Italian ridge of the Matterhorn and the *Brown/Whillans route* on the Blaitière. Malcolm had also done some great routes in the States, such as an early ascent of *Zodiac* on El Cap and Half Dome with Bill Strong. An attempt on *Salathé Wall* with Hugh Banner and routes on the Bugaboos with Chris Radcliff.

Mal climbed extensively on rock throughout the British Isles with many members of the Climbers' Club and Vagabond Club, in particular Roger Bennion, Derek Walker, Hugh Banner, Mike Frith and Mike Pycroft. One of his favourite places was Gogarth where he climbed regularly at E3, doing such classics as *Rat Race*, *The Big Groove*, *The Moon* and just before he went to the Alps in 2000, *Redshift* on Red Wall. Mal's early climbing was with the Vagabonds and he always kept close links with them. When with Mal, the conversation would always come back to climbers associated with the Vags: Pete Minks, Arthur Green and Bryan Mullarkey.

Mal died from rockfall, after completing the *Marchand de Sable* on the Tour Rouge, on the Mer de Glace side of the Aiguilles on Mont Blanc, 9 September 2000. He was climbing with Neil Hitchings and was descending easy ground on his way back to the Envers Hut when the rockfall struck. Mal was a Vice President of the Climbers' Club and an honorary member of that club. He leaves behind his wife Sue and daughter Sally. He will be greatly missed by all who knew him.

John (Fritz) Sumner

Mike Pycroft writes:
The last time I spoke to Mal was the day before he flew out to Chamonix. He had called me to confirm that he still wanted to go to Spain in October and would I book things up. His last words: that it was great to be booking one holiday while packing for another! Still, Chamonix was typical of Mal. A quiet walking holiday with Sue; not quite, as he still squeezed in some climbs. This summed up his attitude – he was always keen to grab another route.

A couple of weeks before his death we had gone to Left Hand Red Wall and climbed *Infidel Direct* (E4). It was the same as usual; Mal would fiddle around sorting his gear, taping his fingers, all the time in the world. Still he cruised the first pitch and enjoyed the last pitch. When we got to the top, after a quick sandwich I persuaded Mal to do *Red Wall* rather than the ice cream he suggested. By the time we topped out it was 8.30, cold and getting dark, but Mal was pleased we had grabbed the route.

It was back to Gogarth a fortnight later. Mal did *Redshift* with Steve Burns and I climbed with Steve Lang. After our routes Mal insisted it was time for ice cream and we sat in the afternoon sunshine making future plans.

The next Sunday he was dead. A tragic loss for Sue and Sally and he is missed by all his friends. It is baffling that he will never appear at our house again on a Sunday morning, playing with Nathan, just 2, whilst we plan the day's climbing. Mal loved 'adventure' climbing and in the two years we spent together we spent many a happy day on Cloggy or Gogarth. Mal had explored sport climbing in the '90s but found little reward in the training and repetition of routes to get another number. In the mountains Mal relished the challenge, be it wet drainpipe cracks on Cloggy or a soaked *Moon* on Gogarth.

In recent times Mal was active a lot. Skiing in March '99 to Chamonix with Sue and Sally. Typically he managed an ice climb on Mont Blanc de Tacul followed by a ski descent of the Mer de Glace. He went back two days later and skied down with Sally, which he was really proud of.

Mal loved Cloggy. We spent a great day up there doing *Troach* and *November*. During the summer Mal had been back there and led *Bow Right Hand*, E3, which gave him a lot of pleasure.

Mal was someone who will be missed by all. He touched so many people's lives, I feel lucky to have known him, even for such a short period. But in that time he provided a breath of fresh air and rekindled the fire inside. We never did *Right Wall* or *Salathé Wall* but his memory will travel there.

Mike Frith writes:
I first met Mal climbing in Cwm Silyn in May 1990, and after sharing a belay ledge for a while and exchanging pleasantries, realised we lived within about five miles of each other. For the next ten years, up to his untimely death, he became a regular climbing partner and close friend. Our frequent weekend climbing venues were the crags of North Wales with occasional trips to the Peak District and beyond, and with another climbing friend, Roger Bennion, we did most of the E2/E3 classics, some of the more popular ones several times.

On the crag, one of Mal's strongest attributes was his attention to safety. He would always double-check belays and protection and was the safest climber I've ever climbed with. Sometimes his attention to detail was a cause of frustration, but it was his way of rationalising the dangers of the sport. Although he enjoyed sport climbing, it was never one of his strong points on our regular Spanish trips. He could never be bothered to work a route, for instance at the Ormes in Llandudno (one of our regular summer evening climbing haunts) for a red-point ascent. His great love was for multi-pitch trad climbing – something he was really beginning to get into again before his accident.

I never got to climb with Mal in the Alps or other mountain ranges, but my favourite memories of him are of climbing sun-drenched rock in such places as Costa Blanca, Mallorca and Las Vegas. Our spring trips for some holiday rock, with our respective wives, were among the highlights of the year. This was the one trip when he really enjoyed climbing on bolts, to get the multi-pitch experience in relative safety. Routes from these holidays included some of the best climbs I ever did with him, especially the six-pitch *Prince of Darkness* (5.10c) at Red Rocks, Nevada; *Costa Blanca* (6c), another six-pitch classic on the Penon de Ifach, near Calpe; and *Sexo Debil* (6b+) at Sa Gubia in Mallorca.

In both his climbing and social life Mal had many friends and acquaintances. He was an active member of the Climbers' Club and an ex Vice President; but I think it was his enthusiasm for all aspects of the sport that he will be remembered for by most people. He was always particularly keen to encourage younger climbers. Mal was the first close friend I've had who has been killed in the mountains. I think most of us believe that it will never happen to us, always trying to concentrate and hold things together in times of high stress and danger, and yet history shows that the most dangerous times are when a climb has been completed. The accident that happened to Mal was a one in a million chance which, as others no doubt have found in the past, makes it much more difficult to accept. He was a kind and generous man and life for his wife Sue, daughter Sally, his family and friends will never be the same again.

Heather Larsen (née Wheeler) 1932–2000

When remembering Heather, there are three things that come immediately to mind. They are her vitality, enthusiasm, and love of fun. She always had a lovely wide smile for everyone.

Heather's childhood was in Essex, and included canoeing in Benfleet Creek – always managing to return just before it became low tide and dark, a skill that served Heather extremely well later in Greenland. Another influence was her great aunt, Winnie Marples, who was a prolific alpinist, putting up many guideless routes between 1920 and 1940.

Heather went to Edinburgh University, studied languages, met climbers, and explored the Scottish mountains in all seasons. *Myrtle Simpson writes*:

Heather soon worked out that action meant the climbing club. Heather's enormous smile, her laugh, her overwhelming presence shone out. Murky bothies, wet tents, bleak bivvies; we were all cold and miserable. Not Heather, she was radiant.

Having gained her MA and BCom, Heather became a money dealer in the City of London; a frenetic life where her personality was an important asset. Climbing was the major activity in every spare moment. From 1961 onwards Heather went out with the Austrian Alpine Club to the Stubai,

Kaunergrat and Ötztal. The Ingham's train was the way that many climbers travelled to the Austrian Alps. Heather met new friends, including Ann Dryland, Ann King, Lizbet Strickland-Constable, Colin Morath and others from the London Mountaineering Club. Peaks included the Zückerhütl, Madatschtürme and Wildspitz.

Meanwhile, she was always encouraging her friends to meet each other, try new routes and visit new ranges. Her enthusiasm was extremely infectious. Also, her parties with themes such as 'Jamaica', 'Jungle' or 'Caribbean' were superb fun.

Some serious climbs, mostly guideless, followed: Aiguilles du Cardinal, du Moine, de l'Evêque and du Chardonnet (by the Forbes Arête), Allalinhorn, Jägigrat, Rimpfischhorn and Weisshorn. Heather was elected to the Ladies Alpine Club in 1964, and was proud to have achieved her ambition to climb the three major summits of the Alps: Mont Blanc, Monte Rosa, and the Matterhorn. But she also enjoyed the fun at the Bahnhof in Zermatt with Bernhard and Frau Biner.

Heather and Lizbet went to the Bernese Oberland. They had no guidebook but this did not stop Heather. She chatted to everyone they met, asking about snow conditions, quality of rock, and exactly where the crevasses were. They went on to the 1966 LAC meet in Saas Fee, and climbed more summits. Tales abound of Heather's Tricouni nails making sparks on the Dri Hörlini slabs. Meanwhile she was a prolific writer for the LAC Journal.

Heather then cast her mountaineering plans wider. She went to the Drakensberg in South Africa with Bill James in 1969. In 1974, with Myrtle Simpson and Bharati Banerjee, Heather climbed Bhunoti (18,5000ft), a peak in the Garhwal–Kumaun Himalaya. However, it was Greenland that became her favourite place. In 1968, after Hugh and Myrtle Simpson had crossed the Greenland ice cap, she flew out to the West Coast with their three small children, to meet them. *Myrtle Simpson describes the excitement of their arrival:*

'There's my mum,' shrieked a shrill voice, as the kids jostled out. Behind came Heather, clutching bags, paper windmills, comics, jerseys and fishing rods. A huge smile beamed out, affecting all. What excitement; letters, presents, and news from home.

Heather lifted the lid from a wooden crate; peaches! 'I bought them in Covent Garden this morning. I think they will be alright.' Again, the great fun Heather always brought to every event.

Heather travelled to Greenland many times. Trips included climbing Hesteskoen in the Staunings Alps, and canoeing to a very northerly point, Segelsälliskapets Fjord. But 1972 was the important year. Heather and the Simpsons had joined some families of hunting Eskimo, and were canoeing near Søndre Strømfjord on the West Coast of Greenland. They had bread and oranges dropped by a light aeroplane. The name of the Danish pilot was Peter Larsen.

Above
54. Sarat Chandra Das (Pundit S.C.D.)
    (*Alpine Club Library Collection*)
    (p191)

Right
55. Rinzin Namgyal (Pundit R.N.)
    (*Alpine Club Library Collection*)
    (p191)

56.   Chola Lake and Pass. Mount Kanchanjanga [*sic*] in the distance. (*Alpine Club Library collection*) (p191)

57. Mont Blanc from Val Veni with (*left*) the Brouillard ridge. (*Manfredo Vanni, 1948*) (p204)

58.   Beatrice Tomasson with the guide Arcangelo Siorpaes on the Becco di Messodi
       near Cortina. (*Carlo Gandini Collection*) (p204)

59. Whymper's guides, Canadian Rockies, 1901.
From left: Christian Kaufmann, Joseph Bossonay, Christian Klucker and Josef Pollinger.
(*Alpine Club Library Collection*) (p204)

60. Mount Marpole and (*left*) Emerald Pass. (*Alpine Club Library Collection*) (p204)

61. Mount Assiniboine from NE with (*centre*) NE ridge and N face.
(*Alpine Club Library Collection*) (p204)

2.   Jim Gavin, 1911-2000, on the Tower Ridge of Ben Nevis, June 1940. (*Ashley Greenwood*)

63. Mal Cameron, 1946-2000, after climbing the North Face of the Grande Casse. (*John Sumner*)

64. Michael Joseph Ball, 1925-2000. (*Frank Fitzgerald*)

Peter soon moved to London, and married Heather in 1977. Their flats in Elizabeth Street were the meeting point for many mountaineers travelling through London. Heather organised several Alpine Club Annual Dinners and, as always, was a great source of inspiration and encouragement for all types of climbing trips.

With ill health beginning to trouble her, she and Peter moved to St Margaret's Bay, near Dover. 'Robin Hatch' enjoyed splendid views over the Channel, and, of course, became a staging post for climbing friends journeying to the Alps. Parties included 'Pirates' and 'Invaders'. In 1998 they visited the upper slopes of Mount Baker in the Cascades and Mount Robson in British Columbia. Shortly before she died, Heather and Peter took a beautiful break in the Scilly Isles, where they were able to walk and see the sky and the views. Heather loved travelling. Like her hero, Nansen, she always wanted to see what was on the other side of the next ridge.

Hywel Lloyd

Paul Henry William Wallace, 1912-2000

Paul Wallace – a bachelor – died peacefully at the age of 87 years at his home in Parkstone, Poole, on 19 June 2000. It came as a shock to all who knew him, as he enjoyed robust good health and, to me at least, appeared ever fit and rugged. Only a month before his death he had enjoyed a walking holiday with a group of ramblers on the Devon Coastal Path.

Paul was born in Halifax, Yorkshire, on 31 October 1912, and in the early 1920s he and his family moved to Poole where he attended Canford School. He came to climbing after World War II, in which he saw active Army service in the Western Desert, Italy and Normandy. I was very fortunate to be introduced to Paul in the late 1960s through my good friend and mountaineering companion Fred Daldry of Bournemouth.

Fred had met Paul a little earlier at a Wessex M.C. meet in North Wales and soon realised he was in the presence of an experienced mountaineer with excellent rock-climbing ability. Paul was tactfully enticed to join Fred and myself on a Bernese Oberland holiday planned for the summer of 1970 and, as luck would have it, he agreed to join us. From that time on, the three of us joined forces and climbed in the Alps every summer for some 15 years or so, recruiting a fourth person whenever possible in order to make up two ropes of two, should it be appropriate.

Paul joined the Alpine Club in 1963 and encouraged, supported and proposed my own membership of the Club in 1976. He was also a founder member of the Wessex M.C. and had been its President for five years. He acknowledged that his own experience and skills owed much to the fine climbing and mountaincraft courses he had earlier attended with the Mountaineering Association and the Austrian Alpine Club, the latter being conducted entirely in German. This gave Paul no problem for he was fluent in German, as well as in French and Italian. For many years he enjoyed working from home translating papers for various clients and agencies. His ability to speak foreign languages gave the rest of us on our Alpine holidays an easy and reassuring time, knowing that good deals for accommodation could be made on our behalf.

Although sound on mixed ground, Paul was always happiest on pure rock, and being a climber from the old school he insisted on doing most of his climbs in mountain boots. He never took gladly to wearing a climbing helmet or to modern mechanical aids. He was, in many ways, very much like an early Victorian mountaineer, with his quiet, well-modulated speaking voice, fund of knowledge and wide interests.

Paul was much involved with the initial opening up of climbs on his nearby Swanage cliffs and for several years he attended – by invitation – the Ladies Alpine Club meets there, to show and assist them with their cliff climbs. He was ever modest about his Swanage climbs but when he invited me to join him on some of his routes there I quickly realised and appreciated his climbing skills and his intimate knowledge of these cliffs. He was always ready to help beginners and encourage them in the art of rock climbing and he devoted much time to various youth groups that Fred Daldry used to bring to North Wales.

Suffice it to say that Paul had an impressive list of Alpine summits and climbs to his credit, many of them being major classic routes; but as he grew older he turned his attention to the Austrian Tirol where the mountain huts were more numerous and comfortable and the mountains less serious. His return to the region was well received by the Austrian Alpine Club who used his diary notes of his hut-to-hut tour in the Venediger Gruppe for their main Newsletter article in the summer edition of 1986 (number 90).

In the 1990s he turned to back-packing the long-distance trails in the British Isles and in Northern France which, considering his advanced years, troublesome knee and metal pin in his hip, was not bad going.

Paul had the most remarkable gifts of patience and endurance and was never known to raise his voice or swear, in spite of being caught out from time to time in conditions serious enough to make a Saint curse. Always solidly dependable and safe and a most interesting companion, he shared his knowledge easily, with no sense of superiority. It was a delight to listen to him talking on such subjects as Botany, Geology and even Philosophy and he was ever eager, in turn, to quiz me and glean some insight into the significance of the laws, theories and advances within modern Science and Technology.

Those who shared Paul's company, whether on a simple country walk or attached to his climbing rope on an arduous route, will, I am sure, forever look back at his memory with admiration and affection; for he was a truly remarkable Gentleman who, for now, has left us but who is, hopefully, enjoying the Celestial Mountains.

Dai Griffiths

Michael Joseph Ball, 1925-2000

Mike Ball, who joined the Club only in 1991 when his Alpine career was past, climbed regularly in Britain throughout his life; Southern Sandstone, the Peak, Yorkshire gritstone, the Lake District, Wales and Scotland all received his attention. He had 16 seasons of winter climbing in Scotland, 21 seasons of summer climbing in the Alps, and he was the doctor on the New Zealand Alpine Club's Himalayan Expedition to the Barun Valley in 1954. Climbing was in his blood – his maternal grandfather was Joseph Collier, the nineteenth century pioneer, a fact of which he was particularly proud.

After Gresham's School, Mike went up to Cambridge to read medicine and was a leading light in the CUMC, visiting the Alps in 1947 with a CUMC party which had the good fortune to be introduced to alpine climbing by members of the Zurich University Mountaineering Club. In 1949, with our late member Tom Bourdillon, he climbed the Mer de Glace face of the Grépon, made the first ascent of Pointe 3050 on the Requin and traversed Les Drus and La Meije, significant expeditions at that time. In the Barun in 1954 he made the first ascent of Chago (22,540ft) with Urkien and was a member of the party that made the first ascent of Pethangtse (22,080) and two other unnamed peaks (20,200ft and 21,300ft). Our first alpine season together, in 1957, was ruined by foul weather but we traversed the Ecandies and climbed the SW Integrale of the Moine.

Although Mike continued to climb regularly in Britain, his activities were restricted by the demands of his surgical career and he did not return to the Alps until 1968. In the interval he had contracted diabetes and management of his condition against the rigours of an Alpine season required considerable skill on his part and a certain vigilance on the part of his companions. We were again troubled by poor weather, but amongst other things traversed the Jägigrat, the Leiterspitzen and the Evêque, climbing the last by a route on its South Face, and we defied the hordes on the Matterhorn in poor conditions which forced many parties to break the expedition at the Solvay refuge. Mike's diabetes might have ended his alpine career but his love of alpine rock, coupled with his fierce determination, carried him through another 18 seasons and ascents including the Dibona South Face, the South Ridge of the Salbitschijen and the Voie Rebuffat on Les Rouies.

In 1971 we climbed in winter on Ben Nevis and in Glencoe, for Mike his first visit since 1946, and for the next eleven years we returned each spring to ascend classic routes such as SC Gully, North Buttress of the Buachaille, the NE Buttress of Ben Nevis, Glover's Chimney and, of course, his grandfather's Tower Ridge. In that time we experienced a revolution in ice-climbing techniques and equipment and especially in foul weather clothing, without which our harvest of routes would have been much smaller. Sadly, Mike's Scottish forays were seriously curtailed after he was badly knocked about in an avalanche in North Gully, but he had already applied Scottish technique to the north faces of the Pigne d'Arolla, Petit Mont Collon, the

Lenzspitze and the Watkins Arête on Mont Blanc de Cheilon. In his later years Mike climbed with a variety of companions, mainly members of the Climbers' Club and his son's ex-Repton school and Reading University friends.

Mike's was a long and distinguished mountaineering career during which he transmitted his unbounded enthusiasm to all with whom he came into contact. He was the friendliest of men, particularly with the young whom he was happy to help and advise. In 1972 he introduced a Reading University party to alpine climbing in the same way that he had been introduced by the Zurich University Club 25 years earlier, leading members up the Ferpècle Arête of the Dent Blanche and the West Ridge of the Dent de Tsalion.

Mike's first allegiance was to the Climbers' Club which he joined in 1946 while President of the CUMC. He served it in a number of capacities, being Vice-President in 1984-87 and he was also an Honorary Member. He will be remembered by all who knew him as one who was not at all concerned with material things, as most of his possessions clearly showed; but he had an abiding interest in what really mattered: climbing and mountains.

Since our respective retirements we tried to climb each month alternately in the Peak and on Yorkshire grit. We met on the A19 in heavy rain only a few weeks before his death and toured North Yorkshire looking for dry rock, finally settling in the Scugdale valley where the weather slowly cleared and we had an excellent afternoon. He was delighted that day to exhibit his remarkable sense of balance which, despite his years, never deserted him. It is hard to believe that I shall never again see the arrival of that battered camper van, and that disreputably clad, gaunt figure, whose first words, whatever the weather, were invariably 'What are we going to do today?'

Mike was a true mountaineer, he faced every obstacle squarely and never gave up. He once told me that no member of his family had survived beyond 55, yet he lived to be very nearly 75 and he filled every available minute. He had a happy, loving family life, unstinting support in all his ventures from Elizabeth his wife, a succeessful professional career and a great life in the hills. What more could one wish for?

Frank Fitzgerald

Robin Cyril Hind 1911–2000

Bob Hind was born in 1911 on a farm in northern Alberta where, as a farm boy, he had to light the morning fires when the overnight temperature within the cabin often plunged to minus 30°C and the water in the pail had frozen solid. He was adept at such things as teaching his sister the knack of trapping muskrats. Following his general education, he graduated in electrical engineering at the University of Alberta and, when the war came, was an officer in the Royal Canadian Navy on a corvette protecting Atlantic convoys.

Bob was a great sportsman, being involved for many years with the Calgary Tennis Club, where he used his skilled techniques to help many students. His first wife Margaret was killed in an avalanche while skiing near Lake Louise, but in 1956 he married Marjory, who also did a great deal of climbing in her younger days, and he was able to tend to all the sporting needs of his daughter and four sons. He was involved with the Scout movement for many years, introducing many to the joys of camping and outdoor life.

But Bob's abiding love was the mountains. He was involved with the Alpine Club of Canada for almost 70 years, serving in many posts – in the Edmonton section (during his university years), in the Calgary section, and in the main club – from chairman of various committees to overall President and finally Honorary President. He first became involved with the Club in 1932 as a camp boy: setting up camp, chopping wood, hauling water and baggage, waiting on tables and dismantling camp, and many other services which generally went unnoticed by the general membership. But over the next few years he mastered the techniques of mountaineering and became an outstanding and noted mountaineer. He led many people confidently on their first climb and, later, on more adventurous trips. He took a whole generation of aspiring leaders under his wing, passing on his knowledge and techniques to this enthusiastic group. Even an accident on Mount Marpole many years ago, in which he severely damaged an ankle, did not deter him for long. He mastered his handicap and continued on as before.

He received many awards – Silver Rope in 1935, Honorary Member 1969, Service Award 1971, Vice President of the ACC 1954-55, President 1964-65, Honorary ACC President 1991 and Legacy Award 1995.

Bob made over 250 climbs, of which 26 were first ascents, and he climbed all the '12,000-footers' in Canada. He also climbed in Britain and the Alps, and did the trek around Annapurna at the age of 72. His application for membership of the Alpine Club in 1961 lists over 90 ascents (at that date) in the Rockies, Selkirks and Purcell Ranges, many, as already mentioned, first ascents. It also includes many British climbs in 1939, 1940 and 1941, mostly with John Barford, and including leading routes such as Central Buttress and Botterill's Slab on Scafell and Belle Vue Bastion on Tryfan. As was stated at his memorial service, he was 'a blazing beacon to mountaineers, a shining inspiration to all who managed to share in some aspects of his life'.

G W Templeman
With thanks to Mrs Marjory Hind

Frederic Sinclair Jackson, 1914 -1999

I first met Fred Jackson (see Obituaries, AJ2000) on the Buachaille Etive Mor. My party had stopped for lunch in a notch in a rib when through the mist and rain came Fred and Alan Fry. Realising that we were from the same area, they paused long enough to swop addresses, and then disappeared back into the mist and rain. Fred and I subsequently climbed together regularly, in College Valley, on Crag Lough, and the Wannies in Northumberland and we were frequent visitors to the Lake District and Scotland, sometimes with his wife Joan. I always remember that while I would be scrabbling for a handhold, Fred would be searching for a rugosity.

Fred was to a degree eccentric and this was illustrated by his purchase of a barrage balloon circa 1944, part of which was used to cover his Lea Francis, while the remainder was used instead of a tent. Needless to say, we were often wet and uncomfortable. He also developed his own specification for headgear. After months of diligent searching he found a suitable hat in a milliner's shop, and the dome-shaped object with a wide circular brim saw him through the remainder of his climbing career.

I joined the Royal Air Force in 1953 and my jaunts with Fred became less frequent. We still made several winter trips to Scotland which were memorable for a lack of snow and consistency of sunshine. Fred was fond of climbing *Church Door Buttress* on Bidean nam Bian in January when some of the cracks were filled with ice. We also met up for a couple of Alpine seasons, the climax of which were ascents of the Ferpècle Arête on the Dent Blanche and the complete traverse of the Aiguilles Rouges d'Arolla.

In 1974, I was leading an expedition to the Sierra Nevada de Santa Marta in Columbia. I wrote to Fred inviting him to join us as a doctor. He replied to say that he would be delighted to come but had that week had a kidney removed and it would be better if we also had someone to keep an eye on him. Thus we left the UK in January 1974 with two eminent physicians to look after our party, the second being Dick Turner from Edinburgh. Fred was then 60 and Dick Turner 65. Despite his fairly recent illness Fred climbed El Guardian (17,139ft).

After retiring from the NHS, Fred and Joan moved to Patterdale, where they entertained many club members. After Joan's death, Fred returned to Northumberland for a while before moving to Zimbabwe to live with his daughter Helen. Fred's other daughter Anthea is a doctor. Both attended a simple ceremony to scatter his ashes in the Cheviots. Fred will be remembered by many as a delightful eccentric with perhaps a slight contempt for both bureaucracy and authority, but an overriding sense of fun.

Norman Ridley

Alpine Club Notes

OFFICERS AND COMMITTEE FOR 2001

PRESIDENT	D K Scott CBE
VICE PRESIDENTS	P F Fagan
	B M Wragg
HONORARY SECRETARY	G D Hughes
HONORARY TREASURER	A L Robinson
HONORARY LIBRARIAN	D J Lovatt
HONORARY EDITOR	
OF THE ALPINE JOURNAL	E Douglas
HONORARY GUIDEBOOKS	
COMMISSIONING EDITOR	L N Griffin
COMMITTEE ELECTIVE MEMBERS	E R Allen
	J C Evans
	W A C Newson
	W J E Norton
	C J Radcliffe
	R M Scott
	R L Stephens
	R Turnbull
	P Wickens

OFFICE BEARERS

LIBRARIAN EMERITUS	R Lawford
HONORARY ARCHIVIST	P T Berg
HONORARY KEEPER OF THE CLUB'S PICTURES	P Mallalieu
HONORARY KEEPER OF THE CLUB'S ARTEFACTS	R Lawford
HONORARY KEEPER OF THE CLUB'S MONUMENTS	D J Lovatt
CHAIRMAN OF THE FINANCE COMMITTEE	R F Morgan
CHAIRMAN OF THE HOUSE COMMITTEE	M H Johnston
CHAIRMAN OF THE LIBRARY COUNCIL	G C Band
CHAIRMAN OF THE MEMBERSHIP COMMITTEE	R M Scott
CHAIRMAN OF THE GUIDEBOOKS EDITORIAL AND	
PRODUCTION BOARD	L N Griffin
GUIDEBOOKS PRODUCTION MANAGER	J N Slee-Smith
ASSISTANT EDITORS OF THE *Alpine Journal*	J L Bermúdez
	G W Templeman
PRODUCTION EDITOR OF THE *Alpine Journal*	Mrs J Merz

ALPINE CLIMBING GROUP

GENERAL, INFORMAL, AND CLIMBING MEETINGS 2000

11 January	General Meeting: Mick Fowler and Steve Sustad, *Arwa Tower*
24 January	Northern Lecture: Peter Gillman, *On Mallory and Everest*
25 January	Informal Meeting: Audrey Salkeld, *The Last Climb*
4-5 February	Scotland Winter Meet
22 February	Informal Meeting: Dennis Gray, *Climbing in South Africa*
March 3-4	North Wales Meet, Dinner & Lecture
14 March	General Meeting: Stephen Venables, Mountains of the Far South
28 March	Informal Meeting: Charles Clarke, *Science, Tibetan medicine and the Nyanchen Tangla*
11 April	General Meeting: Paul Deegan, *Forbidden Summits – Tall Tales from the Pamirs*
18 April	Informal Meeting: Bear Grylls, *Facing Up*
5-7 May	Peak District Meet and Dinner
9 May	General Meeting: Julian Freeman Attwood, *The Mountains of the Antarctic Peninsula*
17 May	Alpine Ski Club Evening
23 May	Informal Meeting: Henry Day, *Annapurna I – 30 years on* (*and three days*)
14 June	Eagle Ski Club Evening
8-15 July	Alpine Meet: (with ABMSAC & CC) Bregaglia Circuit
15 July-12 Aug	Alpine Meet (with ABMSAC & CC) at Pontresina
4-11 September	Joint AC/CC Cornwall meet.
12 September	General Meeting: Tom Chamberlain, *The Lemon Mountains of East Greenland*
21 September	Informal Meeting: Steve Razzetti, *Trekking & Climbing in Nepal*

22-23 Sept.	Lake District Meet
26 September	Informal Meeting: Roger Smith, *European Summits 1999*
4 October	Alpine Ski Club evening
10 October	General Meeting: David Simmonite, *Rock Climbing in England and Wales*
11 October	Northern Lecture: Steve Jackson, *Kangchenjunga 2000*
24 October	Informal Meeting: Hamish Brown, *The Mountains look on Marrakesh* and launch of exhibition of mountain paintings
8 November	Northern Lecture: Marko Prezelj, *Slovenians at home and abroad*
11 November	Annual Symposium and Meet at Plas y Brenin, *Climbing in China, including Tibet*
16 November	Italian Evening: *Val d'Aosta Lecture & opening of 'Theodul Pass' Exhibition*
14 November	General Meeting: Valeri Hardin, *Kyrgyzstan*
28 November	Informal Meeting: Julian Freeman-Attwood, *The British Trans-Himalaya Expedition*
8 December	Annual General Meeting, followed by Sir Chris Bonington, *Around Annapurna – reminiscences of Annapurna II and Annapurna South Face*
9 December	Annual Dinner

The 132nd Annual London Dinner was held on 9 December at The Great Hall, St Bartholomew's Hospital. The principal guest was Joe Brown. The toast to the guests was proposed by Ian McNaught-Davis.

THE BOARDMAN TASKER MEMORIAL AWARD FOR MOUNTAIN LITERATURE

The 18th award ceremony was held at the Alpine Club on 10 November 2000. The judges were Kathleen Jamie (Chairman), Alan Hankinson and Steve Goodwin. The winning book was *The Wildest Dream* by Peter and Leni Gillman (Headline). Other shortlisted books were *Hell of a Journey – On Foot Through the Scottish Highlands in Winter* by Mike Cawthorne (Mercat Press), *Travail So Gladly Spent* by Tom Price (The Ernest Press), *White* by Rosie Thomas (William Heinemann) and *A Slender Thread* by Stephen Venables (Hutchinson).

THE ALPINE CLUB LIBRARY ANNUAL REPORT 2000

Four Council meetings have been held this year, with work proceeding largely on the decisions made in 1999.

In March we published the special Index to the Year Books of the Ladies

Alpine Club 1910-1975, painstakingly compiled by the former Editor of the Alpine Journal, Johanna Merz. This provides a concise history of the remarkable contribution of British women to Alpine climbing in the period before the Ladies Alpine Club merged with the Alpine Club in 1975.

Our Librarian, Margaret Ecclestone, has been occupied with the third and final stage of the cataloguing of the 500 bound volumes of 'tracts', which should be completed early in 2001. [check is it complete?] There are now over 23,000 entries in the Library catalogue database.

As proposed last year, we have embarked on the major project of computerised cataloguing of the Club's unique, mostly handwritten, archives. After seeking professional advice from the Hackney Borough Archivist, in May we engaged a professional archivist, Susan Scott, to work half-time for two years on the project. In considering the best computer system to use, it was decided to adopt ADLIB software and to link together the Library and Archive cataloguing systems so that a common front end would enable the user to draw search results from both databases, or confine the search to the Library or the Archive database. To do this, the existing Library software and computer had to be replaced and a network devised to cover the total Club and Library requirements. As we rely heavily on the voluntary expertise offered by Club members in their spare time, this took much longer to set up than expected; but it is now in place and the archivist busily employed. We are most grateful to the Pilgrim Trust which has now contributed its promised grant of £10,000 towards the costs of this project.

The publicity surrounding the discovery of Mallory's body on Everest on 1 May 1999, and the publication of numerous books and articles about it, has increased the demand for the many unique early Everest photographs held by the Club. To facilitate our relations with the media, these deserve to be freshly catalogued using the latest techniques which would also enable us to duplicate and preserve them from future deterioration. Indeed, with hindsight, we should perhaps have given this project a higher priority than the cataloguing of the written archives. Hopefully we can do both together. A joint AC/RGS three-year 'Everest photo-archive project' has a good chance of raising the necessary funding to employ a photo-archivist to undertake this project in time for the 50th Anniversary of the first ascent of Everest in May 2003, when we expect media interest to peak.

The Library continues to be grateful for donations and gifts in kind. The magnificent Ruskin watercolours bequeathed to us by the late Dr Charles Warren were immediately sought for loan to the Tate Gallery's major exhibition 'Ruskin, Turner and the Pre-Raphaelites', and then went on to the Abbott Hall Gallery in Kendal. This friendly contact with the Tate Gallery has led on to the possibility of an exhibition in their Clore Gallery in Spring 2003 of selected pictures from the Club and other sources to mark the Everest Anniversary. The Club has some 500 pictures, several requiring urgent conservation, and the collection could usefully be digitally scanned as a spin-off from the above much larger photo-archive project. The Library Council has put a proposal to the Club Committee to use a portion of Dr Warren's bequest to the Library for the conservation of the Club's pictures, and to take over responsibility for their curation, as we are already charged to do for the Club's books and photographic collection.

Altogether, this activity is badly in need of further space within the Club's premises. A recent visit to the new premises of the American Alpine Club in Golden, Colorado, made me very envious of the space at their disposal. I very much hope the Club and Library can soon afford to take back either the third or fourth floor of our building when the current leases expire, to give us all some more space for research, reading and informal discussion. We could then feel that the Library was properly addressing its responsibilities for which it was established to curate and support the valuable possessions of the Club.

The Council continues to be greatly indebted to its professional librarian, the new archivist, and to our core of volunteer workers. At the AGM in April there were a number of important changes. Luke Hughes succeeded Peter Ledeboer as Hon Secretary, and Richard Coatsworth took over from John Peacock as Hon Treasurer. Oliver Turnbull joined the Council in place of Christopher Russell. David Baldock succeeded Michael Esten as leader of the joint AC/ACL Computer Working Party. Then, in December, Peter Berg agreed to succeed Livia Gollancz as Hon Archivist. We are most grateful for the services rendered over many years by the previous holders of these positions. Finally, we still urgently seek one or two people interested in books or photographs to take over from our seemingly indispensable Librarian Emeritus, Robert Lawford. Volunteers please!

George Band
Chairman, Alpine Club Library Council

ALPINE CLUB SYMPOSIUM 2002

Next March, the Alpine Club will be holding a symposium similar in format to the highly successful 1999 event 'Climbing into the Millennium'. The subject will be 'Alpine-Style Climbing – Adventure and Commitment' and the organisers have booked an outstanding line-up of lecturers to appear at the Pennine Theatre at Sheffield Hallam University.

• From Slovenia, Silvo Karo will talk on alpinism in Patagonia. Karo recently made the second ascent of the *Slovakian route* on Fitzroy. He has a reputation for climbing long, committing big-wall routes on remote peaks. He has climbed Cerro Torre, and was on the team that put up a major new line on the West Face of Bhagirathi III.

• The famous Polish climber Voytek Kurtyka will give the keynote address, entitled 'No Limits!'. Kurtyka was one of the central figures in Polish Himalayan mountaineering during the 1970s and 1980s, Poland being arguably the most successful nation in the most successful period of Himalayan mountain exploration. In 1985, with the Austrian climber Robert Schauer, Kurtyka made the landmark first ascent of the West Face of Gasherbrum IV.

• Jack Tackle is a leading American alpinist who has climbed in the Himalaya and South America but is best known for over two dozen expeditions to Alaska, which is the subject of his lecture.

• Yasushi Yamano is 36, and one of Japan's leading mountaineers. His climbing resumé includes solo ascents of new routes on Kusum Kanguru, Cho Oyu and Ama Dablam, the latter in winter. He has climbed routes like *Sphinx Crack* (5.13b) in Colorado and *Cosmic Debris* (5.13a) in Yosemite, and he climbed a new route solo on Bublimotin at 5.10/A4.

There will be plenty of British climbers contributing as well: Mick Fowler will be on hand to introduce the day, Simon Richardson will lecture on the vibrant climbing scene in Scotland, Andy Kirkpatrick has done a number of bold ascents around the world, including most recently *Reticent Wall* in Yosemite. Andy Cave will introduce leading female alpinist Louise Thomas who will talk about Baffin Island and Doug Scott will give an overview on the whole question of alpine-style climbing.

Plenty of distractions from the lectures are planned, with a workshop introducing the latest techniques for belaying, hauling and rope-ascending, a bookstall and other stands. The day will end with a party where you can meet the guests. The Alpine Symposium will be an outstanding event and we hope you'll join us. Tickets are available from the Alpine Club at the reduced rate of £13 for members.

THE 14TH INTERNATIONAL FESTIVAL
OF MOUNTAINEERING LITERATURE: 'O CANADA!'

The Festival opened with some nice live Sax and Joni Mitchell on tape. It was a tenuous 'O Canada!' connection, but one that gave Terry Gifford an early chance to muff his lines, describing her as Judy Mitchell when welcoming an audience thinned by Railtrack delays.

The Boardman-Tasker influence then asserted itself with Rosie Thomas talking about and reading from her short-listed novel, *White*. Rosie is an established commercial novelist and, as such, unusual at this festival. She provided some useful insights into the world of popular fiction in her explanation of how she came to write the book. It is her fifteenth novel and, while some might have felt that the extract she read shared some of the more melodramatic elements of 'chiclit', there seemed to be a real attempt to deal with the internal life of the characters, which would later be commended in the Boardman-Tasker judgement. She is clearly a practised speaker, who carefully tailored her remarks to an audience of vastly more experienced mountaineers. Her enthusiasm for her (guided) encounters with mountains won over her audience to the extent that there was no questioning of her motives in writing a novel which echoed so strongly the events of May 1996 and might be expected to enjoy a halo effect in the light of Krakauer's work amongst others.

Continuing a tradition of publishing omnibus editions of the works of major mountain writers, Ken Wilson's latest offering was the *Six Alpine/ Himalayan Climbing Books* by Frank Smythe. Unfortunately publication had not been completed by the time of the festival, but it was a brilliant touch to have the book introduced by Tony Smythe, Frank's son. He surveyed Frank's life and writing with unexpected warmth for a man whom he admitted he scarcely knew after his parents divorced when he was five. His commentary was illustrated with family photos converted to slides and, though Frank Smythe had published 12 volumes of pictures, there remained many fine unpublished slides. The Canadian connection here relied on Frank's trips to climb in that country, but Tony apologetically confessed that in his view those episodes were peripheral to Frank's achievements and philosophy. Handling books of this sheer size one often has the sinking feeling that life is very short, but Wilson is making accessible key works in the history of mountaineering literature at a bargain price, establishing a canon of inspirational, quality writing.

Graham Hoyland, the originator of the project which eventually led to the discovery of Mallory's body, was well placed to question the authors of this year's winner of the Boardman-Tasker prize about their biography *The Wildest Dream: Mallory, His Life and Conflicting Passions.* Since the spate of books on Mallory after the discovery of his body, it was reasonable to ask: why write another? But Peter and Leni Gillman had uncovered new information and emphasised the personal conflicts and complexities of the man; the inner life again. One example was the discovery of a collection of letters substantiating a homosexual affair with James Strachey which one questioner from the audience suggested might have vastly increased the book's commercial appeal, particularly with the emphasis given by the cover of the American edition. Ken Wilson suggested that we have in Mallory a charismatic character on a world scale but, even so, it is interesting to speculate why there should be so much biographical writing in mountaineering literature. Is it the size of the egos involved, the domination of personalised narratives, or the issues of motivation behind gratuitously putting oneself into danger? One person's 'focus' is another's 'selfishness'.

Lunch surprised us, coming over the PA with a shower of rain, so we queued for a distinctly vegetarian choice of food. The break provides an opportunity for those who don't get out much to catch up with the great and good of mountain writing and get their books signed. Browsing the extensive stock displayed by Jarvis Books is mandatory. As usual, people parted with far more money than they'd intended, but then again found just what they'd always wanted despite being previously, perhaps, unaware of its existence.

The afternoon began with Steve Bell attempting to condense his 'Seven Summits' slideshow down from 1½ hours to less than ½ an hour, he told us between plugs for his company. He also amazed his audience with his candour (I think that's the word I want) when he admitted that after finding the writing of the 'Seven Summits' book too time-consuming he decided to package other climbers' contributions instead. Is this literature? At £20 for less than 150 pages it seems a bit steep (sorry!) for what is essentially a picture book for adults. It could have been seen as a cynical promotional exercise, but in fairness he quoted Doug Scott's description of this expensive peak-bagging as a 'disreputable concept', and was clearly prepared to 'take flak' over the effects of guiding trips into some of the world's last unspoilt areas. Unfortunately, disgruntled mountaineers who have found themselves priced out of certain climbing areas had no chance to fire off any salvos as Steve seemed to have overrun. The programme had billed this as an area of debate but sadly this year's festival missed out on that dimension of audience involvement.

Sid Marty, no stranger to the festival, continued with a selection of poems and songs from his new collection, 'Sky Humour'. Despite feeling less than cheerful, 'perhaps through jetlag' he warned us, he interspersed poems about old-timers, Chinooks and literary carnivores in vegetarians' clothing with some nifty guitar work. It was a varied half-hour, both moving and humorous: a hard act to follow as Kym Martindale recognised.

In the past Kym has presented poems commissioned for the Festival, before having been published, so it was good to see her reading from her first collection, '*Jujubes and Aspirins*' (a quotation from Frank O'Hara). Strangely, the poems she read seemed to have little connection with the New York School, and their unremitting seriousness proved difficult to take after Marty's shifts of mood. In her nervousness she managed to hide behind a plastic water bottle balanced on the lectern. A previous review commented that two poets in a row is asking a bit much from an audience, and coupled with the fact that the afternoon session was conducted within a darkened auditorium, heads were nodding.

Then we were into another slide show as Dave Simmonite struggled to capture the individuality of different written contributions accompanying his fine photography in *Rock Climbing in England and Wales*. He finished with a preview of a forthcoming collection of pictures of Scottish climbing.

In her delivery of the Boardman-Tasker judgement Kathleen Jamie was dismissive of photo-books like *Rock Climbing in England and Wales* and *Seven Summits*. After all, this was supposed to be a prize for 'Mountain Literature'. She praised Stephen Venables' book in particular for its reflection of the inner life of the climber in ways that Rosie Thomas had attempted in fiction, but tied herself in knots with comments on high altitude writing. She voiced a disbelief in the capacity of climbers to go up into extremis and bring all the experience back down in their writing, despite the frequent habit of quoting from journals and diaries in expedition books. No, Kath, a notebook doesn't weigh that much compared to the stack of other stuff carried. It may well be that the periods of inactivity enforced by weather or snow conditions are an important factor in the literariness of climbing to which she drew attention in her opening remarks.

Al Alvarez then made a flying visit to the festival. A major figure in English and American literature of the 20th century, Al continued to stir controversy into the 21st. He began by confessing that he didn't read much mountain writing because by and large it wasn't written well enough to be regarded as literature. 'Most of it seems to be written just to finance the next expedition.' Risky stuff, but that's the stock-in-trade of a man who climbed with Mo Anthoine and managed to write about it, stuck his neck out for the poetry he believed in, and plays in international poker tournaments. No wonder his recent autobiography was entitled, *Where did it all go Right?*

Characteristically Alvarez extolled the virtues of a book that is out of print, Cherry-Garrard's *The Worst Journey in the World* because it is 'great literature'. Quoting from the book he praised its spare prose as an epic of fortitude based on essential modesty. It was a commentary spiced with pithy observations such as that about the way men were escaping from the constraints of life in England at the time, from the rigidity and stupidity of people who could even ask Mallory that famous question.

The strangely formulated High/Festival writing competition was, we were told, supposed to be funny. Jan Levi's winning entry, announced by Ian McNaught-Davis, was supposed to be funny too, and Ian Smith did his best to prove it with his reading. It had been a long afternoon.

Tea was preceded by the opening of John Coulton's exhibition of fine chalk drawings and watercolours of British, Alpine and Himalayan subjects. 'The Mountain Seen' continued into December.

After tea a second helping of Sid Marty was served up, this time in prose as he read from his book *Switchbacks*, which won the award for literary merit at the Banff Festival. It is a collection of reflective reminiscences which affectionately recapture the naive youth who still lives in him: 'The child is father to the man,' he quoted Wordsworth. Whether reading about an old rucksack, the character of a 'geriatric' mountain guide, or the fact that 'rum is no burden', there was a potent mixture of humour and fine feeling in the detailed descriptions and illustrative dialogue.

Finally Chic Scott topped the bill with a specially requested focus on the British contribution to Canadian mountaineering, though it was a shame the audience had thinned again. Scott's authoritative history of Canadian climbing, *Pushing the Limits*, is a tremendous achievement, establishing recognition for a whole area of climbing which has tended not to hold centre stage on the world scene. So it is no surprise that Scott and Gifford should hope to highlight the British involvement. Unfortunately the slide show suffered by comparison with the earlier, more spectacular, photo-book presentations. Climbers tend to look much the same under all that hair in any given period, and unfamiliarity with the mountains meant that the portrait gallery of ex-pat Brits did not connect easily with the necessarily brief references to their achievements. Nonetheless, as Terry emphasised, this was a rich vein of British climbing, largely untapped in mountaineering literature, and Chic's book goes far beyond that in its scope and fascination.

So another Festival drew to a close leaving all its participants with plenty to read and to think about. Once again full credit needs to be given to Terry Gifford and his team at Bretton Hall for a smooth piece of organisation.

Dave Wynne-Jones

THE ALPINE CLUB PICTURE COLLECTION IN 2000

The collection of pictures (currently standing at about 550 paintings and engravings) has been greatly enhanced by the recent bequest, from Charles Warren's estate to the Alpine Club Library, of three of the finest John Ruskin watercolours still in private hands. These are: (i) *Grutli - Uri Rostock from Lake Lucerne*, (ii) *Vevay - Sunrise* and (iii) *Moonlight - Chamonix*, dated 1888.

Almost immediately the Tate Gallery approached us to borrow the first and third of these for their major exhibition at Tate Britain 'Ruskin, Turner and the Pre-Raphaelites' from 9 March to 28 May 2000. Subsequently these paintings reappeared at the Abbott Hall Gallery, Kendal, in their 'Ruskin and the Light of Nature' exhibition, from June until October.

During 2001 we intend to hold a small memorial exhibition of all the pictures given by Charles Warren to the Club during his long and expert custodianship of the collection.

Earlier in the year we started what will be a long and fairly extensive (and therefore expensive) programme of conservation of some important paintings in the collection, by having three large oils by Loppé cleaned. Their preservation has been made all the more important by the loss or major damage to 30 of Loppé's works in a fire at the Chamonix museum last year. Our Loppés were cleaned as a gift to the AC from John Mitchell & Sons (picture dealers of New Bond Street) with whom we have had some co-operative association in recent years. We are very grateful to them for their generosity.

Towards the end of the year Tony Astill of Les Alpes Livres approached us to see if he could hold an exhibition of paintings for sale in our clubroom, in exchange for Donkin's memorial picture by Willink, both distinguished mountaineers and early members of the Alpine Club. W F Donkin, Honorary Secretary of the Club from 1885 to 1888, was a pioneer mountaineer and photographer, polymath, scientist and musician. H G Willink, Vice-President from 1899 to 1901, was a distinguished climber and painter. The Club owns ten of his sketches and watercolour drawings.

Donkin and Fox died near Dych-Tau in the Caucasus in 1888. Willink's painting shows Ushba (with Fox in the foreground) in addition to Donkin's portrait and various vignettes associated with Donkin's distinguished and varied life. We were delighted to get this picture after an unsuccessful chase at public auction earlier in the year. The Les Alpes Livres exhibition ran from mid-October until Christmas and may well be repeated next year.

Finally the Montecito Picture Company asked for the loan of some thirty paintings and artefacts which are to appear in a scene called 'the Mountaineers' Club' in a forthcoming feature film *Killing Me Softly* starring Joseph Fiennes. The healthy fee will help to launch our conservation project, although by no means complete it.

Peter Mallalieu
Honorary Keeper of the Club's Pictures

FRANK SMYTHE'S ICE AXE

Peter Steele's recent biography of Eric Shipton revealed that Eric had a tendency to leave ice axes with his various girl friends. Perhaps this was a custom in the 1930s? The Club has just received an ice axe belonging to Frank Smythe which, on his way back from Everest in 1936, he had presented to Jill Henderson, the Himalayan Club's local representative in Darjeeling, who will be remembered as a great friend and link with the Sherpas who were engaged for expeditions. She was married to a tea planter, Jack, and they lived at Rungneet with a magnificent view of Kangchenjunga from their bungalow. We stayed there with them on our way in 1955.

After their retirement, the Hendersons lived in East Meon, Hampshire, until they moved, in the late 1970s, to South Africa where Jill died in 1985. One day in Hampshire their gardener, a Mr Gibb, started to use the axe as a garden implement, but was restrained by his son saying that it came from Frank Smythe and that Jill had eventually intended to present it to the Alpine Club.

Not knowing quite where to send it, the axe remained with the son for over 20 years until, one day, while surfing the Internet, he came upon the Alpine Club website and contacted the Club. I collected the axe from his home in Petersfield on 8 December 2000 and was able to present it to the Club at the AGM that evening.

It is, in fact, an undistinguished ice axe of that era, slightly rusty, with a wooden shaft, and no maker's name engraved upon it. It is remarkably like the first ex WD Army surplus ice axe I owned in the 1950s. I seem to recall a story that at the outbreak of the Second World War in 1939, Smythe was asked to advise on suitable equipment for mountain troops. He duly handed over his ice axe and Bergen rucksack and said 'copy these'. So my ice axe was probably one of thousands based on Smythe's prototype.

George Band

JACK LONGLAND'S CAMERA

A further item of Everest memorabilia has just been generously donated to the Club and brought there by Graham Hoyland, a great-nephew of Howard Somervell. He recently gave a lecture on 'Cameras on Everest'. This camera was used by Jack Longland on the 1933 Expedition. After his death, and that of his son John, it passed to John's wife, now Deborah Newman. At one time, when the Club was in South Audley Street, Deborah was employed as Assistant Secretary, so we are grateful that she should now think of giving the camera a permanent home at the Club.

The camera is well preserved in a leather case. It is a Chronos "C" made by Ernemann, Dresden. It is a folding camera, with a bellows and rising front, f 3.5 – 22, shutter speeds 1 – 1/250 seconds. The body measures 9 x 12 x 5cm and weighs 750gms. A separate film pack and roll film attachment weighs 310gms. Although the shutter clicks convincingly, I am not sure whether it could still be made to work, as I could not find out how the film pack attaches to the body. Hopefully, an expert in antique cameras may be able to renovate it for us.

George Band

HIMALAYAN TRUST

As part of the celebrations for the 50th Anniversary of the historic first ascent of Mt Everest in 1953, the Himalayan Trust UK is to produce a Himalayan Anniversary Calendar, reusable year by year, for recording birthdays and those special anniversaries. Publication is planned for 2002. It is hoped that the calendar will be widely distributed by retailers, but it will also be available direct from the Himalayan Trust UK. Featuring photographs, many of them previously unpublished, from eminent mountaineers including Sir Edmund Hillary, the calendar will be an excellent way to support the work of the Himalayan Trust.

Contact the Hon. Sec., The Himalayan Trust UK, 'Lowecroft', Plains Lane, Blackbrook, Derby, DE56 2DD. Tel/Fax 01773 823831, or email GeorgeandMary@lowecroft.freeserve.co.uk.

Contributors

SVERRE AARSETH was born in 1934 in Norway and is a theoretical astronomer at Cambridge University. He began mountaineering at age 40 but has explored all seven continents, reaching three of the prized summits. He has also been on personal wildlife safaris which form an increasingly attractive alternative to the awesome solitude of the Atacama.

RICHARD ANDERSON is a master at St Edward's School, Oxford. He has climbed, more off than on, since 1958 and tries to escape to high, wild places as often as he can, often with young people.

GEORGE BAND was the youngest member of the 1953 Everest team. In 1955 he made the first ascent – with Joe Brown – of Kangchenjunga, and subsequently climbed in Peru and the Caucasus. More recently he has climbed in Bhutan in 1991, and currently leads treks for 'Far Frontiers' in Nepal, Sikkim and Central Asia. AC President from 1987 to 1989, he is currently Chairman of the Library Council and, as President of the British Mountaineering Council from 1996 to 1999, took on the task of setting up the National Mountaineering Exhibition, which opened in July 2001.

JOSÉ LUIS BERMÚDEZ is a lecturer in the Department of Philosophy, University of Stirling. He took up climbing too late and has been making up for lost time in the Alps, Caucasus and Himalaya. In July 1997 he climbed Gasherbrum I. Co-author, with Audrey Salkeld, of *On The Edge of Europe: Mountaineering in the Caucasus.*

SUE BLACK has been a GP in Bristol for 12 years, having returned to complete her medical training when her three children allowed. She hopes to retire in a few years to build a straw-bale house on the top of a hill and indulge her passion for hill-walking.

ED DOUGLAS is a writer and current Honorary Editor of the *Alpine Journal.* His first book, *Chomolungma Sings the Blues*, won the Special Jury Award at Banff in 1998. His latest book, co-authored with David Rose, is *Regions of the Heart: The Triumph and Tragedy of Alison Hargreaves.* He is currently writing a biography of Tenzing Norgay for National Geographic.

EVELIO ECHEVARRÍA was born in Santiago, Chile, and teaches Hispanic Literature at Colorado State University. He has climbed in North and South America, and has contributed numerous articles to Andean, North American and European journals.

MICK FOWLER works for the Inland Revenue and, by contrast, likes to inject as much adventure and excitement as possible into his climbing ventures. He has climbed extensively in the UK and has been on more than a dozen expeditions to peaks in Peru, Africa, India, Pakistan, Nepal, the former Soviet Union and Canada. His book *Vertical Pleasure* was published in 1995.

PETER GILLMAN has been interpreting the mountaineering world to the general public for most of his career as writer and journalist. His first book, *Eiger Direct*, written with Dougal Haston, described the audacious north face direct ascent of 1966. His biography of George Mallory, written with his wife Leni, won the Boardman Tasker prize in 2000. His Everest anthology, *Eighty Years of Triumph and Disaster*, an updated version of the original 1993 edition, was published this year.

LINDSAY GRIFFIN is a magazine editor and journalist living in North Wales. who, despite dwindling ability, still pursues all aspects of climbing with undiminished enthusiasm. Exploratory visits to the Greater Ranges are his main love, and a return to Bolivia in 1996 marked his first visit to the South American mainland for a decade. Other recent expeditions have included Tibet.

J G R HARDING, formerly a City solicitor and Political Officer in South Arabia but now dividing his time between London and Gower, retains a taste for unusual mountain ranges. His book *Pyrenean High Route*, describing a ski mountaineering traverse of the Pyrenees, was published last year. Vice-President 1996-97.

RAYMOND B HUEY is a professor of zoology at the University of Washington. He normally studies the evolution of physiology in fruit flies and lizards but is also fascinated with analyses of factors influencing success and death of mountaineers on the Himalayan peaks.

HARISH KAPADIA has climbed in the Himalaya since 1960, with ascents up to 6800m. He is Hon Editor of both the *Himalayan Journal* and the *HC Newsletter*. In 1993 he was awarded the IMF's Gold Medal and in 1996 was made an Honorary Member of the Alpine Club. He has written several books including *High Himalaya Unknown Valleys, Spiti: Adventures in the Trans-Himalaya* and, with Soli Mehta, *Exploring the Hidden Himalaya*.

PAUL KNOTT has recently made several changes of continent and now lectures at the University of Canterbury, New Zealand. He delights in visiting obscure mountain ranges and has climbed in most regions of Russia and Central Asia. After three successful trips he also enjoys the adventure provided by the big snowy peaks of the St Elias range in the Yukon.

ANDERS LUNDAHL is Swedish and started climbing in 1973. His main interest has always been new-route exploration, whether on crags or in the mountains. In Norway he has been responsible for some ten first ascents of major big walls. He has a PhD and was elected a member of the Swedish Writers' Union.

JOHANNA MERZ was over 50 when she took up mountaineering. After qualifying for membership of the Alpine Club, she devoted most of her energies to the *Alpine Journal*, first as Assistant Editor, then as Editor from 1992 to 1998, and currently as Production Editor. She enjoys climbing Scottish Munros.

TAMOTSU NAKAMURA was born in Tokyo in 1934 and has been climbing new routes in the greater ranges since his first successes in the Cordillera Blanca of Peru in 1961. He has lived in Pakistan, Mexico, New Zealand and Hong Kong and in the last eleven years has made 19 trips to the Hengduan mountains of Yunnan, Sichuan and South-east Tibet. He is currently auditor of the Japanese Alpine Club.

BILL O'CONNOR is a UIAGM mountain and ski guide who spends much of his time climbing and guiding abroad, with more than 30 summer Alpine seasons and 24 Himalayan expeditions in the bag. A one-time guidebook editor for the AC, he is the author of several books including a soon-to-be-published volume on the Lake District where he lives.

IAN PARNELL worked for the British Mountaineering Council and is now a writer and photographer. An all-round climber, having climbed E6 on sight, Scottish VII and ED2, in 1999 he led an expedition to Kyrgyzstan which established ten new routes. In 2000 he and Jules Cartwright put up a new route on Mount Hunter in Alaska.

RICHARD PASH works in marketing for Unilever in Milan, but has also managed to squeeze in six expeditions to Greenland, Spitsbergen and Sweden in the last ten years. Other travels have included cycling through the Andes in Peru and Chile, motorbiking through the Indian Himalaya, two winters skiing in the Alps, and climbing in the UK, Kenya, Jordan and the Philippines.

MARTIN F PRICE is Director of the Centre for Mountain Studies at Perth College, within the developing University of the Highlands and Islands. His first interest in mountains was climbing, but his academic career in North America and Europe has taken him more into the policy arena (and mountains of paper). He was one of the members of Mountain Agenda, which successfully put mountains on the agenda of the 1992 Earth Summit. He is chair of the Committee of Management of the Mount Everest Foundation, the Mountain Research Group of the Royal Geographical Society, and the European Mountain Forum.

KATH PYKE has been climbing and working on resource management and conservation issues for 15 years. Her climbing includes expeditions and first ascents in Asia, Africa, Europe and North America. She currently resides in Golden, Colorado and works for the Access Fund, a national non-profit climbing-access and conservation organisation.

HERMANN REISACH lives in Munich. A geographer and guide by profession, he climbed the West Face of the Dru and the Triple Direct on El Capitan in the 1970s and is a passionate ski-mountaineer, opening several routes in the Alps. He is a keen mountain historian, with a special interest in the biographies of women mountaineers.

SIMON RICHARDSON is a petroleum engineer based in Aberdeen. Experience gained climbing in the Alps, Andes, Himalaya and Alaska is put to good use most winter weekends whilst exploring and climbing in the Scottish Highlands.

ROBERT ROAF returned from Sikkim to hospital work in Liverpool. He was married in 1939, and after the birth of his first son in 1942, he joined the Merchant Navy as Ship's Surgeon. After contracting brucellosis, he worked for the Emergency Medical Service and in 1946 was appointed orthopaedic surgeon at Liverpool Royal Infirmary. Between 1952 and 1954 he worked in Delhi establishing a post-graduate training scheme. In 1963 he was appointed Professor at Liverpool University. His work with the British Council has allowed him to travel widely and maintain friendships, particularly in Asia. A 'mystical experience' on Simvu led to a lifelong love of the Himalaya which he has revisited many times, the last being in 1998.

DAVID ROBERTS is a recently retired physician who has spent as much time as possible on the crags and hills of the UK and also the Alps, Canadian Rockies, South Africa and the Pamirs – and intends to keep doing so.

C A RUSSELL, who formerly worked with a City bank, devotes much of his time to mountaineering and related activities. He has climbed in many regions of the Alps, in the Pyrenees, East Africa, North America and the Himalaya.

BILL RUTHVEN has been Hon Secretary of the Mount Everest Foundation since 1985. Now confined to a wheelchair, the MEF has provided him with a lap-top computer to ensure that it still gets its 'pound of flesh' from him even during his not infrequent periods in hospital. He is always happy to talk to expeditioners about projects past, present or future

DOUG SCOTT CBE has made almost 40 expeditions to the high mountains of Asia. He has reached the summit of 30 peaks, of which half have been first ascents, and all were climbed by new routes or for the first time in lightweight style. Apart from his climb up the SW Face of Everest with Dougal Haston in 1975, he has made all his climbs in Alpine style without the use of supplementary oxygen. He has reached the highest peaks in all seven continents. He is the current President of the Alpine Club.

DAVID SEDDON is a physician in Nottingham. He has walked, climbed and skied in a number of unusual places, often in the company of John Harding or Derek Fordham. On a good day he has even been known to get to the top of a mountain.

JOHN SLEE-SMITH, printer and professional typographical designer, retired in 1990 to concentrate on converting an old Cumbrian barn into a house. He now spends his time making furniture. He began rock climbing in 1949 and alpine climbing during the late 1970s. With a tally of 200 Munros to date, he hopes to complete these by his 70th year in two years' time.

GEOFFREY TEMPLEMAN, a retired chartered surveyor, has greatly enjoyed being an Assistant Editor of the AJ for the past 29 years. A love of mountain literature is coupled with excursions into the hills, which are becoming less and less energetic.

MICHAEL WARD CBE was a member and Medical Officer of the 1951 and 1953 Everest Expeditions. He is a retired consultant surgeon who has combined exploration in Nepal, Bhutan, Kunlun and Tibet with high-altitude research. Master, Society of Apothecaries of London, 1993-94. Michael Ward was made an Honorary Member of the Alpine Club in 1972.

ATHOL WHIMP is a New Zealander who spent his childhood among the mountains of the Southern Alps, where he developed a passion for mountaineering. At present he lives and works in Melbourne, where he manages his own property development business.

Index

NOTES FOR CONTRIBUTORS

The *Alpine Journal* records all aspects of mountains and mountaineering, including expeditions, adventure, art, literature, geography, history, geology, medicine, ethics and the mountain environment.

Articles Contributions in English are invited. They should be sent to the Hon Editor, Ed Douglas, 181 Abbeydale Road South, Sheffield, S7 2QW (ed_douglas@compuserve.com) or to the Production Editor, Johanna Merz, 14 Whitefield Close, Putney, London SW15 3SS (editor@alpine-journal.org.uk). Articles should be in the form of typed copy or on disk with accompanying hard copy, or as an e-mail attachment with hard copy sent separately by post. Their length should not exceed 3000 words without prior approval of the Editor **and may be edited or shortened at his discretion.** Authors are asked to keep a copy. It is regretted that the *Alpine Journal* is unable to offer a fee for articles published, but authors receive a complimentary copy of the issue of the *Alpine Journal* in which their article appears.

Articles and book reviews should not have been published in substantially the same form by any other publication.

Maps These should be well researched, accurate, and finished ready for printing. They should show the most important place-names mentioned in the text. It is the authors' responsibility to get their maps redrawn if necessary. This can be arranged through the Production Editor if required.

Photographs Prints (any size) should be numbered (in pencil) on the back and accompanied by captions on a separate sheet (see below). Colour transparencies, in 35m format or larger, should be originals **(not copies)**. Please do **not** send photos on CD.

Captions Please list these **on a separate sheet** and give title and author of the article to which they refer.

Copyright It is the author's responsibility to obtain copyright clearance for text, photographs and maps, to pay any fees involved and to ensure that acknowledgements are in the form required by the copyright owner.

Summaries A brief summary, helpful to researchers, should be included with 'expedition' articles.

Biographies Authors are asked to provide a short biography, in not more than 60 words, listing the most noteworthy items in their climbing career and anything else they wish to mention.

Deadline: copy and photographs should reach the Editor by 1 January of the year of publication.